The child's construction
of social inequality

DEVELOPMENTAL PSYCHOLOGY SERIES

SERIES EDITOR
Harry Beilin

Developmental Psychology Program
City University of New York Graduate School
New York, New York

In Preparation

DIANE L. BRIDGEMAN. (Editor). *The Nature of Prosocial Development: Interdisciplinary Theories and Strategies*

EUGENE S. GOLLIN. (Editor). *Malformations of Development: Biological and Psychological Sources and Consequences*

ALLEN W. GOTTFRIED. (Editor). *Home Environment and Early Mental Development*

Published

ROBERT L. LEAHY. (Editor). *The Child's Construction of Social Inequality*

RICHARD LESH and MARSHA LANDAU. (Editors). *Acquisition of Mathematics Concepts and Processes*

MARSHA B. LISS. (Editor). *Social and Cognitive Skills: Sex Roles and Children's Play*

DAVID F. LANCY. *Cross-Cultural Studies in Cognition and Mathematics*

HERBERT P. GINSBURG. (Editor). *The Development of Mathematical Thinking*

MICHAEL POTEGAL. (Editor). *Spatial Abilities: Development and Physiological Foundations*

NANCY EISENBERG. (Editor). *The Development of Prosocial Behavior*

WILLIAM J. FRIEDMAN. (Editor). *The Developmental Psychology of Time*

SIDNEY STRAUSS. (Editor). *U-Shaped Behavioral Growth*

GEORGE E. FORMAN. (Editor). *Action and Thought: From Sensorimotor Schemes to Symbolic Operations*

The list of titles in this series continues on the last page of this volume.

The child's construction of social inequality

Edited by

ROBERT L. LEAHY

Center for Cognitive Therapy
University of Pennsylvania
Philadelphia, Pennsylvania

ACADEMIC PRESS 1983

A Subsidiary of Harcourt Brace Jovanovich, Publishers

New York   London
Paris   San Diego   San Francisco   São Paulo   Sydney   Tokyo   Toronto

ACADEMIC PRESS, INC.
111 Fifth Avenue, New York, New York 10003

United Kingdom Edition published by
ACADEMIC PRESS, INC. (LONDON) LTD.
24/28 Oval Road, London NW1 7DX

Library of Congress Cataloging in Publication Data
Main entry under title:

The Child's construction of social inequality.

   (Developmental psychology series)
   Includes bibliographies and index.
   1. Children--Attitudes--Addresses, essays, lectures.
2. Socialization--Addresses, essays, lectures.
3. Equality--Addresses, essays, lectures. 4. Civil
rights--addresses, essays, lectures. 5. Child
psychology--Addresses, essays, lectures. I. Leahy.
Robert L. II. Series.
HQ783.C544 1983   305.2'3   82-24287
ISBN 0-12-439880-4

41,753

To My Mother

Contents

4 / Children's ideas about intellectual ability   109
STEVEN R. YUSSEN and PATRICK T. KANE

5 / A cognitive–developmental approach to the development of conceptions of intelligence   135
ROBERT L. LEAHY and TERESA M. HUNT

6 / Understanding differences within friendship   161
JAMES YOUNISS

Contributors

Numbers in parentheses indicate the pages on which the authors' contributions begin.

NANCY EISENBERG (179), Department of Psychology, Arizona State University, Tempe, Arizona 85281

WILLIAM S. HALL (253), Department of Psychology, University of Maryland, College Park, Maryland 20742

JAY G. HOOK (207), Department of Psychology, University of Houston, Houston, Texas 77004

TERESA M. HUNT (135), New School for Social Research, New York, New York 10003

PAUL E. JOSE[1] (253), Center for the Study of Reading, University of Illinois at Urbana-Champaign, Urbana, Illinois 61820

PATRICK T. KANE (109), Department of Psychology, University of Wisconsin–Madison, Madison, Wisconsin 53706

PHYLLIS A. KATZ (41), Institute for Research on Social Problems, Boulder, Colorado 80302

ROBERT L. LEAHY (79, 135, 311), Center for Cognitive Therapy, University of Pennsylvania, Philadelphia, Pennsylvania 19104

KATHERINE FROME PAGET (223), Department of Child Study, Tufts University, Medford, Massachusetts 02155

[1] *Present address:* Department of Psychology, University of Illinois at Urbana-Champaign, Urbana, Illinois 61820.

JEANNETTE FLOM PASTERNACK (179), Department of Psychology, Arizona State University, Tempe, Arizona 85281

THOMAS R. SHULTZ (1), Department of Psychology, McGill University, Montreal, Quebec, Canada

JUDITH TORNEY-PURTA (287), Department of Human Development, University of Maryland, College Park, Maryland 20742

JAMES YOUNISS (161), Center for the Study of Youth Development, The Catholic University of America, Washington, D.C. 20064

STEVEN R. YUSSEN (109), Department of Educational Psychology, University of Wisconsin–Madison, Madison, Wisconsin 53705

Preface

Although cognitive–developmental theory is most commonly associated with the study of the child's conception of such nonsocial phenomena as the quantity of liquid in beakers, there has been growing interest in the last decade in the development of social-cognitive functioning. Most recent work in this area has been concerned with the development of moral judgment, descriptions of peers, attribution processes, and conceptions of relationships. The contributors to the present volume generally share a cognitive–developmental perspective on social cognition, although they may differ in the extent to which they view the development of conceptions of social inequality as strictly a structural creation on the part of the child. The title of this book reflects my own Piagetian leanings, and the influence of Lawrence Kohlberg's extension of that model, in that I view the development of conceptions of social inequality as a reflection of a wide range of cognitive attainments: the development of role-taking skills, classificatory operations, and other nonsocial or impersonal cognitive abilities. I imagine that many readers of this volume will be struck by the fact that the child's ideas about inequality are not simply poor reflections of adult views.

Although many people only tangentially familiar with cognitive–developmental theory may believe that it places undue emphasis on the cold, rational, or impersonal qualities of thought, readers more familiar with Piaget and Kohlberg are impressed with their emphasis on the nature of social interactions in the emergence of social cognition. Thus, one emphasis in this volume is on the social origins of conceptions of social inequality. However, the perspective generally taken by most of the contributors appears to reject the argument offered by social learning theorists that children simply imitate adult values. The problem with this mimicking approach to socialization is that it fails to give full credit to the child's qualitatively different view of the impersonal and social world: If adult values are reflected in the child's values, it appears to be essential to know how those values are filtered through the child's cognitive structures.

Given the importance of stratification in the lives of children, it may seem remarkable that a book like the present one has not appeared earlier. This oversight on the part of North American psychologists, ironically, may reflect the bias of the cognitive–developmental model, which attempts to find *universal* patterns of growth, or of the social learning model, which argues for a *general process* view of learning. Stratification has been a topic of interest mainly in attempts to show the "cultural disadvantage" of certain groups. The research and theory reported in this volume take a different road to the study of stratification. These chapters address the question of how children come to understand, and justify or challenge, inequalities in society.

A wide range of content areas of conceptions of social inequality is examined here. The chapter by Shultz begins the volume with a discussion of conceptions of nonsocial inequality that, presumably, are related to the conceptions of social inequality. Katz describes research related to conceptions of gender and race, and Paget discusses developmental work pertaining to conceptions of deviance. Recent work by Yussen, Kane, and Leahy and Hunt is the basis of chapters on conceptions of intelligence. Many of the interpersonal aspects of inequality are addressed in the chapters by Youniss and Eisenberg and Pasternack, which focus on the development of prosocial reasoning. Hook presents his developmental model of equity judgments; Leahy presents his work on the development of class conceptions; and Hall and Jose describe the importance of cultural factors in the conception of equity. The chapter by Torney-Purta describes a number of cultural uniformities and differences in the conception of human rights. In my final chapter, I have attempted to find some uniformities in the development of conceptions of social inequality across a number of topics covered in this volume, recognizing as I do that cognitive–developmental theory may be able to assimilate some data but will eventually have to accommodate to other data.

The present volume should be of interest to a wide variety of readers— developmental and social psychologists, sociologists, anthropologists, and political scientists. Laypersons interested in the social issues that were first addressed by Kenneth Clark in his landmark studies of racial discrimination may find something of relevance in these contributions. Given the scarcity of interdisciplinary research in developmental psychology, the topics reviewed here may help stimulate the interest of psychologists and nonpsychologists in each other's work.

I would like to thank a number of people who have made this project possible. Academic Press was encouraging of the project and understanding of unanticipated delays in bringing this volume to completion. Many of my former students at the Graduate Faculty of the New School for Social Research were instrumental in much of the research reported in my contributions and provided the intellectual repartee that made working with them especially exciting. In particular, I would like to thank Jill Bresler, Jim Briesmeister, Mary Hopkins, Teresa Hunt, Faith Lamb, Pam Lenon, and Stephen Shirk. Finally, I would like to thank the contributors to this volume whose work in this area may help us understand an important foundation of socialization—that is, the child's view of social inequality.

1 / Conceptions of nonsocial inequality

THOMAS R. SHULTZ

Although this book is about the child's developing conceptualizations of *social* inequality, this particular chapter focuses on *nonsocial* concepts of inequality. The inclusion of such a chapter in a book of this sort raises some fundamental questions about the relation between social and nonsocial cognition. For present purposes, this distinction refers, not to the context in which cognition occurs, but to the objects of cognition. Thus, cognition is social insofar as it involves thinking about people; it is nonsocial when focused on other (i.e., nonsocial) objects. Social cognition may focus on individuals, collectivities or groups, or relations among these. An unmarked contrasting term for *social* is quite difficult to find. The term *physical* is not really appropriate, since social entities do in fact have physical instantiations. People are not *nonphysical*. Hence, the distinction is represented here as *social* versus *nonsocial*. Examples of nonsocial concepts that have been investigated from a developmental perspective include conservation, object permanence, and causation.

It is obvious that social and nonsocial cognition can be closely related, since it is easy to conceive of direct social analogues of nonsocial concepts. In addition to studying the child's grasp of the conservation of liquid quantities, for example, one can examine the notion of conservation of personal identity over various transformations (Saltz & Hamilton, 1968; Sigel, Saltz, & Roskind, 1967). Similarly, the infant's developing notion of *person permanence* may be studied. When a person

1

THE CHILD'S CONSTRUCTION
OF SOCIAL INEQUALITY

with whom the child has been in visual contact disappears from view, does the child act as though that person still exists (Bell, 1970)? And just as the child's causal understanding of such basic physical events as the transmission of light or sound (Piaget, 1974; Shultz, 1982) can be assessed, so can his or her causal understanding of human behavior (Shultz, 1980; B. Weiner & Kun, 1976). Such examples suggest that differences between social and nonsocial cognition may be trivial and that each type of cognition can be viewed in terms of the application of a single set of cognitive structures.

Historically, however, it has been far more typical for the study of social and nonsocial cognition to follow largely independent paths, reflecting the predominant influences of social psychology and cognitive psychology, respectively. The present volume is itself an example of this sort of separation, emphasizing as it does the emergence of a particular type of social cognition.

Because of this historical separation, it is perhaps imperative to provide a rationale for including the present chapter on a nonsocial version of the concept of inequality. One consideration is that a number of interesting parallels between social and nonsocial cognition may exist. These parallels make it likely that phenomena discovered in one realm will be discoverable in the other realm. Such influences are already apparent and operate in both directions. Having discovered that young children tend to *center* or focus on one particular aspect of a nonsocial problem to the exclusion other pertinent aspects (Boersma & Wilton, 1974; O'Bryan & Boersma, 1972), it is then possible to search for examples of early centration in social cognition. This would be an example of a nonsocial cognitive phenomenon being extended to social cognition. An example of the reverse direction would be the discounting principle of causal inference. This principle holds that, in a situation where two possible causes are sufficient to produce a given effect, observers tend to discount the operation of one cause if they know the other cause and the effect to have occurred. First used to account for how older children and adults attribute behavior to causes (Kelley, 1973; Shultz, Butkowsky, Pearce, & Shanfield, 1975), the discounting principle could well be extended to the causal understanding of nonsocial events (Kassin, Lowe, & Gibbons, 1980).

A related consideration is that prior developments in one realm may enable subsequent developments in the other realm. It has been proposed, for example, that certain cognitive structures develop out of social interaction (Perret-Clermont, 1980). It is also possible that social concepts have certain cognitive prerequisites that are most discernible in the context of nonsocial problems. Emergence of the concept of social inequality, for example, may require the prior operation of more general concepts of classification, quantity, and equality–inequality.

The purpose of the present chapter is to review and evaluate the available literature on the development of nonsocial concepts of inequality. The chapter poses and attempts to answer a variety of questions. When in development does the child become capable of conceiving of inequality? What are the cognitive prerequisites of inequality judgments? By what strategies or principles is the child able to assess quantitative inequalities? How are quantitative variations interpreted and understood? When do notions of proportional inequality emerge? And what linguistic developments enable the child to express and comprehend inequality through language?

Because notions of inequality generally refer to quantitative variation, the bulk of the chapter focuses on the acquisition of quantitative concepts. But since inequality can also refer to qualitative variation, it is also important to examine the development of cognitive structures that enable the child to make qualitative distinctions. Generally these structures fall under the heading of classification skills. Finally, conclusions are drawn and some implications for the child's comprehension of social inequalities are discussed.

QUANTITATIVE INEQUALITY

As just noted, the most common interpretation of inequality is a quantitative one. To say that two entities are unequal is to imply that they differ in number. This section of the chapter examines the cognitive basis for such judgments. Evidence for the early emergence of equality and inequality concepts is reviewed, and the principles by which judgments are made are identified. Possible asymmetries in the development of equality and inequality concepts are discussed. Then attention is turned to the construction of functions as a mechanism for conceptualizing quantitative variations. Proportional, as opposed to absolute inequality, is examined, and literature on the acquisition of linguistic terms for representing quantitative inequalities is reviewed.

Relations of equality and inequality

Until quite recently, it was widely believed that children younger than about 6 years did not correctly grasp concepts of numerical equality and inequality. The primary evidence for this belief came from Piaget's (1952a) research on establishing the cardinal equivalence of sets of objects. Piaget presented a number of objects of one kind (e.g., flowers) in a row and asked the child to pick out the same number of objects of another kind (e.g., vases). He reported that children's responses to this task formed a three-stage sequence. In the first stage, lasting from about 4:1 to 5:3, children constructed a row of vases of the same length as the row of flowers but often with a different number and density. Children in the second stage, between about 4:5 and 5:7, usually succeeded in picking out the correct number of vases. Typically, this was accomplished by establishing an empirical one-to-one correspondence between the elements of the two sets. That is, the child matched the first vase with the first flower, the next vase with the next flower, and so on until every flower had a vase next to it (see later section on one-to-one correspondence). But these Stage 2 children did reveal an interesting limitation. When Piaget either pushed one of the rows close together or spread one of the rows out, the child judged the two rows to be unequal. In other words, they failed to conserve the cardinal equivalence of the two sets over the transformation of the spatial rearrangement of one of them. Only in the third stage, beginning at about 5:5, did children correctly establish the equivalence of the sets and conserve this equivalence over the spatial transformation.

Despite numerous replications of Piaget's initial findings, there is now substantial reason to doubt the claim that children do not understand equality and inequality relations before about 6 years of age. Much of the newer evidence for young children's comprehension of these relations comes from Gelman's "magic-show" paradigm (Gelman, 1972a, 1972b; Gelman & Gallistel, 1978; Gelman & Tucker, 1975). This is a two-phase paradigm that successfully avoids many of the extraneous difficulties contained in Piaget's procedure, thus providing a more sensitive assessment of the young child's quantitative competence. In the first phase, children are shown two plates containing different numbers of between one and five toys. For example, they might be shown one mouse on one plate versus two mice on another plate, or perhaps three soldiers on one plate versus four soldiers on the other plate. The experimenter designates one of the two plates as the winner and the other as the loser, without making any reference to number. On at least 11 trials, the plates are covered and then shuffled until the child loses track of the winner. Then the child is asked to guess which is the winner, and he or she is allowed to uncover the chosen plate to verify the correctness of the guess and to uncover the other plate if the initial guess is incorrect. The purpose of this first phase is simply to train the child through feedback to identify one of the uncovered plates as the winner. In the second phase of the procedure, the experimenter surreptitiously alters some property of one or both of the sets. These alterations may include spatial arrangements, color, identity, addition, or subtraction. On these trials, the child continues to identify the winner plate and his or her surprise at the alterations is assessed. The child is also asked to justify the choice made, to specify whether anything has happened, to indicate how many objects are presently on each plate, to state whether the game needs fixing, and to suggest how it can be fixed. Any objects needed to fix the game are then provided.

Evidence for comprehension of the equality relation can be found in those trials where the sets were transformed in ways irrelevant to number (e.g., spatial rearrangement or changes in color or identity). Although such alterations were noticed, children as young as 3 years continued to correctly identify the winner plate based on numerical cues alone. They reasoned that, since it still had the same number as before, it was still the winner. Evidence for comprehension of the inequality relation comes from trials that involved addition or subtraction of elements. On these trials, children as young as 3 years indicated that the altered plate was no longer the winner because it now had a smaller or larger number than it had before. Furthermore, they were able to restore a plate's winning status by performing the appropriate adding or subtracting operation.

Inferential use of the inequality relation by 3-year-old children was demonstrated in an experiment by Bullock and Gelman (1977). This experiment too used the magic-show paradigm. In the first phase, children were presented with one object on one plate and two objects on another plate. Children in one condition learned to identify the two-item plate as the winner, whereas children in the other condition learned to identify the one-item plate as the winner. In the second phase, one plate contained three items and the other four items. Here, the 3-year-olds continued to identify as the winner the plate that conformed to the inequality relation they had been trained on. Knowing that two wins over one, they inferred that four wins over three; or knowing that one wins over two, they inferred that three wins over four.

Thus, in contrast to the experiments of Piaget (1952a), Gelman's research demonstrates that children as young as 3 years possess clear notions of equality and inequality. Explanation of the greater sensitivity of Gelman's procedures with young children is presently speculative, but a number of methodological differences have been noted (Gelman, 1972a). First, Gelman used small numbers, between 1 and 5, whereas Piaget used larger numbers, between 6 and 15. It may be that young children fail the Piagetian tasks because of their inability to either estimate correctly or apply their quantitative concepts to these larger numbers. Supporting this view is the finding that 4-year-olds demonstrated conservation of small quantities containing two or three items but not of larger quantities containing five or six items (Winer, 1974a).

A second methodological difference is the greater salience of the transformation and the repetition of the equivalence question in the Piagetian tasks. The objects were rearranged in full view of the children and were followed by a repetition of a question, whereas in Gelman's procedures, the alterations were surreptitious and the children were asked to reidentify the winner. When a salient transformation is followed by a repetition of a question on the equivalence of the two sets, there may be an expectation that something has changed requiring a different answer. In this connection, Rose and Blank (1974) reported that 6-year-olds performed better on conservation tasks requiring only a posttransformation judgment than on standard two-judgment versions.

A third relevant methodological difference concerns the highly verbal nature of the Piagetian procedures, which requires the child to understand a variety of key terms, such as *same, more,* and *less* (see later section on linguistic expression), and to provide a verbal justification for his or her judgments and responses. In contrast, Gelman's procedure circumvented reliance on quantitative terminology and required relatively simple identification responses. The tendency for measures of verbal justification to lag behind judgmental responses has long been noted in developmental research (Brainerd, 1973).

In view of these considerations, the consistently obtained empirical discrepancies between Piaget's and Gelman's research appear quite understandable. If 3–5-year-old children have any limitations in their grasp of number and inequality relations, these limitations must have more to do with performance than with competence factors. They clearly possess the conceptual competence to reason about quantitative inequality, but they may not invariably do so, particularly if the problems presented contain extraneous conceptual difficulties. These sources of performance difficulties need to be more systematically explored in order to understand fully the extent of the child's developing quantitative competence.

If the 3-year-old is truly so competent with quantitative inequality, what about even younger children? What is the extent of their numerical competence, and when does the ability to deal with inequality first appear? An experiment by Starkey and Cooper (1980) suggests that such capacities may be present as early as 22 weeks of age. They measured the infant's duration of first visual fixation of dot patterns in a standard habituation paradigm. Infants were first habituated to arrays containing a particular number of dots and then shown an array possessing a different number. Some conditions involved small numbers (the transition being from two to three dots or from three to two dots), whereas others involved somewhat larger numbers (the transition being from four to six dots or from six to four dots). Dishabituation was evident for transitions of smaller, but not of larger, numbers.

The authors ruled out a variety of alternative explanations for these remarkable results (based on such factors as spatial arrangement, complexity, brightness, and contour) and thus concluded that 5-month-olds do have the ability to discriminate the small numbers two and three. This is perhaps impressive enough, but it appears that their design further enables the conclusion that these infants also discriminated between equality and inequality relations. The small-number conditions of the experiment are pictured in Figure 1.1. The habituation arrays, symbolized by H1 and H2, were presented randomly in each of the two transition conditions, and infants habituated to both of them. Note that the H1 and H2 arrays were equal in number but different in either length (Condition 2→3) or density (Condition 3→2). In each condition, the transition to the posthabituation trials, symbolized by PH, involved a clear change in number but not in length and density. In Condition 2→3, for example, the PH array has the same length as the H1 array and the same density as the H2 array. Infants revealed an appreciation of the equality relation by habituating to equal arrays (H1 and H2) and an appreciation of the inequality relation by dishabituating to the unequal array (PH).

Strategies for establishing quantitative equality and inequality

The evidence presented by Gelman and by Starkey and Cooper for early understanding of equivalence relations is impressive, but it leaves unanswered the question of how the young child makes such judgments. A variety of different strategies or mechanisms for quantitative judgments have been suggested, and a good deal of controversy has been generated over which of them is the most fundamental in a de-

Figure 1.1. Schematic description of the small-number conditions. (From Starkey, P., & Cooper, R. G. Perception of numbers by human infants. *Science*, 1980, *210*, 1033–1035. Copyright 1980 by the American Association for the Advancement of Science.

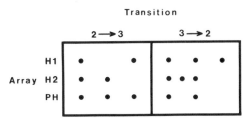

velopmental sense. They include one-to-one correspondence, spatial strategies, counting, and subitizing. Evidence for each of these strategies is discussed in turn.

ONE-TO-ONE CORRESPONDENCE

Piaget (1952a) was strongly influenced by the logicists' attempts to reduce mathematics to logic. The logicists held that the cardinal equivalence of two or more sets was based on a term-to-term correspondence between the sets. In other words, two sets can be said to have the same number if their members can be put into one-to-one correspondence. In similar fashion, the notion of inequality could presumably be derived from a lack of such correspondence; after each item of one set has been matched with those of another set, any left over or unmatched items indicate that the sets are unequal. Empirical support for the use of one-to-one correspondence in establishing quantitative equivalence was provided by Piaget's (1952a) Stage 2 and Stage 3 children (older than 4:5), as reviewed earlier. The use of one-to-one correspondence has also been noted among certain African tribal societies as a means to avoid directly counting taboo items, such as cattle, people, and valuable possessions (Zaslavsky, 1973). The solution is to establish a one-to-one correspondence between a collection of taboo items, which cannot be counted, and a collection of nontaboo items, which can be counted. The nontaboo items are then counted, and the number of taboo items is inferred to be the same. Thus, it is clear that one-to-one correspondence is used by ordinary individuals to establish quantitative equivalence. What is not so clear is whether this strategy represents the child's initial and most fundamental means for knowing about equality and inequality. What do younger children, for example, do when asked to verify or establish the equivalence of sets?

SPATIAL STRATEGIES

According to Piaget's (1952a) evidence, children between 4:1 and 5:3 utilize a variety of spatial strategies to assess quantity. For linear arrays, these strategies focus on either the length or density of the array. Analogous strategies would presumably focus on area for nonlinear two-dimensional arrays and on volume for three-dimensional arrays. As noted earlier, Piaget (1952a) reported that 4-year-olds matched the length of a linear array but not necessarily the density or number. Older children tended to vacillate between the two spatial properties, sometimes judging equivalence on the basis of length and other times on the basis of density. And finally, at about age 6 years, children achieved a coordination of the relations between length and density and correctly based their judgments on number.

A number of experiments have examined young children's use of length and density cues somewhat more systematically (Lawson, Baron, & Siegel, 1974; Pufall & Shaw, 1972; Smither, Smiley, & Rees, 1974). For the most part, these more recent experiments have employed a format in which the child is asked to judge the equivalence of static linear configurations of objects. Thus, none of them enabled the child to establish the equivalence of sets through one-to-one correspondence as Piaget's technique had. Likewise none of these studies assessed the child's belief in conservation of equivalence over a spatial transformation. Instead, children between about 3 and 6 years of age were presented with pairs of static linear arrays that varied in number, length, or density, and were asked to indicate whether or not the two arrays were equivalent on one of these dimensions.

Pufall and Shaw (1972) found evidence from this paradigm for a three-stage theory somewhat different from Piaget's (1952a). They reported that children first used either length or density information and then length alone before achieving a coordination of the two. Lawson *et al.* (1974) challenged the hypothesis that young children based their number judgments on length. Their evidence indicated that questions about number and questions about length were both answered in terms of number. From these results, Lawson *et al.* concluded that, whereas young children often confused concepts of number and length, length was not a more potent cue than number. Instead, it was just the opposite, with children often basing their length judgments on number.

An experiment by Smither *et al.* (1974) largely resolved these discrepancies while confirming the strong effects of perceptual cues on equivalence judgment tasks. They found that children used length information on some problems and number information on other problems, depending on the particular perceptual arrangement. Length was favored when numbers were large and number differences were small, whereas number was favored when numbers were small and number differences were substantial. No particular developmental trends between ages 3 and 6 were noted. In other words, children in this age range utilized whatever source of information was most salient and easiest to process. There was no evidence that the concepts of number and quantitative equivalence were based fundamentally on the factors of length and density. Similarly, Gelman (1972a) found with a matching procedure that 4–7-year-olds judged the quantitative equivalence of small sets using number information. The conclusion is that young children use spatial strategies to judge quantitative equivalence only when the numbers involved are too large for them to deal with directly and the spatial information is perceptually salient. Judgment of continuous quantities, such as sand, liquid, or clay, would presumably involve very large numbers of very small units and thus be susceptible to such spatial strategies.

The foregoing studies do indicate that young children correctly conceptualize the relations between number and a single spatial factor, such as the length or the density of the array. They realize that number varies proportionately with either length or density. However, other research has revealed that a complete inferential grasp of the two-variable function relating the number of items in a linear array to the length and density of the array ($n - 1 = dl$) is not achieved until 12–15 years of age (Shultz, Wells, & Clarke, 1981). In that experiment, children were asked to infer one variable from another, with the third variable either fixed or left unknown. The results indicated that children as young as 3 years recognized that number varied proportionately with each of the spatial variables but the full set of relations among all three variables was not comprehended until 12 years. The latter limitation was revealed by the failure of children below age 12 to take into account the status of the third variable while relating the other two. For example, a denser array may not actually contain more items if it is significantly shorter than a less dense array. Failure to take account of length differences in such a case yields an incorrect inference.

COUNTING

If asked how young children manage to assess quantities, the ordinary observer would probably suggest counting. A good deal of evidence indicates that counting is indeed a pervasive strategy in the quantitative judgments of young children. Gelman (1972a; Gelman & Gallistel, 1978) has conducted a wide variety of experiments on the child's grasp of number and has noted that counting is a salient behavior whenever the experimental context permits it and sometimes even when it does not. Children were observed to count when they were allowed to, to ask if they could count when they were unsure if it was permitted, and to complain when they were not allowed to count. In the magic-show paradigm, for example, Gelman (1972a, 1972b) found a tendency for 3- and 4-year-olds to count aloud when trying to determine whether unexpected alterations in small arrays (in spatial arrangement or number) actually affected winner status. They also tended to count when asked to justify their judgments about which plate was the winner. In another experiment, Gelman and Tucker (1975) asked 3-5-year-olds to indicate how many items were present in linear two-dimensional arrays of between two and five items. As the exposure time of the array was increased, counting occurred more often and judgments were more accurate. Russac (1978) contrasted the counting ability of 5-8-year-old children with their ability to use the one-to-one correspondence strategy. They were asked to use each of these strategies to evaluate the equivalence or nonequivalence of pairs of arrays containing 7-10 items. At each age level, children were more accurate with counting than with one-to-one correspondence. Thus, not only is counting very pervasive, but it is also relatively likely to generate correct quantitative conclusions, even in the preschool years.

The most extensive research on the development of counting skills has been done by Gelman and Gallistel (1978), who have begun to analyze the various components involved. Gelman and Gallistel have identified the five essential components as one-to-one, stable order, cardinality, abstraction, and order irrelevance. Perhaps the most interesting feature of their research is the assessment of each of these individual components independently of completely accurate counting. Thus, they are able to characterize the child's partial abilities at counting in terms of missing components or faulty coordination of existing components. Evidence for the operation of the components was derived both from the magic-show experiments, in which children were not asked to count, and from a separate experiment in which 2-5-year-olds were videotaped while following instructions to count sets ranging from 2 to 19 items.

The *one-to-one* principle refers to the necessity of noticing each item in the array once and only once. This principle itself requires the coordination of two subcomponents: partitioning and tagging. *Partitioning* involves the step-by-step construction of two categories of items: those already counted and those to be counted. *Tagging* refers to the assignment of distinct tags to each item as the count proceeds. Such tags may consist of the conventional number words of the language, but they can also include any arbitrary, distinct tags used in a fixed order. Some children, for example, were observed to use the letters of the alphabet in their enumeration of objects. Partitioning and tagging are coordinated as the child assigns a distinct tag to each item at the moment it is transferred from the "to be counted" to the "counted" category. The gesture of pointing to the item being counted seems to facilitate this coordination for the vast majority of young children. In both experimental paradigms, children from 2 to 3 years of age utilized the same number of tags as there were items in the array, at least with arrays of five or fewer items. Four- and 5-year-olds used the correct number of tags even for arrays of up to 19 items. The tendency to use the correct number of tags was present even in children who did not use the conventional number words. For example, counts of 2, 6 and *A, B* were considered to conform to the one-to-one principle for a two-item array. Violations of this principle were very rare, and when they did occur, they tended to reflect errors of partitioning (e.g., counting an item more than once or omitting an item) or of coordinating partitioning with tagging (e.g., failing to stop at the terminal element and thus counting one too few or one too many). An earlier experiment by Potter and Levy (1968), who asked children to touch each object in an array just once, had established that children as young as 3 years could partition arrays successfully.

The *stable-order* principle refers to the utilization of a fixed order of tags, even if these tags happen to be unconventional. Again, children as young as 2–3 years were observed to use consistent orders in both the magic-show and the videotaped counting experiments. The *cardinality* principle holds that the last number applied in counting represents the cardinal value of the set. Cardinality logically presupposes both the one-to-one and the stable-order principles. The criterion for identifying cardinality was that the child should either repeat or stress the last of a fixed ordered and correct number of tags. For example, a child counting a two-item array as ''2, 3; there are 3'' would be credited with the cardinality rule. Under these criteria, the majority of 3-year-olds applied cardinality to two- to four-item arrays, and the majority of 5-year-olds did so with arrays of up to 11 items. Only about one-half of the 2-year-olds applied cardinality to two-item arrays. Successful coordination of these first three principles was evident on small arrays of two to three items. As set size increased, children began to experience difficulty with the one-to-one principle and ceased to use cardinality. On the largest arrays, children would typically attempt, but fail, to apply the one-to-one rule, while continuing to maintain a stable order of tags. Generally, this pattern held at all age levels, but the performance of younger children tended to break down on smaller arrays than did the performance of older children.

The *abstraction* principle specifies that the foregoing three principles can be applied to any array, whether represented by concrete objects or not. One of the issues relevant to the abstraction principle is whether arrays composed of heterogeneous items are more difficult for young children to count than arrays composed of homogeneous items. Siegel (1974) reported that 4–5$\frac{1}{2}$-year-olds had more difficulty assigning cardinal numbers to heterogeneous than to homogeneous arrays. In contrast, Gelman and Tucker (1975) reported that 3–5-year-olds were just as accurate in judging the cardinal value of heterogeneous as homogeneous arrays. Gelman and Gallistel (1978) suggested that this discrepancy may reflect Siegel's (1974) use of a discrimination learning format wherein children were required to associate cardinal numbers with one of three arrays. They supported this interpretation by noting that learning is often impeded by the introduction of irrelevant stimulus dimensions, as would be provided by heterogeneous items. However, if children in both experiments were using the counting strategy, then it is doubtful that children were *learning* to any greater extent in Siegel's (1974) than in Gelman and Tucker's (1975) experiment. The role of item heterogeneity in counting would seem to require more systematic study.

Theoretically, one might expect heterogeneous items to actually be easier to count than homogeneous ones, as their heterogeneity might well facilitate partitioning as discussed earlier. The counter could conceivably use perceptual differences among the items to help keep track of which have been counted and which have not. Conversely, heterogeneity might be expected to interfere with the child's conception of the items as belonging to a single set or class. Such theoretical considerations could guide future experimentation on the conditions under which item heterogeneity facilitates or interferes with counting. Furthermore, it would seem desirable to broaden the study of the abstraction principle beyond the confines of the issue of heterogeneity. In broader terms, what are the limitations of the sorts of items that young children consider countable?

The *order irrelevance* principle refers to the fact that the order in which items are counted does not affect the resulting cardinal value. Gelman and Gallistel (1978) assessed the emergence of this idea by asking 3-, 4-, and 5-year-old children to count a set of five objects under certain constraints. On repeated trials, the child was asked to assign different tags to the same object (e.g., to take the second object counted and make it Number 1, then Number 3, etc.) or to assign the same numerical tag to two different objects. Children of 4 and 5 years of age could perform these tasks, but 3-year-olds had considerable difficulty.

It can be concluded that counting is both pervasive and accurate for assessing small quantities by about 3 years of age. As far as the components of counting ability are concerned, children use a stable order of tags by 2 years, the correct number of tags shortly thereafter, and the last tag to represent the cardinal value of the set by 3 years. By 4 years of age, children consider the order of counting to be irrelevant to the result obtained. Emergence of the concept that these counting principles can be applied to any sort of set requires further theoretical and empirical work.

SUBITIZING

In contrast to the methodical strategies of one-to-one correspondence and counting, subitizing is thought to consist of an extremely rapid perceptual process that enables the immediate apprehension of small quantities (Klahr, 1973; Klahr & Wallace, 1976). One merely glances at two dots, for example, and knows right off, without having to count, that there are two of them. Early studies of subitizing (reviewed by Klahr, 1973) focused on the question of whether the time required to identify the quantity of small arrays was indeed independent of the quantity. Early results were mixed, but eventually a consensus emerged that the reaction time function had a shallower slope for small quantities than it did for larger quantities.

Sample data from such an experiment (Chi & Klahr, 1975) are presented in Figure 1.2. In this experiment, 12 children aged 5 and 6 years and 12 adults were asked to verbalize the number of dots they saw in random arrangements with unlimited exposure times. Both percentage of errors and mean reaction times are plotted in Figure 1.2 for each age

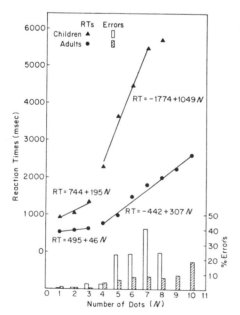

Figure 1.2. Reaction times and errors for children and adults as a function of size of array (from Chi & Klahr, 1975).

group as a function of the quantity in the array. The apparent discontinuities in the reaction time slopes (between $N=3$ and $N=4$) were investigated with separate analyses of variance with trend analysis for $N=1-3$, $N=1-4$, and so on, until a significant quadratic component appeared (at $N=1-4$). Then linear regressions were computed separately for arrays of fewer than four and arrays of four or more. Error rates were found to be significantly higher in both age groups for the larger than for the smaller arrays. Thus, for adults, judgment of one to three items was essentially error free and occurred at the rate of 46 msec per item, whereas judgments of four to ten items produced more errors and proceeded at the rate of 307 msec per item. For children, the increases in reaction time slope and errors also occurred at four items, but both slopes were steeper and reaction times considerably slower than for adults. Children's processing was at 195 msec per item for small arrays and at 1049 msec per item for larger arrays. Klahr (1973) has argued that, for adults, the steeper upper slope in such data represents the process of counting, whereas the shallower lower slope represents the process of subitizing.

That it would take longer to count more items is obvious, but the presence of a slope in the subitizing section of the function is more problematic. Why should it take longer to subitize, say, three items than two items? Klahr (1973) proposed that subitizing involves a serial self-terminating scan of short-term memory for a match between the encoded array and a short, ordered list of number symbols that are transferred from long-term memory. Sternberg (1967) had reported that reaction time in short-term memory processing was in part a function of the serial position of the item in the list, with mean serial position rates ranging between 22 and 240 msec for individual subjects. This range of slopes easily encompasses the subitizing rates reported by Chi and Klahr (1975). Assuming that the number symbols are processed in order from smallest to largest, it is then reasonable to conclude that reaction time increases with quantity across the subitizing list. Interpretation of the slower reaction times and processing rates in children than in adults is difficult to interpret. Chi and Klahr (1975) suggested that children are relatively slow counters because they count one by one, whereas adults use a combination of subitizing and cumulative adding for the upper range of items. As for the lower range, Chi and Klahr raised the possibility that children are simply slower subitizers than are adults. However, this is inconsistent with the finding that the number recitation rate for children is nearly equal to that for adults (Landauer, 1962).

The question was raised earlier as to which strategy for evaluating quantity is the most fundamental in a developmental sense. Current researchers appear to favor either counting (Gelman & Gallistel, 1978) or subitizing (Klahr & Wallace, 1976) as the leading candidate for most fundamental quantitative strategy. Thus, the question has become one of whether children first learn about subitizing through counting or first learn about counting through subitizing. Or put another way, when young children begin to judge quantities, do they use counting or subitizing? Firm evidence has so far been difficult to obtain. Starkey and Cooper (1980) argued that the ability of their 5-month-old infants to discriminate small quantities (as reported earlier) was probably based on subitizing. In support of this interpretation, they noted the restricted numerical range of the phenomenon ($N = 3$) and the "unlikelihood" that infants of 5 months are able to count. Such an argument merely begs the question at issue, since early counting ability is also likely to be limited to small numbers (Gelman & Gallistel, 1978) and there is no existing evidence to support the view that infants cannot count.

An early study by Beckmann (1924; cited in Gelman, 1972a) has been interpreted by Gelman (1972a) to support the view that children count before they subitize. Beckmann presented 4–6-year-old children with arrays of two to six objects and asked them to indicate the quantity of each array. He classified children as counters or subitizers according to their method of approach and explanations of how their judgments were reached. Children categorized as *counters* were observed to count the items before answering and said that they counted when asked to explain their judgment. *Subitizers* were those who responded very rapidly without any obvious indication of counting. When asked to explain how they arrived at their answers, subitizers said that they could simply see what the quantity was. Measured in this fashion, counting was found to decrease with age and increase with the quantity of the array. Precisely the opposite trends were characteristic of subitizing, since all children were classified as either counters or subitizers.

It is the age trends that Gelman focused on to support the preeminence of counting. Presumably, since counting decreased and subitizing increased with age, and since developmentally advanced strategies eventually replace developmentally primitive strategies, counting is developmentally more primitive than subitizing. However, there are a number of difficulties with this conclusion. One is that counting could have occurred in nonobvious ways, subvocally and without pointing, and thus have gone undetected. If so, the observed age trends could be interpreted as a decrease in obvious counting and an increase in nonobvious counting, with the total extent of counting at each age level unknown. A second difficulty is that Beckmann's procedures may have assessed strategies of grouping and cumulative adding rather than subitizing per se. That is, older children may have perceptually divided the array into small groupings, whose quantities could have been either counted or subitized and then cumulatively summed. The fact that five- and six-item arrays, known to be too large even for adults to subitize (Klahr, 1973), failed to produce any discontinuities in the data is consistent with this view. Still another problem is that the children in Beckmann's study, aged 4–6 years, may have been too old to be useful subjects for the study of the origin of quantitative strategies. More recent research, reviewed earlier, suggests that, by 4 years, children may already possess a variety of strategies for judging quantity. Efforts to determine the fundamental basis for the emergence of these strategies may have to focus on younger children or even infants. Finally, one can reach the opposite conclusion from Gelman's (1972a) merely by focusing on the effects of quantity of the array rather than on the effects of age. As the size of the array increased, counting increased and subitizing decreased. Since it can safely be assumed that children master small arrays before large ones, it could be concluded (following Gelman's, 1972a, argument) that it is subitizing that is developmentally primitive and counting that is developmentally advanced. Such an alternative would be subject to the three criticisms just advanced, but it would fit Beckmann's data just as well as Gelman's interpretation does.

A study by Walters and Wagner (1981), which appears to avoid these limitations, suggests that subitizing may indeed precede counting. The authors conducted longitudinal observations of the symbolic development of nine children from 1 to 6 years of age. As part of this project all videotaped instances of numerical behavior were analyzed. The results indicated that 2- and 3-year-old children used the words *two* and *three* accurately before using counting to compute quantities. The words *two* and *three* frequently occurred in situations with no visible counting and often were employed as a prelude to counting, as in the case of a boy age 2:5 who said, "There are 2 ducks here; 1, 2" (Walters & Wagner, 1981, p. 9). Nonobvious counting and grouping and adding strategies would be rather unlikely to affect the results for children so young and quantities so small. However, since observational data based on such a small number of children are not substantially more rigorous than anecdotes, more systematic investigation of this issue seems warranted. Unfortunately, the reaction time procedures used with individuals of 5 years and older may not prove feasible with younger children and infants, who are typically distractable and not likely to provide the large number of repetitive responses that are required.

CONCLUSIONS ABOUT STRATEGIES

It is clear that young children have a variety of strategies at their disposal to assess quantities and thus relations of equality and inequality. The rapid perceptual process of subitizing may be the most primitive of these strategies, perhaps appearing in the second and third years for small quantities of two and three. Counting is both pervasive and accurate (at least for small arrays) by about 3 years, with fundamental components such as the fixed ordering of number tags being functional at 2 years. Spatial strategies involving such cues as the length, density, and area of the array are available from about 3 years but are restricted to judging relatively large numbers in situations where the spatial information is perceptually salient. Setting the items of different arrays into one-to-one correspondence appears by about $4\frac{1}{2}$ years and is likely to be used when quantities are large and perceptual differences between the arrays are not especially salient. It is reasonable to assume that the emergence of each of these later-developing strategies is based on the functioning of an earlier strategy, but no direct evidence for this is yet available. The child may notice, for example, that arrays counted to be relatively large tend to occupy more space than arrays counted to be small. If so, it could be claimed that spatial strategies derive from earlier use of counting.

Asymmetry in the development of concepts of equality and inequality

At first glance, it would seem correct to assume that the child's concepts of quantitative equality and inequality emerge at the same time. After all, the two notions appear to represent merely opposite ends of a single dimension of meaning. However, there are theoretical reasons to expect that the concept of equality might develop before that of inequality, and empirical reasons to suggest just the reverse. Theoretically, it is noteworthy that, whereas equality represents the positive or unmarked end of the dimension, inequality represents the negative or marked end. Since the concept of negation is well known to be cognitively more complex to deal with than that of affirmation (e.g., H. H. Clark, 1969; Haygood & Bourne, 1965; Wason, 1959), the relatively late emergence of the notion of inequality could be expected. The author was not able to find evidence on developing concepts of equality and inequality supporting this theoretical position. He did encounter, though, some evidence indicating that cases of equivalence are more difficult for children to accurately assess than cases of inequivalence. Russac (1978), in a study reviewed earlier on strategies of counting and one-to-one correspondence, reported that 5–8-year-olds were more accurate judging unequal than equal arrays. Does such evidence demonstrate that children develop the concept of inequality before that of equality?

There would appear to be a major logical stumbling block for an affirmative answer. This logical stumbling block is undoubtedly the source of the commonsense view that, of course, the two concepts develop together. It consists, in essence, of the idea that, since neither concept can be defined without the other, neither can be understood without the other also being understood. *Unequal* can only be interpreted to mean *not equal;* and *equal* can only be interpreted as *not unequal.* Hence, understanding of *equal* entails understanding of *unequal,* and vice versa. To not understand that would be to fail to understand the meaning of either term.

How then can findings such as Russac's (1978) be explained? One possibility is that they represent, not asymmetries in conceptual development, but the differential impact of errors in strategy implementation for equal and unequal arrays. It is well known that, when young children employ a quantitative strategy such as counting, they do commit errors (Gelman & Gallistel, 1978, as reviewed earlier). Often these errors are quite small, as in failures to stop at the terminal item and thus count one too many or one too few. When arrays are equal, these small errors will likely produce incorrect judgments. But when arrays are unequal, small errors may not alter the inequality judgment, especially when the size of inequality is large. If this analysis is correct, one could expect to find accuracy of equivalence–inequivalence judgments to be greatest for widely differing arrays, less for moderately differing arrays, and least for equal arrays. Arrays that differ by one element only should be nearly as difficult to judge as arrays that are equal.

Written and oral expression of equality relations in mathematical sentences

Evidence reviewed so far indicates that children develop a firm conception of equality and inequality relations by about 3 years of age. However, an interview study by Behr, Erlwanger, and Nichols (1976) suggests that children develop a misunderstanding of equality as expressed in mathematical sentences that persists well into the elementary school years. They conducted loosely structured interviews with first through sixth graders on mathematical sentences expressing addition and reflexivity. The results suggested a tendency for children in these grades to conceive of the = symbol in terms of action rather than as representing an identity or equivalence of meaning. Addition sentences of the form $a+b=\square$ were interpreted as a stimulus calling for an answer to be placed in the box. When the order of such addition sentences was reversed, $\square=a+b$, first and second graders resisted, either reversing the order (to $a+b=\square$) or interchanging the operator symbols (to $\square+a=b$). Such misinterpretations appeared to be somewhat more frequent for written than for verbal expressions. Reflexive sentences containing no + signs or more than one + sign presented particular difficulties for children in first through sixth grades. Sentences with no plus signs were rejected and modified to include + signs. A sentence of the form $a=a$ might be changed to $a+0=a$; $a=b$ might be changed to $a+b=\square$ or $a-b=\square$. Some of the children were tested with sets of real objects and were found, as in the literature reviewed earlier, to understand equality very well. Their difficulty seems to reside in abstracting a relational statement (e.g., $a=a$) to represent the equality of sets of objects. Sentences with two + signs ($a+b=c+d$) were likewise construed as signals to perform an action rather than as equalities. A + sign inserted between two numbers seemed to demand that a sum is to be computed. Even if a sentence such as $2+3=3+2$ was accepted (perhaps on the grounds that it has the same digits on each side), a sentence such as $4+1=2+3$ might have been rejected (because it does not have the same digits). Again, orally presented statements were somewhat less likely than written statements to be misinterpreted.

Behr *et al.* (1976) expressed the view that such misconceptions of equality relations reflect "a deep-seated mind set which produces rigid reactions [p. 10]." Ginsburg (1977) has expressed the alternate view that they reflect only the ordinary demands of the classroom. Since mathematical sentences often do require children to perform a calculation, Ginsburg believes that their interpretations and expectations will be shaped accordingly. Experiments that attempt to teach children that symbolic representations of equality refer to relations and not only to actions could presumably resolve the issue of how deep seated the misconceptions are. In any case, it is clear from Gelman's (1972a, 1972b; Gelman & Gallistel, 1978) work reviewed earlier that even 3-year-olds understood equality and inequality relations. Thus, the difficulty that Behr *et al.* (1976) have observed with equality relations in mathematical sentences likely concerns the highly symbolic format of the problems. This provides a good example of the general principle that conceptual understanding can occur at different levels and that not all of these levels emerge at the same point in development (see section on implications for understanding social equality).

The author has not been able to locate any literature on children's understanding of the written mathematical symbols representing inequality ($>,<$). However, since these inequality symbols are not often used in a computational context (e.g., $a+b>\square$), it is doubtful (at least in Ginsburg's, 1977, view) that children would develop the same misconceptions about them as they do about the $=$ sign. Thus, it would be expected that sentences of the form $a+1>a$ would be readily understood and accepted. If so, this would constitute still more evidence that inequality is understood sooner than equality (see earlier section on asymmetrical development of these concepts). But following earlier arguments, it should not be concluded that such differences reflect asymmetries in conceptual development. It is more likely that they reflect differences in symbolic instruction and practice.

Functions as a means of conceptualizing quantitative variation

Children's concepts of inequality relations are not restricted to mere detection or identification; they also may come to interpret or understand inequalities in various ways. Perhaps the most important conceptual structure for understanding inequalities is that of the mathematical function. A function expresses a dependent relationship between two or more quantitative variables. If for each quantitative value of variable x there corresponds a definite quantitative value of variable y, then y is considered to be a function of x, expressed as $y=f(x)$. Inequalities or variations in one variable may be related to variations in another variable, and thus the initial inequalities may be better understood or at least may be placed in a conceptually richer context.

One of the best illustrations of this comes from Szeminska and Piaget's experiment on the equalization and estimation of inequalities reported in their book on functions (Piaget, Grize, Szeminska, & Vinh Bang, 1977). The procedure began with the experimenter distributing an equal number of tokens to herself and the child. Then the experimenter took away some number of tokens from the child, adding them to her own collection, which was hidden from view. This created an inequality that the child was then asked to redress by taking additional tokens from a reserve. The number of tokens (y) needed to restore the equality could be conceptualized as a linear function of the number of tokens (x) that had been transferred from the child to the experimenter, $y=2x$. In other words, for every token taken by the experimenter, the child had to withdraw two tokens from the reserve to eliminate the inequality.

A sequence of four developmental stages was noted. In the first stage, between 3 and 6 years, children first acted as though $y=x$ and then later as though $y=mx$, with m varying unsystematically. That is, children began by withdrawing from the reserve the same number of tokens that had been taken by the experimenter. Somewhat later in this first stage, they withdrew some multiple of the number taken by the experimenter, but that multiple varied irregularly from trial to trial. Stage 2 children, 5–6 years of age, constructed certain regularities but failed to apply them in a general way. For example, they acted as though $y=2x$ when the initial collections were small (say, three items each) but reverted back to $y=x$ for larger collections (say 17 items each). The third stage, 6–9 years, was characterized by the gradual, inductive discovery that $y=2x$. Children in the fourth stage, 9–11 years, comprehended the problem sufficiently to explicitly deduce that the relation must be $y=2x$.

The results of this experiment illustrate a number of principles regarding the development of reasoning with the logic of functions. One principle is the *progressive quantification* of functions. With development, children exhibit an increasing tendency to precisely quantify functions that had earlier been conceptualized in a rougher, qualitative fashion. Even the Stage 1 children knew that they had to add tokens to their collection following the transfer by the experimenter; their limitation was that they did not know exactly how many to add. That is, Stage 1 children behaved in a manner consistent with the qualitative direction of the function ($y \propto x$) without yet constructing the precise quantitative relation ($y=2x$). Numerous other examples of the progressive quantification of functions are presented by Piaget *et al.* (1977).

A second principle demonstrated by these results is that of *extension to larger numbers*. Reminiscent of the work on quantitative estimation reviewed earlier, children first master small quantities and then only gradually extend their understanding to larger quantities. In this experiment, Stage 2 children applied the correct functions to small collections but reverted back to Stage 1 errors for large collections. As yet, this appears to constitute the only demonstration of the extension to larger numbers principle with functions.

A third principle of functional logic, not revealed by this particular experiment, is that *directly proportionate variation* is understood *before inversely proportionate variation*. A number of demonstrations of this principle are now reported in the literature on functions (Piaget *et al.*, 1977; Shultz *et al.*, 1981; Slovic, 1974). For example, in the Shultz *et al.* (1981) experiment reported earlier, children were found to understand that number is directly proportionate to the length and density of linear arrays ($n \propto l$; $n \propto d$) before understanding that length and density are inversely proportionate to each other ($l \propto 1/d$). Shultz *et al.* (1981) found the same pattern in children's construction of the function relating the velocity of moving objects to the distance and time of the movement ($v=d/t$). The directly proportionate relations between velocity and distance ($v \propto d$) and between distance and time ($d \propto t$) were comprehended before the inversely proportionate relation between velocity and time ($v \propto 1/t$). In fact, evidence from a variety of sources (Piaget *et al.*, 1977; Shultz *et al.*, 1981; Slovic, 1974) indicates that there is a tendency for observers to interpret inversely proportionate functions as if they were directly proportionate. Such a misconception might lead the young child, for example, to claim that, for two cars traveling the same distance, the faster car travels for a longer time than does the slower one (Shultz *et al.*, 1981).

Another principle of the development of functional reasoning is that of *inclusion of more variables*. With development, the child becomes capable of constructing functions containing more variables. So far, the study of this principle has been limited to a comparison of single-variable to two variable functions (Piaget *et al.*, 1977; Shultz *et al.*, 1981). The results consistently indicate that single-variable functions are comprehended before two-variable functions. For example, in their study of the two-variable function relating the number of a linear array to its length and density ($n - 1 = dl$), Shultz *et al.* (1981) found that, although some single-variable relations ($n \propto d$; $n \propto l$) were understood as young as 3 years, children did not begin to take all three variables into account until 12–15 years. This was also true of their results for the two-variable function relating velocity to the distance and time of moving objects ($v = d/t$). It is not yet clear to what extent ordinary individuals attain an intuitive understanding of functions with more than two variables.

A final principle concerns the relation between functional and causal reasoning, which has become a matter of some controversy. Piaget *et al.* (1977) claimed that causal reasoning is based on and derives from the prior understanding of functions. In support of this idea, Piaget *et al.* reported evidence suggesting that children could learn certain functions through repeated observations of the variables without being able accurately to predict those functions in advance of the observations. However, Shultz and Asselin (1981) argued that both incorrect functional predictions and correct functional learning are probably based on causal interpretation. Prior to the observations, the child may construct an inappropriate causal model that is later altered to fit the observed facts.

Shultz and Asselin (1981) proposed an alternate model in which the recognition of causal connections provides a natural context for the construction of functional relations. In support of this position, they reported an experiment in which 4–11-year-old children were shown a piston-like mechanism that translated rotational into linear motion. Children's understanding of the portrayed sine function was assessed by asking them to predict the linear position from information about the rotational position. The results indicated that visual access to the underlying causal mechanism (a connecting rod) enhanced understanding of the functional relationship, particularly for younger children. These results were more consistent with the view of Shultz and Asselin (1981) that functional understanding derives from causal understanding rather than with the opposite view expressed by Piaget *et al.* (1977). The latter theory, that causal reasoning derives from functional reasoning, would have predicted no effect of visual access to the causal mechanism.

It was further noted that the supported psychological analysis paralleled certain historical and philosophical analyses of causal and functional understanding. A variety of philosophers of science have noted that mathematical functions do not express all the essential aspects of causal connections (Bunge, 1979; Mackie, 1974; Wright, 1974), and historians of science and mathematics have claimed that functions were initially embedded in a physical context and only gradually abstracted to the realm of pure mathematics (Newman, 1967; Piaget *et al.*, 1977). Thus, a final principle of the conceptual development of functions concerns a shift from *causal to functional relations.* Even young children may be expected to interpret inequality relations by attributing them to causes. Knowing how an inequality has been produced and how it can be redressed provides the child with, not only a greater depth of understanding, but a possible course of future action.

Proportionality or relative inequality

An interesting complication of the problem of judging inequality relations is that of proportionality. Proportionality is itself a relational concept consisting of the ratio between one cardinal number and another. It refers essentially to the notion of relative number and thus opens up the possibility of relative equality or inequality. As such, proportionality is likely to figure importantly in certain areas of social cognition. Members of a large social group, for example, may predominate in certain positions in absolute terms but not in relative terms. There may exist a numerically smaller group having a proportionately greater number of members in those positions. As this hypothetical example reveals, it is important to distinguish between the evaluation of inequalities based on proportionality and those based on absolute number or sheer numerical magnitude.

A good example of a technique enabling this distinction is provided by Nelson, Zelniker, and Jeffrey (1969). In an extension of a technique developed by Bruner and Kenney (1966), they asked 5- and 7-year-olds to judge the relative fullness of two beakers. A schematic drawing of three sample pairs of beakers is presented in Figure 1.3. Children who

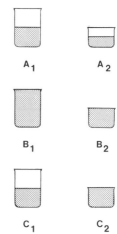

Figure 1.3. Sample proportionality problems used by Nelson, Zelniker, and Jeffrey (1969).

judged fullness in terms of absolute quantity would presumably maintain that beaker A_1 is fuller than beaker A_2, beaker B_1 is fuller than beaker B_2, and beakers C_1 and C_2 are equally full. In contrast, children judging fullness proportionately would say that beakers A_1 and A_2 are equally full, as are beakers B_1 and B_2, whereas beaker C_2 is fuller than beaker C_1. The results indicated that 7- but not 5-year-olds could be trained to base their judgments on proportionality or relative fullness.

In an earlier study, Bruner and Kenney (1966) had concluded that 6-year-olds based their spontaneous judgments on the heights of the columns of liquid, that 10-year-olds based their judgments on the volumes of liquid, and that neither age group relied on the proportion of filled to empty space. These findings were confirmed in an experiment by Siegler and Vago (1978), who in addition pinpointed the difficulty as one of combining the various components of the problem (i.e., attending to both empty and filled spaces, labeling the proportions correctly, and comparing the proportions). Thus, it may be concluded that the ability to assess proportionality develops after the ability to deal with comparisons of absolute quantities, the ability to deal spontaneously with proportions does not appear before adolescence, and children as young as 6 or 7 years can be trained to use proportionality.

Just as it is important to distinguish the concept of proportionality from that of sheer quantity, so it is critical to distinguish between the concepts of probability and proportionality. Probability refers to the assessment of the likelihood of a hypothetical event actually occurring. The fact that probabilities are often expressed as proportions has made them easy to confuse. Indeed, a number of contemporary investigators have treated the concepts of probability and proportion interchangeably (e.g., Chapman, 1975; Ginsburg & Rapoport, 1967; Hoemann & Ross, 1971).

There are two ways to describe the essential differences between assessment of these two concepts. One is to note that, even though a given probability can be expressed as a proportion, an evaluation of the equality of two probabilities may be based on the comparison of sheer magnitudes rather than proportions. This can occur whenever either the two denominators or the two numerators are equal. When the denominators are equal (as in 1/3 versus 2/3), all one needs to do is note that 2>1 in order to conclude that the second event is more probable than the first. When the two numerators are equal (as in 3/4 versus 3/7), one needs only to note that 4<7 to conclude that the first event is more probable than the second. This is likely to be more difficult for young children than the previous decision (with equal denominators), since here there is an inverse relation between size of the number and size of the probability. The other way to demonstrate the difference between the concepts of probability and proportion is to note that one can evaluate the equality of proportions referring to actual objects or events, rather than to hypothetical events. In such a case, the notion of probability does not even arise. Examples include the proportionality techniques used by Bruner and Kenney (1966), Nelson *et al.* (1969), and Siegler and Vago (1978), as described earlier.

Probabilities, then, are not identical to proportions. Probabilities, referring to the likelihood of hypothetical events, may be based on either sheer magnitude or proportion. One of the best examples of the assessment of probability concepts in children is provided by Piaget and Inhelder (1976). One of their techniques consisted of a lot drawing task in which there were a number of wooden discs, some of which had a cross carved on their face. The experimenter constructed two collections of counters with differing proportions of crosses (e.g., 2/4 with crosses versus 1/3 with crosses). After the child had examined these collections face up, the counters were turned over and then scrambled within each collection. The child's task was to judge whether he or she had a better chance of drawing a counter with a cross from one collection or the other. A variety of such problems were administered, some of which were quite easy since the denominators were equal (e.g., 2/4 versus 0/4) and others of which were more difficult because they required a comparison of proportions (as in 2/4 versus 1/3).

In typical Genevan fashion, Piaget and Inhelder (1976) noted three developmental stages, corresponding roughly to the major developmental periods. The preoperational children failed to apply any particular probabilistic strategy to the problems. Concrete operational children attempted to quantify the probabilities, but they repeatedly made a particular sort of error. This was to predict probabilities on the basis of the absolute number of crosses in each collection, rather than in terms of the proportion of counters with crosses to the total number of counters in each collection. Consequently, they were correct on those problems requiring only magnitude estimates (e.g., 2/4 versus 0/4; 2/3 versus 1/3), and incorrect on those problems requiring a comparison of proportions (e.g., 1/2 versus 2/5). Piaget and Inhelder (1976) argued that formal operational skills were required to reason in terms of probabilities, and their data seemed to bear this out. Very few children below about 10–11 years solved all types of problems correctly. Within the framework described here, it would be more correct to conclude that their concrete operational children accurately based probability comparisons on sheer number but not on proportions and that formal operational children accurately based probability comparisons on either proportions or magnitudes as required.

Quite a number of North American investigators have claimed evidence for understanding of proportionality and/or probability based on proportionality by preadolescents (Davies, 1965; Ginsburg & Rapoport, 1967; Hoemann & Ross, 1971; Yost, Siegel, & Andrews, 1962). Unfortunately, every one of these studies has confounded true proportionality with magnitude estimation and thus has failed to demonstrate anything other than probability judgments based on comparisons of sheer magnitudes. Experiments that were careful to avoid this confounding (e.g., Chapman, 1975) have reported data supporting Piaget and Inhelder's (1976) conclusion that understanding of probability based on proportion is very rare before adolescence.

Perhaps the simplest way to characterize conceptual development in this area is by postulating the following four-stage model. In Stage 1, the child is able to compare absolute numbers or magnitudes related to concretely present objects or events. Evidence reviewed earlier indicates that this ability is clearly present by 3 years and perhaps even younger. The Stage 2 child (4–5 years) is further able to assess the probabilities of hypothetical objects or events based on a comparison of absolute numbers or magnitudes. It is only in the third stage that children develop a concept of true proportionality, enabling them to accurately contrast the proportions referring to actually present objects or events. Without training, this ability seems to be restricted to adolescents or adults, but with training it seems to be within the grasp of children as young as 6 or 7. The Stage 4 child successfully bases probability comparisons on these proportions. Only adolescents and adults have so far been observed to perform at Stage 4, but extension of the highly successful training procedures used with proportionality concepts may serve to lower this age estimate somewhat.

Thus, the proposed four-stage model emphasizes two developmental trends. One is the transition from judging the quantitative characteristics of the concretely present to estimating the probability or likelihood of the hypothetical; the other is the transition from comparing absolute quantities to comparing true proportions. The proposed model is also characterized by the incorporation of primitive concepts into more advanced ones. Stage 4 functioning presupposes the proportionality concept of Stage 3 and the probability concept of Stage 2; Stage 3 functioning in turn presupposes the absolute quantitative comparisons of Stages 1 and 2; and Stage 2 functioning presupposes the absolute quantitative comparisons of Stage 1. Although the model appears to fit the existing data contained in disparate studies, a comprehensive, systematic evaluation in a single experiment is in order before drawing firm conclusions or extrapolating to the domain of social cognition.

Linguistic expression of equality and inequality relations

Many of the important cognitive acquisitions in children are paralleled, or perhaps followed, by analogous developments in language. Children are often able to verbalize aspects of their conceptual structures and are likewise often able to understand the verbalizations of others about these structures. Almost certainly, this is true for concepts of equality and inequality. The key linguistic expressions for these concepts are such lexical entries as *more, same,* and *less.* And fortunately for purposes of this discussion, it is precisely these terms that have been the focus of a good deal of recent theoretical and empirical work in developmental psycholinguisitcs. Generally speaking, individual studies have focused on comparisons of either *more* versus *less* or *more* versus *same.*

MORE *AND* LESS

For some years, the most influential theoretical position regarding the acquisition of the terms *more* and *less* has been the semantic feature hypothesis proposed by the Clarks (E. V. Clark, 1973; H. H. Clark, 1970). This position specifies that, in learning the meaning of bipolar adjectives, such as *more* and *less,* the child first acquires knowledge of the so-called unmarked or positive end of the dimension and interprets both expressions as representing that end. This is based on the idea that word meanings are represented in terms of underlying semantic features. It is the acquisition of these features that governs the process of lexical development. For example, the complete meaning of *more* can be described in terms of the combination of the features + *quantity* and + *polarity;* the mature meaning of *less* can be rendered within this system as + *quantity,* − *polarity.* On the assumption that the polarity dimension is acquired later than the quantity dimension, it is predicted that, for the young child, *more* and *less* are interpreted synonymously as meaning more. If the child is asked to make a quantity less, he or she may respond by increasing it. Or if asked which of two quantities is less, the child may choose the one containing more.

Support for the prediction that *less* initially means *more* has been at best equivocal (e.g., Bartlett, 1976; Eilers, Oller, & Ellington, 1974) and at worst lacking (e.g., Nelson & Benedict, 1974; Palermo, 1973; Townsend, 1974; Townsend & Erb, 1975). But evidence that *more* is acquired before *less* has been generally confirmatory (Donaldson & Balfour, 1968; Estes, 1976; Holland & Palermo, 1975; Palermo, 1973; S. L. Weiner, 1974). A major interpretational problem for all these studies is the possibility that nonlinguistic factors could be contributing to the results. For example, Trehub and Abramovitch (1978) discovered a general bias among young children for selecting arrays with more items regardless of the task. In their experiment, 3–4-year-old children were required to identify which of two arrays had either more or less or to simply point to either one of the arrays. The results incidated that children consistently selected the array with more on all three tasks. In a similar vein, Carey (1977) found that those 3–4-year-olds who treated *less* as *more* also treated the nonsense word *tiv* as *more.* This was in response to such instructions as, ''Would you please make it so I have tiv tea in here?'' Again, the implication is that young children are biased toward perceiving and creating large quantities, not that they interpret a particular lexical term as being synonymous with its semantic opposite.

MORE *AND* SAME

The term *same* has not so far been included in analyses of semantic features. There are nonetheless some empirical studies of its acquisition, particularly in relation to the acquisition of *more.* Lapointe and O'Donnell (1974) asked 2–5-year-olds to make equality judgments of pairs of arrays containing four or five items and varying in length, density, and number. For each pair of arrays, the child was first asked, ''Does this bunch have the same number of things as this bunch?'' and then, ''Does one bunch have more things?'' Because of an apparent bias toward positive responses, 2- and 3-year-olds produced largely inconsistent answers, suggesting that they did not yet grasp the logical relation between *same* and *more*. Using somewhat smaller arrays of two and three items, Laxon (1981) reported better success on *same* and *more* with 3-year-olds. The tasks involved either the comparison of static arrays or the comparison of an array before and after it was added to. The results indicated that, by 3 years of age, about one-half of the children responded accurately, provided the children themselves constructed the comparison arrays. When yes–no judgments were required relating to arrays constructed by the experimenter, the age at which at least half responded correctly increased to 5 years. The terms *more* and *same* appeared to be equally difficult as did array comparisons that were equal or unequal.

It can be concluded that the terms *more*, *less*, and *same* are correctly understood by English-speaking children by about 5 years of age, with *less* appearing somewhat later than the other two. Not surprisingly, then, linguistic expressions for equality and inequality relations emerge shortly after the cognitive ability to judge such relations.

QUALITATIVE INEQUALITY

It was noted at the beginning of the chapter that inequality relations do not always involve quantitative variation but can instead involve qualitative variation. Two entities may be unequal by virtue of the fact that they possess different qualities. The assessment of such variations in quality generally falls under the heading of classification skills. Entities may be classified or categorized on the basis of their respective qualities. In some cases, qualitative inequalities may be constructed simply by imposing a dichotomous classification scheme onto an inherently quantitative dimension. A hypothetical example from the realm of social cognition is the observer who sees other individuals as being either smart or stupid. In other cases, the classification scheme may be inherently qualitative, as when individuals are categorized into various racial or ethnic groups. In these cases, classification may set the stage for further evaluation of quantitative differences among the groups. For example, members of one racial or ethnic group may be seen as possessing more or less of some quantity than do the members of another group. Thus, it is important for the student of the child's construction of various kinds of social inequality to become familiar with the literature on classification skills in children.

As it happens, many of the major figures in cognitive psychology have at some time examined this topic (Bruner, Olver, & Greenfield, 1966;

Inhelder & Piaget, 1964; Kagan, Moss, & Sigel, 1963; Vygotsky, 1962; Werner, 1948). Generally, the methodology has consisted of presenting children with a set of objects and asking them to group together those things that are most alike. In some studies, only a single classification is requested, but in other studies, the children are asked to make several alternate classifications (e.g., "Can you do it a different way?"). Some examiners also request the children to explain the bases of their classifications. The findings of these studies have been quite uniform, regardless of the particular objects employed.

From 2 to 4 years of age, children ordinarily sort objects haphazardly, and their rationales are highly idiosyncratic and personalized, often based on individual preferences. By 5 and 6 years, children begin to classify on a more systematic basis, such as function or quality. At this age, however, children are not terribly consistent in their application of classification principles. They often change the criterion from one trial to the next or even from one item to the next. Seven- and 8-year-olds are generally more consistent in their classification and begin to construct hierarchical and multiplicative categories (discussed later). Besides increasing their consistency, children also come to utilize more abstract and more subtle criteria as they get older. Young children tend to favor salient features (such as color), whereas older children may use less obvious qualities (such as the presence of acute angles).

Although the foregoing trends are indeed consistent across many studies, a few investigations suggest that very young children are not totally devoid of classification skills. Denney (1972) presented 2-, 3-, and 4-year-old children with a set of 32 cardboard figures, which included four different shapes, two different sizes, and four different colors. The results indicated that 50% of the 2-year-olds and 89% of the 3- and 4-year-olds constructed classifications based on some sort of similarity. Similarly, Ricciuti (1965) found that it was possible to train 2-year-olds through imitation to classify geometric figures on the basis of shape, size, or color. And Nelson (1974) found that even younger children classified objects, though not on these conventional perceptual attributes. She found that 12–24-month-olds sorted objects primarily on the basis of the functions the objects could be made to perform. Objects were likely to be classified, for example, as edible, rollable, throwable, or pushable; not as red, blue, large, or small. This is consistent with Piaget's (1952b) view that the infant's conceptions of objects are in terms of the action schemes that can be applied to them.

Inhelder and Piaget (1964) also noted certain limitations to the young child's classification skills, which they discussed in terms of the so-called logical groupings that emerge with the transition to concrete operations.

One of these groupings dealt with the addition of classes (also known as class inclusion) and another concerned the multiplication of classes. According to Inhelder and Piaget, the preoperational child fails to see the state of reversible equilibrium existing between a superordinate class and its subclasses. This was revealed on the standard class-inclusion problem in which they showed the child a bunch of, say, 10 flowers, most roses and some not. Preoperational children correctly classified the flowers as to type (say, roses versus nonroses) and correctly indicated that they were all flowers. But when asked whether there were more flowers or more roses, the preoperational child maintained that there were more roses, seemingly disregarding the hierarchically additive composition of the classes and comparing instead the two subclasses.

Though this basic result has been confirmed in a number of replications, a number of investigators have disputed Inhelder and Piaget's interpretation of the failure of preoperational children on class-inclusion problems. They argued that failure is due, not to lack of cognitive structure, but rather to the interference of misleading perceptual cues of various kinds (Ahr & Youniss, 1970; Kalil, Youssef, & Lerner, 1974; Tatarsky, 1974; Wohlwill, 1968). But since other experiments have confirmed Inhelder and Piaget's findings even while controlling for these noncognitive influences, it would seem premature to abandon their analysis (Brainerd & Kaszor, 1974; Winer, 1974b). There is also evidence that, even when young children succeed on class-inclusion problems, it may be due to empirical assessments of the quantities involved rather than to the logic inherent in the additive composition of the classes (Markman, 1978).

Class multiplication involves the ability to conceptualize the logical product or intersection of two or more classes. For example, Inhelder and Piaget (1964) presented the child with a horizontal row of pictures of different-colored leaves. This horizontal row, representing the class of leaves, met to form a right angle with a vertical column of pictures of blue objects of various kinds, representing the class of blue objects. The child's task was to describe the sort of picture that could be placed at the intersection of the two classes—namely, a blue leaf. As with class inclusion, Inhelder and Piaget (1964) found that successful performance on class multiplication did not appear until 8–10 years of age (see Parker & Day, 1971, for a replication).

Thus, whereas rudimentary classification skills may be found in the second year, children do not appear to have mastered some of the logical properties of classification until middle childhood. Also, it must be remembered that the qualities children use to guide their classifications increase in subtlety and abstraction with increasing age.

CONCLUSIONS AND IMPLICATIONS

This chapter was meant to provide a comprehensive review of the literature on the development of concepts of nonsocial inequality. It is hoped that students of developing concepts of social inequality may find it useful to have this material summarized and interpreted in a systematic fashion. No attempt is made here to spell out in detail all the many specific implications this research may have for the study of social cognition. Such a task is left in some measure to the editor and in larger measure to future investigators. It is, in fact, quite difficult at this point to predict exactly what will prove most relevant to research in the social arena. With these considerations in mind, it may now be appropriate to summarize the main conclusions offered by this literature and to discuss some general implications for the study of social cognition.

Conclusions

The concepts of quantitative equivalence and inequivalence are clearly within the grasp of 3-year-old children and may emerge even earlier. These concepts are based on the child's ability to evaluate cardinal numbers, and it is evident that young children possess several strategies for doing this. Subitizing may be the most fundamental of these strategies, appearing between 2 and 3 years of age in the assessment of small arrays of two and three items. Children are able to count arrays of this size by about 3 years of age. On large arrays, 3-year-olds utilize spatial strategies based on a variety of cues, such as length and density and perhaps area and volume as well. By $4\frac{1}{2}$ years, the strategy of one-to-one correspondence becomes available. It is important to note that the accuracy of some of these strategies, particularly subitizing and counting, is severely limited by the size of the array. Even in adults, subitizing does not go beyond about four to five items, and it takes at least a few years for counting skills to be extended to the larger numbers. Children of 3 years are also well aware of the impact of number-relevant transformations, such as addition and subtraction, on equality relations. And they realize that certain other transformations (e.g., of shape, color, or identity) do not alter either number or the relation of equality. The evidence suggests that the concepts of equality and inequality emerge together and that any apparent asymmetry in their development is due to the differential frequency of errors in the application of certain strategies to equal and unequal arrays.

By 4 or 5 years of age, the child begins to use functions to interpret quantitative inequalities. The burgeoning literature on functional reasoning suggests a number of developmental trends or principles: (*a*) progressive quantification of functions; (*b*) extension to larger quantities; (*c*) directly to inversely proportionate variation; (*d*) inclusion of more variables; and (*e*) causal to purely functional relations.

The concept of proportionality emerges relatively late but, when operative, enables the child to conceive of proportional or relative inequality. Adolescents utilize proportional concepts spontaneously, and children of 6–7 years can be trained to do so. It is important for research in this area to clearly distinguish proportionality from both magnitude estimation and probability. It was noted that assessments of the probability or likelihood of hypothetical events can be applied to either sheer magnitudes or proportions.

Linguistic expressions for relations of equality and inequality, such as *more* and *same*, appear by about 5 years of age, with *less* appearing somewhat later. This is in general conformity with the idea that linguistic development follows closely upon cognitive development.

The child's understanding of qualitative inequalities is based on the emergence of classification skills. The evidence indicates that the rudiments of classification are present during the second year and that further developments take place in terms of the subtlety and abstractness of the criteria for classification. The ability to reason about hierarchical and multiplicative classification does not seem to develop until about 8–10 years of age.

Implications for understanding social inequality

It is likely that research discussed elsewhere in this book will indicate that certain aspects of social inequality are not correctly understood by children below particular levels of development. The proper interpretation of such failures to understand in young children is not always straightforward. Research reviewed here on children's developing conception of nonsocial inequality points to a number of possible interpretations. One is that children fail to show understanding of a particular social concept because they have not yet developed that concept. The correctness of this interpretation becomes increasingly likely insofar as the nonsocial analogue concept is a late-appearing one, such as proportionality. It is not so likely in the case of an early-developing nonsocial analogue concept, such as inequality (unless the child is under about 3 years of age). In such cases, it would be wise to look instead for difficulties in evocation or implementation. The situation may not successfully evoke conceptual structures that children do indeed possess; or even if it does, there may be difficulties in the implementation of these structures leading to errors or misconceptions. Such *false negatives* in developmental diagnosis are often due to the use of overcomplicated tasks. These are tasks that are too difficult for children for nonconceptual reasons. There may be too much information, or the information may be presented in a way that is too difficult to process, or the child's attention may be diverted elsewhere. Studies attempting to assess concepts of equality and inequality by presenting children with overly large arrays are a good example of this. A critical feature of many studies of social cognition is the manner in which information is presented. It has been demonstrated that young children do far better with information presented live or on videotape than they do with verbal stories (e.g., Chandler, Greenspan, & Barenboim, 1973; Shultz & Butkowsky, 1977).

Just as investigators must guard against false negatives, they must also beware of *false positives*—that is, inferring from successful performance of a task that the child possesses the presumed underlying conceptual structure. This danger was well illustrated in research on the concept of proportionality. Successful performance on tasks that could be solved by mere magnitude estimation was falsely interpreted as evidence of use of the proportionality concept. False negatives and false positives are both illustrations of the general principle that a given behavior can often be accounted for by different conceptual structures.

The other side of this diagnostic coin is that there are a number of different ways in which a child may possess a given concept. And these different ways appear to form a regular developmental sequence. The child may reveal a concept in his or her behavior before being able to use it as a basis for cognitive judgments. Laxon's (1981) evidence on the earlier understanding of the terms *more* and *same* with behavioral rather than with judgmental measures provides an example. Judgmental measures, in turn, typically reveal earlier understanding than do measures of verbal justification. The greater sensitivity of Gelman's (1972a, 1972b) magic-show paradigm compared to Piaget's (1952a) conservation procedure is a case in point. Additional examples of this principle from the realms of social cognition (Wells & Shultz, 1980) and metalinguistic development (deVilliers & deVilliers, 1972) are available.

It is hardly ever a trivial matter to determine precisely what cognitive structures are available to a given child. It is hoped that the diagnostic problems encountered and dealt with in the study of nonsocial concepts of inequality will prove helpful to those interested in studying the development of concepts of social inequality.

REFERENCES

Ahr, P. R., & Youniss, J. Reasons for failure on the class-inclusion problem. *Child Development*, 1970, *41*, 131–144.

Bartlett, E. J. Sizing things up: The acquisition of the meaning of dimensional adjectives. *Journal of Child Language*, 1976, *3*, 205–219.

Behr, M., Erlwanger, S., & Nichols, E. *How children view equality sentences.* Tallahassee: Florida State University, 1976. (ERIC Document Reproduction Service No. ED 144 802)

Bell, S. M. The development of the concept of object as related to infant–mother attachment. *Child Development*, 1970, *41*, 291–311.

Boersma, F. J., & Wilton, K. M. Eye movements and conservation acceleration. *Journal of Experimental Child Psychology*, 1974, *17*, 49–60.

Brainerd, C. J. Judgments and explanations as criteria for the presence of cognitive structures. *Psychological Bulletin*, 1973, *79*, 172–179.

Brainerd, C. J., & Kaszor, P. An analysis of two proposed sources of children's class-inclusion errors. *Developmental Psychology*, 1974, *10*, 633–643.

Bruner, J. S., & Kenney, H. J. On relational concepts. In J. S. Bruner, R. R. Olver, & P. M. Greenfield (Eds.), *Studies in cognitive growth.* New York: Wiley, 1966.

Bruner, J. S., Olver, R. R., & Greenfield, P. M. *Studies in cognitive growth.* New York: Wiley, 1966.

Bullock, M., & Gelman, R. Numerical reasoning in young children: The ordering principle. *Child Development*, 1977, *48*, 427–434.

Bunge, M. *Causality and modern science* (3rd rev. ed.). New York: Dover, 1979.

Carey, S. Less may never mean more. In P. Smith & R. Campbell (Eds.), *Proceedings of the Stirling Conference on the Psychology of Language.* New York: Plenum, 1977.

Chandler, M. J., Greenspan, S., & Barenboim, C. Judgments of intentionality in response to videotaped and verbally presented moral dilemmas: The medium is the message. *Child Development*, 1973, *44*, 315–320.

Chapman, R. H. The development of children's understanding of proportions. *Child Development*, 1975, *46*, 141–148.

Chi, M. T. H., & Klahr, D. Span and rate of apprehension in children and adults. *Journal of Experimental Child Psychology*, 1975, *19*, 434–439.

Clark, E. V. What's in a word? On the child's acquisition of semantics in his first language. In T. E. Moore (Ed.), *Cognitive development and the acquisition of language.* New York: Academic Press, 1973.

Clark, H. H. Linguistic processes in deductive reasoning. *Psychological Review*, 1969, *76*, 387–404.

Clark, H. H. The primitive nature of children's relational concepts. In J. R. Hayes (Ed.), *Cognition and the development of language.* New York: Wiley, 1970.

Davies, C. M. Development of the probability concept in children. *Child Development*, 1965, *36*, 779–788.

Denney, N. W. Free classification in preschool children. *Child Development*, 1972, *43*, 1161–1170.

deVilliers, P. A., & deVilliers, J. G. Early judgments of semantic and syntactic acceptability by children. *Journal of Psycholinguistic Research*, 1972, *1*, 299–310.

Donaldson, M., & Balfour, G. Less is more: A study of language comprehension in children. *British Journal of Psychology*, 1968, *59*, 461–472.

Eilers, R. E., Oller, D. K., & Ellington, J. The acquisition of word meaning for dimensional adjectives: The long and the short of it. *Journal of Child Language*, 1974, *1*, 195–204.

Estes, K. W. Nonverbal discrimination of more and fewer elements by children. *Journal of Experimental Child Psychology,* 1976, *21,* 393–406.

Gelman, R. The nature and development of early number concepts. In H. W. Reese (Ed.), *Advances in child development and behavior* (Vol. 7). New York: Academic Press, 1972. (a)

Gelman, R. Logical capacity of very young children: Number invariance rules. *Child Development,* 1972, *43,* 75–90. (b)

Gelman, R., & Gallistel, C. R. *The child's understanding of number.* Cambridge, Mass.: Harvard Univ. Press, 1978.

Gelman, R., & Tucker, M. F. Further investigations of the young child's conception of number. *Child Development,* 1975, *46,* 167–175.

Ginsburg, H. *Children's arithmetic: The learning process.* New York: Van Nostrand, 1977.

Ginsburg, H., & Rapoport, A. Children's estimate of proportions. *Child Development,* 1967, *38,* 205–212.

Haygood, R. C., & Bourne, L. E. Attribute- and rule-learning aspects of conceptual behavior. *Psychological Review,* 1965, *72,* 175–195.

Hoemann, H. W., & Ross, B. M. Children's understanding of probability concepts. *Child Development,* 1971, *42,* 221–236.

Holland, V. M., & Palermo, D. S. On learning "less": Language and cognitive development. *Child Development,* 1975, *46,* 437–443.

Inhelder, B., & Piaget, J. *The early growth of logic in the child: Classification and seriation.* London: Routledge & Kegan Paul, 1964.

Kagan, J., Moss, H., & Sigel, I. Psychological significance of styles of conceptualization. *Monographs of the Society for Research in Child Development,* 1963, *28,* 73–112.

Kalil, K., Youssef, Z., & Lerner, R. M. Class-inclusion failure: Cognitive deficit or misleading reference? *Child Development,* 1974, *45,* 1122–1125.

Kassin, S. M., Lowe, C. A., & Gibbons, F. X. Children's use of the discounting principle: A perceptual approach. *Journal of Personality and Social Psychology,* 1980, *39,* 719–728.

Kelley, H. H. The processes of causal attribution. *American Psychologist,* 1973, *28,* 107–128.

Klahr, D. Quantification processes. In W. G. Chase (Ed.), *Visual information processing.* New York: Academic Press, 1973.

Klahr, D., & Wallace, J. G. *Cognitive development: An information processing view.* Hillsdale, N.J.: Erlbaum, 1976.

Landauer, T. Rate of implicit speech. *Perceptual and Motor Skills,* 1962, *15,* 646.

Lapointe, K., & O'Donnell, J. P. Number conservation in children below age six: Its relationship to age, perceptual dimensions and language comprehension. *Developmental Psychology,* 1974, *10,* 422–428.

Lawson, G., Baron, J., & Siegel, L. The role of number and length cues in children's quantitative judgments. *Child Development,* 1974, *45,* 731–736.

Laxon, V. J. On the problems of being more or less the same. *Journal of Experimental Child Psychology,* 1981, *31,* 531–543.

Mackie, J. L. *The cement of the universe: A study of causation.* Oxford: Clarendon, 1974.

Markman, E. M. Empirical vs. logical solutions to part–whole comparison problems concerning classes and collections. *Child Development,* 1978, *49,* 168–177.

Nelson, K. Concept, word, and sentence: Interrelations in acquisition and development. *Psychological Review,* 1974, *81,* 267–285.

Nelson, K., & Benedict, H. The comprehension of relative, absolute, and contrastive adjectives by young children. *Journal of Psycholinguistic Research,* 1974, *3,* 333–342.

Nelson, K., Zelniker, T., & Jeffrey, W. E. The child's concept of proportionality: A reexamination. *Journal of Experimental Child Psychology,* 1969, *8,* 256–262.

Newman, R. (Ed.). *The Harper encyclopedia of science* (rev. ed.). New York: Harper, 1967.

O'Bryan, K. G., & Boersma, F. J. Movie presentation of Piagetian tasks: A procedure for the assessment of conservation attainment. *Journal of Genetic Psychology*, 1972, *121*, 295–302.

Palermo, D. S. More about less: A study of language comprehension. *Journal of Verbal Learning and Verbal Behavior*, 1973, *12*, 211–221.

Parker, R. K., & Day, M. C. The use of perceptual, functional, and abstract attributes in multiple classification. *Developmental Psychology*, 1971, *5*, 312–319.

Perret-Clermont, A.-N. *Social interaction and cognitive development in children*. New York: Academic Press, 1980.

Piaget, J. *The child's conception of number*. New York: Humanities, 1952. (a)

Piaget, J. *The origins of intelligence in children*. New York: International Universities Press, 1952. (b)

Piaget, J. *Understanding causality*. New York: Norton, 1974.

Piaget, J., Grize, J.-B., Szeminska, A., & Vinh Bang. *Epistemology and psychology of functions*. Dordrecht, Holland: D. Reidel, 1977.

Piaget, J., & Inhelder, B. *The origin of the idea of chance in children*. New York: Norton, 1976.

Potter, M. C., & Levy, E. I. Spatial enumeration without counting. *Child Development*, 1968, *39*, 265–272.

Pufall, P. B., & Shaw, R. E. Precocious thoughts on number: The long and the short of it. *Developmental Psychology*, 1972, *7*, 62–69.

Ricciuti, H. Object grouping and selective ordering behavior in infants 12–24 months old. *Merrill-Palmer Quarterly*, 1965, *11*, 129–148.

Rose, S. A., & Blank, M. The potency of context in children's cognition: An illustration through conservation. *Child Development*, 1974, *45*, 499–502.

Russac, R. J. The relation between two strategies of cardinal number: Correspondence and counting. *Child Development*, 1978, *49*, 728–735.

Saltz, E., & Hamilton, H. Concept conservation under positively and negatively evaluated transformations. *Journal of Experimental Child Psychology*, 1968, *6*, 44–51.

Shultz, T. R. Development of the concept of intention. In W. A. Collins (Ed.), *The Minnesota Symposium on Child Psychology* (Vol. 13). Hillsdale, N.J.: Erlbaum, 1980.

Shultz, T. R. Rules of causal attribution. *Monographs of the Society for Research in Child Development*, 1982, *47*(1, Serial No. 194).

Shultz, T. R., & Asselin, J. A. *The role of causal mechanism in the understanding of functional relations*. Unpublished manuscript, McGill University, 1981.

Shultz, T. R., & Butkowsky, I. Young children's use of the scheme for multiple sufficient causes in the attribution of real and hypothetical behavior. *Child Development*, 1977, *48*, 464–469.

Shultz, T. R., Butkowsky, I., Pearce, J. W., & Shanfield, H. Development of schemes for the attribution of multiple psychological causes. *Developmental Psychology*, 1975, *11*, 502–510.

Shultz, T. R., Wells, D., & Clarke, K. *Conception of two-variable functions involving time or number*. Unpublished manuscript, McGill University, 1981.

Siegel, L. S. Heterogeneity and spatial factors as determinants of numeration ability. *Child Development*, 1974, *45*, 532–534.

Siegler, R. S., & Vago, S. The development of a proportionality concept: Judging relative fullness. *Journal of Experimental Child Psychology*, 1978, *25*, 371–395.

Sigel, I. E., Saltz, E., & Roskind, W. Variables determining concept conservation in children. *Journal of Experimental Psychology*, 1967, *74*, 471–475.

Slovic, P. Hypothesis testing in the learning of positive and negative linear functions. *Organizational Behavior and Human Performance*, 1974, *11*, 368–376.

Smither, S. J., Smiley, S. S., & Rees, P. The use of perceptual cues for number judgment by young children. *Child Development*, 1974, *45*, 693–699.

Starkey, P., & Cooper, R. G. Perception of numbers by human infants. *Science*, 1980, *210*, 1033–1035.

Sternberg, S. Retrieval of contextual information from memory. *Psychonomic Science*, 1967, *8*, 55–56.

Tatarsky, J. H. The influence of dimensional manipulations on class-inclusion performance. *Child Development*, 1974, *45*, 1173–1175.

Townsend, D. J. Children's comprehension of comparative forms. *Journal of Experimental Child Psychology*, 1974, *18*, 293–303.

Townsend, D. J., & Erb, M. Children's strategies for interpreting complex comparative questions. *Journal of Child Language*, 1975, *2*, 1–7.

Trehub, S. E., & Abramovitch, R. Less is not more: Further observations on non-linguistic strategies. *Journal of Experimental Child Psychology*, 1978, *25*, 160–167.

Vygotsky, L. *Thought and language*. Cambridge, Mass.: MIT Press, 1962.

Walters, J., & Wagner, S. *The earliest numbers: A longitudinal study of children's number word acquisition and counting development*. Paper presented at the meeting of Society for Research in Child Development, Boston, April 1981.

Wason, P. C. The processing of positive and negative information. *Quarterly Journal of Experimental Psychology*, 1959, *11*, 92–107.

Weiner, B., & Kun, A. The development of causal attributions and the growth of achievement and social motivation. In S. Feldman & D. Bush (Eds.), *Cognitive development and social development*. Hillsdale, N.J.: Erlbaum, 1976.

Weiner, S. L. On the development of *more* and *less*. *Journal of Experimental Child Psychology*, 1974, *17*, 271–287.

Wells, D., & Shultz, T. R. Developmental distinctions between behavior and judgment in the operation of the discounting principle. *Child Development*, 1980, *51*, 1307–1310.

Werner, H. *Comparative psychology of mental development*. New York: Harper, 1948.

Winer, G. A. Conservation of different quantities among preschool children. *Child Development*, 1974, *45*, 839–842. (a)

Winer, G. A. An analysis of verbal facilitation of class-inclusion reasoning. *Child Development*, 1974, *45*, 224–227. (b)

Wohlwill, J. F. Responses to class-inclusion questions for verbally and pictorially presented items. *Child Development*, 1968, *39*, 449–466.

Wright, G. H. von. *Causality and determinism*. New York: Columbia Univ. Press, 1974.

Yost, P. A., Siegel, A. E., & Andrews, J. M. Nonverbal probability judgments by young children. *Child Development*, 1962, *33*, 769–780.

Zaslavsky, C. *Africa counts*. Boston: Prindle, Weber, & Schmidt, 1973.

2 / Developmental foundations of gender and racial attitudes[1]

PHYLLIS A. KATZ

At birth, the newborn has little knowledge of where he or she ends and the rest of the world begins. That same child will enter school, however, with a fairly well-differentiated sense of self, together with some clearly defined notions about many social groups and their distinguishing characteristics. The relative status of each group vis-à-vis one another and how each group is evaluated within the larger society will also be common knowledge. Moreover, much of the child's own developing sense of identity will be based on this knowledge of how the social world is organized.

This chapter will attempt to describe the nature and sequencing of this early development and the types of maturational and psychological processes that may underlie it during the first 6 years of life. These processes can be conceptualized as significant forerunners of later intergroup attitudes held by older children, adolescents, and adults. Of primary interest will be the early learning and cognitions with regard to both gender and race. Each of these dimensions, of course, constitutes the basis for group classifications that have long been regarded as particularly significant in our society.

[1]Preparation of this chapter was assisted by Contract No. N01–HD–92820 from the National Institute of Child Health and Human Development, Phyllis A. Katz, principal investigator.

41

THE CHILD'S CONSTRUCTION
OF SOCIAL INEQUALITY

The general issue of which particular person attributes are actually employed as a basis for grouping is an interesting one to consider in its own right. Clearly, the neonate enters a world where these basic decisions have already been made, and thus, an important part of the child's early learning is composed of ascertaining which particular perceptually distinctive cues also have social significance. It should be noted, however, that there is wide societal diversity with regard to the kinds of cues used to define social groups. Moreover, even cues that appear to be universally employed to categorize individuals (such as gender) are not necessarily equally important in different cultures (Barry, Bacon, & Child, 1957; Mead, 1961), and the particular sets of expectations associated with similarly defined groups vary widely across cultures (Sanday, 1981). This cross-cultural perspective underscores the arbitrariness of all definitions of social groups in spite of their seeming necessity within a given culture. The point being made is simply that innumerable options are available as ways to classify individuals. In practice, however, those that have been culturally selected are often regarded as either the only or the most cogent way of organizing one's social environment.

A related issue has to do with why individuals need to be grouped at all. The question could be raised as to why each person is not responded to solely in terms of his or her own unique set of characteristics. Although the tendency to classify individuals appears to be universal, we might still speculate about how essential it is. Perhaps the dynamics underlying the need for social classification are similar to those that Bruner, Goodnow, and Austin (1956) suggest are generally at the root of any type of concept formation—namely, a desire to reduce an overwhelming amount of stimulus information and, consequently, simplify one's perceptual world. It should be noted, however, that such simplification when applied to the social world also has some inherent disadvantages. Langer (1979) has commented on the negative consequences for both social interaction and thought processes when person categories are mindlessly maintained. The very process of learning categorizations may also have insidious perceptual effects that may enhance the development of prejudice. The learning and usage of group labels have been shown to minimize the perception of intragroup differences, while accentuating intergroup ones (Katz, 1973; Tajfel, 1969). The relation of these basic perceptual processes to intergroup attitude development will be delineated further in subsequent sections.

The organization of this chapter will be both age related and topical. The first section will concern itself with the first 3 years of life. For this age group, three subsections will be used to describe (*a*) the development of gender awareness; (*b*) the development of racial awareness; and (*c*) the similarities and differences between the two. Analogous developmental processes with regard to the preschool period (ages 3–6) will then be discussed and elaborated.

THE FIRST THREE YEARS

There is a perceptual prerequisite involved in learning any category system. Prior to being able to define a social group, the child must be able to discriminate between groups and learn which cues are relevant for group inclusion or exclusion. Learning about people is analogous to all early concept formation. For instance, the category "cow" is defined (for young children) by the sound it makes, which is different from sounds other animals make. During early language development, young children receive considerable training of this kind and parental rewards for correct classification responses. When the child correctly verbalizes "meow" to the pussycat and "bowwow" to the puppy, parents express their pleasure. Thus, it may be that both this extensive practice with classification skills and the associated reinforcement may generalize and increase a child's predisposition for categorizing people.

Because of the perceptual prerequisite, young children's initial classifications are based on cues that are easily discernible. This is undoubtedly why both gender and race are learned so early. It also accounts in part for why religion and nationality cues are learned at much later stages. It is interesting to note, in this regard, that the absence of clear perceptual cues for classifying certain ethnic groups has occasionally led governments to add them. In Nazi Germany, Jews were forced to wear Stars of David so that they could be more easily identified. In Truffaut's movie "The Last Metro," a story based in German-occupied Paris in 1942, a Nazi radio announcer decries the fact that it is so difficult to tell who is Jewish: "Wouldn't it be nice," he asks, "if they just all had blue skin?"

The cues for learning about gender and race are more readily apparent than those for religion, particularly to a young child. Between the two, it would appear that gender cues are more physically complex than racial ones, since the former vary with the age of the person. This complexity, however, appears to be compensated for by the fact that information relevant to gender is enormously redundant and overdetermined throughout the life span (Katz, 1979).

Gender awareness in the first three years

There are two interrelated modes in which an infant learns about gender cues. The first has to do with direct adult input and treatment—that is, how he or she is responded to. The second has to do with the child's direct repeated observations of adults and children in his or her social environment. Both of these processes begin at birth. Let us consider each of them in turn.

ADULT INPUT AND TREATMENT

So concerned is the social environment with gender that it is highly probable that the first words the baby hears uttered relate to it. At delivery, the child's sex is usually announced. Thus, the first words probably heard by the infant are either "It's a boy" or "It's a girl," underscoring immediately the primacy of gender categories.

One of the most consistent findings in the research pertinent to early parent–infant interaction is that adults respond differently to the child as a function of gender. One study by Rubin, Provenzano, and Luria (1974), for example, found that parents of day-old sons viewed their babies as bigger than parents of day-old daughters. In actuality, the infants did not differ in either weight or length. Other kinds of stereotypes were also exhibited by these parents in the first 24 hr of their babies' lives. Girls were described as "softer," "finer," and "little," whereas sons were perceived as "firmer," "more alert," and "stronger."

In another study, conducted by the present author and colleagues (Seavey, Katz, & Zalk, 1975), the same 3-month-old infant was introduced to nonparent adults with either a girl's name, a boy's name, or no name (and thus no gender information). In subsequent play activity, the adults used a doll more frequently when they believed the child to be a girl. Moreover, the subjects exhibited considerable discomfort in the condition where no gender information was given. When interviewed afterward, all subjects indicated that they had indeed attributed a particular gender to the child and used "appropriate" cues to buttress their decision. Those who thought the child to be a boy (70%, despite the fact that the infant was female) commented on such things as its firm grip and absence of hair, whereas those who thought it was a girl mentioned such attributes as the softness of its skin and its cuddliness. These results have recently been replicated by Sidorowicz and Lunney (1980), utilizing similar procedures.

In a similar vein, Condry and Condry (1976), found differential reactions to the same videotaped 9-month-old infant as a function of the attributed gender label. In this study, the child's emotional responsivity was judged by adults. An infant who cried in response to a jack-in-the-box was reported to be "angry" when they thought it was a boy but "fearful" when the child was identified as a girl. In addition, the same infant when given a male name was judged to be more active and potent than when it was associated with a female name. Differences in toy handling and stimulation as a function of attributed gender have also been reported by Will, Self, and Datan (1976) with a baby dressed as either a girl or boy. Similarly, Smith and Lloyd (1978) found that the perceived sex of an unfamiliar 6-month-old infant affected both toy choices and the degree to which gross motor behavior was encouraged. When the baby was introduced as a boy, a toy hammer was selected and the child was verbally encouraged to engage in large-scale vigorous play. When the baby was introduced as a girl, however, a doll was offered as a play object and gentler vocalizations were used.

Each of these studies make substantially the same point: Adults treat boys and girls differently from birth as a function of perceived gender cues. This differentiation occurs even when objective differences with regard to the infants are absent. It should be noted that an alternative explanation is often given for socialization differences based on differential adult reactivity. It is commonly believed that adults treat boys and girls differently as a response to the different behavior patterns they exhibit. Outside of a laboratory situation, of course, it is impossible to disentangle how much of the differential treatment is responsive and how much is based on earlier expectations and stereotypes that have nothing to do with the child's behavior. It is clear from the studies cited here, however, that expectations can substantially influence adult behavior even when all else is held constant. Behavior based on such expectations may subsequently become self-fulfilling in terms of its effects on children.

If such potent effects of gender labels can be demonstrated in the laboratory, where the adults have not had much contact with an infant, the magnitude of gender typing in the real world must be very great indeed. Even casual observation reveals that there is scarcely an area untouched by sex typing. It is difficult to purchase a gift for an infant without the salesperson asking the sex of the child and directing one to the "appropriate" items. In addition to the obvious clothing and color differences (e.g., pink versus blue and dress versus pants), manufacturers offer an astounding array of masculine and feminine styles in many diverse items, including booties (ballet slippers for girls, running shoes for boys) and rubber pants (pink ruffles versus blue denim). Even with regard to toys for young infants, stuffed kittens and bunnies are recommended for girls, whereas stuffed lions and tigers are seen as more appropriate for boys. If stores are indeed reflecting parental sentiment, it would appear that mothers and fathers are very desirous of announcing the sex of their child to the world. This in turn sets up an inexorable chain of events. As the earlier-cited studies show, adults will react to infant gender cues with differential social responses and differential expectations. Ruffles elicit one set of responses, whereas "little slugger" t-shirts elicit another, and there is remarkable consistency within each category.

In addition to differences in social treatment, the actual physical environments of male and female infants have been found to differ widely (Rheingold & Cook, 1975). This is reflected in both room decor and toy availability. A "softer" environment is generally provided for girls, and differences are both obvious and subtle. Even where pinks and blues are not used for differentiation, colors in girls' rooms are more likely to be pastel and muted, rather than bright. Sex-appropriate female patterns tend to have smaller prints and more detail, rather than the bold stripes or animals typically selected for boys' rooms. Similar differences are seen in fabric used for boys' and girls' clothing. It does not seem too far-fetched to assume that such consistent differences have psychological significance as well, although these have never been specifically assessed. A muted, soft environment may well be more calming on both the infant and the caretakers. In contrast, a visual environment that is bolder, brighter, and livelier may well have potential energizing effects. Although we cannot ascertain what specific results might occur as a function of continued exposure to a very lively versus a very serene environment, it does not seem too remote to anticipate that there may well be both emotional and behavioral ramifications.

In addition to these global environmental differences, parents, grandparents, and friends supply the young infant with an array of toys, and these often vary by gender. Not all toys designed for infants are sex typed. In fact, the proportion of sex-typed toys young children play with probably increases with age during early childhood. Even when a toy is gender neutral, however, cues are often added that assist the stranger in discovering the baby's gender. Rattles and teething rings, for example, while ostensibly gender neutral, come in an assortment of colors and patterns that are themselves sex typed—parents simply do not buy pink rattles for their sons.

Although we have discussed a number of factors that enable the infant to learn about gender, parents themselves probably constitute the most significant social influence in this area. A considerable body of research has demonstrated that both fathers and mothers treat their sons and daughters differently from birth. Personality stereotypes and behavioral expectations exist prior to birth, and these clearly affect subsequent interactions. For example, boy infants appear to be valued more and preferred, especially by fathers (Coombs, Coombs, & McClelland,

1975; Hoffman, 1975). Hoffman (1977) found that women typically expect daughters to be more obedient, and thus easier to raise, but think sons will be more pleasing to their husbands.

Unlike the very clear-cut differences that emerge with regard to toys and physical environments, early interaction patterns are vastly more subtle and not consistent across age. During the first 3 months of life, for example, male infants are touched more frequently by their mothers than are female infants (Lewis, 1972a). Boys are rocked and handled more frequently but also less gently than girls (Moss, 1967; Parke & O'Leary, 1976; Yarrow, Rubenstein, & Pederson, 1972). At this early age, girls are touched less, but they are talked to and looked at more, particularly by their mothers (Lewis & Cherry, 1977; Lewis & Goldberg, 1969; Moss, 1967).

One can only speculate on why these differences exist. It may be that boys are initially touched more because, as noted earlier, they are more highly valued. In addition, male infants tend to be more physically vulnerable in the early months (Garai & Scheinfeld, 1968) and thus may elicit more soothing and gentle behavior from their parents. Whatever the reason, the pattern of sex differences observed in interaction during the first 3 months of life reverses itself at 6 months (and thereafter). By the middle of the first year, girls are touched more frequently, and mothers' touching behavior with regard to their sons decreases markedly (Lewis, 1972b). Thus, by 6 months of age, infants are treated differentially by their caretakers in a manner that both approximates and encourages future sex-appropriate behavior: Within our society, touching and physical expression of affection are considered more appropriate for females than for males.

Similar patterns are evident in other interactional sequences as well. Female infants typically receive more social stimulation of all kinds, including more verbal interaction (Lewis, 1972a; Thoman, Leiderman, & Olson, 1972). Although the effects remain to be documented, we can again speculate on what the long-term consequences of this phenomenon might be. The exposure of the female to richer and more frequent vocalizations may account for her later superior verbal skills. On the other hand, the combined effects of greater maternal touching, looking, and socialization may well enhance the female's social involvement, while her brother is busier exploring and manipulating the world of inanimate objects.

These environmental and social differences in the treatment of male and female infants may well have a considerable and long-lasting impact on the developing child's cognitive style, personality pattern, and future interests. Each of the previously discussed phenomena have immediate effects as well in terms of laying the groundwork for the establishment of one's core gender identity during the first 2 years of life.

THE CHILD'S COGNITION AND PERCEPTION

There are two interrelated cognitive aspects to gender identity development. The first involves the application of the correct gender label to oneself and the consequent elaboration of its meaning. The second concerns the ability to differentiate other persons with regard to gender cues. These two components probably develop concurrently, although the second (i.e., differentiation of others) is observable at somewhat earlier maturational levels.

Correct self-labeling and gender conceptualization is a lengthy developmental process, requiring cognitive skills that are not yet present in the first 2 years. Some environmental precursors of this, however, can be found in the differential treatment of boys and girls discussed in the preceding pages. In addition to the differences previously discussed, the very frequent use of gender labeling by others should also be mentioned. Statements such as, "Aren't you a strong little boy," and "What a pretty little girl you are," are made with such frequency that we hardly notice them. From the child's point of view, however, the repeated use of such labeling may represent an important rudimentary way of organizing social experience. With the exception of one's first name (which itself is ordinarily gender linked), few words are used toward the infant with such consistency as *boy* or *girl*. Probably because of this, most children can correctly label themselves with a fair degree of accuracy by 2 years of age (Kuhn, Nash, & Brucken, 1978; Slaby & Frey, 1975).

Before infants are capable of using words in this way, however, most children have exhibited the ability to differentiate some aspects of gender in others. The process by which this occurs is not entirely clear. A number of preverbal gender cues are probably used at varying points in the first 2 years. Voice pitch is undoubtedly a significant one. It has been found, for example, that young infants condition more quickly to high-pitched than to low-pitched voices (Blehar, 1980; Wolff, 1963). This suggests not only a perceptual skill but perhaps also an innate adaptive mechanism that enables the infant to readily seek out those persons (typically female) who are the sources of primary reinforcement. It would be of interest to see whether infants whose primary caretaker is male (admittedly rare) may come to exhibit a preference for low-pitched voices.

Other distinctions that are probably salient relatively early in life include olfactory, tactile, and visual cues. In the olfactory area, for instance, women's cosmetics are perfumed. There are also systematic differences in the way male and female adults handle infants. Although considerable within-gender variability exists in the manner that infants are picked up and held, men often exhibit more initial awkwardness and discomfort. Differential visual cues occur in a number of areas, such as stature and dress. Height differences between male and female adults may be observable to the infant at various phases of development, perhaps beginning when the child becomes locomotory. Before this time, adults bend toward infants in cribs and so systematic height differences might not be easily visible to the child. It is possible, however, that even during these early months, an infant might notice different vantage points as a result of being picked up by a male or a female; that is, they are typically held higher by a male. Systematic differences in dress and hairstyle may also be apparent. At a proximal level, skin contact with a male or female is also a differential experience. One does not usually feel stubble on mommy's face. Thus, in all sense modalities, gender cues are potentially discriminative, although their salience may not be pronounced during the first year. Perhaps the most significant gender cue, however, has to do with differential availability: Mommy (or a female substitute) is there; daddy is usually not. (Once again, some interesting but as yet unconducted research suggests itself with male primary infant caretakers.)

Parents are delighted to discover that their child's first words usually include *mommy* and *daddy*. The child's correct use of these nouns, together with their incorrect generalization to other adults shows that children clearly have rudimentary gender concepts by the time they can speak. While the use of the word *daddy* for a strange male adult might be embarrassing to a parent, the fact that it is almost never used in conjunction with a strange female adult suggests that, although the child's concepts are rudimentary, they are already accurate by about 18 months of age.

The child's increasing ability to discriminate gender cues during the first 3 years has been demonstrated with regard to peers as well. Lewis and Brooks (1975) found that as early as 10 months of age infants fixate more to photographs of a same-sex infant than an opposite-sex one. This preference is particularly interesting given that adults were unable to discern the gender of the photographed babies. This preference for and enhanced attention to same-sex children has also been observed in the social behavior of $2\frac{1}{2}$-year-olds. Within a laboratory situation, Jacklin and Maccoby (1978) found that young children responded more (in both positive and negative ways) to same-sex than to opposite-sex children they had not previously met. One of the particularly interesting features of this study is that the children were not told each other's name or sex, and all children were similarly dressed in pants. Thus, some of the more usual visual cues for distinguishing gender were absent. Nevertheless, boy–boy and girl–girl pairs exhibited higher rates of social interaction than did mixed-sex dyads. The underpinnings of this peer preference behavior are not well understood.

Three additional trends, describing concurrent developmental phenomena, appear to be conceptually relevant to gender identity formation and deserve mention. First, preferences for sex-appropriate toys have been found in children as young as 2 years of age (Blakemore, LaRue, & Olejnik, 1979; Fagot, 1974, 1977a), indicating that both knowledge and prior learning have occurred. This knowledge of sex typing has also been obtained with regard to adult possessions (Weinraub, Brown, Sockloff, Ethridge, & Gracely, 1982) and jobs (Kuhn *et al.*, 1978) between 2 and 3 years of age. Second, correct verbal identification of one's own and other people's gender is present before age 3 (Thompson, 1975). Finally, the intriguing findings of Money, Hampson, and Hampson (1957) with anatomically atypical children have shown how psychologically problematical it is to surgically change a child's gender after 2 years of age (cf. Money & Ehrhardt, 1972). Although gender development is far from complete and considerable gender confusion is still to be found, an amazing amount of gender awareness does develop in the first 3 years of life.

In summary, it would appear from the diverse findings discussed here that children's main achievements in the area of sex roles by 3 years of age include (*a*) the development of the ability to differentiate both children and adults on the basis of gender; and (*b*) the correct classification of themselves and others on the basis of gender cues. This primary gender identity seems relatively resistant to change and already includes information about what things constitute gender-appropriate behavior. Possible factors that underlie these developmental processes include (*a*) the salience of gender for adults; (*b*) the redundancy of sex-typed cues; and (*c*) the differential social and physical environments of male and female infants.

Racial awareness

As is evident from the previous section, much remains to be understood about the processes involved in gender awareness. Even less is known, however, about the development of racial awareness during the first 3 years of life. This is undoubtedly because less systematic research has been conducted with very young children in the racial area, probably reflecting the fact that gender is a more significant cue than race for children (Katz & Zalk, 1974).

In the mid-1970s, the present author noted (Katz, 1976) that no studies of racial awareness had been conducted with children below 3 years of age, and this still remains largely the case. Consequently, discussions concerning the development of racial perception during the first 3 years of life will be necessarily speculative. Such speculation may be important to engage in, however, for at least two reasons. First, it may serve to stimulate needed research. The second reason stems from the repeated finding that a sizable proportion of 3-year-old and most 4-year-old children do exhibit awareness of racial cues, as well as preferential patterns. If this is indeed the case (a topic that will be discussed in more detail in a subsequent section), then it is clear that the underlying developmental processes must have taken place during the earlier period.

The overwhelming majority of recent studies of children relevant to the racial area have been conducted with regard to perceptions and attitudes about white–black differences. Thus, generalizations about racial and ethnic cue perceptions to other groups or other pairs of groups may not be warranted. As noted earlier in this chapter, ethnic group differences that are based on cues more subtle than skin color are not readily perceived by children until much later in their development. In this regard, Cairns (1978), for example, has shown that the majority of children in Northern Ireland do not accurately discriminate between Catholic and Protestant names until age 11, despite the fact that this categorization is indeed a salient one within the society. Other studies have shown, however, that one's own religious group is known by age 7 or 8 (Radke & Sutherland, 1949).

Thus, it would appear that the more readily visible the differentiating cues, the earlier the child will utilize them. This may well account for the emphasis on black–white differences, since it is typically assumed that these represent maximal visibility. Parenthetically, it might be noted that this belief has not actually been tested. It may be that other racial groups (such as Oriental–black) are seen as more distinctive by children. The white–black emphasis may indeed be reflecting both historical American race relations concerns and investigator ethnocentrism. An interesting study conducted with congenitally blind children in South Africa (Bhana, 1977) suggests that in some instances visibility may not even be a necessary precondition for prejudice to occur. In South Africa, the political salience of race questions may actually overcome the need for vision, since white children who were blind were found to hold negative attitudes toward blacks.

When early studies on children's racial awareness were first published (e.g., Clark & Clark, 1947; Goodman, 1952), considerable surprise was expressed at the fact that young children even noticed skin-color differences. Indeed, many people still believe that children, in Rousseau-like innocence, are color-blind with respect to people. The present author has encountered several school administrators who believe that assessing the racial attitudes of grade school children would cause them to suddenly pay attention to race for the first time. Such beliefs are clearly not supported by the evidence. Upon reflection, they are somewhat peculiar. Very young infants are obviously capable of distinguishing color cues (Fagan, 1974). Why, then, should people be exempted from this perceptual process? A study by the present author and her students conducted with 3-day-old infants (Rose, Katz, Birke, & Rossman, 1977) found not only that facial-like configurations of varying hues were discriminated but that infants preferred high-contrast stimuli. Thus, they followed a white face against a brown background and a brown face against a white background more actively than they followed a white face against a pink background. It may be that in very early infancy anything that visually stands out becomes a compelling stimulus. Newborns seem to be sensitive to color cues, figure–ground contrast, border illumination discrepancies, and configurational details as well. So much for color blindness!

That children by age 3 should employ skin color cues as a basis for person classification, therefore, should not be surprising. Much of a child's early cognitive training employs the teaching of colors and their use as classification devices. What may be more surprising, however, is that nursery school children exhibit differential evaluative responses to different skin colors. White children clearly prefer the color white in both nonhuman and human pictures, and until relatively recently, young black children also exhibited a prowhite bias.

Two theories have been proposed to account for these phenomena; an earlier one by Allport (1954) and a more recent view by Williams and his colleagues (Williams, 1972; Williams & Morland, 1976).

Allport (1954) has suggested that children evaluate individuals of other races negatively as one instance of general fear of strange and unfamiliar things. Fear of the strange may be elicited by inanimate objects, unexpected occurrences, and, perhaps, people who look very different to the child. Allport further suggests that visible differences between people may imply other real differences to the child as well. This last possibility is also in accordance with cognitive-developmental theory (e.g., Piaget). Allport's notions were vividly brought home to the present writer when she visited a foundling home in a remote part of China several years ago. The children in the home had not had any exposure to whites, and when our group walked in, several of the children between 6 and 12 months became obviously fearful, avoided us, and began to cry. Since this reaction was not elicited by other unfamiliar Chinese adults, it was clear that more than simple stranger anxiety was involved.

Although the possibilities suggested by this view are intriguing, no systematic work with young children deriving from Allport's theory has been conducted. Thus, even assuming the validity of the "strange person" phenomenon, we do not know whether or how this earlier fear relates to subsequent attitude development. Similarly, the age when such events would have maximal developmental impact is not known. Whether such fear develops at all would seem to depend on happenstance occurrences, and thus could not readily account for the very systematic effects we see later in development. Allport's reasoning suggests a modification technique that has not always been successful. It could be argued that fear of the strange might be reduced by early and frequent interracial contact. Although several studies suggest that increasing familiarity may also increase liking for previously unfamiliar stimuli (Cantor, 1972; Zajonc, Swap, Harrison, & Roberts, 1971), anecdotal evidence suggests occasions when the opposite may be true, particularly with prolonged exposure. The rearing of upper-class southern white children by black women did not apparently inoculate them against negative racial attitudes.

Williams has posited an even more far-reaching theory. His position suggests that early racial preferences of whites (and some blacks) reflect primitive feelings about day and night. In an excellent review of work in the area, Williams and Morland (1979) argue that the development of the concept of race is inextricably bound up with the symbolism associated with color usage. This argument is based on several pieces of evidence. First, the color names *black* and *white* are the most frequently encountered color terms in almost all known languages (Hays, Margolis, Naroll, & Perkins, 1972). Second, considerable cross-cultural research has demonstrated that the color white is associated with positive attributes in most cultures and the color black with negative ones. Williams and Morland go on to suggest that such affective connotations generalize to skin color cues. A basic question that needs to be addressed, however, has to do with the origin of these very common linguistic patterns. These investigators speculate that prowhite bias originates from a basic human tendency to prefer light over darkness. Darkness, it is argued, is intrinsically aversive because it elicits visual disorientation that leads both humans and nonhuman primates to avoid it. Because of this, darkness comes to be associated with fear, whereas lightness is associated with fear reduction. Generalization of these trends is presumed to occur along many dimensions, including language, color, and race. Thus, it is argued that preference for lightness over darkness may be the developmental forerunner of the preference for white skin. The cultural factors (i.e., language connotations, lower status associated with dark skin, etc.) merely serve to reinforce these initial tendencies.

Ontogenetically, this fascinating theory implies that there should be a relation between a young child's fear of the dark and the subsequent negativity of his or her attitudes toward blacks. In the only empirical effort to test this notion (Boswell & Williams, 1975), a modest correlation ($r = .40$) was found between white–black color bias in 37 5-year-olds and their mothers' reports about their aversive responses to darkness. Further work in this area is clearly warranted and needed.

To summarize, by age 3, many children already exhibit some awareness of racial cues, although the processes underlying this development are not well investigated or understood. Children are capable of making the requisite perceptual differentiation on the basis of skin color (and possibly on the basis of facial features as well) quite early in life, but whether racial concepts are indeed formed seems quite dependent on such specific experiential factors as whether the child lives in a predominantly racially homogeneous or heterogeneous environment. Two theoretical viewpoints have been offered to account for differential evaluations of racial groups. Allport has suggested that fear of the unfamiliar underlies much of a child's response to people of other races. In contrast, Williams has argued that all children begin life with a preference for light colors and an aversion to darkness, a tendency that continues in white children but is counteracted by other factors in dark-skinned minority children.

Parallels between early gender and racial awareness

There are both similarities and differences between gender and race awareness development in the early stages of life. The most obvious similarity is that by age 3 the rudiments of gender and race categorization have been mastered by the majority of children. During this period of development, perceptual processes undoubtedly represent the most important factors for both race and gender knowledge. Gender awareness appears to be pervasive and inevitable, given the usual conditions under which most children are reared. In contrast, racial awareness is not, particularly for white children growing up in segregated environments. Thus, the foundations of racial awareness and concepts probably develop somewhat later and are more variable. Some support for this view can be seen by comparing several studies with $2\frac{1}{2}$-year-olds, one by Boswell (cited in Williams & Morland, 1976) on black–white preference in white children and the others by Blakemore *et al.* (1979) and Kuhn *et al.* (1978) on male–female toy preferences and stereotypes. The two studies conducted with sex stereotyping revealed that consistent sex-appropriate choices were being made by $2\frac{1}{2}$-year-olds (and in some instances by younger children), whereas strong distinctions were not yet being made on the basis of color. In the Boswell study, children in a free-play situation chose black and white toys with equal frequency, although they did exhibit some tendency in a forced-choice situation to associate more positive adjectives with the white toys. The relative availability of other-sex versus other-race models undoubtedly has a profound impact upon both early awareness and later attitudes. Moreover, preference for and knowledge of one's own gender and racial group comes before knowledge of others'.

In considering the mechanisms underlying this early learning about race and gender, it may be useful to distinguish between the inevitability of the outcome itself and the near universal conditions of child rearing that may account for it. It might be instructive for the reader to consider, at least hypothetically, what would happen to gender awareness and salience if (*a*) males and females were equally available to a child as caretakers; (*b*) clothing, hairstyle, and infant handling patterns did not vary systematically with sex of adult; (*c*) adult expectations and behavior did not differ systematically as a function of the sex of the child; and (*d*) consequent differences did not occur between the social and physical environments of male and female children. A similar and analogous exercise in the race awareness area is to consider the experiences of a child being reared in a biracial environment. Since the second ''natural experiment'' is considerably more probable than the first, such families have, in fact, been studied (albeit infrequently) by social scientists. These studies (e.g., Gunthorpe, 1977; Jacobs, 1978; Payne, 1977) have focused on the difficult adjustment problems often encountered by interracial children. Two points, however, have received insufficient theoretical attention. First, within the nuclear biracial family, gender and race cues are ordinarily confounded, although this has not been considered. Investigation of this factor could shed some light on the relative salience of race versus gender as factors in the process of identity development. Does an interracial child identify more with a same-sex parent, even when skin color differs greatly? A second question is how racial and gender identity develop when they are not completely confounded. One possibility here is to look at families where transracial adoption has occurred. Another might be to look at later-born children of large extended biracial families where, for example, a child might have a black mother and a white sister. Although such families are unusual, the use of such groups might help clarify some of our conceptions about identity development.

THE PRESCHOOL PERIOD

The period between 3 and 6 years of age has been particularly crucial for investigating both sex role and racial awareness and attitudes. It has been the most frequently investigated age group by those interested in gender awareness. For example, of the 1600 studies reviewed by Maccoby and Jacklin (1974) in their now classic work, over 75% of the studies were conducted with children in this age range. The preschool period has also been the one most frequently studied with regard to racial knowledge, but by a somewhat narrower margin.

Gender-role development

The sheer volume of studies in gender-role development with this age group precludes the possibility of any comprehensive review in this chapter. The literature through 1974 has been excellently reviewed by Maccoby and Jacklin, although it probably needs updating in view of the changing concerns exhibited by investigators over the past decade.

Prior to 1970, most sex-role research with children sought to document two areas: (*a*) knowledge about and preference for sex-typed activities; and (*b*) areas in which the sexes differed. Indeed, a goodly portion of Maccoby and Jacklin's book is concerned with assessing the status of the research on sex differences.

The trends exhibited in more recent investigations are somewhat different, however. First, there is less concern with the documentation of sex differences per se. Second, preference for sex-stereotyped toys and activities, while conceptually regarded as evidence of sex-role learning, is not necessarily treated as the sine qua non of the socialization process. In view of newer and broader conceptions of sex roles, particularly those that suggest that psychological advantages may be associated with non-sex-typed or androgynous patterns (e.g., Bem, 1975, 1977; Hemmer & Kleiber, 1981; Lott, 1978), departures from traditional sex-typed patterns in children are no longer regarded as invariably deviant as they once were (e.g., Sutton-Smith & Rosenberg, 1960). Third, more theoretically guided research has been conducted, particularly in the cognitive area. Finally, in accordance with the conceptualizations of androgyny referred to earlier, many attempts to modify stereotyping in children's responses have been reported, utilizing variations in such things as nursery school environments, reinforcement procedures, and television programs (e.g., DiLeo, Moely, & Sulzer, 1979; Flerx, Fidler, & Rogers, 1976; Kliman, 1978; Lutes-Dunckley, 1978; Nilsen, 1977; Robinson & Hobson, 1978; Serbin & Connor, 1979; Serbin, Connor, & Iler, 1979).

This section of the chapter will focus on the various mechanisms that have been theoretically proposed as underlying the development of the child's awareness of and conceptualizations about gender. In contrast to the first 3 years of life, when the largely nonverbal child is the recipient of gender-role information and differential socialization practices, in the preschool period, the child is a very active participant in the whole process. The age period between 3 and 6 has been considered by many investigators of varying theoretical persuasions as being very significant for sex-role socialization, and we might consider why this is the case.

On a behavioral level the preschool period is marked by rapid learning of the culturally designated gender-appropriate categories in many areas, including toys, activities, future occupations, and domestic roles. A very broad literature shows this to be true for a wide variety of responses, including verbal responses expressing preferences and knowledge of stereotypes, nonverbal preferences, play behavior, choice of playmates, choice of books, favorite television characters, some personality attributes, and the sex-typing of others (e.g., R. J. Barry, 1980; Birnbaum, Nosanchuk, & Croll, 1980; Birns, 1976; Blakemore et al., 1979; Connor & Serbin, 1977; Eisenberg-Berg, Boothby, & Matson, 1979; Gold & Berger, 1978; Haugh, Hoffman, & Cowan, 1980; Peterson & McDonald, 1980). There is probably no other area in the child's life (with the possible exception of language) that is as overlearned as this one. Even in adult populations, where norms have been changing rapidly, sex stereotypes have shown remarkable stability over the past 20 years (Ruble & Ruble, 1980). There may well be 5-year-olds that do not know the alphabet or color names, but there probably is not one who does not recognize the separate toy domains of boys and girls. Money and Ehrhardt (1972) have gone so far as to suggest that imprinting may be involved, given the comprehensiveness of gender differentiation.

Theorists in the sex-roles area have exhibited particular interest in the preschooler for a variety of reasons, depending on their point of view. In reviewing this issue in an earlier publication (Katz, 1979), the present author noted that four theoretical views have been particularly prominent in this area, each stressing the significance of different mechanisms. These include (a) shaping or reinforcement paradigms; (b) modeling theories that stress observational learning; (c) parental bonding and identification (psychoanalytic theory); and (*d*) cognitive-developmental theory.

The last two, best exemplified by the writings of Freud (1927) and Kohlberg (1966), respectively, postulate the occurrence of specific critical events during the 3–6-year-old period that are presumed to have lasting effect upon sex-role development. Within psychoanalytic theory, the child of 3 or 4 is expected to form a strong positive attachment to the opposite-sex parent and a concomitant hostility toward the same-sex one. The conflict that this state of affairs engenders in the child, however, is considerable and is resolved (by age 6) when the child relinquishes desires for the opposite-sex parent and identifies with the same-sex one. Within psychoanalytic theory, this identification constitutes the end of the basic sex-role socialization process.

Cognitive-development theory, on the other hand, postulates two entirely different events as critically important. The first is the occurrence of correct self-labeling as to gender, which is present in most children by age 3 (and usually before). According to Kohlberg, the gender label is generalized to "boy" or "girl" things; the appropriate category takes on enhanced value to the child and is actively sought out. This process, then, is conceived of as an active and self-reinforcing one. Its cognitive culmination comes at approximately 5 or 6 years of age with the achievement of *gender constancy*. This refers to the recognition that one's gender is an unmodifiable trait, despite changes in age and outward appearance.

Thus, cognitive and psychoanalytic theories, while postulating very different kinds of critical events, both regard the preschool period as the most salient. In contrast, the other two views (i.e., shaping and observational learning) are not tied to particular ages, since these processes can occur at any time. The preschool period is, nevertheless, still regarded as one in which an exceptional degree of reinforcement and modeling occurs. These four views, then, have all stressed the importance of focusing on the preschool child and on parents as the major sex-role socializers.

The present author has previously questioned (Katz, 1979) the narrowness of this focus, both from the point of view of development level and particular socialization agents. Considerable evidence has been amassed since these older views were espoused that suggests that an individual's sex role continues to develop and change throughout childhood, adolescence, and adulthood (e.g., Feldman, Biringen, & Nash, 1981; Fischer & Narus, 1981; Katz, 1979; Rebecca, Hefner, & Oleshansky, 1976; Urberg & Labouvie-Vief, 1976). Furthermore, no evidence exists that the degree of stereotyping existing at one period is related to any other period. Moreover, the general assumption made by earlier theorists that children will imitate, identify, and generally be more similar to their same-sex parent than to anyone else has not been empirically substantiated (e.g., see Fling & Manosevitz, 1972; Hetherington, 1965; Lazowick, 1955; Lott, 1978; Maccoby & Jacklin, 1974; Rosenberg & Sutton-Smith, 1965; Troll, Neugarten, & Kraines, 1969). This suggests, therefore, that there are many other socialization influences that play a significant role in sex-role development.

As a result of this reasoning, Katz (1979) has postulated that there may be three distinctive but overlapping developmental stages in sex-role acquisition that need to be looked at across the life span: (a) the learning of child sex roles (i.e., what is appropriate for boys and for girls); (b) the preparing for adult sex roles (i.e., putting aside child things and considering future occupational, courtship, sexual, and domestic aspects of sex roles); and (c) developing and executing these adult roles. Different substages within each period are delineated for males and females, each with differing crises and milestones. Finally, differing sets of socialization agents are assumed to be operative at varying points in the life cycle.

Although this paradigm is quite new and has not yet received much empirical support, it is interesting to note that there is some literature, even with regard to the preschool child, that clearly demonstrates the broad social context in which sex-role learning occurs. Although parents have been found to be important socializers along a number of dimensions of sex typing (Downs & Langlois, 1977; Fagot, 1978a; Greif, 1979), it is clear that many additional sources of social influence are evident, including picture books (e.g., LaDow, 1976; Mortimer, 1979; St. Peter, 1979), nursery school teachers (Fagot, 1978b, 1979), television (McArthur & Eisen, 1976; Sprafkin & Liebert, 1978), siblings (Brown & Weinraub, 1981; Katz & Rank, 1981), and most importantly, peers (Downs & Langlois, 1977; Fagot, 1977b, 1978b, 1979; Lamb & Roopnarine, 1979; Serbin et al., 1979).

Of all the theoretical positions previously described, the one that has stimulated the greatest amount of recent research with preschool children has been the cognitive-developmental approach. This author has argued elsewhere (Katz, 1976) that a child's social cognitions cannot be adequately understood without an accompanying understanding of both the social and cognitive context in which they occur. The various components of the social environment influencing gender knowledge have been outlined earlier. It should be noted, however, that the cognitive level of the preschool child is particularly conducive to the formation of stereotypes. Between ages 3 and 6, the child is at the preoperational level, according to Piaget. This means that, with regard to inanimate objects, the child is not yet capable of conserving certain aspects of situations, such as number and quantity, and is very much affected by the changing perceptual qualities of objects. The absence of gender constancy may, in fact, be simply one more manifestation of the child's inability to conserve. The child at this age also exhibits a peculiarly illogical type of reasoning, called *transductive reasoning*—making conclusions on the basis of going from one particular to another particular. Moreover, the child is especially interested in learning about his or her body and those of others. Finally, the child is particularly prone to understanding concepts in terms of their opposites, which forms a ready cognitive basis for the simplistic kinds of "us" versus "them" beliefs associated with both sex role and racial attitudes. Urberg (1979) has presented some data suggesting that children indeed perceive more overlap between the characteristics of males and females as they enter the period of concrete operations (i.e., ages 6–7) than they do at earlier stages. At age 5, there is a particularly strong tendency to attribute positive things to one's own sex and negative attributes to the other, a trend that becomes less pronounced with age, but that is still evident in middle childhood (Zalk & Katz, 1978). Evidence supports some of these other suppositions as well, in that positive relationships have been obtained between gender concepts and other measures of cognitive maturity (Coker, 1977; Marcus & Overton, 1978).

Several conceptual questions remain, however, with regard to some cognitive aspects of sex-role learning. The age at which gender constancy occurs is not entirely clear, nor is the relation of gender constancy to preferences for sex-typed toys and activities. With regard to the age issue, Kohlberg has indicated that gender constancy should be accomplished by 6 years, although there appears to be considerable variation in the findings reported. Some studies report finding it at age 3 (Kuhn *et al.*, 1978), whereas others (Emmerich, Goldman, Kirsh, & Sharabany, 1977) indicate it may not consolidate until 8 years. These variations may be attributable to measurement differences. The findings with regard to gender constancy and knowledge of stereotypes are also equivocal, with some studies finding significant relationships (Kuhn *et al.*, 1978) and others (Marcus & Overton, 1978; Wehren & De Lisi, 1981) reporting none. Thus, despite a considerable amount of research in the cognitive components of gender roles, the specific antecedents and consequences of gender constancy remain to be ascertained with certainty.

In summary, the preschool child appears to go through a very active "gender curriculum" (Luria, 1980). Gender cues are particularly salient to children during this period, and considerable time and effort is devoted to their elaboration. By 6 years of age, children's knowledge about toy sex typing is similar to that of adults (Masters & Wilkerson, 1976). They also know a good deal about sex typing with regard to personality attributes (Williams, Bennett, & Best, 1975) and occupational and family role stereotypes (Flerx *et al.*, 1976; Kuhn *et al.*, 1978). Information about gender roles comes not only from parents but from a number of other sources as well, including siblings, peers, and the media. Children's concepts about gender appear to be related to their general level of cognitive maturation, and a considerable body of research has investigated the cognitive components of sex-role learning. Future research needs to be directed toward the issue of how the cognitive and social components interact within a developmental context.

Racial awareness and attitudes

As was noted earlier, racial awareness during the first 3 years is more variable and less investigated relative to gender. Nevertheless, the behavioral manifestations of racial awareness and incipient attitudes show systematic development during the preschool period. Beginning with the original Clark and Clark study in 1947, numerous investigators have shown that most children between ages 3 and 6 can correctly categorize themselves as to racial group. Moreover, these children exhibit distinctive preferences for certain skin colors over others. In most earlier studies (i.e., prior to 1972), both white and minority preschool children exhibited preferences for white-skinned dolls, pictures, and playmates (Goodman, 1952; Morland, 1966; Porter, 1971). More recent studies suggest that this pattern may be changing and that children may now be exhibiting same-race preferences for both symbolic stimuli and friendship choices (e.g., Banks, 1976; Braha & Rutter, 1980; Feinman, 1979; Morland & Suthers, 1980; Schofield, 1978; Stephan & Rosenfield, 1979). Although this issue is not without controversy (cf. Banks, McQuater, & Ross, 1979; Williams & Morland, 1979), the preponderance of evidence seems to suggest a growing shift toward greater minority self-esteem and positive racial identification, both historically (Butler, 1976) and ontogenetically (H. P. McAdoo, 1977). Black preschool children now show either no bias or a same-race preference in choice tasks.

It has become fashionable recently to criticize the older doll-choice studies, and the present author has been among those (Katz, 1976) who have pointed out some of their methodological shortcomings and possible overinterpretations of findings. We should not, however, lose sight of the fact that the Clark and Clark study is one of the few in the history of psychology to significantly alter history and social policy. The use of a task that was simple enough for nonsocial scientists to understand undoubtedly helped to win its acceptance by the Supreme Court as a basis for banning school segregation in the famous 1954 *Brown* v. *Board of Education of Topeka, Kansas* case. The psychological damage evidenced by young black children who preferred to be white was a powerful argument against the inequality inherent in the "separate but equal" doctrine that had been declared valid by the courts for decades.

It should be noted that, although responses of black children have changed, the responses of young white children have not. White children almost never express a preference to be a member of any racial group but their own. Moreover, a multitude of studies have shown that children as young as 3–4 have strong positive associations to both the color and the racial group labeled "white" and negative ones to "black" in both its abstract and skin-color designations (Asher & Allen, 1969; Fox & Jordan, 1973; Greenwald & Oppenheim, 1968; Hardin, 1977; Hraba & Grant, 1970; Morland, 1966, 1972; Renninger & Williams, 1966; Stevenson & Stewart, 1958; Williams, Boswell, & Best, 1975). Although it is generally assumed that skin color is the most salient cue for differentiating race, two rather interesting studies looked at the role of other physiognomic cues. One conducted by Sorce (1979) found that physiognomic features were more salient than skin color and that white children were more aware of hair features than skin color. This latter finding is particularly interesting, since most doll-choice tasks vary both skin, hair, and sometimes eye color simultaneously. Thus, a brown-skinned, brown-eyed, and brown-haired doll is usually paired with a pink-skinned, blue-eyed, blonde-haired one. A study by Katz and Zalk (1974) that varied *only* skin color within male and female doll pairs (all dolls had brown hair and eyes) did not, in fact, find clear-cut preferences for white dolls. It was suggested in that study, therefore, that children may, like the proverbial "gentlemen," simply prefer blondes. A study by Lacoste (1978) with 3–4-year-old white children found that they were able to classify facial features of blacks and whites even when differentiated skin-color cues were absent. As in the previously mentioned study, hair differences were particularly salient.

At least three mechanisms have been proposed as major determinants of preschool racial awareness and attitude development. These include learning factors, cognitive factors, and perceptual mechanisms. Within each rubric, several varying theoretical emphases have been proposed.

The mechanism of reinforcement has frequently been offered as an explanation of how children acquire racial attitudes. The most active proponent of a reinforcement view has been John Williams, whose theory was discussed in a previous section. It can be recalled that Williams and his colleagues suggest that all children develop a positive bias toward light colors and consequent aversion to darkness because of our diurnal rhythm. This is reflected in the language of most cultures, which contain positive associations to the color white and negative ones to the color black. This reinforces the child's predilections in this area, which generalize to skin-color cues. Finally, the pervasive racist attitudes within our society further serve to reinforce such connections for white children. Black children, according to Williams, begin life with the same preferences for brightness, but positive associations to darker colors (due to contact with dark-skinned adults) soon come into play to counteract these earlier tendencies. Although Williams does not specifically discuss it, the other side of the coin should be equally true; that is, to the extent that black children have negative experiences with white racism, they should begin to devalue both the color white and the racial group.

Williams and his colleagues and students have conducted a number of studies with preschool and young grade school children that have demonstrated that (*a*) colors are evaluated in accordance with the theory, particularly by majority group children; and (*b*) these associations do generalize to pictures of people. Two measures are used to assess these trends: the Color Meaning Test (Williams & Roberson, 1967), which consists of pairs of objects or animals alike in all respects but color, and the Preschool Racial Attitude Measure (PRAM) (Williams, Best, Boswell, Mattson, & Graves, 1975), which assesses children's association of positive and negative adjectives to pairs of child and adult figures varying in skin color.

One of the interesting implications of this position is that, if associations are formed by reinforcement, these same associations should be modifiable when the reinforcement contingencies are changed. The whole issue of attitude modification has become more prominent since the early 1970s, and the number of change attempts has been proliferating. When the present author reviewed this literature in 1974, she noted the paucity of modification studies conducted with young children. This was also noted by Proshansky (1966) in an earlier review and by Balch and Paulsen (1979), who more recently discussed some of the historical trends. Over the past decade, however, many change studies have been conducted using a variety of techniques, such as increasing interracial contact at the preschool level (e.g., Goldstein, Koopman, & Goldstein, 1979; Palmer, 1977), positive television portrayals of minorities (Goldberg & Gorn, 1979), increasing multicultural experiences (Blackwell, Silvern, & Yawkey, 1976), perceptual differentiation techniques (Katz & Zalk, 1978), and attempting to change prowhite–antiblack bias by negatively reinforcing traditional responses or by positively reinforcing problack–antiwhite responses (Chamberlin-Robinson, 1977; J. L. McAdoo, 1970; Shanahan, 1972; Spencer & Horowitz, 1973; Traynham, 1974; Williams & Edwards, 1969). In general, this last technique has been successful, particularly when used at the preschool level, although its long-term effectiveness has not been ascertained (Balch & Paulsen, 1979).

A number of investigators have proposed that cognitive components are central to any understanding of racial attitude acquisition. The general expectation, discussed in the previous section on sex-role development, that children's group concepts should reflect their general level of cognitive maturity is equally relevant to the racial area. Less cognitively mature children, for example, should accentuate racial differences and assume that they imply the existence of other differences as well. Young children should also not recognize that racial cues are unmodifiable. Some support for these expectations has been obtained by Semaj (1980).

Clark, Hocevar, and Dembo (1980) reported findings relevant to how well children (between $2\frac{1}{2}$ and $10\frac{1}{2}$ years of age) understood the origins of race. These investigators found that children's reasoning about race followed a seven-stage developmental hierarchy: (*a*) lack of comprehension; (*b*) reference to supernatural powers; (*c*) reference to arbitrary causality; (*d*) inaccurate physical explanations; (*e*) accurate physical attribution without an accompanying explanation; (*f*) accurate physical attribution and explanation but without reference to genetics; and finally (*g*) genetic explanation. Only six levels were obtained from the children studied; none of the 10-year-olds were able to give the highest level of response. These investigators additionally found, in accordance with Semaj (1980) and Katz (1976), that a child's level of reasoning about skin color was related to his or her scores on physical conservation tasks. This again underscores the importance of the cognitive context of attitude development. Clark *et al.* found subtleties with regard to the expression of racial preferences as a function of the race of the examiner. This result substantiated earlier findings by the present author and her colleagues (Katz, Sohn, & Zalk, 1975; Katz & Zalk, 1974, 1978) and suggests that measurement of racial attitudes is quite complex even with young children.

A somewhat different cognitive emphasis has been proposed by Tajfel and his colleagues (Tajfel, 1969, 1973, 1979; Tajfel & Billig, 1974). This investigator has looked at the consequences of group categorization on both cognitive and intergroup behavior in a very interesting series of studies. Tajfel has argued that classifications into nationalities or racial groups are, by their nature, discontinuous and that this discontinuity elicits a tendency to exaggerate the differences between the classes on any given continuous dimension and to minimize the differences within each of the classes. Tajfel and Wilkes (1963) conducted a study using lines to demonstrate this phenomenon. Three groups of subjects were shown eight lines varying in length and asked to estimate the length of each. The group that was asked to label the four shorter lines ''A'' and the four longer ones ''B'' did in fact exaggerate the difference in length between the ''boundary'' items much more so than did a group with either no labels or one that associated the letter with the lines in alternation sequence. Similar trends have been found for social stimuli as well (Tajfel, 1959; Tajfel, Sheikh, & Gardner, 1964). Other studies have demonstrated the relationship of this phenomenon to social groups. When schoolchildren are divided into groups with different labels, even on the basis of arbitrary and meaningless criteria, they tend to value others in their group more positively than those in the out-group (Billig & Tajfel, 1973; Tajfel & Billig, 1974).

Tajfel has clearly tapped an important underlying dimension of social categorization relevant to both gender and racial categorization. Although much of his work has been conducted with older children and adults, his results are very similar to those obtained in studies with younger children conducted by the present author and colleagues. We have preferred, however, to discuss the phenomenon as a perceptual rather than a cognitive one. For example, a study conducted by Katz (1973) used a two-choice discrimination learning task, and nursery school and kindergarten children were tested with either brown, pink-tan, or green faces that varied in shade. In accordance with prediction, black children had more difficulty learning to discriminate pink-tan shades, whereas white children exhibited more difficulty learning to distinguish the brown shades. The rationale underlying this expectation assumes that the process of group differentiation is composed of two related but separable processes: (*a*) increased attention to between-group differences; and (*b*) a concomitant decrease in the perceptual distinctiveness among the individual members of a group. The effects of labels would be expected to enhance each of these phenomena, in accordance with Dollard and Miller's (1950) hypotheses regarding the acquired distinctiveness and equivalence of cues. The Katz (1973) study further argued that if unfamiliarity with other-race faces is the major factor (rather than acquired distinctiveness or equivalence), then green faces should be the most difficult to distinguish. In fact, however, the green-face condition did not differ from the same-race one, suggesting that by age 4 children have already undergone considerable socialization with regard to race and hold differential perceptions of their own and other races.

In a further demonstration of how these processes might operate on a perceptual level, Katz and Seavey (1973) assessed the relation between type of label and perception of faces. In this study conducted with somewhat older children, four schematic line drawings of faces were used. The faces varied along two dimensions; color (purple versus green) and facial expression (smile versus frown). There were four experimental groups: One learned to associate two names to the four faces on the basis of color cues; a second learned two names for the four faces on the basis of expression; a third group learned four names for the four faces; and finally, a control group viewed the stimuli for the same number of trials without names. Following this training, subjects were shown all possible pairs of faces at rapid exposures and asked to judge how similar they were. Results indicated that the type of label used significantly affected perceptual judgments. Labels based on color cues increased the perceived distinctiveness of color variations, whereas those associated with facial expression augmented differentiation of expressions. When different names were associated with each of the faces, both color and expression differences were equally highlighted. Finally, when no names were given, all faces were perceived as more similar to one another. This perceptual approach has considerable ramifications for modification as well. Both Tajfel's work and the present writer's position suggest that any technique that increases individuation of other-race individuals should decrease negative attitudes toward that group by focusing attention on within-group rather than between-group differences. Support for this has been found with older children (e.g., Katz, Sohn, & Zalk, 1975; Katz & Zalk, 1978), but the question of whether such techniques might also be effective for younger children remains to be assessed.

Two additional issues merit consideration regarding the development of racial attitudes. The first has to do with who transmits information to the child. The second has to do with the relative salience of racial as opposed to other person cues.

With regard to the first issue, the situation is quite comparable to the sex roles area. Commonsense notions strongly suggest that parents are the primary socializers, but research has not substantiated this supposition (Bird, Monachesi, & Burdick, 1952; Byrne, 1965; Frenkel-Brunswick & Havel, 1953; Pushkin, 1967; Radke-Yarrow, Trager, & Miller, 1952). As was the case with gender stereotypes, an increasing body of work is pointing to television (Barry & Sheikh, 1977; Greenberg, 1972;

Zuckerman, Singer, & Singer, 1980) and books (Wirtenberg, 1978; Zimet, 1976) as important sources of information. Even though things have changed since the 1960s, a report of the U.S. Commission on Civil Rights (1979) suggests that race and sex stereotyping on television continues. The President's Commission on Mental Health suggests that inadequate representation of minority groups assists in the stereotyping process. Finally, the role of peers is probably significant as well, although little work has been done with this age group.

In reviewing the earlier work on preschool racial awareness, it sometimes appears that young children are quite bigoted. A number of investigators, however, have begun to question whether race is really that salient or whether our assessment techniques (i.e., forced-choice questions) may have exaggerated its importance to children. Data to date seem to suggest that it may not be as salient as previously thought. In open-ended interviews, race does not seem to be spontaneously mentioned very often by children (Lerner & Buehrig, 1975; Semaj, 1981). Moreover, racial cues appear to be less important to children than gender (Katz & Zalk, 1974; Van Parys, 1981), cleanliness (Epstein, Krupat, & Obudho, 1976), physical attractiveness (Langlois & Stephan, 1977), and age (Van Parys, 1981).

Similarities and differences between gender and racial learning

As was the case with the first 3 years of life, there are some striking parallels between the development of gender and racial awareness during the preschool period. Between ages 3 and 6, children appear to be particularly active in learning to understand both of these dimensions of social groups. Considerable effort is devoted by the child to the development of gender identity, and the sex typing of items in the child's environment is learned during this time. For nonminority children, the understanding of racial cues is not as time consuming a task as for minority children, but it is clear that all children become aware of racial differences during this period and can correctly identify themselves along this dimension. Minority children are more precocious in this regard.

The major similarity between racial and gender development, therefore, is that many of the perceptual and the basic cognitive processes underlying this development are complete for both of these dimensions by the time the child is ready to enter school. Children realize that race and gender are significant within our society for person classification.

Moreover, they can readily use these cues to accurately classify themselves, other children, and adults.

Another important similarity is that not only are preschool children actively using these cues for categorization but they are always using them in evaluative ways. The evidence with regard to race shows that, until fairly recently, children of all races evaluate white-skinned individuals more positively than dark-skinned ones. More recent studies with black children suggest that this phenomenon may be changing, with some investigators finding no preference and others reporting more positive evaluation of blacks than whites. This same-race preference appears to be becoming more pronounced in minority children at the grade school and secondary school levels. For white children, same-race preference appears to be a constant phenomenon. Evaluations with regard to gender group during the preschool period are more clear-cut; each gender prefers its own. Some studies suggest that, at older age levels, girls may have more conflict about their gender identity than do boys. Thus, with regard to both age and gender, the relative status that society confers upon groups is reflected in children's feelings about their own group. Male children rarely wish to be female, and white children never want to be black.

There is a strong tendency to think in terms of opposites at the preschool level of cognitive development. This has the effect of augmenting perceived differences between groups. In large part, children develop both gender and racial identity by learning which group they are in and assuming that the "other" group is different along most dimensions. Thus, the possibility of overlap is not great in either perception or behavior. If you are a boy, you do not play with "girl" things. In view of the overlearning and particularly dichotomous nature of sex-role learning, this tendency is undoubtedly more pronounced with regard to gender than race.

Another similarity in the preschooler's cognitive processes underlying the two categories is the recognition that both racial and gender characteristics are immutable in terms of group categorization. This recognition has been widely discussed with regard to gender under the rubric of gender constancy. It has been less widely discussed with race, although the present author has postulated a similar concept of racial constancy (Katz, 1976), and some evidence (Semaj, 1980) supports the use of such a concept. The immutability of gender groups may be somewhat more difficult for children to grasp, since some anatomical gender cues do change as a function of growth.

The complexity of gender as a cognitive concept may, in fact, underlie an important difference between children's understanding of race and

gender. Comprehension of gender roles is age related not only phys-
iologically but psychologically as well. Thus, differential expectations
are associated with different development levels, and learning about
these is an active and ongoing process. In contrast, however, race is a
more fixed category in that it does not change with age and thus is not
as subject to essential revisions in thinking. This may account for why
an individual's concepts about race often remain more primitive.

CONCLUDING REMARKS

The emphasis in this chapter has been on the early developmental
forerunners of racial and sex-role attitudes, and it is for this reason that
the primary focus was on the first 6 years. This focus is not meant to
imply that everything is fixed before the child enters school or that development does not continue in each of the areas addressed. The present author has, in fact, previously delineated the importance of some of
these later developmental sequences in both the racial (Katz, 1976) and
sex-role (Katz, 1979) areas. In general, both concepts and attitudes continue to be elaborated throughout childhood. Peers and the media become particularly important socializers of both racial and sex-role
attitudes during the grade school period. Racial attitudes tend to crys-
tallize by about 10 or 11 years of age (Katz, 1976; Proshansky, 1966),
whereas sex-role expectations and perhaps attitudes continue to change
over the life span (Katz, 1979). Adolescence may, in fact, be a particularly important age period for sex-role attitude development. The foundations of both types of attitudes are pretty firmly ensconced, however,
by the time the child enters school.

Interestingly, although the preschool child has learned quite a bit
about the types of social groups society regards as important, the actual
cues used in differentiating people may be somewhat different from the
defining characteristics employed by adults. In the case of race, for example, there is some suggestion in the literature that children use hair
type and facial features more than skin color. Analogously for gender
classification, hair length, body type, and clothes are more powerful indicators of gender for preschool children than are genital differences
(Conn, 1940; Katcher, 1955; Thompson & Bentler, 1971).

It was noted at the outset of this chapter that children are born into
a situation in which society has already designated the cues that are
significant for classifying and conferring status upon individuals. There
is little question that, within our own society, racial and gender cues
are particularly salient ones for understanding social organization and

that consequently these are transmitted to children at remarkably early ages—long before they are capable of reading or doing arithmetic. These groups become so real that when the "immutability" changes, considerable trauma is involved. Consider, for example, the plight of the transsexual and societal reactions to such individuals. Although racial change is even rarer than gender change, a disease called vitiligo does occasionally change an individual's skin color, and a newspaper account (Firstman, 1981) of a 41-year-old black woman who had this disease and turned completely white reported profound psychological trauma. Stories like these point out the absurdity underlying the social reality of our so-called irrevocable group distinctions. At the very least, it suggests that there may be alternative, perhaps better, ways of dividing up the human race.

ACKNOWLEDGMENTS

The author wishes to express particular gratitude to Carol Hathaway-Clark, who most ably assisted in the library research for the chapter, and Susie Gulbrandsen, whose secretarial and editorial skills are without equal.

REFERENCES

Allport, G. W. *The nature of prejudice.* Reading, Mass.: Addison-Wesley, 1954.
Asher, S. R., & Allen, V. L. Racial preference and social comparison processes. *Journal of Social Issues,* 1969, *25,* 157–165.
Balch, P., & Paulsen, K. *Strategies for the modification and prevention of racial prejudice in children: A rereview.* Paper presented at the 59th Annual Meeting of the Western Psychological Association, San Diego, April 1979.
Banks, W. C. White preference in blacks: A paradigm in search of a phenomenon. *Psychological Bulletin,* 1976, *83,* 1179–1186.
Banks, W. C., McQuater, G. V., & Ross, J. A. On the importance of white preference and the comparative difference of blacks and others: Reply to Williams and Morland. *Psychological Bulletin,* 1979, *86,* 33–36.
Barry, H., Bacon, M. K., & Child, I. L. A cross-cultural survey of some sex differences in socialization. *Journal of Abnormal Social Psychology,* 1957, *55,* 327–332.
Barry, R. J. Stereotyping of sex role in preschoolers in relation to age, family structure and parental sexism. *Sex Roles,* 1980, *6*(6), 795–806.
Barry, T. E., & Sheikh, A. A. Race as a dimension in children's T.V. advertising: The need for more research. *Journal of Advertising,* 1977, *6*(3), 5–10.
Bem, S. L. Sex-role adaptability: One consequence of psychological androgyny. *Journal of Personality and Social Psychology,* 1975, *31,* 634–643.
Bem, S. L. Probing the promise of androgyny. In A. G. Kaplan & J. P. Bean (Eds.), *Beyond sex-role stereotypes: Reading toward a psychological androgyny.* Boston: Little, Brown, 1977.

Bhana, K. The relationship between perception and racial attitudes. *Behavioral Science,* 1977, 2(4), 253–258.

Billig, M., & Tajfel, H. Social categorization and similarity in intergroup behavior. *European Journal of Social Psychology,* 1973, 3, 27–51.

Bird, C., Monachesi, E. D., & Burdick, H. Infiltration and the attitudes of white and Negro parents and children. *Journal of Abnormal Social Psychology,* 1952, 47, 688–699.

Birnbaum, D. W., Nosanchuk, T. A., & Croll, W. L. Children's stereotypes about sex differences in emotionality. *Sex Roles,* 1980, 6(3), 435–443.

Birns, B. The emergence and socialization of sex differences in the earliest years. *Merrill-Palmer Quarterly,* 1976, 22(3), 229–254.

Blackwell, J., Silvern, S. B., & Yawkey, T. D. *Effects of early childhood multicultural experiences on black preschool children's attitudes toward themselves and whites.* Paper presented at the Annual Meeting of the American Educational Research Association, San Francisco, April 1976.

Blakemore, J. E. O., LaRue, A. A., & Olejnik, A. B. Sex-appropriate toy preference and the ability to conceptualize toys as sex-role related. *Developmental Psychology,* 1979, 15(3), 339–340.

Blehar, M. *Development of mental health in infancy.* NIMH Science Monograph No. 3, 1980.

Boswell, D. A., & Williams, J. E. Correlates of race and color bias among preschool children. *Psychological Reports,* 1975, 36, 147–154.

Braha, V., & Rutter, D. R. Friendship choice in a mixed-race primary school. *Educational Studies,* 1980, 6(3), 217–223.

Brown, L. M., & Weinraub, M. *Sibling status: Implications for sex-typed toy preferences and awareness of sex-role stereotypes in 2- to 3-year old children.* Paper presented at the 1981 Biennial Meeting of the Society for Research in Child Development. Boston, April 1981.

Bruner, J. S., Goodnow, J. J., & Austin, J. A. *A study of thinking.* New York: Wiley, 1956.

Butler, R. O. Black children's racial preference: A selected review of the literature. *Journal of Afro-American Issues,* 1976, 4(1), 168–171.

Byrne, D. Parental antecedents of authoritarianism. *Journal of Personality and Social Psychology,* 1965, 1, 369–373.

Cairns, E. *The development of ethnic discrimination in children in Northern Ireland.* Paper presented at the Northern Irish B.P.S. Conference on Children and Young People in a Society under Stress, Belfast, 1978.

Cantor, G. N. Effects of familiarization on children's ratings of pictures of whites and blacks. *Child Development,* 1972, 43, 1219–1229.

Chamberlin-Robinson, C. *Strategy to modify racial attitudes in black and white preschoolers.* Paper presented at the Biennial Meeting of the Society for Research in Child Development, New Orleans, March 1977.

Clark, A., Hocevar, D., & Dembo, M. H. The role of cognitive development in children's explanations and references for skin color. *Developmental Psychology,* 1980, 16(4), 332–339.

Clark, K. B., & Clark, M. P. Racial identification and preference in Negro children. In T. M. Newcomb & E. L. Hartley (Eds.), *Readings in social psychology.* New York: Holt, 1947.

Coker, D. R. *Development of gender concepts in preschool children.* Paper presented at the Annual Convention of the American Psychological Association, San Francisco, August 1977.

Condry, J., & Condry, S. Sex differences: A study of the eye of the beholder. *Child Development,* 1976, 47(3), 812–819.

Conn, J. H. Children's reactions to the discovery of genital differences. *American Journal of Orthopsychiatry*, 1940, *10*, 747–755.

Connor, J. M., & Serbin, L. A. Behaviorally based masculine- and feminine-activity-preference scales for preschoolers: Correlates with other classroom behaviors and cognitive tests. *Child Development*, 1977, *48*(4), 1411–1416.

Coombs, C. H., Coombs, L. C., & McClelland, G. H. Preference scales for number and sex of children. *Population Studies*, 1975, *29*, 273–298.

DiLeo, J. C., Moely, B. E., & Sulzer, J. L. Frequency and modifiability of children's preferences for sex-typed toys, games and occupations. *Child Study Journal*, 1979, *9*(2), 141–159.

Dollard, J., & Miller, N. *Personality and psychotherapy.* New York: McGraw-Hill, 1950.

Downs, A. C., & Langlois, J. H. *Mother and peer influences on children's sex-role play behaviors.* Paper presented at the Annual Meeting of the Midwestern Psychological Association, Chicago, May 1977.

Eisenberg-Berg, N., Boothby, R., & Matson, T. Correlates of preschool girls' feminine and masculine toy preferences. *Developmental Psychology*, 1979, *15*(3), 354–355.

Emmerich, W., Goldman, K. S., Kirsh, B., & Sharabany, R. Evidence for a transitional phase in the development of gender constancy. *Child Development*, 1977, *48*, 930–936.

Epstein, V. M., Krupat, E., & Obudho, C. Clean is beautiful: Identification and preference as a function of race and cleanliness. *Journal of Social Issues*, 1976, *32*(2), 109–118.

Fagan, J. F., III. Infant color perception. *Science*, 1974, *183*, 973–975.

Fagot, B. Sex differences in toddlers' behavior and parental reaction. *Developmental Psychology*, 1974, *10*, 554–558.

Fagot, B. *Sex determined parental reinforcing contingencies in toddler children.* Paper presented at the Biennial Meeting of the Society for Research in Child Development, New Orleans, March 1977. (a)

Fagot, B. I. Consequences of moderate cross-gender behavior in preschool children. *Child Development*, 1977, *48*, 902–907. (b)

Fagot, B. I. The influence of sex of child on parental reactions to toddler children. *Child Development*, 1978, *49*, 459–465. (a)

Fagot, B. I. *The consequences of same-sex, cross-sex and androgynous preferences.* Paper presented at the Annual Meeting of the Western Psychological Association, San Francisco, April 1978. (b)

Fagot, B. I. *Play styles in early childhood: Continuity and change as a function of sex.* Paper presented at the meeting of the International Society for the Study of Behavioural Development, Lund, Sweden, June 1979.

Feinman, S. Trends in racial self-image of black children: Psychological consequence of a social movement. *Journal of Negro Education*, 1979, *48*, 488–499.

Feldman, S. S., Biringen, Z. C., & Nash, S. C. Fluctuations of sex-related self-attributions as a function of stage of family life cycle. *Developmental Psychology*, 1981, *17*(1), 24–35.

Firstman, R. C. Black, white: Woman just wants to be whole. *Daily Camera*, June 12, 1981, pp. 1; 11.

Fischer, J. L., & Narus, L. R., Jr. Sex-role development in late adolescence and adulthood. *Sex Roles*, 1981, *7*,(2) 97–106.

Flerx, V. C., Fidler, D. S., & Rogers, R. W. Sex role stereotypes: Developmental aspects and early intervention. *Child Development*, 1976, *47*, 998–1007.

Fling, S., & Manosevitz, M. Sex typing in nursery school children's play interests. *Developmental Psychology*, 1972, *7*, 146–152.

Fox, D. J., & Jordan, V. B. Racial preference and identification of black, American Chinese and white children. *Genetic Psychology Monographs*, 1973, *88*, 229–286.

Frenkel-Brunswick, E., & Havel, J. Prejudice in the interviews of children: Attitudes toward minority groups. *Journal of Genetic Psychology*, 1953, *82*, 91–136.

Freud, S. Some psychological consequences of the anatomical distinction between the sexes. *International Journal of Psychoanalysis*, 1927, *8*, 133–142.

Garai, J. E., & Scheinfeld, A. Sex differences in mental and behavioral traits. *Genetic Psychology Monographs*, 1968, *77*, 169–299.

Gold, D., & Berger, C. Problem-solving performance of young boys and girls as a function of task appropriateness and sex identity. *Sex Roles*, 1978, *4*(2), 183–193.

Goldberg, M. E., & Gorn, G. J. Television's impact on preferences for non-white playmates: Canadian "Sesame Street" inserts. *Journal of Broadcasting*, 1979, *23*(1), 27–32.

Goldstein, C. G., Koopman, E. J., & Goldstein, H. H. Racial attitudes in young children as a function of interracial contact in the public schools. *American Journal of Orthopsychiatry*, 1979, *49*(1), 89–99.

Goodman, M. *Race awareness in young children*. Cambridge, Mass.: Addison-Wesley, 1952. (2nd ed., New York: Crowell-Collier, 1964)

Greenberg, B. S. Children's reactions to T.V. blacks. *Journalism Quarterly*, 1972, *49*(1), 5–14.

Greenwald, H. J., & Oppenheim, D. B. Reported magnitude of self-misidentification among Negro children—Artifact? *Journal of Personality and Social Psychology*, 1968, *8*, 49–52.

Greif, E. B. *Sex differences in parent–child conversations*. Massachusetts, December 1979. (ERIC Document Reproduction Service No. ED 174 337)

Gunthorpe, W. W. Skin color recognition, preference and identification in interracial children: A comparative study (Doctoral dissertation, Rutgers University, 1977). *Dissertation Abstracts International*, 1977, *38*, 3468B–3469B. (University Microfilms No. 77-27, 946)

Hardin, M. *Examination of examiner effects on performance of the Preschool Racial Attitude Measure Test II (PRAM II): A replication*. Unpublished master's thesis, University of Arizona, 1977.

Haugh, S. S., Hoffman, C. D., & Cowan, G. The eye of the very young beholder: Sex typing of infants by young children. *Child Development*, 1980, *51*, 598–600.

Hays, D. G., Margolis, E., Naroll, R., & Perkins, D. R. Color term salience. *American Anthropologist*, 1972, *74*, 1107–1121.

Hemmer, J., & Kleiber, D. Tomboys and sissies: Androgynous children. *Sex Roles*, 1981, *7*(12), 1205–1212.

Hetherington, E. M. A developmental study of the effects of sex of the dominant parent on sex-role preference identification and imitation in children. *Journal of Personality and Social Psychology*, 1965, *2*, 188–194.

Hoffman, L. W. The value of children to parents and the decrease in family size. *Proceedings of the American Philosophical Society*, 1975, *119*, 430–438.

Hoffman, L. W. Changes in family roles, socialization and sex differences. *American Psychologist*, 1977, *32*, 644–657.

Hraba, J., & Grant, G. Black is beautiful: A reexamination of racial preference and identification. *Journal of Personality and Social Psychology*, 1970, *16*, 398–402.

Jacklin, C. N., & Maccoby, E. E. Social behavior at 33 months in same-sex and mixed-sex dyads. *Child Development*, 1978, *49*(3), 557–569.

Jacobs, J. H. Black/white interracial families: Marital process and identity development in young children (Doctoral dissertation, Wright Institute, 1977). *Dissertation Abstracts International*, 1978, *38*, 5023B.

Katcher, A. The discrimination of sex differences by young children. *Journal of Genetic Psychology*, 1955, *87*, 131–143.

Katz, P. A. Perception of racial cues in preschool children: A new look. *Developmental Psychology,* 1973, *8*(2), 295–299.

Katz, P. A. The acquisition of racial attitudes in children. In P. A. Katz (Ed.), *Towards the elimination of racism.* New York: Pergamon, 1976.

Katz, P. A. The development of female identity. *Sex Roles,* 1979, *5*(2), 155–178.

Katz, P. A., & Rank, S. A. *Gender constancy and sibling status.* Paper presented at the meeting of the Society for Research in Child Development, Boston, April 1981.

Katz, P. A., & Seavey, C. Labels and children's perception of faces. *Child Development,* 1973, *44*(4), 770–775.

Katz, P., Sohn, M., & Zalk, S. R. Perceptual concomitants of racial attitudes in urban grade-school children. *Developmental Psychology,* 1975, *11*, 135–144.

Katz, P. A., & Zalk, S. R. Doll preferences: An index of racial attitudes? *Journal of Educational Psychology,* 1974, *66*(5), 663–668.

Katz, P. A., & Zalk, S. R. Modification of children's racial attitudes. *Developmental Psychology,* 1978, *14*(5), 447–461.

Kliman, D. S. Avoiding sexism in early childhood education. *Day Care and Early Education,* 1978, *6*(1), 19–21.

Kohlberg, L. A cognitive developmental analysis of children's sex-role concepts and attitudes. In E. E. Maccoby (Ed.), *The development of sex differences.* Stanford, Calif.: Stanford Univ. Press, 1966.

Kuhn, D., Nash, S. C., & Brucken, L. Sex role concepts of two- and three-year-olds. *Child Development,* 1978, *49,* 445–451.

Lacoste, R. J. *Young children's ability to match facial features typical of race.* San Antonio: University of Texas at San Antonio, 1978. (ERIC Document Reproduction Service No. ED 156 312)

LaDow, S. *A content-analysis of selected picture books examining the portrayal of sex-roles and representation of males and females.* Urbana-Champaign: University of Illinois. September 1976. (ERIC Document Reproduction Service No. ED 123 165)

Lamb, M. E., & Roopnarine, J. L. Peer influences on sex-role development in preschoolers. *Child Development,* 1979, *50,* 1219–1222.

Langer, E. Rethinking the role of thought in social interaction. In J. Harvey, W. Ickes, & R. Kidd (Eds.), *New directions in attribution research* (Vol. II). Hillsdale, N.J.: Erlbaum, 1979.

Langlois, J. H., & Stephan, C. The effects of physical attractiveness and ethnicity on children's behavioral attributions and peer preferences. *Child Development,* 1977, *48,* 1694–1698.

Lazowick, L. M. On the nature of identification. *Journal of Abnormal Psychology,* 1955, *51,* 175–183.

Lerner, R. M., & Buehrig, C. J. The development of racial attitudes in young black and white children. *Journal of Genetic Psychology,* 1975, *127,* 45–54.

Lewis, M. Parents and children: Sex-role development. *School Review,* 1972, *80*(2), 229–240. (a)

Lewis, M. State as an infant–environment interaction as a function of sex. *Merrill-Palmer Quarterly,* 1972, *18,* 95–121. (b)

Lewis, M., & Brooks, G. Infant's social perception: A constructivist's view. In L. B. Cohen & P. Salapatek (Eds.), *Infant perception: From sensation to cognition* (Vol. 2). New York: Academic Press, 1975.

Lewis, M., & Cherry, L. Social behavior and language acquisition. In M. Lewis & L. Rosenblum (Eds.), *Interaction, conversation and the development of language: The origins of behavior* (Vol. 2). New York: Wiley, 1977.

Lewis, M., & Goldberg, S. Perceptual-cognitive development in infancy: A generalized expectancy model as a function of the mother–infant interaction. *Merrill-Palmer Quarterly*, 1969, *15*(1), 81–100.

Lott, B. Behavioral concordance with sex-role ideology related to play areas, creativity and parental sex-typing of children. *Journal of Personality and Social Psychology*, 1978, *36*, 1087–1100.

Luria, Z. *Kids' discretionary choices: The peer group and its importance.* Paper presented to the Ford Foundation Conference on Research on Female Gender Role Development, Southbury, Connecticut, May 1980.

Lutes-Dunckley, C. J. Sex-role preferences as a function of sex of storyteller and story content. *Journal of Psychology*, 1978, *100*, 151–158.

McAdoo, H. P. *The development of self-concept and race attitudes in black children: A longitudinal study.* 1977. (ERIC Document Reproduction Service No. ED 148 944. Not available separately; see UD 017 651)

McAdoo, J. L. *An exploratory study of racial attitude change in black preschool children using differential treatments.* Unpublished doctoral dissertation, University of Michigan, 1970.

McArthur, L. Z., & Eisen, S. V. Television and sex-role stereotyping. *Journal of Applied Social Psychology*, 1976, *6*(4), 329–351.

Maccoby, E. E., & Jacklin, C. N. *The psychology of sex differences.* Stanford, Calif.: Stanford Univ. Press, 1974.

Marcus, D. E., & Overton, W. F. The development of cognitive gender constancy and sex role preferences. *Child Development*, 1978, *49*, 434–444.

Masters, J. C., & Wilkerson, A. Consensual and discriminative stereotypy of sex-type judgments by parents and children. *Child Development*, 1976, *47*, 208–217.

Mead, M. Cultural determinants of sexual behavior. In W. C. Young (Ed.), *Sex and internal secretions* (Vol. 2). Baltimore: Williams & Wilkins, 1961.

Money, J., & Ehrhardt, A. A. *Man and woman, boy and girl.* Baltimore & London: Johns Hopkins Press, 1972.

Money, J., Hampson, J. G., & Hampson, J. L. Imprinting and the establishment of gender role. *A.M.A. Archives of Neurology and Psychology*, 1957, *77*, 333–336.

Morland, J. K. A comparison of race awareness in northern and southern children. *American Journal of Orthopsychiatry*, 1966, *36*(1), 22–31.

Morland, J. K. Racial acceptance and preference of nursery school children in a southern city. In A. R. Brown (Ed.), *Prejudice in children.* Springfield, Ill.: Charles C Thomas, 1972.

Morland, J. K., & Suthers, E. Racial attitudes of children: Perspectives on the structural-normative theory of prejudice. *Phylon*, 1980, *41*, 267–275.

Mortimer, M. Sex stereotyping in children's books. *Australian Journal of Early Childhood*, 1979, *4*(4), 4–8.

Moss, H. A. Sex, age and state as determinants of mother–infant interaction. *Merrill-Palmer Quarterly*, 1967, *13*, 19–36.

Nilsen, A. P. Alternatives to sexist practices in the classroom. *Young Children*, 1977, *32*(5), 53–58.

Palmer, E. L. *The public kindergarten concept as a factor in racial attitudes.* Davidson College, 1977. (ERIC Document Reproduction Service No. ED 129 936)

Parke, R. D., & O'Leary, S. E. Family interaction in the newborn period: Some findings, some observations and some unresolved issues. In K. Riegel & J. Meacham (Eds.), *The developing individual in a changing world.* Vol. II: *Social and environmental issues.* The Hague, Netherlands: Mouton, 1976.

Payne, R. B. Racial attitude formation in children of mixed black and white heritage: Skin color and racial identity (Doctoral dissertation, California School of Professional Psychology, 1977). *Dissertation Abstracts International,* 1977, *38,* 2876B. (University Microfilms No. 77-27, 605)

Peterson, C., & McDonald, L. Children's occupational sex-typing. *Journal of Genetic Psychology,* 1980, *136*(1), 145–146.

Porter, J. *Black child, white child: The development of racial attitudes.* Cambridge, Mass.: Harvard Univ. Press, 1971.

Proshansky, H. The development of intergroup attitudes. In I. W. Hoffman & M. L. Hoffman (Eds.), *Review of child development research* (Vol. 2). New York: Russell Sage Foundation, 1966.

Pushkin, I. *A study of ethnic choice in the play of young children in three London districts.* Unpublished doctoral thesis, University of London, 1967.

Radke, M., & Sutherland, J. Children's concepts and attitudes about minority and majority American groups. *Journal of Educational Psychology,* 1949, *40*(8), 449–468.

Radke-Yarrow, M., Trager, H., & Miller, J. The role of parents in the development of children's ethnic attitudes. *Child Development,* 1952, *23,* 13–53.

Rebecca, M., Hefner, R., & Oleshansky, B. A model of sex role transcendence. *Journal of Social Issues,* 1976, *32,* 197–206.

Renninger, C. A., & Williams, J. E. Black–white color connotations and race awareness in preschool children. *Perceptual and Motor Skills,* 1966, *22,* 771–785.

Rheingold, H. L., & Cook, K. V. The contents of boys' and girls' rooms as an index of parents' behavior. *Child Development,* 1975, *46,* 459–463.

Robinson, B. E., & Hobson, C. F. Beyond sex-role stereotyping. *Day Care and Early Education,* 1978, *6*(1), 16–18.

Rose, S., Katz, P. A., Birke, M. S., & Rossman, E. Visual following in newborns: The role of figure–ground contrast and configurational detail. *Perceptual and Motor Skills,* 1977, *45,* 515–522.

Rosenberg, B. G., & Sutton-Smith, B. Family interaction effects on masculinity–femininity. *Journal of Personality and Social Psychology,* 1965, *8,* 117–130.

Rubin, J., Provenzano, F., & Luria, Z. The eye of the beholder: Parents' views on sex of newborns. *American Journal of Orthopsychiatry,* 1974, *44*(4), 512–519.

Ruble, D. N., & Ruble, T. L. Sex stereotypes. In A. G. Miller (Ed.), *In the eye of the beholder: Contemporary issues in stereotyping.* New York: Holt, 1980.

St. Peter, S. Jack went up the hill . . . but where was Jill? *Psychology of Women Quarterly,* 1979, *4*(2), 256–260.

Sanday, P. R. *Female power and male dominance: On the origins of sexual inequality.* Cambridge: Cambridge Univ. Press, 1981.

Schofield, J. School desegregation and intergroup relations. In D. Bar-Tal & L. Saxe (Eds.), *Social psychology of education: Theory and research.* Washington, D.C.: Hemisphere Publishing Company, 1978.

Seavey, C. A., Katz, P. A., & Zalk, S. R. Baby X: The effect of gender labels on adult responses to infants. *Sex Roles,* 1975, *1,* 103–109.

Semaj, L. The development of racial evaluation and preference: A cognitive approach. *The Journal of Black Psychology,* 1980, *6*(2), 59–79.

Semaj, L. T. The development of racial-classification abilities. *Journal of Negro Education,* 1981, *50*(1), 41–47.

Serbin, L. A., & Connor, J. M. *Environmental control of sex related behaviors in the preschool.* Paper presented at the Society for Research in Child Development, San Francisco, March 1979.

Serbin, L. A., Connor, J. M., & Iler, I. Sex-stereotyped and non-stereotyped introductions of new toys in the preschool classroom: An observational study of teacher behavior and its effects. *Psychology of Women Quarterly*, 1979, 4(2), 261–265.

Shanahan, J. K. *The effects of modifying black–white concept attitudes of black and white first grade subjects upon two measures of racial attitudes.* Unpublished doctoral dissertation, University of Washington, 1972.

Sidorowicz, L., & Lunney, G. S. Baby X revisited. *Sex Roles*, 1980, 6, 67–73.

Slaby, R. G., & Frey, K. S. Development of gender constancy and selective attention to same-sex models. *Child Development*, 1975, 46, 849–856.

Smith, C., & Lloyd, B. Maternal behavior and perceived sex of infant: Revisited. *Child Development*, 1978, 49, 1263–1265.

Sorce, J. F. The role of physiognomy in the development of racial awareness. *Journal of Genetic Psychology*, 1979, 134, 33–41.

Spencer, M. B., & Horowitz, F. D. Effects of systematic social and token reinforcement on the modification of racial and color concept attitudes in black and white children. *Developmental Psychology*, 1973, 9, 249–254.

Sprafkin, J. N., & Liebert, R. M. Sex-typing and children's television preferences. In G. Tuchman, A. K. Daniels, & J. Benet (Eds.), *Hearth and home: Images of women in mass media*. New York: Oxford Univ. Press, 1978.

Stephan, W. G., & Rosenfield, D. Black self-rejection: Another look. *Journal of Educational Psychology*, 1979, 71(5), 708–716.

Stevenson, H. W., & Stewart, E. C. A developmental study of race awareness in young children. *Child Development*, 1958, 29, 399–410.

Sutton-Smith, B., & Rosenberg, B. G. Manifest anxiety and game preferences in children. *Child Development*, 1960, 31, 307–311.

Tajfel, H. Quantitative judgment in social perception. *British Journal of Psychology*, 1959, 50, 16–29.

Tajfel, H. Cognitive aspects of prejudice. *Journal of Social Issues*, 1969, 25, 79–97.

Tajfel, H. The roots of prejudice: Cognitive aspects. In P. Watson (Ed.), *Psychology and race*. Chicago: Aldine, 1973.

Tajfel, H. Individuals and groups in social psychology. *British Journal of Social and Clinical Psychology*, 1979, 18, 183–190.

Tajfel, H., & Billig, M. Familiarity and categorization in intergroup behavior. *Journal of Experimental Social Psychology*, 1974, 10, 159–170.

Tajfel, H., Sheikh, A. A., & Gardner, R. C. Content of stereotypes and the inference of similarity between members of stereotyped groups. *Acta Psychologica*, 1964, 22, 191–201.

Tajfel, H., & Wilkes, A. L. Classification and quantitative judgment. *British Journal of Psychology*, 1963, 54, 101–114.

Thoman, E. B., Leiderman, P. H., & Olson, J. P. Neonate–mother interaction during breast feeding. *Developmental Psychology*, 1972, 6, 110–118.

Thompson, S. K. Gender labels and early sex role development. *Child Development*, 1975, 46, 339–347.

Thompson, S. K., & Bentler, P. M. The priority of cues in sex discrimination by children and adults. *Developmental Psychology*, 1971, 5(2), 181–185.

Traynham, R. M. *The effects of modifying color meaning concepts on racial concept attitudes in five- and eight-year old children.* Unpublished master's thesis, University of Arkansas, 1974.

Troll, L. E., Neugarten, B. L., & Kraines, R. J. Similarities in values and other personality characteristics in college students and their parents. *Merrill-Palmer Quarterly*, 1969, 15, 323–336.

U.S. Commission on Civil Rights. *Window dressing on the set: An update.* Washington, D.C.: U.S. Government Printing Office, 1979.

Urberg, K. *Sex role concepts.* Paper presented at the Biennial Meeting of the Society for Research in Child Development, San Francisco, March 1979.

Urberg, K. A., & Labouvie-Vief, G. Conceptualizations of sex roles: A life span developmental study. *Developmental Psychology,* 1976, *12*(1), 15–23.

Van Parys, M. *Preschoolers in society: Use of the social roles of sex, age and race for self and others by black and white children.* Unpublished master's thesis, University of Denver, 1981.

Wehren, A., & De Lisi, R. *Self and other gender constancy: A dimensional analysis.* Paper presented at the Biennial Meeting of the Society for Research in Child Development, Boston, April 1981.

Weinraub, M., Brown, L., Sockloff, A., Ethridge, T., & Gracely, E. The development of sex role stereotypes in preschoolers: Relationship to gender knowledge, gender identity, sex-typed toy preference and family characteristics. Manuscript, November 1982.

Will, J. A., Self, P. A., & Datan, N. Maternal behavior and perceived sex of infant. *American Journal of Orthopsychiatry,* 1976, *46,* 135–139.

Williams, J. E. *Racial attitudes in preschool children: Modification via operant conditioning and a revised measurement procedure.* Paper presented at the American Psychological Association, Honolulu, September 1972.

Williams, J., Bennett, S., & Best, D. Awareness and expression of sex stereotypes in young children. *Developmental Psychology,* 1975, *11,* 635–642.

Williams, J. E., Best, D. L., Boswell, D. A., Mattson, L. A., & Graves, D. J. Preschool racial attitude measure II. *Educational and Psychological Measurement,* 1975, *35,* 3–18.

Williams, J. E., Boswell, D. A., & Best, D. L. Evaluative responses of preschool children to the colors white and black. *Child Development,* 1975, *46,* 501–508.

Williams, J. E., & Edwards, C. D. An exploratory study of the modification of color concepts and racial attitudes in preschool children. *Child Development,* 1969, *40,* 737–750.

Williams, J. E., & Morland, J. K. *Race, color and the young child.* Chapel Hill: Univ. of North Carolina Press, 1976.

Williams, J. E., & Morland, J. K. Comment on Banks' "White preference in blacks: A paradigm in search of a phenomenon." *Psychological Bulletin,* 1979, *86*(1), 28–32.

Williams, J. E., & Roberson, J. K. A method for assessing racial attitudes in preschool children. *Educational and Psychological Measurement,* 1967, *27,* 671–689.

Wirtenberg, J. *Cultural fairness in materials development.* Paper presented at the skills workshop of the Women's Educational Equity Act Program, Washington, D.C., April 1978. (Abstract)

Wolff, P. H. Observations on the early development of smiling. In B. M. Foss (Ed.), *Determinants of infant behavior, II.* New York: Wiley, 1963.

Yarrow, L. J., Rubenstein, J. L., Pederson, F. A., & Jankowski, J. J. Dimensions in early stimulation and their differential effects on infant development. *Merrill-Palmer Quarterly,* 1972, *18,* 205–218.

Zajonc, R. B., Swap, W. C., Harrison, A. A., & Roberts, P. Limiting conditions of the exposure effect: Satiation and relativity. *Journal of Personality and Social Psychology,* 1971, *18,* 384–391.

Zalk, S. R., & Katz, P. A. Gender attitudes in children. *Sex Roles,* 1978, *4*(3), 349–357.

Zimet, S. G. *Print and prejudice.* Kent, England: Hodder & Stoughton Educational, 1976

Zuckerman, D. M., Singer, D. G., & Singer, J. L. Children's television viewing, racial and sex-role attitudes. *Journal of Applied Social Psychology,* 1980, *10*(4), 281–294.

3 / The development of the conception of social class

ROBERT L. LEAHY

INTERVIEWER: *What are rich people like? How would you describe them?*
BILL: *They feel they are modern, filter tip, like a high-rise apartment . . .*

This metaphoric description by a 17-year-old, working-class black male begins a rather poignant interview in which he reflects on class consciousness, equity, social structure, and the possibility of equality. His interview, articulate and moving, suggests the richness of the clinical method introduced to developmentalists by Piaget (1932). In this chapter, I will review the theoretical foundations and empirical findings of a study of 720 children and adolescents in which conceptions of economic inequality were investigated. But to give the reader a sense of the quality of what was said, I would like to begin by contrasting this interview with Bill with an interview with a 6-year-old white male named Joe.

BILL: *They probably are missing a certain part of life. They only know the good side of life, they miss the bad side. They feel they are over poor people and they shouldn't be in their society. That's why rich businessmen in New York who run this city don't live here. They don't know about the apartments, what's bad about them. They live in the suburbs.*
INTERVIEWER: *Anything else to describe rich people?*
BILL: *Some are very nice, they care about people, help people. But then there's the bad, too.*

Contrast Bill's comments about class antagonism between the rich and the poor, the political power of the rich, and his qualifications of the attitudes of some of the rich with Joe's perspective on the wealthy.

JOE: *They got yachts, got big boats, got crazy outfits. They got horses, dogs, and cats.*

Bill's awareness of class conflict and the reduced life chances of the poor is reflected in his comments about how he would describe poor people.

BILL: *Poor people have to struggle. Every day is a bad day it seems like to them. Some really don't care if they are poor or not, as long as they are living. Then, the kids, they forget they need education to get out of the poorness. Without it, they won't make it. Since their parents are poor, they should realize that.*

On the other hand, Joe's view of the poor is focused on the peripheral or observable qualities of poverty—food and clothes.

JOE: *No food. They won't have no Thanksgiving. They don't have nothing. They don't have no shirts. They don't have no shoes.*

In comparing the rich and poor, Bill once again sees life chances— that is, the opportunities to gain access to social goods—as an important distinguishing difference.

INTERVIEWER: *How are rich and poor people different?*
BILL: *One is the money. They can go where they want when they want. I feel they have certain more rights than poor people. They can get better lawyers than poor people. Poor people get lawyers who don't care really because they are not getting the money the city is paying.*
INTERVIEWER: *Any other differences?*
BILL: *They have better advantages. Rich people's life is easy for them.*
INTERVIEWER: *Anything else?*
BILL: *I feel rich people feel more happier about life than poor people.*

Joe's conception of difference is entirely focused on the peripheral dimensions that define economic class for him.

JOE: *Because rich people have crazy outfits and poor people have no outfits.*
INTERVIEWER: *Anything else?*
JOE: *Rich people have more money and poor people don't and rich people have everything if they want and if they want everything they could have it. The poor people can't get nothing. They could buy rings, the poor people can't.*

Although Bill's emphasis on class conflict and life chances may at first make him reluctant to see any similarities between the rich and poor, he is able to cite obligations to the law (i.e., taxes), family life, and aspirations as points of commonality across class lines.

INTERVIEWER: *How are rich and poor people the same?*
BILL: *I can't even see what they have in common.*
INTERVIEWER: *How do you think they are the same?*
BILL: *They pay the same taxes.*
INTERVIEWER: *Anything else?*
BILL: *They work. Everyday life. They care for their family, love them, try to look out for them. They want their kids to be better than they are in life.*

In contrast, once having classified the rich and poor as different, Joe is unable to find any points of commonality.

JOE: *They ain't the same.*
INTERVIEWER: *Isn't there anything that is the same about them?*
JOE: *No, because one's rich and they got fancy outfits and the other ain't.*

When Bill explains wealth and poverty, he emphasizes differences in individual inputs, especially effort, that are believed to relate to differences in income. Furthermore, the reason why poor people are believed to have less ability to achieve wealth is seen by Bill to be a consequence of environmental differences—for example, poor education.

INTERVIEWER: *Why is it that some people are rich while others are poor?*
BILL: *Some strive for their goal, believe in it. They have this certain adrenaline in their system that they want to be rich, and they can make it, be successful. Some people are poor because they let this happen to them. They didn't want to learn so they suffer the consequences.*
INTERVIEWER: *Any other reasons why some people are rich?*
BILL: *Some are born rich because their families are rich. Then they get all the money and believe there is nothing to work for because they have it. Some people are poor because they are born in the world poor. They can't help it to get out of the slum. Poor education, poor teaching, poor environment.*

Joe's explanation of poverty is focused on the importance of jobs. Similar to a number of other young children in this study, Joe believes that one reason why people are poor is that they cannot afford to ''buy'' a job.

JOE: *Because they got to work and they work in real business and they get money every day. The poor people don't have no jobs. They couldn't pay for no jobs because they don't have no money to get a job.*
INTERVIEWER: *Why is it that some people are poor?*
JOE: *Because they live in Africa and nobody gives them no food and they have to eat out of the garbage.*

Despite Bill's awareness of the reduced life chances associated with poverty, he does believe that wealth is justified if it results from individual differences in effort and ability. But poverty is viewed as unfair because he believes that poor people suffer and that part of recognizing human dignity is to set a minimum standard of living.

INTERVIEWER: *Do you think that some people should be rich while others are poor?*

BILL: *No. That's really discriminating. That you are in favor of somebody being poor. That's disliking and saying you don't want them in your environment or in your world. Keep them on the dark side of the street.*

INTERVIEWER: *Any other reasons why you don't think some people should be poor?*

BILL: *I feel people are people, we breathe the same air, drink the same water. I don't feel there should be no discrimination against that.*

INTERVIEWER: *Do you think that some people should be rich?*

BILL: *People who strive to be rich, try to be rich, yes, I feel they should be rich. But being that this world is dog eat dog, it's hard to get rich, because everybody is competing for the same goal.*

INTERVIEWER: *Anything else?*

BILL: *They are the more aggressive in the world. They try to go out and seize success, but they fail.*

INTERVIEWER: *Who?*

BILL: *The poor. People who try to go out in life and be successful, they should be rich. People who can help society with their money should be rich, who care about others.*

Joe, on the other hand, sees no justification for extremes of wealth, because he believes that poor people should not suffer and that people should be equal.

JOE: *No, because it ain't fair. Some people have money and poor people don't. It ain't fair.*

INTERVIEWER: *Why isn't it fair?*

JOE: *Because the rich people could buy whatever they want and the poor, they're left with nothing. The rich people should share with the poor people. The rich people should have 50 and the poor people should have 50. It would be even.*

In their conceptions of social mobility of the poor, Bill and Joe have different ideas about the importance of values, motivation, and education. Given Bill's emphasis on equity as a source of inequality, it is not surprising that he believes that mobility can be achieved through the poor attaining the requisite motivation and training to achieve wealth.

INTERVIEWER: *How could a poor person get rich someday?*

BILL: *There are a lot of things. He or she can get a better education, go out and look for better jobs, and make money. Try to get out of that poor system environment. Try to believe they are not poor, have confidence they can make it.*

Joe believes that the acquisition of a job is a means of mobility, but he also believes that the rich could give money to the poor. This reflects the egocentric-dependent view of social mobility and social change given by a number of these younger children. According to this view, wealth is partly a consequence of generosity of others toward poor individuals.

JOE: *They could get a job. People could give them money.*
INTERVIEWER: *Who would give them money?*
JOE: *The rich people.*

Similar to his conception of mobility of the poor, Joe's conception of his own mobility reflects a belief that jobs are important and that others could give him money. As with a number of the young children, mobility is also understood in simple definitional terms, in which the way to get rich is simply to acquire goods.

INTERVIEWER: *How could you get rich someday?*
JOE: *Get a job.*
INTERVIEWER: *Anything else?*
JOE: *Keep clothes, buy clothes to wear and you have a nice place to live.*
INTERVIEWER: *How else could you get rich someday?*
JOE: *People give you money. You have food to eat.*

Bill's view of mobility suggests that he understands that occupations are stratified with regard to income and that the possibilities of success in work will be related to expansions within different sectors of the economy. Furthermore, Bill believes that it is important to have a variety of goals or options. Regardless of his recognition of the importance of plans in achieving goals, Bill, like a number of working-class adolescents, rejects wealth as an important goal for himself.

BILL: *Choose a field that I know I can make a certain amount of money, that I can live well off. Like, say, computers, major in that and I know that later on in life our society will need people to operate them. So I'll think ahead so I'll be ready for life.*
INTERVIEWER: *Anything else?*
BILL: *Have more goals than one just in case you don't make it in one field there is a shot for another.*
INTERVIEWER: *Anything else?*
BILL: *I wouldn't really want to become rich. I'd just like to become well off.*
INTERVIEWER: *Why wouldn't you want to become rich?*
BILL: *Becoming rich, people who are rich feel they are so superior and people who are poor are so inferior that they forget about them. But I feel money isn't everything, so I feel if I have a certain amount I'm happy with, that's all I need.*

Finally, in their conceptions of social change Bill and Joe focus on different sources of economic function. Joe believes that jobs would be important but also that others would have to help the poor. In contrast, Bill's emphasis is on changing the competitive values that he believes underlie the present social system. Part of this change, according to Bill, would entail change in the political system.

INTERVIEWER: *What would have to happen so that there would be no poor people?*
JOE: *They would have to get a job.*
INTERVIEWER: *Anything else?*
JOE: *People would have to give them money.*

Bill's conception is less concrete, reflecting psychological qualities of economic stratification and the importance of economic class.

BILL: *Darwin's theory about survival of the fittest would have to change. It would have to be everybody is happy, take a piece of my bread, share and share alike.*
INTERVIEWER: *Anything else?*
BILL: *The government would have to change, too. Better jobs, better education, better property. Make everybody equal and happy.*
INTERVIEWER: *Anything else?*
BILL: *Also, to force the poor not to feel that they are poor, make them feel important, not left out. No more rich people. Make everybody equal, middle class, a certain amount of money in each person's pocket.*

As the preceding quotations and comments indicate, there appears to be a considerable difference in the responses given by these subjects of different ages. In this chapter, I will attempt to outline briefly issues in the development of conceptions of social class and to suggest some cognitive-developmental qualities in societal conceptions. Furthermore, I will report the results of an extensive study of children and adolescents in the United States that assessed their conceptions of economic inequality. Finally, I will offer a three-level developmental model of class conceptions based on the data of this study.

EPISTEMOLOGY OF SOCIAL CLASS CONCEPTS

Developmental models of cognitive or social cognitive processes often imply some end point or idealized quality toward which growth proceeds (Harris, 1959). Such an end point need not be teleological in the sense that earlier stages or points in development are directed by the final product or are considered reducible to that product. In fact, in considering "advanced" conceptions of social class, we may be confronted with the recognition that such conceptions are seldom realized in lay epistemology and may reflect the conceptions of unusual individuals who live within a specific historical period.

The selection of some theoretical conceptions rather than others as representative of "advanced" conceptions of social class may appear to imply that these conceptions are veridical, whereas other unselected conceptions or conceptions considered less advanced are less veridical. However, satisfactory criteria as to the veridicality of one conception of class over another are elusive and, indeed, useless in the context of the present study. First, they are elusive in that no empirical test of the historical or ethical value of these potential theories—for example, Marxist, functionalist, or Weberian theory—presents itself as a clear criterion for resolving conflicting claims to veridicality. And, second, even if satisfactory criteria could be imposed for deciding which theory of class is veridical, this does not necessarily imply that such a conception is developmentally more advanced. Such a developmental model must address itself to the natural ordering of concepts (in which structural hierarchy is implied) and the relationship of chronological age to the utilization of such concepts.

The epistemology of the development of class conceptions must consider three questions:

1. What are the conceptions of social class held by leading sociological theorists? Are there common elements among these theoretical positions?
2. What would be the expected developmental ordering of class concepts?
3. What role does experience play in the development of class conceptions?

Sociological theories of social class

It is far beyond the scope of this chapter to describe adequately sociological theories of social class. However, I will briefly discuss the views of Marx and Weber, who appear to share a similar understanding of the meaning of social class. Both argue that classes are not simply collections of individuals. Rather, classes entail common social constructions of reality held by members of a class, and classes occupy different positions within the perspectives of other groups within society. That is, members of a class share a common perspective (e.g., class consciousness or communalization), and they are the object of the common perspective of some other groups (e.g., political power and prestige). In addition, Weber argues that classes differ in their *life chances*—that is, the opportunities for the quality of life explicitly resulting from class position. These life chances are not limited to a single moment in the life of an individual, but rather they are assumed to extend throughout long periods and to pervade a variety of areas of life. Thus, classes have common perspectives, are the object of perspectives of others, and can have extended opportunities resulting from class position and political power.

Developmental ordering

Learning theory generally assumes that the development of conceptions of society is a process reflecting the learning of factual information. The epistemology of a cognitive-developmental model is somewhat different. Societal concepts are viewed as developing in a sequential pattern, such that conceptions developed later are more general and abstract and may require knowledge at earlier levels. We are familiar with the idea of a natural ordering of concepts in Piaget's (1970) and Kohlberg's (1969) theories. For example, the ability to perform transformations on abstract symbols presumes the ability to perform transformations on concrete objects (i.e., formal and concrete operational thought). The epistemology of class concepts guiding this study suggests that a possible ordering might be the following: (*a*) distinguishing groups from one another on external criteria (e.g., wealth); (*b*) attributing characteristics to these groups that might account for these classifications (e.g., intelligence, motivation); and (*c*) indicating how these classes relate to one another within a coordinated (or uncoordinated) societal framework (e.g., class consciousness).

Cognitive-developmental theory suggests that the ordering of societal conceptions will be similar to the ordering of other kinds of social cognition, such as moral judgment, person descriptions, and attributions for achievement. This is based on the idea that intelligence is *organized*— that is, common structures will be applied to a variety of contents (Piaget, 1932).

Experience and class conceptions

Two central assumptions of cognitive-developmental theory are that change comes about through experiences that are optimally challenging (i.e., that provide some degree of structural match with the individual's cognitive level) and that at the same time challenge existing structures. Piaget refers to *equilibration* in describing this process of change. According to this view, cognitive level limits the effect of experience since cognitive structures have a self-regulating function. Consequently, even though young children may be exposed to sophisticated political reasoning (e.g., supply-side economics), their societal conceptions will not reflect a true copy of these external stimuli. Thus, young children may attempt to comprehend economic functioning by relating market relationships (e.g., buyer–seller) to a role structure with which they are familiar (e.g., parent–child).

The second assumption—that of cognitive challenge—suggests that acceleration in the development of class concepts will be greatest for those exposed to conflicting information about class. The difficulty inherent in this disequilibrium model is that it is almost impossible to operationalize cognitive conflict. The problem is further compounded when we speak in such elusive terms as "conflicting information about class." Consequently, it is difficult to derive clear predictions about the role of experience from the cognitive-developmental model.

In contrast, sociological theories of class diverge considerably in their descriptions of the role of class (as an index of experience) in the development of class conceptions. Two sociological theories are relevant to the issue of conflict in conceptions of stratification. On the one hand, *functionalist* theory suggests that individuals in society share common beliefs as to the nature of social class. This consensus presumably serves the function of stabilizing societal institutions and indicating to individuals the rationale or justification of and the means of mobility within the class system (Merton, 1957; Parsons, 1960). In contrast to this consensus model, other theories of stratification stress the importance of *conflict* within society, such that unequal distribution of social goods is viewed as associated with differences in constructions of social reality (Marx, 1844/1966; Weber, 1946). Consequently, from functionalist theory we might expect wide consensus among classes in their conception of economic class, and with increasing age (as an index of socialization), we might expect to find increasing justification of inequality. In contrast, conflict theories suggest that classes will differ considerably in their conception of inequality and that these differences will be greatest in regard to the evaluation (i.e., justification) of class differences.

DEVELOPMENTAL RESEARCH ON
CLASS CONCEPTS

Most previous research on the development of conceptions of social class has focused on age and class differences in children's knowledge or recognition of attributes associated with class position. Stendler (1949) presented pictures to first- through eighth-grade subjects. These pictures depicted the investigator's judgment of class differences in residence, recreation, clothes, and jobs. Her findings indicated that with increasing age there is increasing agreement with adult ratings of pictures. Another variation of the use of a classifying technique to test class awareness was employed by Jahoda (1959) in a study of children between 6 and 10 years of age. Subjects were presented with puzzle drawings depicting three social classes as indicated by external criteria (e.g., possessions and appearances). Jahoda found that first-grade children performed at better than chance level in assigning pieces to "appropriate" puzzles.

Tudor (1971) also employed a classifying method in her study of children in the first through sixth grades. First, subjects were requested to match families (i.e., mother, father, children), houses, and automobiles depicted in photographs. Second, subjects indicated which father figure attended college. Finally, subjects were asked whether the middle- or lower-class child is disliked by the upper-class child. Tudor's findings indicate that, although the first graders performed better than chance in sorting families with houses and autos and in indicating which father attended college, these abilities increased between the first and sixth grades. Finally, although there were no significant age trends for evaluation (i.e., which child is more disliked), even first-grade children indicated that the lower-class child is more disliked. The findings from these studies suggest that, by the first grade, children may recognize that possessions, residence, and possibly education are associated with social class status.

Another factor traditionally viewed as relevant to class is occupational ranking. Two studies have focused on developmental trends for this issue. DeFleur and DeFleur (1967) presented children (ages 6–13) with cartoon pictures of occupations varying in prestige according to adult rankings. There was a substantial increase between ages 6 and 13 in the concordance of adult and subject ratings of the status of occupations. Simmons and Rosenberg (1971) found that even third graders show agreement with adult ratings of the prestige of occupations. There was a substantial increase between elementary school and high school age in the claim that people do not have equal opportunity to achieve success. However, it is interesting to note that 97% of subjects for each social class claimed that they have "as good" a chance or a "better" chance to rise in the world compared to most other individuals. Apparently, even though children and adolescents may believe that others will be handicapped by stratification, they perceive their own opportunities in an optimistic light. Simmons and Rosenberg interpret these findings in terms of Davis and Moore's (1945) theory of stratification: Specifically, motivation to attain higher status presumably depends on the individual's *knowledge* of status rankings and *optimism* about one's own chances.

One study specifically concerned with class differences among children in conceptions of inequality was conducted by Estvan (1952). Subjects were 10- and 11-year-old children from upper- and lower-class backgrounds. Awareness of poverty was determined by responses to two pictures depicting social-problem situations—that is, problems of food, clothing, and shelter, although the specific content of the pictures is unclear from Estvan's monograph. Furthermore, Estvan gives little rationale for the selection of categories used for scoring subjects' responses or for why class differences in responses should be expected. Of the many statistical comparisons made between upper- and lower-class children, only a few were significant. Upper-class children were more likely to mention slums (i.e., location of shelter) and facilities for recreation, whereas lower-class children were more likely to mention personal health habits and quantity of clothing.

With the exception of the Simmons and Rosenberg study in which class concepts are related to functionalist theory, most previous research on the development of class concepts appears to lack a coherent theoretical rationale. The finding that age is associated with agreement with adult stereotypes is not surprising: Could one imagine that as children or adolescents become more similar to adults in age that they would become *less* like adults in their social concepts? If anything, these studies share an implicit assumption that age is an index of experience and that experience is associated with knowledge of the stratification system. Moreover, these studies do not address questions central to most sociological or political theories of stratification—namely, evaluations, explanations, and conceptions of mobility and social change. Previous developmental research on class concepts appears to delineate deficits in knowledge of children of different ages or classes. Such an approach, as Piaget has argued, may obscure the qualitative differences associated with age in conceptions of the world. The present study was largely guided by such a cognitive-developmental perspective.

DEVELOPMENTAL TRENDS IN
PERSON DESCRIPTIONS

According to cognitive-developmental theory, the development of conceptions of social class should reflect qualitative differences in the categories used by children of different ages in conceptualizing their social world. According to this cognitive-developmental approach, conceptions of social structure should reflect other aspects of social and nonsocial cognition that, presumably, develop in parallel with one another. A number of studies on the development of person perception indicate that between 7 and 10 years of age children show an increasing tendency to refer to the *central* aspects of others, such as their thoughts, feelings, traits, and motivations (Bigner, 1974; Livesley & Bromley, 1973; Scarlett, Press, & Crockett, 1971). There is a corresponding decrease during this age period in references to the *peripheral* characteristics of others, such as their appearances, behaviors, possessions, or habits. Similarly, the first sex-role stereotypes learned refer to the behavioral rather than dispositional qualities of persons (Williams, Bennett, & Best, 1975) or the physical appearance associated with sex or occupational role (Kohlberg, 1966, 1969). Conceptions of deviance or disorder also undergo change with age, with younger children defining deviance in terms of behavioral differences and adolescents defining deviance in terms of violations of social norms or disorders in perspectives (Coie & Pennington, 1976). Consequently, one expectation in the present study was that younger children would emphasize peripheral qualities (e.g., possessions, behaviors, and appearance), whereas adolescents would emphasize inferred psychological characteristics (e.g., traits, thoughts, and motivations) in describing the rich and poor.

Conceptions of social class, however, are not entirely reducible to the development of descriptions of individuals. Sociological conceptions of economic inequality emphasize differences among classes in life chances (Davis & Moore, 1945; Parsons, 1960; Weber, 1946) and class consciousness (Dahrendorf, 1959; Ossowski, 1963). The recognition of these factors would appear to involve an understanding of the long-term consequences of social structure for individuals belonging to different classes and the effect of social structure on attitudes or thoughts toward other classes or toward one's own class within the social structure. Developmental investigations of the awareness of social structure have indicated that not until adolescence do subjects manifest an understanding of the relationship between individual actions and social structure (Adelson, Green, & O'Neil, 1969; Adelson & O'Neil, 1966), which these authors describe as *sociocentric* conceptions. Furthermore, the recognition that people belonging to different classes may have different perspectives would appear to entail nonegocentric thought. This ability to recognize differences in individual perspective develops by 9 years of age (Chandler & Greenspan, 1972), whereas recognition of differences in perspective within a social system—*social systems role taking*—does not develop until adolescence (Selman, 1976).

Cognitive level may also be implied by the ability to recognize similarities between groups already classified by the child as different. The recognition that persons may be grouped by any consistent attribute (e.g., wealth or poverty) reflects an ability to classify persons according to an exhaustive sorting strategy. For classification of physical stimuli, this ability develops by age 4 or 5 and may underlie early gender constancy (Inhelder & Piaget, 1964; Kohlberg, 1969). Since Jahoda (1959) found that 5-year-old children share adult stereotypes of certain characteristics of the rich and poor, we may assume that these young children are able to apply simple classificatory operations to the classes of rich and poor. Classificatory operations, however, undergo modification between ages 5 and 8, with older children recognizing that classes of physical stimuli may be subsumed by other superordinate classes and that classes may intersect each other at points of common properties. The implication of the development of these classificatory operations is that with increasing age there should be increasing recognition of the similarities (or intersecting qualities) of different social classes and a decrease in the claim that classes do not share similar characteristics. Thus, the development of the conception of similarities and differences in social classes that later come to be recognized as sharing similar superordinate qualities (e.g., both are people) or qualities marking an intersection of class boundaries (e.g., some of each have similar needs or thoughts) will be expected.

As the foregoing discussion suggests, we would expect young children (age 6) to find some difficulty in recognizing similarities between social classes. As reclassification skill develops, the first basis of similarity should be peripheral qualities (e.g., both are people), with recognition of central (or psychological) and sociocentric similarities becoming more frequent during adolescence.

DEVELOPMENTAL TRENDS FOR EXPLANATIONS AND JUSTIFICATIONS

Piaget (1932) has proposed that between early and later childhood there is a shift in conceptions of distributive justice. According to Piaget, the young child (age 5) judges behavior in terms of obedience to authority. By age 7 or 8, with increasing interaction within peer groups, the child shifts to equality in the conception of justice. By age 11 or 12, there is a further shift toward equity, as the peer group becomes more differentiated and the child takes into account individual differences (Piaget, 1932, p. 320).

Although empirical research on the development of equity has produced mixed findings (Hook, Chapter 8, this volume), Piagetian theory does suggest that justifications of economic inequality would show marked age trends. Specifically, we would expect that between ages 6 and 10 there would be an increase in equality challenges to class, but that these would be offset during early adolescence by equity justifications. Moreover, the cognitive-developmental quality of this sequence suggests some uniformity among classes in the ordering of these concepts.

DEVELOPMENTAL TRENDS FOR CONCEPTIONS OF SOCIAL CHANGE AND MOBILITY

According to cognitive-developmental theory, the development of social concepts reflects changes in the nature of social interaction (Leahy, 1981a). For the young child (age 5 or 6), social interactions presumably focus on unilateral respect for adult authority in which the child is largely deferent toward and dependent on adult sanctions and rewards (Piaget, 1932). Although the older child (age 10 or 11) may also defer to adult authority, his or her social concepts will also reflect consideration of peer society and acculturation to the ethic of progress (or developmental and individual differences) characteristic of school culture.

The dual influence of peer society and school culture may be reflected in the increasing belief during middle childhood of a link between individual differences in work and rewards—that is, the emergence of nominal equity concepts (Hook & Cook, 1979). The younger child may transfer his or her dependent role within the family to a conception of the economy as a system of benevolently motivated superior and subordinate relationships. For the younger child, then, the emphasis on social change or individual mobility is on the expansion of these dependencies—that is, others will help the poor (just as adults will help children). In contrast, at age 10 or 11, the child shifts responsibility to the individual, emphasizing work or motivational factors in achieving change.

This proposed developmental trend should also show a marked change during later adolescence when the individual is able to conceptualize the possible role of the social system in determining unequal distribution of social goods and unequal opportunities to achieve the means for successful competition. These sociocentric conceptions should be reflected in an increase during adolescence in the claim that change can come about, not simply by changing individuals, but also by changing the social and economic structure.

THE STUDY OF CONCEPTIONS OF
SOCIAL CLASS

Overview of the study

The study reported here was an attempt to investigate the development of spontaneous conceptions of economic inequality. The choice of spontaneous descriptions, rather than an expression of preferences for predetermined responses, was based on the consideration that the open interview method would reveal more clearly the qualitative aspects of children's responses. As indicated, previous research that demonstrated the deficit in children's knowledge of class failed to elicit the actual conceptions of class held by these children. In the absence of a strong empirical (or even theoretical) basis for predicting what the younger children might say, the choice of a Piagetian clinical method seemed most appropriate.

The expectations guiding this study were that developmental trends in class conceptions would follow a sequence from peripheral to central to sociocentric conceptions. On the basis of Piagetian theory, I expected to find a curvilinear (inverted U) age trend for equality conceptions, followed by an increasing emphasis during later childhood and early adolescence on the use of equity concepts. In conceptions of social change and mobility, it was expected that younger children (age 6) would emphasize dependency, older children (age 11) would emphasize equity (e.g., work and motivation), and adolescents would emphasize changes in social structure.

Furthermore, the present study allowed comparisons of functionalist and conflict theories of class concepts. Functionalist theory would be supported by general uniformity among classes and races in conceptions of economic inequality; conflict theory would lead to the prediction that classes would diverge in their conception of class. Moreover, functionalist theory would suggest that with increasing age (as an index of socialization experience) there would be increasing adherence to the legitimacy of economic inequality.

The study tested 720 children and adolescents. Except for 67 adolescents who responded to the same questions on open-ended questionnaires, all subjects were individually interviewed. Subjects came from four social classes, ranging from lower (primarily welfare recipients) to upper or upper middle (primarily professionals); 188 were black. All subjects came from the metropolitan areas of Washington, D.C., Boston, and New York City.

The following questions were asked:

1. Describe rich people. What are they like?
2. Describe poor people. What are they like?
3. How are rich people different from poor people?
4. How are rich people the same as poor people? What do they have in common?
5. Why are some people rich while others are poor?
6. Why are some people poor?
7. Should some people be rich while others are poor? Why?
8. Should some people be poor while others are rich? Why?
9. How could a poor person get rich someday?
10. What would have to happen so that there would be no poor people?
11. How could you get rich someday?

A content analysis of responses was conducted, with categories for analysis derived from literature on person descriptions, attribution, sociological theories of class (e.g., Marx, Weber), and interviews. Interjudge reliability for placing subjects' statements into categories was reasonably high (see Leahy, 1981b, 1983). In the sections to follow, I present the summary of the analyses of the categories for subsets of questions regarding descriptions, comparisons, explanations, and conceptions of mobility and individual change. Individual analyses for each question are reported in detail in other publications (Leahy, 1981a, 1983).

Describing the rich and poor

References to possessions showed a substantial decrease with age, whereas references to appearances and residence increased between ages 6 and 11 and decreased during adolescence. As expected, references to peripheral descriptions decreased between ages 6 and 11. Descriptions of the central and sociocentric qualities of the rich and poor increased in frequency between childhood and adolescence. Unexpectedly, class consciousness was seldom used in describing the poor, but it was more often mentioned by adolescents than by children in describing the rich.

There were no race differences and few class differences for descriptions of the rich and poor. Lower-class subjects were more likely than middle- or upper-middle-class subjects to mention life chances of the rich. This finding would be consistent with a conflict theory of class concepts: Lower-class individuals may be more aware of the long-term quality of life affected by social class because of the economically depriving and therefore conflicting experiences in their own life histories.

Other class differences are also consistent with conflict theory: Lower-class subjects were more likely to emphasize the thoughts of the poor, whereas upper-middle-class subjects were more likely to emphasize the traits of the poor. This finding suggests that lower-class individuals may be taking the role of other poor people in describing their perspectives. Research on differences between self and other attributions indicates that when describing other people we tend to attribute their behavior to dispositions or traits (Jones & Nisbett, 1971). The fact that upper-middle-class subjects are more likely to describe poor people in trait terms suggests that they may view the poor as the "other"—that is, as individuals with whom they have less in common. Although these findings are suggestive of conflicting class perspectives, it should be noted that one essential aspect of class conflict was not demonstrated here— that is, there were no race or class differences in references to class consciousness.

Comparisons of the rich and poor

The percentages of responses for the two questions, "How are the rich and poor different (the same)?" are presented in Leahy (1981a). Analyses of variance (ANOVAs) for these data indicated that references to differences in possessions and appearances decreased with age, whereas references to thoughts increased with age. References to differences in central qualities (i.e., traits, thoughts, motivation) increased during adolescence, and there was a marginal ($p < .05$) tendency for sociocentric conceptions of difference to increase with age. (Most of these sociocentric responses referred to the life chances associated with class.) Peripheral responses decreased during late adolescence. Although sociological indices of class and discussions of stratification emphasize class differences in occupation, education, race, rights (or power), and membership in organizations (such as unions), not a single one of these categories accounted for 3% of responses.

Conceptions of similarities of the rich and poor showed a curvilinear age trend for peripheral categories. Peripheral similarities increased between ages 6 and 11 but decreased during adolescence. Of these peripheral responses, almost half were claims that the rich and poor are both people. Consistent with the Piagetian model of classification development, there was a substantial decrease with age in denying the similarity of the rich and poor or in giving "don't know" responses.

Similarities in the central and sociocentric qualities of the rich and poor showed increases with age. Sociocentric qualities referred to the life problems that were seen as independent of social class. (This category was viewed as analogous to life chances.) References to similar rights or obligations under the law (e.g., paying taxes) were almost never mentioned.

Examples. The emphasis on peripheral aspects of class are reflected in the interviews with the 5- and 6-year-old children. Sandra, age 6, claims that the rich "have clothes . . . money . . . food to eat," whereas the poor "don't have no food to eat . . . they don't have a place to live." However, like many 6-year-old children, Sandra sees no similarity between the rich and poor. The emphasis on psychological, or central, conceptions is reflected in the interviews of children between ages 10 and 14. Maria, age 13, claims that the rich are "smart" and that they have "different personalities." To Lenny, age 12, poor people are "lazy. They are poor because they don't want to work." In comparing the rich and poor, the older children are able to recognize the peripheral similarities of people—for example, "they're both human beings." Henry, age 14, claims, "They're both normal. Like they're built the same way. They've got the same bodies." Finally, by later adolescence some subjects have become aware of life chances and class consciousness. Maureen, age 18, says that poor people "are not being recognized as part of the system. They are neglected, ignored, treated wrong." Similarly, Mike, age 17, claims that the rich are "stuck up, conceited." Their similarities are viewed in psychological terms: "They all have the same needs—to be loved and understood," claims Maureen.

Summary: descriptions and comparisons

These data offer considerable support to the cognitive-developmental approach to class concepts. First, almost all significant effects were associated with age, rather than class or race, suggesting considerable uniformity in developmental trends and raising questions about the presumed developmental lag of allegedly disadvantaged children. Second, the age trends for descriptions largely replicate and extend other findings on person descriptions, demonstrating that younger children are more likely than older children to emphasize the external, observable qualities of people. In contrast, older children and adolescents place increasing emphasis on the inferred psychological qualities of people. Third, consistent with the proposal that adolescents show increasing awareness of the role of social structure (Adelson & O'Neil, 1966; Kohlberg, 1969), the present findings indicate that sociocentric conceptions of social class become increasingly more salient during adolescence.

What are the possible implications of these age trends? First, the scarcity of class and race differences for descriptions may reflect a stabilizing function in the shared ideology of stratification among American youth. We will address this issue when we discuss the data on justifications, explanations, and conceptions of change and stability. Second, an indication of the increasing emphasis on central qualities is what I would call the development of a psychological model of inequality. By this I mean an interpretation of inequality as associated with or due to the personality characteristics of people occupying different strata. For the younger child, social class is determined by the observable characteristics presumed to reflect status—that is, possessions, appearances, behaviors, or residence. The first shift in focus appears to occur at age 10 when class is viewed by the child as reflective of inferred psychological qualities, such as traits, motivation, thoughts, or feelings. This psychological definition of class may, for some of these subjects, become a basis of justifying the unequal distribution of social goods. Thus, once class is viewed as reflective of individual differences in relevant inputs (such as motivation), these differences may become a basis of distributive justice conceptions (such as equity). We will examine the data on explanations and justifications to assess this interpretation.

Finally, for a small minority of adolescents, descriptions and comparisons of class entail sociocentric qualities, such as life chances and class consciousness. The emergence of these sociocentric qualities of class, especially class consciousness, reflects the recognition of possible class conflicts. It is noteworthy that these conceptions are infrequent (relative to peripheral or central conceptions), that they are used more frequently in describing the class consciousness of the rich rather than the poor, and that there is a similarity among classes and between races in the use of these conceptions.

I will offer a tentative developmental sequence that I believe reflects the age trends for descriptions of the rich and poor and conceptions of differences between classes. The three levels are *peripheral, central,* and *sociocentric.* I would suggest that these levels reflect progressive changes in *decentration.* Peripheral concepts are centrated on the observable, external qualities, whereas central concepts refocus from the observable to the internal, psychological qualities of people. Finally, sociocentric concepts reflect a more abstract decentering in that they indicate a refocusing from individuals or groups to their relationships within a social structure. Thus, a perspective of class that takes the perspective of social structure not only recognizes the relevance of the coordination of interests across class (as reflected in law, social order, or convention considerations) but also may recognize conflicting interests among classes in their claims to social goods. Consequently, for some adolescents, developmental progress may entail greater *disequilibrium*—that is, the recognition of conflict within society rather than a coordination or uniformity of class perspectives.

Explanations of inequality

Responses to the questions of why some people are rich (poor) are given in Leahy (1983), along with the results of ANOVAs for these responses. Of particular relevance to Piagetian theory are the age trends for explanations based on equity principles—that is, conceptions of individual differences in such inputs as work, effort, education, and intelligence. As reflected in the data, the age trend for equity was primarily due to the increase between ages 6 and 10 in these explanations for both wealth and poverty. The 6-year-old children were more likely than others to focus on peripheral qualities as explanations—that is, on "having (or not having) possessions."

Of particular relevance to conflict theory is the fact that the upper-middle-class subjects were the ones most likely to explain poverty by equity principles ($\bar{x}$'s $= 55.2$ versus 39.9, 42.3, 41.0, respectively, for the four classes). Sociocentric explanations (such as economic or political factors) were infrequent.

Examples: As noted earlier, Bill (the 17-year-old) explains wealth and poverty by referring to motivation ("adrenalin"), inheritance, and education. In contrast, Joe (the 6-year-old) explains inequality by referring to the poor person's inability to buy a job or because of his residence ("Africa"). The emphasis on definitional explanations by the youngest children is reflected in 6-year-old John's interview: "[Why are people rich?] Because they find money on the ground, a lot of money . . . they found money in their pockets. . . . [Why are people poor?] They don't got enough food, that's why we bring food for the poor people." The shift to equity concepts is reflected in the interviews of the 10- and 11-year-olds. According to Pete (age 10), people are rich "because they save their money and they earn it. They work as hard as they can . . . they don't just go around and buy whatever they want to buy." And people are poor "because they don't want to work hard, they're lazy . . . they spend their money unwisely." Finally, by late adolescence the emphasis is on both equity and environmental factors determining inequality. Rose (age 17) claims that people are rich "because they are born into wealth . . . or because they really want to be rich and they start at the bottom and they work themselves up to it . . . because of their determination." Similarly, she views poverty as due to the family coming from a "slum area . . . and the kids grow up and this is all they know . . . so they drop out of school. . . . You know if you are poor there are opportunities open to you—education . . . and making yourself better . . . [but] they don't have the ambition to see it.''

Justifications of and challenges to inequality

The percentages of responses to the questions ''Should some people be rich (poor)?'' are given by Leahy (1983). There were significant increases with age in equity and fatalistic justifications for both questions. Emphasis on equalizing wealth (i.e., the rich should help the poor, or equality challenges) manifested curvilinear age trends, increasing between childhood and early adolescence and tending to decrease by late adolescence. There were decreases with age in definition, justifications of wealth (e.g., ''They should be rich because they have a lot of money''), and in ''don't know'' responses.

Several race and class effects were revealed by these analyses. First, whites were more fatalistic than blacks about wealth ($\bar{x}$'s = 9.2 and 2.4). Second, concern for consequences to the poor was more common among lower-class subjects ($\bar{x}$'s = 18.5, 18.7, 21.5, and 32.7, for Classes I-IV). Third, upper-middle-class subjects were more likely than others to use equity justifications of wealth ($\bar{x}$'s = 55.2, 39.9, 42.3, and 41.0 for Classes I-IV).

Examples: The analyses of the challenges and justifications to inequality reflect a developmental shift from concern for consequences to the poor (the only category used frequently by the 6-year-olds), to equality, to equity, and fatalistic conceptions given by the adolescents. The interviews of Joe and Bill reported earlier reflect these changes. Mary, age 6, challenges inequality because ''some people don't got no refrigerators, nothing to eat . . . if they don't eat, they gonna die.'' By age 12, some children believed that equality should be the norm: ''I think that they should all be the same,'' claims Dean, age 12, ''each have the same amount of money because then the rich people won't think they're so big.'' At age 17, Rose recognizes the conflict inherent in inequality: ''If you look at it one way you say, 'Why? It's so unfair . . . Like why can't it be equally balanced?' But I guess people who are rich, they work for what they have.'' John, at 17, also justifies poverty by referring to equity (lack of motivation): ''They don't want to go for a job, it's their own fault. They deserve to be poor . . . they're just hanging out, doing nothing. A person like that deserves to be poor.'' Debbie, whose father is an executive, is more fatalistic: ''There will always be poorer people, no matter whether they deserve it or not. That's just the way the world is set up.''

Conceptions of individual mobility

Responses to the questions of how others (or the self) could become rich are shown in Leahy (1983). "Asking others for money" decreased sharply between ages 6 and 10, whereas references to work showed a curvilinear age trend, increasing between ages 6 and 11 and decreasing thereafter. Emphasis on education and effort increased substantially between childhood and adolescence. Claims that the subject did not wish to be rich also increased between childhood and late adolescence.

Lower-class 17-year-old subjects were the most likely to claim that they did not wish to be rich. This is interesting in light of both functionalist and dialectical theory: The fact that some of the poorest adolescents may reject wealth as a goal may serve a stabilizing function in the economy. Similarly, lower-class subjects in general were more likely than others to view work (i.e., having a job) as the major means of gaining wealth. Again, the stabilizing nature of this class difference may be to assure that those who are least deprived believe that individual improvement can be achieved by membership in the work force.

Examples: The changing emphasis from dependency conceptions ("Ask others for money") to emphasis on work, education, and effort is reflected in the interviews with Bill and Joe. The egocentric-dependent conception of mobility is also seen in the interviews with two 6-year-old children, Mary and John. Mary says that poor people can become rich by going "to the store and they give them money" and that she can become rich if "your husband gives you money and your grandmother or your grandfather." John, age 6, also says that "we [can] give money to the poor people." The increasing emphasis by age 10 on work and saving is reflected by Pete (age 10): "They [the poor] save their money and work as hard as they can to get money . . . If their wife wants something, they don't buy it. They just save it up." The emphases on education and effort are major concerns of older subjects.

Tony (age 18) claims that the poor could "start up all over . . . by going back to school, try and get a better education" and that he could become rich by "taking up accounting. That's one of the pretty good fields. There's a need for that. . . . The most you can do is try."

Conceptions of social change

Percentages of responses to the question of what would have to happen so that there would be no poor people are shown in Leahy (1983). Claims that poverty could end by getting rid of people or by others giving money decreased with age. Equity concepts (e.g., work, education, effort) increased between ages 6 and 11, while denying the possibility of change and advocating changing the social structure increased between childhood and adolescence.

Blacks were more likely than whites to emphasize changing the social structure, and middle-class whites emphasized the impossibility of social change. Of particular interest is the fact that 17-year-old lower-class subjects were considerably more likely than others to claim that the rich would resist change.

Examples: The analyses reveal a shift between childhood and adolescence from emphasis during childhood on egocentric-dependent or concrete conceptions to the adolescent's emphasis on equity, social structure, and fatalism. For example, John (age 6), claims that the poor "got to die." At age 12, Tom argues for redistribution of wealth: "We should send more to the poor people." Pete (age 10) emphasizes frugality: "The poor would have to stop spending money unwisely and save it and work hard for it." Debbie (age 16) offers a sociocentric conception of change: "Everything. You would have to change the government. You'd have to change business because there are different levels and they all get different incomes." On the other hand, Tony (age 18) sees poverty as inevitable: "That would be hard because there's too many poor people in this world to change it . . . I don't think they will ever do it." Tony goes on to indicate that the reason inequality is fated is because of resistance to change: "Because the rich people are the powerful people . . . they have more ways of getting around it. I think they're never going to change that because they're powerful, they'll always want what they have. They'd say, 'Why should we give everything we got. They didn't work for it. We did.'"

Summary: explanations, justifications, and conceptions of social mobility and social change

The findings from these questions lend considerable support to the cognitive-developmental model. According to this model, the young child focuses on the external qualities of people (or institutions), personifies the economy, and transfers a dependent role. These characteristics are reflected in the definitional explanations and justifications, the concrete references to "getting rid of the poor," and the belief either that others should give money to the poor or that the self can achieve wealth by asking people for money.

By age 10 or 11, there is a shift toward either equality or equity conceptions. Although Piagetians might argue that equality norms would occur earlier in development, I would suggest that the increase in equality conceptions by age 10 reflects increasing cognitive level. Specifically, in a closed system (of constant absolute wealth), an increase for one dimension or class (i.e., the poor) might require a compensating decrease for another class (i.e., the rich). This recognition of compensations in equalization is similar to the requirements of traditional Piagetian conservation tasks—a fact that has encouraged me to refer to this as "conservation of wealth" (Leahy, 1983). These equality norms give way to equity norms during adolescence—a finding consistent with Piagetian theory.

Finally, the increasing emphases on social structure and class conflict (resistance to change) are consistent with other cognitive-developmental findings (Adelson & O'Neil, 1966; Kohlberg, 1969). It is interesting to note that class and race differences, favoring blacks and lower-class subjects, were found on these sociocentric conceptions. This fact suggests that the disequilibrium inherent in class position may accelerate the recognition of class structure. Of course, this finding is also consistent with dialectical theory.

These questions on explanations, justifications, social change, and mobility were the ones most likely to elicit class and race effects. While dialectical theory may be supported by these class and race differences, functionalist theory receives support from the finding that adolescents were more likely than younger children to justify inequality and to claim that poverty was an immutable characteristic of nature. Thus, while race and class differences may suggest some divergence of evaluative perspectives on class, the course of development among these subjects appears to result in an adherence to stratification of groups.

LEVELS OF CLASS CONCEPTIONS

On the basis of the numerous age trends for descriptions, comparisons, explanations, justifications, and conceptions of mobility and social change, I shall propose a tentative developmental model of the development of conceptions of social class. I am hesitant at this time to label these as "stages" of class conceptions. A variety of factors offer grounds for such hesitancy, including the following: lack of cross-cultural replication, lack of longitudinal data of individual growth patterns, lack of correlational data regarding the relationship between cognitive level and class conceptions, and lack of evidence of the stability of such conceptions. In fact, I would argue that all the criticisms leveled by Kurtines and Greif (1974) against Kohlberg's model might fruitfully be leveled against my model. That is why I shall present it as tentative and invite the interested reader to explore the validity of the model through empirical inquiry.

The value of the model, I believe, is twofold. First, it provides a heuristic for reducing the variety of data obtained in the present study—it helps order our findings. Second, and not unrelated to the first point, is the need for a cognitive-developmental model of political socialization—that is, a model that both incorporates our knowledge of the development of cognitive structures (both social and nonsocial) and is relevant to existing data on political conceptions of children and youth. In fact, the need for such a psychological model is reflected by the fact that political socialization research is often not reported in psychological journals. The present model suggests that conceptions of social class may bear some resemblance to other psychological processes.

Let us turn to the levels of social class conceptions. In Figure 3.1, I

I. *Peripheral-Dependent Conceptions: Ages 6–11*
The focus in descriptions is on the observable, external qualities of class, such as possessions and appearances. Explanations of class differences lack causal reasoning and focus on the definitional or peripheral aspects of wealth and poverty. Although there is concern for consequences to the poor, class differences may be justified because the rich and poor meet the definitional criteria of class. Mobility and social change are largely viewed in terms of either the rich or others helping people by giving them money. The child views the economy as functioning out of benevolence for the poor or for the child's own interests.
II. *Psychological Conceptions: Ages 11–14*
At this level, classes are described in terms of their inferred psychological qualities, such as traits, thoughts, and motivations. Classes are seen as being similar primarily because they share peripheral commonalities (e.g., "Both are people"). Inequality is explained in terms of differences in work, education, effort, and intelligence. Class differences are challenged by equality principles or justified by equity considerations. Mobility is seen largely in terms of education, effort, work, and investment. Social change is viewed in terms of either the rich sharing their wealth or the poor gaining education, working hard, and getting jobs. The economy is seen as rewarding merit reflected by individual differences in inputs.
III. *Sociocentric Conceptions: Ages 14–17*
Descriptions focus on differences in life chances and class consciousness. Classes are viewed as similar because they share psychological commonalities. Explanations still focus on equity. There is an increasing emphasis on the difficulty of changing the social system and claims that social change would meet with resistance by the rich. Changing the social structure is viewed as one way to change poverty. The economy is seen as being largely functionally based on equity principles, although there is a recognition of competing class interests. The economy is viewed in impersonal terms such that its functioning is seen as a reflection of the invisible hand of earned merit or as the expression of the interests of the wealthy. Emphasis is either on conflict (e.g., class consciousness) or the futility of conflict (e.g., fatalism).

Figure 3.1. Levels of class conceptions.

have presented the characteristic conceptions found at three levels—peripheral-dependent, psychological, and sociocentric conceptions. Because older and younger subjects often share some similar conceptions (e.g., both describe rich and poor in terms of peripheral characteristics), I have chosen to indicate some age overlap for levels. In fact, many of the characteristic responses given by younger subjects are also given by adolescent subjects, who might be categorized as sociocentric: To some extent, development is not entirely a total restructuring of earlier conceptions in this model.

As inspection of Figure 3.1 reveals, the children between ages 6 and 11 focus on the external qualities of class (e.g., possessions, appearances, behaviors). The general structural quality of this stage appears to be centration: Thus, conceptions focus on the external, figurative, or observable qualities, with young children offering an egocentric-dependent conception of the economy. This egocentric-dependent notion—that others will take care of the poor or of the child—is, I suggest, a reflection of two related processes. The first of these is the general tendency of young children to confuse their perspectives with those of others, the consequence of which is often to conclude that others may share the child's perspective that the child's needs (or the needs of other "dependent" persons, such as the poor) are of central importance. This is similar to Furth's (1979) observation that young children may believe that the bus driver and storekeeper are motivated by concern for children. A second factor contributing to this egocentric-dependent conception is what Hess and Torney (1967) call "role transfer"—that is, the tendency of children to overgeneralize from their role as dependents within a presumably benevolent family structure. Thus, the young child views the adult world of political institutions and wealthy adults as an extension of the family's caretaking function.

The second level, characteristic of children between ages 11 and 14, stresses the nature of psychological factors in poverty and wealth. The rich and poor are seen as different kinds of people—that is, they are viewed as having different thoughts, feelings, and traits. This is an important transition in the emergence of equity conceptions in that individual differences become the basis for conceptions of merit, especially earned merit.

The idea of equalization of wealth—that is, the view that the rich should help the poor or that people should be equal—also emerges for some subjects at this age. I would suggest that one factor accounting for conceptions of equalization is the recognition that an increase in wealth for the poor must be compensated by a decrease in wealth for the rich—that is, a recognition of conservation of absolute wealth. Conceptions at this level reflect inferences of covert processes or states (i.e., central or psychological qualities) that may form the basis for some subjects for conceptualizing changes in poverty. At the second level, then, conceptions are decentered from the external or peripheral to the unobservable or psychological qualities of persons.

One might argue that class conceptions do not arise until the level of sociocentric conceptions. According to this view, social class implies a recognition of the importance of social structure in determining the life chances and class consciousness of people. The sociocentric adolescents in this study appear to conceptualize class in terms of the conflicting perspectives and needs of classes, and they view social structure as something that may be resistant to change. However, what is somewhat striking about the explanations offered by these American youth is their failure to mention social structure in explaining inequality. Very few subjects mentioned economic or political factors or even demographic factors, such as race or age, in accounting for inequality. The reader may share my suspicion that youth in more traditionally rigid class societies (such as France, Italy, or the United Kingdom) would be more likely to mention social structure in explaining inequality. Probably because of the general belief in the Horatio Alger ideal in American culture (Handlin & Handlin, 1970), American youth rely on equity and psychological explanations rather than on sociocentric explanations. Of course, these speculations argue for cross-cultural comparisons.

The ability to discern similarities of the rich and poor appears to lag behind the ability to recognize criteria of differences between classes. Thus, the children at Level I often find no basis for similarity, whereas Level II subjects view similarity in terms of peripheral qualities (e.g., ''Both are people''). Finally, Level III subjects view classes as similar in terms of psychological similarities. The failure of some 6-year-olds at Level I to mention similarities may reflect their inability to employ a multiple-classificatory structure. The generality of this limitation is reflected in our other findings indicating that 6-year-olds have more difficulty than older children in finding a basis of similarity of intelligent and unintelligent people (Leahy & Hunt, Chapter 5, this volume) and in our finding that children who fail a multiple-classification task of physical stimuli also fail to recognize that some boys and girls may exhibit behavior that is viewed as more stereotypical of one gender (Leahy & Shirk, in press). Furthermore, our findings on the development of conceptions of intelligence suggest that between ages 6 and 11 there is a qualitative shift in emphasizing peripheral-obedience aspects (age 6) to emphasizing psychological aspects (age 11) of intelligent and unintelligent people (Leahy & Hunt, Chapter 5, this volume).

SUMMARY

Most previous research on conceptions of economic stratification has failed to consider qualitative changes in conceptualizing inequality. The research reported here draws upon cognitive-developmental theory and research and suggests that there are different levels of conception of economic class—peripheral-dependent, central (or psychological), and sociocentric. These levels of conception appear to show a similar age course for children and adolescents regardless of their economic or racial background. With increasing age, generally regardless of the child's group membership, there is increasing justification of economic inequality. The findings of the present study of social inequality should be viewed as only a tentative beginning to elaborating a cognitive-developmental approach to this topic. Future research is needed to explore class concepts in other cultures, using other methods, and more directly testing levels of conception.

REFERENCES

Adelson, J., Green, B., & O'Neil, R. The growth of the idea of law in adolescence. *Developmental Psychology*, 1969, *1*, 327–332.

Adelson, J., & O'Neil, R. The growth of political ideas in adolescence: The sense of community. *Journal of Personality and Social Psychology*, 1966, *4*, 295–306.

Bigner, J. A Wernerian developmental analysis of children's descriptions of siblings. *Child Development*, 1974, *45*, 317–323.

Chandler, M., & Greenspan, S. Ersatz egocentrism: A reply to H. Borke. *Developmental Psychology*, 1972, *7*, 104–106.

Coie, J. D., & Pennington, B. F. Children's perception of deviance and disorder. *Child Development*, 1976, *47*, 407–413.

Dahrendorf, R. *Class and class conflict in industrial society*. Stanford, Calif.: Stanford Univ. Press, 1959.

Davis, K., & Moore, W. E. Some principles of stratification. *American Sociological Review*, 1945, *10*, 242–249.

DeFleur, M. L., & DeFleur, L. B. The relative contribution of television as a learning source for children's occupational knowledge. *American Sociological Review*, 1967, *32*, 777–789.

Estvan, F. J. The relationship of social status, intelligence, and sex of ten- and eleven-year-old children to an awareness of poverty. *Genetic Psychology Monographs*, 1952, *46*, 3–60.

Furth, H. Young children's understanding of society. In H. McGurk (Ed.), *Issues in childhood social development*. London: Methuen, 1979.

Handlin, O., & Handlin, M. *Facing life*. New York: Free Press, 1970.

Harris, D. *The concept of development*. Minneapolis: Univ. of Minnesota Press, 1959.

Hess, R., & Torney, J. *The development of political attitudes in children*. New York: McGraw-Hill, 1967.

Hook, J., & Cook, T. D. Equity theory and the cognitive ability of children. *Psychological Bulletin*, 1979, *86*, 429–445.

Inhelder, B., & Piaget, J. *The early growth of logic in the child: Classification and seriation.* New York: Norton, 1964.

Jahoda, G. Development of the perception of social differences in children from six to ten. *British Journal of Psychology,* 1959, *50,* 159–196.

Jones, E. E., & Nisbett, R. *The actor and the observer: Divergent perceptions of the causes of behavior.* Morristown, N.J.: General Learning Press, 1971.

Kohlberg, L. A cognitive-developmental analysis of children's sex-role concepts and attitudes. In E. Maccoby (Ed.), *The development of sex differences.* Stanford: Stanford Univ. Press, 1966.

Kohlberg, L. Stage and sequence: The cognitive-developmental approach to socialization. In D. A. Goslin (Ed.), *Handbook of socialization: Theory and research.* New York: Rand-McNally, 1969.

Kurtines, W., & Greif, E. B. The development of moral thought: Review and evaluation of Kohlberg's approach. *Psychological Bulletin,* 1974, *81,* 453–470.

Leahy, R. L. Parental practices and the development of moral judgment and self-image disparity during adolescence. *Developmental Psychology,* 1981, *17,* 580–594. (a)

Leahy, R. L. The development of the conception of economic inequality. I. Descriptions and comparisons of rich and poor people. *Child Development,* 1981, *52,* 523–532. (b)

Leahy, R. L. The development of the conception of economic inequality. II. Explanations, justifications, and conceptions of social mobility and social change. *Developmental Psychology,* 1983, *19,* 111–125.

Leahy, R. L., & Shirk, S. The development of classificatory skills and sex-trait stereotypes in children. *Sex Roles,* in press.

Livesley, W., & Bromley, D. *Person perception in childhood and adolescence.* London: Wiley, 1973.

Marx, K. [Economic and philosophical manuscripts] (T. B. Bottomore, Trans.). In E. Fromm (Ed.), *Marx's concept of man.* New York: Ungar, 1966. (Originally published, 1844.)

Merton, R. *Social theory and social structure.* Glencoe, Ill.: The Free Press, 1957.

Ossowski, S. *Class structure in the social consciousness.* New York: The Free Press, 1963.

Parsons, T. *The social system.* Glencoe, Ill.: The Free Press, 1960.

Piaget, J. *The moral judgment of the child.* London: Kegan Paul, 1932.

Piaget, J. Piaget's theory. In P. H. Mussen (Ed.), *Carmichael's manual of child psychology* (3rd ed., Vol. 1). New York: Wiley, 1970.

Scarlett, H., Press, A., & Crockett, W. Children's description of peers: A Wernerian analysis. *Child Development,* 1971, *42,* 439–453.

Selman, R. Social cognitive understanding: A guide to educational and clinical practice. In T. Lickona (Ed.), *Morality: A handbook of moral development and behavior.* New York: Holt, 1976.

Simmons, R., & Rosenberg, M. Functions of children's perceptions of the stratification system. *American Sociological Review,* 1971, *36,* 235–249.

Stendler, C. *Children of Brasstown.* Urbana, Ill.: Bureau of Research and Service, 1949.

Tudor, J. The development of class awareness in children. *Social Forces,* 1971, *49,* 470–476.

Weber, M. [*Essays in sociology*] (H. Gerth & W. Mills, Trans.). Oxford: Oxford Univ. Press, 1946.

Williams, J., Bennett, S., & Best, D. Awareness and expression of sex stereotypes in young children. *Developmental Psychology,* 1975, *11,* 635–642.

4 / Children's ideas about intellectual ability[1]

STEVEN R. YUSSEN
PATRICK T. KANE

This chapter reports the findings from an ongoing project concerned with how children understand the concept of intelligence and other terms denoting kinds of intellectual ability. The seminal investigation was a broad-based interview study, in which 75 elementary school children were asked to respond to a number of questions and rating scales surveying several different issues. Since this investigation has been reported in detail elsewhere (Yussen & Kane, in press), we will attempt only to summarize it briefly here. The first investigation led us down several additional paths of inquiry. These involved sharpening up our evidence regarding how finely young children are able to distinguish among different kinds or senses of ability. The seminal study had uncovered a predictable pattern of change from early to late childhood in which young children did not differentiate intellectual ability from other kinds, but older children did. An additional investigation was then pursued to determine just what kinds of distinctions younger children might

[1]The authors are indebted to the many teachers and students who participated in the research reported here and to the Wisconsin Center for Education Research, which supported the research through funds provided to it as a national research and development center from the National Institute of Education (Center Grant No. NIE-G-81-000-9). The opinions herein do not necessarily reflect the position or policy of the National Institute of Education, and no official endorsement by the National Institute of Education should be inferred.

109

be able to make among kinds of ability and under what circumstances they might make them. We also sought more precise information about how children define intelligence or ability in age or stage terms. That is, to what extent do children conceptualize ability as having different core manifestations at different points in the life span?

The concept of intelligence looms large in the history of psychology. Beginning in 1905 with the development in Europe by Binet and Simon of the first tests to measure it through to our present-day inheritance from the early psychometric movement (e.g., Eysenck, 1979), few other topics of inquiry have had as great an impact on the field of psychology or society at large. The measurement of intelligence has influenced the evolution of applied statistics, measurement theory, theories about cognition and human development, and the practice of clinical, industrial, and school psychology. Formal measures of intelligence have permeated virtually every other aspect of scientific inquiry in the field as well, providing a salient and precisely quantifiable dimension along which people can be described and differentiated.

A careful survey of the literature revealed that there is little formal research on the commonsense notion of intelligence held by nonpsychologists. (A salient exception is Sternberg, Conway, Ketron, & Bernstein, 1981.) Just as psychologists have developed elaborate models of intelligence around specific tests or cognitive functions, so too, the layperson has probably acquired, through learning and development, a number of meanings for the term *intelligence.* These meanings may be intuitive, loosely formulated and incomplete, but they are there nevertheless. And it is likely that this meaning system operates in much the same way as others—for example, contributing to the individual's assessment of personal competence, influencing the individual's attribution about the competence of others, and guiding his or her choice of friends and acquaintances. Since there appeared to be little prior research and since we believed the concept to be important, we designed a wide-ranging study to take a broad look at this notion in children.

THE SEMINAL STUDY

Without a clear tradition of research to fall back upon, we necessarily made a number of arbitrary decisions in approaching the design of this first investigation.

First, and perhaps most importantly, the target population selected was elementary school children—first, third, and sixth graders to be exact. As developmental psychologists, we were interested in tracing age-related changes in the meanings children attribute to the concept of intelligence. There is now a vast literature on elementary school children's developing concepts of a number of mental and social items, such as memory, the brain, justice and morality, religion, and friendship (e.g., Flavell, 1981; Wellman, in press). We expected to uncover a number of specific meanings associated with children's concepts of intelligence (which seems to be both mental and social in nature). But at the same time, we anticipated that the developmental pattern of change would reflect some of the same dimensions of change noted in the other literatures. For example, we expected to find evidence for conceptual differentiation across grades. That is, children's notions about intelligence should become increasingly differentiated as they become older. They should offer multiple ideas about what it is and see intelligence as multifaceted. We also expected to see increasing evidence of conceptual abstractness across grades. That is, children should increasingly characterize intelligence in more abstract terms. The younger children would be likely to depict intelligence in terms of the concrete things people do and say, whereas the older ones would be more likely to depict it in terms of qualities and traits in individuals. Finally, we expected to find evidence of increasing internalization with age. This is closely associated with conceptual abstractness, but in principle, separable from it. Specifically, we expected that children would be increasingly likely to characterize intelligence as something inside the person (e.g., in the mind, qualities of the brain) as opposed to something overtly visible or present in the external world.

A second feature of the investigation was that many parts consisted of unstructured interview questions. From the beginning, we were well aware of the pitfalls of this approach. Differences in motivation, talkativeness, and verbal fluency could all obscure what the children know and believe. To hedge against this problem, some of the items called for children to make choices among finite alternatives. And, in two of the studies to be reported later in the chapter, we have supplemented the evidence from this first investigation with more analytical techniques.

Third, there is the matter of what specifically to ask the children. What pertaining to intelligence might be in their commonsense notions of the concept. We considered and rejected a number of plans, ranging from writing a series of questions on a specific theory of intelligence (e.g., Guilford's Structure of Intellect Model or Piaget's genetic epistemology) or a single issue (e.g., "Is intelligence a single ability or several abilities?" "Are there different types of intelligence?") to questions requiring the children to identify instances of intelligent behavior.

We finally settled on questions (items) derived from historically prominent issues in the study of intelligence. In the history of the study of intelligence, it is possible to identify a number of continuing concerns lasting well beyond the popularity or acceptance of a single theory and that continually find themselves redefined and rearticulated. They are sufficiently general that they are likely to be with us for a long time to come and sufficiently practical in the sense that social debates have often centered on them. Perhaps most fortunate from our perspective is that the issues hold up no standard of truth against which to contrast the children's conceptions. They are rather dimensions (and important ones at that) along which people may fix their ideas about intelligence. These issues permit us to examine where children stand on significant matters related to intelligence without a preconceived notion of what is actually true.

The specific issues surveyed were

1. *Visible signs of intelligence*—questions concerned with whether it is possible to spot intelligence in people from overt things they do
2. *Qualities associated with intelligence*—questions concerned with whether intelligent people can be distinguished from others on the basis of a number of mental, school-related, physical, and social skills
3. *The influence of nature and nurture on intelligence*—questions concerned with the origin of intelligence and the relative contribution of inheritance and various kinds of experiences to it
4. *The constancy or malleability of intelligence*—questions concerned with whether bright (i.e., very intelligent) or dull (i.e., not so intelligent) individuals necessarily remain so throughout childhood and, if not, what factors might contribute to change

In addition to questions addressed to these issues, the study also called for children to offer

5. *A general definition of intelligence*—with a pair of questions asking them what it means to say that someone is smart or intelligent
6. *An assessment of their own relative intelligence*—with a simple scale

We also assessed each child's verbal ability by administering the Peabody Picture Vocabulary test. This was to provide standardized information on the children's actual intellectual functioning and to test the intriguing possibility that individual differences in psychometrically tested IQ are associated with individual differences in one or more aspects of children's ideas about intelligence.

A sample of 71 elementary school children was tested in first, third, and sixth grades. All the children were white and, based on our impressions of the community, came from lower-middle- to middle-middle-class families. Each child was administered the Peabody Picture Vocabulary test first, followed by the entire questionnaire that appears in the appendix. Details of the sample and procedure appear in Yussen and Kane (in press).

A very brief summary of the major findings is presented here. For more details, see the full report in Yussen and Kane (in press).

Actual IQ scores

First, let us consider the children's actual IQ. The means and standard deviations for the Peabody Picture Vocabulary test for the three groups were: first grade—103.8 (SD = 15.0); third grade—106.4 (SD = 11.0); and sixth grade—107.9 (SD = 13.7). In other words, each age group had a fairly similar distribution and mean level of IQ, and the sample of children had a relatively average IQ.

Definition of intelligence

For both questions designed to elicit a general definition of intelligence for children (1 and 2 on the questionnaire), the protocols were examined for the number of different ideas or concepts generated by a child as well as the qualitative nature of the concept offered. An example of the quantitative analysis can be given with the following response offered by a first grader: "It means they know a lot of stuff. 10 + 10 is 20. Some people are smart to do a lot of nice things for a lot of poor people like give them money." This protocol was scored 2. There were basically two concepts—that smart people know a lot and that they perform nice acts. The remaining talk was viewed as an elaboration of these concepts. Predictably, there was an increase across grades in the number of concepts offered by children to each of the first two items on the questionnaire. This is captured in Table 4.1. A one-way analysis of variance for grade revealed the effect to be significant for the first question only.

More interestingly, there were qualitative changes in the nature of the concepts offered by the children at the different grades. This is illustrated in Table 4.2. The youngest children identified interpersonal skills and behaviors as essential components, but the older children did not. (Note the row labeled "social skill" in this table. This is the effect we are referring to.) Conversely, the older children prominently identified

Table 4.1. Mean Number of Different Concepts Offered in Response to Question I-1 (Smart) and I-2 (Intelligent) by Grade

| | Grade | | | | | |
| | 1 | | 3 | | 6 | |
Question	$\overline{X}$[a]	SD	$\overline{X}$	SD	$\overline{X}$	SD
I-1 Smart	1.20	.41	1.20	.42	1.90	1.00
I-2 Intelligent	1.00	0	1.33	.59	1.53	.92

[a] Responses were tabled only for those children who offered at least one concept in response to each question, establishing an arbitrary floor of 1 in the scale. This was a conservative procedure to hedge against finding age differences due to the simple increase in the number of children at the older grades who offered at least some response to the questions.

proficiency in academic skills (e.g., reading and writing) as a defining feature of intelligence, whereas younger children were less likely to do so (see the row labeled "academic skill"). At all grades, children felt that the amount of information or knowledge a person has is an important part of the concept (see the row labeled "knowledge"). These age trends were supported by appropriate 1 by 3 chi-square tests.

Visible signs of intelligence

Table 4.3 summarizes the results for three of the questions in this part of the survey. A quick summary is that the youngest children had a greater likelihood than did the third and sixth graders of answering that it is possible to spot intelligence in people from overt things they do and

Table 4.2. Percentage of Time Different Types of Concepts Were Offered in Response to Question I-1 (Smart) by Grade

| | Grade | | |
Concept	1	3	6
Knowledge	38	30	28
Thinking	0	11	4
Problem solving	4	15	2
Academic skill	13	26	46
Social skill	25	0	2
Arrogance	4	0	4
Good	4	15	4
Same	0	0	9
Miscellaneous	12	4	0

Table 4.3. Percentage of Children at Each Grade Who Answered Questions about the Visible Signs of Intelligence Affirmatively (Yes)

Question	Grade		
	1	3	6
II–4 Look different?	40	13 **	9 **
II–5 Talk differently?	52	22 **	30 *
II–6 Act differently?	64	35	48

*Significantly different from chance (50%), $Z > 1.96$, $p < .05$.
**Significantly different from chance (50%), $Z > 2.59$, $p < .01$.

say. As can be seen in the table, for two of the three questions, the third and sixth graders offered such an opinion very infrequently. (Note the low percentage of yes responses.)

Self-assessment

For self-assessment, the linear scale required that each child pinpoint his or her relative level of intelligence (from least intelligent to most intelligent person in the world) on a line 6 in. long. A score ranging from 0 (least intelligent) to 6 (most intelligent) was assigned to the nearest 1/16 (taken from the nearest 1/16 in on the scale). The means and standard deviations for self-assessment are shown in Table 4.4.

As can be seen in the table, the first graders have the highest average assessment, the third graders have the next highest, and the sixth graders have the lowest. T tests for pairwise differences among means revealed that first graders estimated a relatively higher level of average intelligence than both third and sixth graders ($p < .01$), but the difference between third and sixth graders in the same direction was not significant. Interestingly, the amount of variation in these judgments was almost twice as great for the first graders as it was for the sixth graders. So, in addition to having the highest average assessment, the youngest children also had the greatest variability in responses.

Table 4.4. Self-Assessment of Intelligence Means and Standard Deviations by Grade

	Grade		
	1	3	6
M	4.04	2.92	2.55
SD	(1.99)	(1.33)	(1.02)

Qualities associated with intelligence

The frequency with which children affirmed that each of the 16 qualities distinguished between an average and a smart or intelligent person
is shown in Table 4.5. (Refer here to question 8 in the interview.) The
table reports the number of children who responded yes to at least three
of the four questions for a particular group of qualities (e.g., general
mental). We grouped responses this way to gain a better impression of
grade-related differences in responding and to reduce reliance on the
large chance factor of 50% for any single item. From the table, it appears
that first and third graders evidence less differentiation among categories than do sixth graders. For three of the four categories, roughly
half of the younger children identify the subsumed attributes as distinguishing between average and bright people. They seem to distinguish
only the physical category from the others, with substantially fewer children identifying physical attributes as a basis for separating average and
bright people. By contrast, for sixth graders, there appear to be three
groupings—general mental qualities are seen as distinguishing characteristics more frequently than are academic and social qualities. Physical
qualities are identified least frequently.

The influence of nature and nurture on intelligence

Across the different items designed to tap this issue (Questions 9–15),
there was some inconsistency among children. However, to the extent
a pattern could be detected, there was a greater tendency for the youngest children than for the older ones to identify intelligence as something
we are born with. For example, when asked the classic question ''Is it
nature, nurture, or both?'' they opted for nature (or what we were born

Table 4.5. Percentage of Children Who Affirmed that at Least Three of the Qualities in a
Group Distinguished between an Average and a Smart–Intelligent Person[a]

	Grade		
Group of qualities	1	3	6
General mental	43	42	44
Academic	46	50	28
Physical	29	13	4
Social	57*	46*	24

[a] The likelihood of answering three of four questions affirmatively by chance is .31. There are exactly five patterns of answers that can yield at least three correct, and each pattern has the probability of occurring by
chance of $(.5)^4$, or .0625.
* The percentage differs significantly from chance at $Z > 2.59$, $p < .01$.

Table **4.6.** Percentage of Children at Each Grade Who Selected the Different Options in Response to Question V–12 (paraphrased): *Are both experience and what we're born with important or is one more important than the other?*

	Option		
Grade	Born	Experience	Both
1	59	18	22
3	52	35	13
6	13	57	30

with) most of the time. Older children generally emphasized experiences. This finding is shown in Table 4.6. As we see in the table, the modal response for first graders is *born* or nature, whereas the modal response for sixth graders is *experience*.

The constancy and malleability of intelligence

There are five questions (16–20) calling for children to indicate whether a person's level of intelligence can change. The first one posed this as a general matter, while two considered specifically whether bright individuals could subsequently become dull (17, 20) and two considered specifically whether dull individuals could subsequently become bright (18, 19). Among the last four questions, two asked whether the change could occur with the benefit of specific experiences. A summary of the children's responses to these questions is provided in Table 4.7. The overwhelming impression is that children at all grades tend to answer

Table **4.7.** Percentage of Children Who Indicated in Response to Each of the Questions Listed that a Person's Level in Intelligence Can Change, by Grade

	Grade		
Question	1	3	6
V–16 Can they change?	80**	91**	96**
V–17 Change from bright to dull?	48	70*	65
V–18 Change from dull to bright?	92**	96**	83**
V–19 Change from dull to bright via experiences?	76**	91**	78**
V–20 Change from bright to dull via experiences?	56	83**	83**

* Significantly different than chance, $Z > 1.96$, $p < .05$.
** Significantly different than chance, $Z > 2.58$, $p < .01$.

frequently that intelligence can change. To the extent that there is a discriminating attitude, it appears more prominently in the first graders' responses. Although first graders deem it possible to change in general (Question 16) and change from dull to bright (Questions 18, 19), they are less likely to agree that people can change from bright to dull (Questions 17, 20). Thus, they seem to possess a belief about unidirectional change. We can become smarter but are not likely to become dumber. A formal statistical test supports this observation for the first graders. The proportion of change responses offered to Questions 18 and 19 is significantly greater than the proportion of change responses offered to Questions 17 and 20. An inspection of third and sixth graders' responses suggests a similar trend; however, statistical comparisons equivalent to the preceding one did not support the unidirectional belief about change at either grade.

Miscellaneous findings

We tested for a number of possible individual differences in the findings of the investigation (e.g., sex differences and differences according to the children's tested level of ability). Surprisingly, there were few meaningful sex differences or differences between the verbally brighter and duller children (as measured by actual Peabody performance). However, one striking result did surface. For each grade, a separate correlation was computed between each child's Peabody score and his or her self-assessed intelligence as judged by Item 7 (judged distance on the line). For sixth graders only, there was a highly significant positive correlation ($r = .63$, $p < .001$) indicating that the higher the child's actual Peabody score, the higher was the self-assessment. The correlations for children in the other grades were small and nonsignificant. Thus, within the limits of the particular sample tested and the particular ability measure employed, it seems fair to conclude that if you want to know how intelligent sixth graders are just ask them.

Brief comment on the seminal study

There was clear and repeated confirmation that younger children's concepts and ideas were less differentiated than those of older children. This was evidenced in their open-ended definitions of smartness and intelligence (Questions 1 and 3), the particular signs they identified as visible indicators of a person's intelligence (Questions 4, 5, 6), the qualities they believed to be associated with intelligence (Question 8), and their beliefs about the origins of intelligence (Question 9).

There was less direct evidence for the expectation that with increasing age children's answers would become conceptually more abstract. In retrospect, we recognize that this is the result of our (perhaps overly) optimistic hope that children would spontaneously state matters in a way that would permit clear distinctions between such entities as traits versus behaviors, or general ideas versus specific examples. Perhaps, if such distinctions had been posed directly or by implicit contrasts, our success would have been greater.

There was modest support for the expectation that with increasing age children would be increasingly likely to characterize intelligence as an internalized quality. We may infer this indirectly from the older children's reticence to identify the quality as something that is visible (Questions 4–6) and more directly from their tendency to identify personal characteristics as the origin of intelligence (Question 9) and the source of change (Questions 17, 18, 20). At the same time, however, it must be admitted that the younger children also hinted at the internal status of the quality. A modest number of them included "knowledge" as an element of being smart (Question 1) and indicated that a good tactic for telling whether a person was smart or intelligent is to observe their intellectual performances (Question 3).

STUDY 2: CHARACTERISTICS REVISITED

A second investigation was undertaken to pursue some logical questions we had about one part of the broad interview study—the *characteristics* children use to distinguish among levels of intelligence. This corresponds to Part IV of the earlier survey (i.e., Question 8 and its associated 16 characteristics). Study 2 was an attempt to be more analytic in designing an appropriate task to gauge what children might think, as well as to provide the younger children with an opportunity to exhibit greater cognitive differentiation than we had given them credit for. A number of features of the earlier probes may have obscured younger children's ability to offer useful distinctions among the proffered qualities—the abstract nature of the characteristics mentioned to them (e.g., learning), the need to consider the whole dimension of smartness or intelligence (from dull to bright) while making judgments about each ability, and the crude yes–no judgments called for.

Inspired by an approach taken by Heller and Berndt (in press), the second study was crafted in a very different way. Specifically, we asked children to imagine a hypothetical person of their own sex and age who is either (*a*) smart or (*b*) not smart. Each child was faced with one description only—so half judged "smart" and the other half judged "not smart." Whereas in the earlier investigation, we generated 16 gross categories of functioning for judgments (e.g., remembering, understanding), here we identified 16 *concrete behaviors* that a person could do with varying degrees of competence (e.g., remembering the words in a song) and that had ecological validity for children. Representative behaviors appear in Table 4.8 and, by intended design, reflect the same four dimensions we studied earlier—physical, social, academic, and cognitive. Finally, we required children to rate the degree of performance to be expected of the hypothetical child using a visual scale with seven discrete, Likert-type alternatives. The alternatives ranged from none (or not at all) to perfect performance. To ensure that all children were using the rating scales in sensible ways, there were also three filler items that served as manipulation checks.

So, in this second study, we were making the young child's task easier (*a*) by having the child imagine only one value of intellectual prowess (i.e., whether a person is smart or not smart); and (*b*) by calling for judgments about concrete behaviors rather than about abstract categories. And by offering a discrete rating scale, we built in the power to draw quantitatively precise inferences about children's judgments (that are not plagued by guessing and chance factors).

In all, we tested 48 children—24 first graders and 24 sixth graders from a community similar to that of the first study. Each child judged all 16 target behaviors in a single session lasting about 20–25 min, with the order of presenting items completely randomized across children. Table 4.9 summarizes the major findings of this study. For simplicity, we have summed ratings across each general a priori category that the specific behaviors were thought to fit. (There are no hidden surprises lurking behind this handy summation. For example, in virtually every

Table 4.8. Representative Target Behaviors Rated on a Seven-Point Scale in Studies 2 and 3

General category	Behavior
Physical	1. Suppose (Tom, Alice) is having a jumping contest with (his/her) friends. How often will (he/she) jump the farthest and win the contest?
Social	2. Suppose (Tom, Alice) is asked to help (his/her) family do chores around the house. How much of the time will (he/she) help?
Academic	3. Suppose (Tom, Alice) is taking a test. How many of the questions will (he/she) get right?
Cognitive (Study 2 only)	4. Suppose (Tom, Alice) hears a new song. How much of it will (he/she) remember the next day?

Table 4.9. Mean Ratings for Target Figures Described as "Smart" or "Not Smart," by Behavioral Category Rated and Grade: Study 2[a]

| Behavioral category | Grade of child and ability of target figure | | | |
| | 1 | | 6 | |
	Smart	Not smart	Smart	Not smart
Physical	18.38	15.75	16.75	13.75
Social	22.25	16.38	23.75	16.38
Academic	23.13	14.13	21.25	12.50
Cognitive	20.50	8.88	19.63	12.00

[a] Each mean is based on 12 subjects, each of whom rated 4 behaviors. The summed ratings of the 4 behaviors could range from 4(1) = 4 to 4(7) = 28. Thus, each mean is the average of summed ratings.

case, the data would look the same if we tabled the results for single behavioral items.)

There are three quite striking findings. Each is supported by planned comparisons in a preliminary analysis of these means. First, the means generally reflect a higher judged performance for smart individuals than for those depicted as not smart. This holds across descriptive categories and for both first graders and sixth graders. Second, the gap between ratings for smart and not smart is relatively small for the category of physical behaviors but relatively large for the remaining categories. Finally, this gap is about the same for first and sixth graders.

It appears that, given the appropriate task parameters, young children give as differentiated a picture of intelligence (here gauged by reactions to "smartness") as do older ones. And, unlike our earlier findings, here both the younger and older children view interpersonal behaviors as reflecting different degrees of intelligence. Surprisingly, there was less differentiation among categories of behavioral items than we had anticipated. That is, children generally thought a smart person would outperform one who is not smart in most ways. The only dimension of performance not applicable to such a distinction was physical behaviors.

STUDY 3: A SPECIFIC INTELLECTUAL ABILITY

Although the second study improves upon the earlier design by including concrete behaviors to judge, it ignores a second consideration that is probably critical as well. As Robert Sternberg's work has shown (Sternberg *et al.*, 1981), we have to be careful in specifying what intellectual ability is being assessed. For adults, for example, it makes a substantial difference whether subjects evaluate *academic* as opposed to *practical* intelligence or *academic* versus *social* intelligence. For children, the problem is even more acute, since the meanings children attach to a particular ability label are likely to undergo significant changes during childhood.

In Study 3, we considered this problem and responded to it by again shifting from asking questions abstractly ("academic intelligence" and "general intelligence" are, after all, quite abstract notions for children) to posing them more concretely. Specifically, we asked children to offer judgments about the likely behavioral performances of same-sex peers who are either good or poor readers. Reading is construed as a highly important intellectual activity to most children and adults in our society. And it is an activity with which elementary school children are likely to have vast prior experience. The goal was to determine the implicit personality theory children might have of hypothetical peers who are good or poor readers. As in the previous study, children rated the level of expected performance of the hypothetical target figure on a number of concrete behaviors (the list was similar to the one shown in Table 4.8). Some of the behaviors were academic and so were expected to be aligned either positively or negatively with reading. Others were behaviors associated with physical motor or social interpersonal skills. We expected that by focusing on the specific task of reading, we might be able to demonstrate greater domain restriction in the qualities perceived to be associated with this ability. That is, unlike smartness (investigated in Study 2), which children viewed as composed of all three domains of social, cognitive, and academic skills, perhaps reading ability would produce a narrower definition.

A group of 48 children was again tested—half were first graders and half were sixth graders. At each grade, half of the children rated a hypothetical good reader, while the others rated a poor reader. All children were from the same general community as those tested earlier, and there was an approximately even distribution of boys and girls at each age. Each child judged all 12 target behaviors in a single session lasting about 20–25 min, with the order of items randomized. Table 4.10 summarizes the major results in a fashion similar to the summary for Study 2. The major result here is that, for both first graders and sixth graders, good readers were perceived as likely to perform better on academic tasks than were poor readers. However, in the perceptual motor and social interpersonal realms, any difference between good and poor readers was perceived as minimal. This verbal summary is supported by statistically significant planned comparisons. And again, an item-by-item breakdown revealed this pattern to be uniform with only one exception. (For

Table 4.10. Mean Ratings for Target Figures Described as "Good Readers" or "Poor Readers," by Behavioral Category and Grade: Study 3[a]

	Grade of child and ability of target figure			
	1		6	
Behavioral category	Good reader	Poor reader	Good reader	Poor reader
Perceptual motor	16.67	15.83	16.50	17.75
Social interpersonal	21.25	20.75	20.33	16.91
Academic	22.58	10.92	22.50	11.42

[a] Each mean is based on 12 subjects, each of whom rated 4 behaviors. The summed ratings of the 4 behaviors could range from 4(1) = 4 to 4(7) = 28. Thus, each mean is the average of summed ratings.

sixth graders, one item in the social interpersonal realm yielded a gap between good and poor readers, thus accounting for the mean difference of about 3.4 in the rating. When this single item is eliminated, the two means are virtually identical.)

So, in the present study, the young children evidenced a greater ability to make very precise discriminations among high- and low-ability individuals than they had in the previous studies. And again, their degree of differentiation seemed to match that evident in the older sixth-grade children. Good readers as opposed to poor readers were thought to excel on only one category of behaviors—academic. Perceptual motor and social interpersonal qualities were not thought to distinguish between them. The key to this finding, we believe, is that the discrimination called upon subjects to consider a very specific type of ability—reading. It did not call for a global assessment of ability (e.g., as in assessing someone who is "smart," Study 2). Of course, it remains an open and intriguing prospect to discover whether children are similarly able to offer precise personality profiles of (hypothetical) others whose intellectual abilities are of a different sort—for example, exhibiting skill in mathematics, writing, communicating, or remembering. There is no reason to suspect, a priori, that the same findings uncovered here will apply to other such cases. Children's knowledge bases about other behavioral (or skill) domains may differ considerably, and their concepts about them may entail narrower or broader attributions.

STUDY 4: ABILITY ACROSS THE LIFE SPAN

Most experts agree that intellectual ability ought to be viewed as a dynamic entity whose manifestations are likely to change across different epochs in development (e.g., Resnick, 1976; Sternberg, 1979; Yussen

& Santrock, 1982, Chapter 8). However, the studies reported so far ignored this issue. Children were asked to make judgments about the nature of ability without consideration of the developmental maturity of the hypothetical person being evaluated. The present study was a first effort in that direction. It was inspired, in part, by an investigation reported by Robert Siegler and Dean Richards (1982). Siegler and Richards examined the concept of intelligence in a group of undergraduate psychology students who were asked to state defining characteristics of intelligence in a 6-month-old, a 2-year-old, a 10-year-old, and an adult. The adult students were fairly consistent in their definitions of what intelligence is at any specific age. The definitions of intelligence, however, differed significantly across the ages of the hypothetical people being described (i.e, the infants, child, and adult). For example, for infants, the raters identified the following key characteristics as signaling intelligence: recognizing people and objects, motor coordination, alertness, and awareness of the environment. By contrast, for adults, the following characteristics were deemed to be central: reasoning, verbal ability, problem solving, learning ability, and creativity. The study by Siegler and Richards is a good starting point, but it is limited to the perceptions of adults, and highly knowledgeable ones at that (students in a human development course at Carnegie-Mellon University).

The focus of our efforts, by contrast, has been to examine how conceptions of ability change during childhood. To that end, Study 4 was designed to examine the concepts of ability in children and adults asked to focus on hypothetical others (targets) at four different points in the life span. The goal was to determine if children share the same ideas as adults of how ability is manifested at different periods in development.

The study was quite simple. As part of a lengthier interview about intellectual ability, subjects were asked to describe all the concrete ways one might know if a person has high ability for four hypothetical target figures: an infant, a 10-year-old, an adult, and an older adult. For children, each target figure was defined by a picture, and in addition, they were told that the infant depicted was 1 year old, the adult was about their parents' age, and the older adult was an "older adult" who had retired from work. In all cases, the photos depicted Caucasians of the same sex as the child. For adults, the pictures were supplemented with relevant age information for all the target figures. In addition to the 1-year-old infant and 10-year-old child, the adult was said to be 35 years old and the older adult to be 65 years old.

There were 48 subjects tested in all—16 third graders, 16 sixth graders, and 16 adults. The children were drawn from the same community as the first three studies, and the adults were undergraduates at the

University of Wisconsin-Madison. There was an approximately equal number of males and females at each age and all subjects were Caucasian.

The procedure was to ask each subject to list all the ways he or she could tell if the relevant target figure was "intelligent" or "smart." (These terms were used interchangeably after each subject had engaged in a discussion of what each adjective meant prior to the procedure proper.) Each subject reacted to all four target figures. There were several orders of presenting target figures for rating, generated by a Latin Square design. An audio and written record was maintained for each subject. From this was created an exhaustive list of every idea mentioned by every subject for each target figure. The two authors deleted obvious duplications and repetitions and then proceeded to create a set of descriptive categories (as was done for many parts of Study 1) to cover as many of the subject's ideas as possible. The data yielded rich and surprising information about the conception of ability across the life span. A summary is provided in Tables 4.11-4.14.

Rather than try to detail the frequencies with which particular categories were selected (since we have not yet reached mathematical precision and reliability on this analysis), we will communicate informal prototypes generated by each group of subjects for each target figure described. The categories appearing in the tables reflect relatively frequent responses offered by at least one group of subjects. The check marks indicate that the particular group in question offered a number of responses that fit the corresponding response category.

Turning first to Table 4.11, we see the responses given to characterize a hypothetical infant. Common to everyone's definition of ability is the infant's progress in fine and gross sensorimotor control (e.g., holding cup for the former, and standing, crawling, and throwing for the latter),

Table 4.11. Qualities Characterizing Intellectual Ability in an Infant, by Subject Group

Qualities	Third grade	Sixth grade	Adults
Sensorimotor control			
Fine motor	✓	✓	✓
Gross motor	✓	✓	✓
Self-control and independence	✓	✓	✓
Social knowledge	✓	✓	
Language	✓	✓	✓
Learning ability		✓	✓
Motivation and curiosity			✓
Activity level			✓

Table 4.12. Qualities Characterizing Intellectual Ability in a 10-Year-Old, by Subject Group

Qualities	Subject group		
	Third grade	Sixth grade	Adult
School performance	✔	✔	✔
Reading	✔	✔	
Mathematics	✔	✔	
Knowledge	✔	✔	✔
Social skill	✔	✔	✔
Physical skill (e.g., sports)	✔	✔	
Motivation (effort, curiosity)			✔
Learning (speed, potential)			✔
Thinking abstractly			✔
Peer affiliation			✔
Independence and creativity			✔

the tendency to do things without help (what we have called self-control and independence), and evidence of precocious language acquisition (e.g., speaking in intelligible words, talking early). Common to the responses of both grade school groups of children (but not the adults) was a number of ideas about infants knowing what they ought to do and ought not to do in particular circumstances (what we have termed social knowledge). Both sixth graders and adults repeatedly and explicitly referred to the child's speed or ability to learn (learning ability) as important. Finally, adults (and only adults) prominently mentioned that motivation and curiosity signaled infant intelligence (e.g., "curious,"

Table 4.13. Qualities Characterizing Intellectual Ability in an Adult (35-Year-Old), by Subject Group

Qualities	Subject group		
	Third grade	Sixth grade	Adult
Home skills	✔	✔	
Work accomplishments	✔	✔	✔
Managing money and finances	✔	✔	
Child care	✔	✔	
Teaching others	✔	✔	
Driving	✔	✔	
Sports	✔	✔	
Physical skills	✔	✔	
General psychological traits			
Social adjustment			✔
Motivational			✔
General cognitive			✔
Values			✔

Table 4.14. Qualities Characterizing Intellectual Ability in an Older Adult (65-Year-Old), by Subject Group

	Subject group		
Qualities	Third grade	Sixth grade	Adult
Attention to physical well-being–physical limitations	✓		
Teach–help children	✓	✓	✓
Hobbies	✓	✓	
Work	✓	✓	
Memory–knowledge	✓	✓	✓
Wisdom			✓
Personal adjustment			✓
Sharing knowledge			✓
Keeping alive intellectually			✓

"explorative," "has an alert look") along with a high activity level (e.g., "very active," "be active").

Turning next to Table 4.12, we see the responses given to characterize a hypothetical 10-year-old. All age groups mentioned superior school performance as a typical characteristic of a bright youngster, but whereas everyone mentioned a variety of general kinds of knowledge and performance indicators, only the children emphasized the importance of excelling in the specific activities of reading and mathematics. All groups mentioned a variety of social skill indicators, ranging from being helpful to others and being an adaptable member of the group to the more trait-like pronouncements of the adult subjects (e.g., "develop moral values"). Among the characteristics that discriminated among the groups of subjects was mention of physical skills (e.g., "sports," "baseball"), which only the children mentioned prominently, and a series of characteristics that only the adult subjects mentioned—motivation, learning, thinking abstractly, showing interest in and affiliation with peers (peer affiliation), and exhibiting independence and creativity.

Table 4.13 summarizes the responses used to characterize a hypothetical adult. Here we noted the greatest divergence between children and adults. The characteristics stated by the children on the one hand and the adults on the other were surprisingly nonoverlapping. Children focused on how well adults manage specific tasks—managing the household (home skills), excelling at a job (work accomplishments), taking care of and earning money (managing money and finances), and dealing with and teaching children (child care and teaching others). The grade schoolers also valued the adult's ability to drive (driving) and perform athletic (sports) and manual skills (physical skills).

By contrast, the adults had little to say about specific activities or competencies. Virtually all their responses were general or stressed abstract qualities. The qualities mentioned were quite diverse, and we simply flag the diversity by listing general categories that easily subsume the responses—social adjustment (e.g., "well-rounded person," "do what is right," "be independent," "treat people with respect and understanding"), motivational (e.g., "enjoy life," "enjoy career," "trying new things," "like security," "do things to be happy"), general cognitive (e.g., "abstractness," "depth of knowledge," "knowing that much is beyond understanding"), and values (e.g., "open mindedness," "join special-interest groups," "get politically active").

Table 4.14 summarizes the responses used to characterize a hypothetical older adult. Again, there was substantial divergence between the types of responses given by children and those offered by adults. The third graders were particularly preoccupied with older adults' physical limitations, health-related problems, and infirmities. To the extent the target figure reckoned with these difficulties and took sensible steps to protect him- or herself from unfavorable circumstances, the children deemed the person intelligent (attention to physical well-being, etc.). Children also emphasized that bright older adults have rich knowledge and memories (memory–knowledge) and can teach youngsters many things and impart much knowledge (teach–help children). Finally, children repeatedly mentioned older adults finding both recreational outlets for themselves (hobbies) as well as formal work for pay (work). Although the adult subjects shared two of the response types with children (teach–help children and memory–knowledge), the more dramatic finding is the substantially different categories of responses adults came up with in addition. These include comments reminding us of Clayton and Birren's (in press) description of wisdom in the elderly (e.g., "ingenuity," "perceptiveness," "relate experience to growth," "relate to people differently as the result of changing times"), a sense of personal adjustment (e.g., "keep interested in life," "incorporate new ways into life with ease," "a sense of accomplishment"), sharing knowledge (e.g., "teach others," "explain things to people") and keeping alive intellectually (e.g., "remain active," "continue to grow intellectually," "like a book," "realize learning is unfinished").

To summarize the findings of Study 4, then, we note two important trends. First, just as Siegler and Richards (1982) found that the presence of intelligence is signaled by different behaviors and skills at different ages, so have we. Common to everyone's definition of intelligence is this: Infants are deemed bright by virtue of sensorimotor precocity, independence and self-control, and language skill; and school-aged children by their performance in school and general knowledge. Second, and the novel finding of this investigation, is that the defining features of intelligence also differ significantly depending on the age (maturity) of the person doing the defining. Adults define intelligence very differently than do grade school children, especially when the target figures being described are adults or older adults.

The one common denominator evident across all the hypothetical figures being described was in the definitions given by adults. Adults saw others' levels of motivation and learning potential to be a core defining feature of intelligence regardless of the others' ages.

CONCLUDING THOUGHTS

The investigations reported in this chapter cover quite a lot of ground. Each considers the meaning of terms associated with ability in elementary school children. And each offers some unique perspective on conditions that constrain and influence the nature of these meanings. The research began with the wide-ranging interview study reported at the outset (Study 1) and described in much greater detail elsewhere (Yussen & Kane, in press). As should be evident from earlier remarks, that initial investigation is a goldmine of information about likely developmental changes in the conception of intelligence. It cries out for tighter methodology, expansion, and analytical fleshing out. One such further effort is reported in Studies 2 and 3, where children are asked to distinguish high- and low-ability individuals in concrete behavioral terms. Whereas Study 1 supported the conclusion that young children tend to see high-ability individuals as being different in most or many respects from low-ability individuals—and hence tend to be fairly global in implicitly defining intelligence—Studies 2 and 3 suggest otherwise. It appears that young elementary school children can be less global and more discriminating when the ability domain is stated in specific and concrete terms and when potential characteristics are stated specifically and concretely. Such an outcome has important implications for the study of children's attributions in general (e.g., Heller & Berndt, in press; Leahy and Hunt, Chapter 5, this volume) as well as the narrower domain of ideas about intelligence discussed here. It suggests an important object lesson in the appropriate use of methodology with young children to avoid the common trap of underestimating what they are capable of cognizing.

Study 4 represents a second effort to expand upon the initial investigation. It takes seriously the notion that intellectual ability may be defined very differently depending on the age or perceived maturity of the target individual being evaluated. Ability in an infant is a very different entity than ability in a child or ability in an adult—or is it? The children and adults tested here answered the question affirmatively, although their conceptions of just what ability is like at different ages was not consistent. We do not consider the results of Study 4 final, in any sense. Having generated a large pool of responses from our subjects, the next step will be to pursue the definitional issue with more analytical techniques, of the sort that Sternberg and his students have employed with adults (Sternberg *et al.*, 1981). Only by having children sort available response alternatives or rate the applicability and centrality of various response items to the definition of some prototypical ability (e.g., intelligence, smart) will we be able to state with confidence how definitions of ability change across the life span.

APPENDIX: QUESTIONNAIRE ON INTELLIGENCE

Part I. Definition of intelligence

I'd like to ask you some questions about what it means to be "smart" or "intelligent." Everyone has different ideas about these things and I want to know what you think. The questions are fun to think about and whatever you say is the right answer because everybody has different ideas. I just want to know what your ideas are.

1. First of all, what does it mean to say that someone is *smart?*
2. What does it mean to say someone is *intelligent?*

From now on, I'm just going to use the words "smart" and "intelligent" as the same words. Sometimes I'll say "smart" and sometimes "intelligent," but they'll mean the same thing. OK?

Part II. Visible signs of intelligence

3. If you meet a person, how do you know if they are (smart/intelligent?) (Can you tell?)
4. Does a(n) (smart/intelligent) person look different in any way than an average person? How? Can you explain/tell me more?
5. Does a(n) (smart/intelligent) person talk differently in any way than an average person? (prompt)
6. Does a(n) (smart/intelligent) person act differently or do anything differently than an average person? (prompt) What?

Part III. Self-assessment of intelligence

7. Suppose we used this to show all the people in the world from the most (smart/intelligent) to the least (smart/intelligent). Let's suppose that this person is the most (smart/intelligent) and this person is the least (smart/intelligent). Everyone else is along the line. Put your finger on the line to show where you are.

Least Intelligent   (actual line length = 6 in.)   Most intelligent

Part IV. Qualities associated with intelligence

I'm going to say some things that we do every day. I'd like you to tell me whether a very (smart/intelligent) person does these things differently than an average person. If the average person does these things the same as the very (smart/intelligent) person, then just say, "there is no difference." Or the average person may do things differently than the very (smart/intelligent) person and I'd like to know that, too. OK?

8. "Does a very (smart/intelligent) person _____ differently than a person who is (average/not as [smart/intelligent])?

A (Mental)	B (Physical)
a. learn things	e. see
b. remember things	f. run
c. understand things	g. lift things
d. talk (speak)	h. jump

C (School)	D (Social)
i. read	m. help people
j. write	n. smile a lot
k. draw	o. have good manners
l. follow instructions	p. share with others

Part V. The influence of nature and nurture on intelligence

9. Where does a very (smart/intelligent) person get their ("smartness"/"intelligence"); where does it come from?
10. If a person is very (smart/intelligent), were they born that way?

11. If a person is very (smart/intelligent), is it because of the things they've done or experiences they've had?

12. Some people think that what we are born with and the things we've done (experiences we've had) are both important for causing us to be smart (in determining how intelligent we become). Do you think both are important, things we've done (experiences we've had) are more important, or what we're born with is more important?

13. Some people think that the things we do (experiences we have) as we grow up cause us to be smart (determine how intelligent we become). I'm going to say some kinds of things that we do.
    I'd like you to tell me how important you think each one is in causing us to be smart (determining how intelligent we become).
    I want you to use this to tell me if these things will be "not important at all," "not too important," "medium important," "pretty important," or "very important." OK?
    How important do you think _____ are in causing us to be smart (determining how intelligent we become)?"
    a. _____ things we do with our family
    b. _____ things we do with our friends
    c. _____ things we do at school

14. If a person's parents are very (smart/intelligent), will that person be very (smart/intelligent) too? Why?

15. What else causes people to be (smart/intelligent)?

Part VI. The constancy or malleability of intelligence

16. Will a person always be the same in how (smart/intelligent) they are or can they change?

17. If someone is (smart/intelligent) as a child, can they be not so (smart/intelligent) when they grow up? How?

18. If someone is not so (smart/intelligent) as a child, can they be (smart/intelligent) when they grow up? How?

19. If a person is not so (smart/intelligent), can they become (smart/intelligent) by the things they do and/or the experiences they have? Like what? What kinds of things?

20. If a person is (smart/intelligent), can they become not so (smart/intelligent) by the things they do and/or experiences they have? Like what? What kinds of things?

REFERENCES

Clayton, V., & Birren, J. E. Age and wisdom across the life-span: Theoretical perspectives. In P. B. Baltes & O. Brim, Jr. (Eds.), *Life span development and behavior* (Vol. 3). New York: Academic Press, in press.

Eysenck, H. J. *The structure and measurement of intelligence.* New York: Springer-Verlag, 1979.

Flavell, J. H. Monitoring social cognitive enterprises: Something else that may develop in the area of social cognition. In J. H. Flavell & L. Ross (Eds.), *Social cognitive development.* Cambridge: Cambridge Univ. Press, 1981.

Heller, K., & Berndt, T. J. Developmental changes in the formation and organization of personality attributions. In S. R. Yussen (Ed.), *The growth of reflection.* New York: Academic Press, in press.

Resnick, L. B. (Ed.). *The nature of intelligence.* Hillsdale, N.J.: Erlbaum, 1976.

Siegler, R. S., & Richards, D. D. The development of intelligence. In R. J. Sternberg (Ed.), *Handbook of human intelligence.* New York: Cambridge Univ. Press, 1982.

Sternberg, R. J. The nature of mental abilities. *American Psychologist,* 1979, *34,* 214–230.

Sternberg, R. J., Conway, B. E., Ketron, J. L., & Bernstein, M. People's conceptions of intelligence. *Journal of Personality and Social Psychology,* 1981, *41,* 37–55.

Wellman, H. M. A child's theory of mind: The development of conceptions of cognition. In S. R. Yussen (Ed.), *The growth of reflection.* New York: Academic Press, in press.

Yussen, S. R., & Kane, P. Children's concept of intelligence. In S. R. Yussen (Ed.), *The growth of reflection.* New York: Academic Press, in press.

Yussen, S. R., & Santrock, J. W. *Child development* (2nd ed.). Dubuque: Brown, 1982.

5 / A cognitive-developmental approach to the development of conceptions of intelligence

ROBERT L. LEAHY
TERESA M. HUNT

One of the major dimensions of stratification of individuals in contemporary society is intelligence. This is especially salient in the school culture in which children may be tracked or isolated from "normal" peers on the basis of intellectual ability. Given the fact that the primary purpose of educational settings is to enhance the development of intellectual skills, it is surprising that so little research has been conducted on the development of conceptions of intelligence and conceptions of the role of the school or parents in facilitating the development of intelligence. Not only can the study of children's conceptions of intellectual inequality broaden our knowledge of social cognitive processes, but it also may provide a conceptual framework for the application of that knowledge for educators. In particular, educators may wish to know how children interpret the goal of education (i.e., "What is intelligence?") and how this set of skills may be acquired. The purpose of this chapter is to provide a cognitive-developmental perspective to the study of these questions, to review our empirical findings of an interview study of children's conceptions of intelligence, to suggest a series of cognitive-developmental levels of conceptions of intelligence, and to indicate the practical implications for educators of these proposed levels.

THE CHILD'S CONSTRUCTION
OF SOCIAL INEQUALITY

SOCIAL-COGNITIVE DEVELOPMENT

In our study of conceptions of intelligence, we were interested in exploring the implications of Piaget's (1932) and Kohlberg's (1969) cognitive-developmental theories. According to this approach, social concepts show qualitative, structural changes with age that are reflective of other nonsocial cognitive attainments (e.g., the acquisition of classification skills and decentration). The development of these social conceptions, however, is not entirely reducible to nonsocial cognition; rather, social cognitive development also reflects changes in the structuring of social interactions (Kohlberg, 1969; Leahy, 1981a; Piaget, 1932; Youniss, 1979).

Our cognitive-developmental model stresses five qualitative changes in social cognition that are relevant to the development of conceptions of intelligence: the development of moral reasoning, the emergence of psychological conceptions of individuals, social comparison, the development of internal standards, and classificatory skill. The approach that we advance draws upon the theoretical perspectives advanced by Piaget, Kohlberg, and Werner. We shall suggest how conceptions of intelligence may undergo modification as general developmental processes and the nature of social interactions change between childhood and adolescence.

Moral judgment and intelligence

Piaget (1932) claims that the young child's moral judgments are characterized by *moral realism*, which he defines as rule-bound concern for the letter rather than the spirit of the law and concern with objective rather than subjective responsibility. Piaget claims that concern for intentions arises through cooperation and mutual respect, which necessarily entail a change from relationships of obedience to adult constraint to the relationships of mutuality with peers.

Piaget (1932) claims that young children emphasize retribution (or expiation) in punishment, according to which violations of rules should be followed by consequences that cause harm to the protagonist. In contrast, older children presumably emphasize the preventative (educative or reforming) quality of punishments, such that the consequences following a violation of a rule should change the protagonist's behavior to be more consistent with a desirable goal. If young children equate intelligence with obedience (as Piagetian theory implies), then we could expect that young children would advocate punishment for people who are not "smart." Furthermore, older children would be expected to argue that the consequence of lack of intelligence should be educational intervention to help improve that person's performance.

Kohlberg's (1969, 1976) substantial modification and extension of Piaget's theory indicates that during adolescence there is a marked shift in moral reasoning. In particular, the adolescent judges behavior in terms of the expectations of others (Stage 3) or in terms of maintaining the social order (Stage 4). Kohlberg has argued that the development of role-taking skill underlies this development of conventional moral reasoning. Empirical support for this view is found in a number of studies (e.g., Selman, 1976, 1980; Walker & Richards, 1979). In an attempt to explore some implications of Kohlberg's theory, Leahy has suggested that conventional judgments are role dependent—that is, competent or appropriate behavior is defined by performing in a manner consistent with a widely held stereotype shared by both actor and audience (Leahy, forthcoming; Leahy & Eiter, 1980). An implication of this development of moral thought is that *intelligence* may come to imply competence in role enactment, including the ability to recognize the perspectives of others, to get along with others, or to adapt to individual differences among people. Sternberg, Conway, Ketron, and Bernstein's (1981) study of adults' conceptions of intelligence indicates that social competence is a major component of popular beliefs about intelligence. The question addressed in our study was: At what age do these conceptions develop?

Concrete operational thinking and intelligence

The cognitive-developmental model suggests that the development of conceptions of intelligence will reflect structural changes in nonsocial cognition. Of particular interest to us in the present study is the transition from preoperational to concrete operational thought. Specifically, preoperational thinking is reflected by perceptual focus on the external dimensions of stimuli, inflexible classification of objects, and lack of awareness or concern regarding the perspectives of others (Piaget, 1970).

Perceptual versus psychological qualities

As a number of studies indicate, the younger child's descriptions of peers focus on the external, observable, or peripheral qualities of people, such as their appearances and behaviors, whereas the older child recognizes the covert, inferred, or psychological qualities of people, such as their thoughts, traits, or feelings (e.g., Leahy, 1981b; Livesley & Bromley, 1973; Peevers & Secord, 1973). In defining *intelligence*, we may differentiate its overt components (e.g., motor skills, reading out loud) from the processes that are presumed to account for or describe individual differences (e.g., traits, motivation, self-direction). In fact, one might argue that the inference of psychological qualities (e.g., traits) may presume the prior recognition of behavioral uniformities—that is, the child first begins with the observation of behavioral similarity across situations or time and then classifies these into trait terms (Barenboim, 1981; Shirk & Leahy, Note 1). On the basis of this rationale, we expected that conceptions of intelligence would reflect an increase between 6 and 10 years of age in references to psychological qualities and a decrease with age in references to peripheral qualities.

Comparisons

The recognition of differences between stereotypical groups is found in preschool children for comparisons of races (Katz, Chapter 2 this volume), classes (Leahy, Chapter 3 this volume), and genders (Williams, Bennett, & Best, 1975). In fact, the ability to consistently sort physical objects along a single dimension (e.g., color) is found in children as young as 3 and 4 (Schultz, Chapter 1, this volume). However, once the young child sorts objects or people into distinct groups, he or she may fail to recognize similarities of these groups. This inflexibility of children limited to consistent sorting ability eventually gives way to more flexible, multiple sorting ability—for example, objects may be sorted on the basis of either color or form, and males and females may be classified as different in some respects but similar in others (e.g., both are people) (Leahy, 1981b; Leahy & Shirk, in press). This structural limitation would be expected for conceptions of intelligence—that is, the younger child, limited in classificatory skill, would be expected to fail to recognize the similarities of intelligent and unintelligent people.

Social comparison

One way individuals assess intelligence or ability is to compare their performance with that of others (Festinger, 1950, 1954). An interesting series of studies by Ruble and her colleagues indicates that young children are quite unlikely to engage in social comparison—that is, to request information about the performance of other people (Ruble, Feldman, & Boggiano, 1976; Ruble, Parsons, & Ross, 1976). The cognitive-developmental approach would suggest that a number of cognitive limitations may account for this lack of social comparison among young children. First, young children lack the ability to decenter—that is, they tend not to refocus on two or more dimensions and to coordinate these dimensions by systematic comparisons (Feffer, 1970; Piaget, 1970). Although decentration is generally viewed as an important ability for conservation tasks, it has relevance to social comparison in that social comparison involves the comparison among a set of performances by different people using a systematic standard (e.g., test scores). Decentration is also involved in role-taking ability in that the child who takes the perspective of others must recognize the differences between self and others in subjective experiences (Chandler & Greenspan, 1975). Similarly, interest in the performance of others entails the comparison of the abilities of self and others as these are judged by a uniform criterion. A second factor contributing to social comparison conceptions may be the development of seriation skills—that is, the ability to spontaneously order stimuli along an ordinal scale from "least" to "most." As Piaget and others have shown, the ability to engage in seriation increases during later childhood (Liben, 1976). The relevance of this ability to social comparison and conceptions of intelligence is that the older child may be able to use and be interested in using a standard reference (such as test performance) to assess inequality of performances.

Internal control of behavior

A variety of developmental theories propose that increasing age is associated with increasing reliance on internal standards for behavior, such as standards of competence, moral principles, or conscience (Freud, 1933/1965; Glick & Zigler, forthcoming; Kohlberg, 1969; Leahy, 1981a; Yando, Seitz, & Zigler, 1978). For example, Zigler and his colleagues have indicated that increasing age and IQ are associated with a more positive (or demanding) ideal self-image (Achenbach & Zigler, 1963; Katz & Zigler, 1967) and less imitativeness (Achenbach & Zigler, 1968; Yando et al., 1978). Similar to Kohlberg's (1969) cognitive-developmental model, Zigler's theoretical position is that the individual forms an internal representation of competence and this standard then guides the self's behavior. Lower levels of developmental functioning are characterized by outer-directedness precisely because the child lacks a standard of competent performance and therefore relies on others to guide his or her behavior: Consequently, once internal standards are articulated, dependency diminishes. Thus, from this perspective, as well as from our foregoing argument that obedience and imitation are reflective of moral realism, we should expect a decrease with age in emphasis on imitation as a defining attribute of intelligence and an increase with age in reliance on internal standards as indicative of intelligence.

From a somewhat different perspective, Soviet developmental theory

(Luria, 1961; Vygotsky, 1978) has proposed that increasing age is associated with the internal regulation of behavior through the functions served by internalized speech. Meichenbaum and his colleagues have been especially successful in advancing cognitive-behavioral interventions that emphasize the directive and regulative role in inner speech for the control of impulsive behavior (Meichenbaum, 1977). The cognitive-behavioral view of development is not entirely clear as to the child's understanding of cognitive processes, although Meichenbaum and Asarnow (1979) have suggested some educational implications of such abilities. However, their model would suggest that increasing age might be associated with an increasing emphasis on the child's ability to recognize the self-directive quality of intelligence—that is, the problem solving strategies employed in setting goals and developing plans. Consequently, we were interested in trends in the development of conceptions of self-direction and decreases with age in emphasis on obedience and imitation in conceptions of intelligence.

A STUDY OF THE DEVELOPMENT
OF CONCEPTIONS OF INTELLIGENCE

Details of our investigation of the development of conceptions of intelligence are reported elsewhere (Leahy, Note 2; Leahy & Hunt, Note 3). At the inception of our data collection, very little was known about children's conceptions of intelligence (see Yussen & Kane, forthcoming, for an exception to this). Given our Piagetian perspective, it should not surprise the reader that we used a modification of the clinical method of interviewing. We chose this method because we lacked a strong empirical basis on which to test recognition (although one might argue that with adult subjects such an empirical or theoretical basis did exist; see Sternberg *et al.*, 1981). As in the study of conceptions of economic inequality (Leahy, 1981b; 1983), we might have had some reasonable expectations of what young children might say, but we recognized that in such a pilot study we might not be able to anticipate the unusual constructions of younger children. There are considerable disadvantages in using the interview method, including social desirability, language deficiency, competence and performance differences, and even the possibility that subjects might simply spout off opinions they heard from others without reflecting on these issues (Cannell & Kahn, 1968; Maccoby & Maccoby, 1954). Certainly the use of a recall technique might have underestimated the competence of younger children whose abilities might be accurately assessed using recognition tests.

Notwithstanding these methodological disclaimers, we believe that valuable data are obtained by interview methods because they appear to represent the spontaneous, everyday conceptions of children—that is, they reflect what children *do* say, not what they *could* say in an optimum testing situation removed from the realities of conversations among individuals. However, we also suggest that future research should employ a variety of recognition or even behavioral techniques to assess conceptions of intelligence.

The subjects in this study were 119 children and adolescents forming three age groups—6, 10, and 16. They were enrolled in either public or parochial schools located in the metropolitan area of New York City.

The interview was quite simple. Each child was tested individually by a graduate student, who asked the following questions:

1. What does it mean to be smart?
2. What does it mean not to be smart?
3. and 4. How are smart people and people who are not smart different from (the same as) one another?
5. and 6. Why are people smart (not smart)?
7. What could someone do to get smart?
8. and 9. What could parents (the school) do to make someone smarter?

Interviewers were instructed to minimize their probes of subjects in order to provide similar interview conditions for all subjects. Interviewers did ask for clarification of statements by subjects and for "any other" material that subjects could offer. An advantage of this limitation on probes is that interview conditions may be replicated by other researchers and that the interview might be replicated for older subjects using questionnaire techniques. A disadvantage is that further inquiry might have revealed more detailed (or developmentally optimum) performance.

Responses were tape-recorded and transcribed. Each response to each question was classified as falling within a set of specific categories such that these categories reflected typical person description categories (e.g., traits, emotions, actions), theoretical models of intelligence (e.g., specific and general abilities, heritability, factual knowledge), achievement attributions (e.g., effort), and categories derived from cognitive-developmental theory and research related to moral judgment and social cognition (e.g., obedience, peer conformity, self-control, and social competence). Interrater reliability was high ($r = .85$), with raters able to classify over 95% of responses.

RESULTS: LEVELS OF CONCEPTION

The details of Age (3) × Sex (2) analyses of variance (ANOVAs) are reported elsewhere (Leahy, Note 2; Leahy & Hunt, Note 3). Our review of the data suggests that three general levels of conceptions of intelligence are manifested. The qualities of these levels are shown in Figure 5.1.

Level I: peripheral–obedient

The first level, most characteristic of the younger children, emphasizes the peripheral and obedience qualities of individuals. These include references to simple actions, reading, and knowledge of specific facts. For example, several younger children mentioned "tying your shoes" or being able to "dress yourself" as indicative of intelligence. Most children could not find a basis of similarity for these groups.

The emphasis on reading and obedience as the defining attributes of intelligence is found in a number of interviews. (Fictional names are assigned to subjects here.) Marc, age 6, says that intelligent people "know how to read" and people are not intelligent "because they don't listen." The passive dependence on adults is reflected in Carol's (age 6) claim that someone could become intelligent "if they'd . . . listen more and if they really didn't know something they could ask someone." For Brenda (age 6) intelligence means that you are "good" and

I. *Peripheral-Obedient*
    Intelligence is defined by actions, reading, knowledge of specific facts, and obedience to adult authority. Causes and changes in intelligence are conceptualized by passive obedience to adult authority or attendance at school. The view at this level is that the school should punish children who are not smart. Children deny the similarity of intelligent and unintelligent people.
II. *Psychological Conceptions*
    Intelligence is defined by performance on tests, with an increased awareness that the intelligent and unintelligent groups are similar in that they both are people and both can learn. Differences are attributed to motivation, studying, and training. Moral evaluations emerge, focusing on the lack of motivation presumed to characterize the unintelligent. Emphasis is on special tutoring and classes for the unintelligent.
III. *Social Interaction Conceptions*
    There is emphasis on specific intellectual abilities associated with different kinds of intelligence. Intelligence is viewed as involving social competence, with groups of intelligent and unintelligent people seen as differing in personality traits. Differences in intelligence are attributed to social conformity and self-direction. Changes in intelligence are seen as resulting from psychological or motivational support and association with others.

Figure 5.1. Levels in the conception of individual differences in intelligence.

lack of intelligence means that you are "bad . . . You get out of your seat." She continues:

INTERVIEWER: *How are they different?*
BRENDA: *One is bad and the other is good.*
INTERVIEWER: *How are they the same?*
BRENDA: *I don't know. No. They're not.*
INTERVIEWER: *How could someone who's not smart get smarter?*
BRENDA: *They work good—listen to the teacher.*
INTERVIEWER: *What could a mother or father do?*
BRENDA: *Punish him. Put him to sleep.*

Joe, age 6, also believes that reading, obedience, and attention are the hallmarks of intelligence. A person could become intelligent "if they know how to read. Like when you listen a lot and you go out to the reading group and pay attention." And people who are not intelligent "fool around so much. They don't look at the blackboard and they don't know what they're doing, and they turn around and say 'I don't know.' " Tom (age 6) believes that people are not smart "because they see too much TV and they play around and don't listen to their parents." Consistent with this, Tom believes parents should "take out the wire so that he doesn't see the TV." The interviewer inquired, "How would that help?" and Tom replied, "No wire, no more TV."

Thus, at Level I the emphasis is on specific behaviors, reading, and obedience. Intelligence does not seem to imply motivation or psychological traits. Because intelligence is reflected by behavior, reading, or rule compliance, children at this level appear to believe that it is easy to see that someone is intelligent. There are no references to the heritability of intelligence, so intelligence appears to be a changeable quality.

Level II: psychological conceptions

At age 10 (and during adolescence), many subjects emphasize the inferred psychological qualities that distinguish intelligent from unintelligent people. At this level, emphasis shifts to performance on tests as a measure for social comparison, and intelligence is attributed to motivation and study. Groups seem similar in that they both are human.

The emphasis on grades and tests is seen in a number of interviews with the 10-year-olds. Mike says that if "you're smart you get good grades and can pass and go to the next grade." Jim claims you can get smarter "by studying hard and really concentrating on what you want to do" and people are not smart "because they don't like to do that stuff. They don't study." The negative psychological qualities associated with lack of intelligence are referred to by Wendy: For people who are not smart "sometimes it's upsetting and you blame yourself for it and you're disappointed and want to stay away and there's a lot of problems to get your mother and father, to get them understanding." Jim also sees negative consequences for those who are not intelligent: "Like if you're not smart, lots of people won't like you that much and they'll call you 'Dopey'. . . . If somebody asks you what you got on your test and you didn't do well, you might feel like a little sad somebody got a higher mark than you."

The importance of motivation, especially valuing education, is emphasized by Frank, who claims that people who are not intelligent "don't care about school. They want to get married first." Some people are not intelligent, Jill says, "because they're too lazy to study." Lee has an optimistic view about intelligence: "You can be smart if you want to be smart but you have to really work on it."

Whereas the younger children believed that simply going to school would enhance intelligence, the children at Level II believe that individual differences in ability warrant specific interventions (e.g., special classes or tutoring). Donna (age 11) claims "if they had a tutor it would help them because the tutor is telling them what the teacher said." Lee believes in the value of compensatory education that will make up for the intellectual handicap of some children: "They can ask them for summer school and they could learn a little bit more about the year next to them and then they can go to the next grade."

These interviews reflect the important change at Level II—the emergence of conceptions of individual psychological differences. These differences are viewed as due to motivational and intellectual deficits that can be altered by special tutoring or classes that take into consideration the "special" nature of the child who is not intelligent.

Level III: social interaction conceptions

The distinguishing quality of conceptions at Level III is the idea that intelligent people are able to engage in competent social relationships and that changes in intelligence are related to social conformity, belonging to the appropriate group, or psychological and motivational support from others. Furthermore, the adolescent at this level emphasizes the self-direction necessary to form plans and carry them out: There is considerable emphasis on having the appropriate attitude toward work, including an interest in pursuing goals and the ability to analyze problems. Groups are viewed as similar in psychological qualities.

The ability to set goals and carry them through using problem solving strategies is indicated by a number of adolescents. Rose (age 16) believes someone can become more intelligent if he has "his own goals—what he wants out of life. . . . They become intelligent to reach specific goals or be more accepted." This emphasis on general problem solving strategies is considerably different from the younger child's emphasis on knowledge of facts. For the adolescent, intelligence involves more general gathering, processing, and utilization of information. We shall return to this issue later to suggest that an important change appears to be the spontaneous emphasis on the processes (e.g., problem solving) rather than the content (e.g., words) of thought in conceptions of intelligence.

The social competence of intelligence is mentioned by Rose: "Say my brothers took something of mine. I would sit down and think, 'They took it. Why don't I ask why they took it?' Or, 'Could they give it back?' Somebody who's not intelligent would go up there and start fighting with them real quickly. That's somebody who's dumb. . . . [It's the way] they handle themselves with other people." Mary (age 16) emphasizes the social cognitive (role-taking) qualities of intelligence: "To be grown-up and understand other people's ideas and their feelings. . . . To be aware of other people. . . . Not go around trying to step on other people." For Juan, a 16-year-old Hispanic, being intelligent means being "able to understand the community."

Just as social competence and social interaction are seen as important elements of intelligence, the adolescent may argue that socialization (i.e., the general home environment) may affect the development of intelligence. Andrea (age 14) believes that people may not be intelligent "because of this environment. If you take one person from the ghetto and another from a good home, maybe the person from the ghetto won't be intelligent because they might not have the learning to get somewhere."

At this level, the adolescent believes that social support (e.g., counseling and encouragement) will help the unintelligent student overcome his or her lack of intelligence. The emphasis on this supportive educational role is seen in the interview with Bob (age 16):

INTERVIEWER: *What could the school do?*
BOB: *They should get a teacher who cares. They can't get just any teacher because your mind breaks when you try and no one cares. Let them be with the smarter students—that'll help them be more motivated.*

Although Level III subjects do claim that psychological differences are important, they appear to view these in terms of successful interactions with a supportive social environment. Unlike the Level I subject, who argues for unilateral respect for adults, the Level III subject believes that encouragement, positive regard, and socially competent peers will enhance intelligence.

FROM OBEDIENCE AND RETRIBUTION TO
SOCIAL COMPETENCE AND EDUCATION

According to cognitive-developmental theory, the young child is primarily concerned with obeying the sanctions of adult authority. This moral realism emphasizes an inflexible set of adult-defined rules such that individual differences in intentions, efforts, needs, and abilities are not considered relevant to judgments of transgression or claims for distributive justice (Damon, 1977; Kohlberg, 1969; Piaget, 1932). The purpose of punishment at this early level is concerned with causing suffering to the transgressor. The findings of the present study suggest that the young child's conceptions of intelligence are similar to this heteronomous morality.

By far the most common explanations of intelligence by the 6-year-olds refer to obedience, training by teachers, and attending school. Each of these clearly reflects a deference to the unilateral authority of adults. The passive quality of this educational relationship has an interesting parallel with the empiricist model of John Locke, who portrayed the young mind as a template upon which the impressions of the world would be stamped.

The young child's conceptions of how intelligence can be increased also reflect a belief in retribution: Since lack of intelligence is viewed as defiance of authority, the young child believes that the unintelligent person should obey or suffer consequences. For example, among the 6-year-olds, over half of the responses to the question of what parents could do refer to the use of punishment, requests for compliance, or insistence on the child attending class. Similarly, the young child believes that the school authorities should use punishment or request compliance.

By age 10, there is an increasing emphasis on equity-related factors in intelligence, includng motivational conceptions (e.g., study and effort) as reasons accounting for intelligence. These psychological conceptions remain salient during adolescence, when there is an increase in references to intelligence as social competence, social interaction, and self-direction. Thus, for the adolescent, to be intelligent involves being able to conform to the expectations of others and being able to understand other people. Many of the conceptions of social competence involve reference to social cognitive skills that involve role taking. For some adolescents, intelligence suggests the ability to adapt to individual differences.

This change in conceptions reflects an increasing tendency of adolescents to view behavior in role-dependent terms. Roles serve to unify the expectations of actor and audience: A person acting in role anticipates the reactions of others and conforms to those expectations. As Mead (1934) has suggested, this process of role taking is a central factor in the socialization of individuals in that the individual learns to understand the values of the group by taking the perspective of others toward behavior or toward the self. From this model, the failure to engage in role taking involves a failure in socialization.

Similarly, Piaget (1932), Kohlberg (1969), and others (Damon, 1977; Leahy, 1981a; Sarbin, 1954; Selman, 1980) view role taking as an important factor underlying social development. For Piaget the transition to autonomous morality and for Kohlberg the transition to conventional morality are characterized by concern for the opinions of others. Thus, the adolescent's emphasis on social competence (especially, social cognition) as a factor underlying intelligence is reflective of these concerns. According to the adolescent, intelligence can be increased by changing one's associations with peers. In fact, low intelligence is attributed at times to the belief that by associating with unintelligent people you become unintelligent.

This emphasis on social interaction and adapting to the perspectives of others is a central issue in cognitive-developmental theory of social development. Piaget (1970) claims that development is marked by the construction of shared meaning, symbolization, and coordination of perspectives. He refers to this as *socialization of thought,* suggesting that the older child's thinking is no longer limited to specific individual actions or egocentric perspectives: Thinking becomes "socialized" in that thinking develops through dialogues with others in which symbols come to have a meaning shared with others, in which one's views may be checked with others, and in which individual interests are considered within the context of the interests of the group.

What implications does this broad theoretical metaphor have for our understanding of conceptions of intelligence? We suggest that two possibilities might be relevant. First, intelligence is viewed by the older child as a reflection of thinking rather than doing. Thinking has as its object the perception and interpretation of the nature of reality. Such a conception of intelligence places considerable emphasis on the validity of such thoughts—that is, the view that different thoughts are invalid or inferior thoughts. It is at this stage that our subjects emphasize social comparison or test performance to evaluate the nature of intelligence. This is also the age period that Coie and Pennington (1976) found that children and adolescents mention distorted perspectives as a criterion for defining deviance.

The second factor is that intelligence comes to signify the ability of the individual to form a cohesive bond with group members—that is, intelligence describes the reification of the group's attractiveness. Thus, individuals who achieve the goal of socialized thought may be described as "socially competent" as intelligence comes to be equated with reputation. Furthermore, because lack of intelligence is viewed as the failure to form a bond with the group, enhancement of intelligence is urged by emotional support and changing peer associations.

FROM BEHAVIORAL TO PSYCHOLOGICAL QUALITIES

The younger child is more likely than the older child to define intelligence in terms of observable behaviors, such as knowing acts ("how to tie your shoes") and specific abilities ("reading"). Similarly, many references to obedience and attendance at school entail peripheral or behavioral descriptions ("do what the teacher tells you" or "go to school"). As these behavioral conceptions decline in frequency, references to inferred qualities increase at ages 10 and 16. These include references to traits and motivations and an increasing emphasis on emotional support as a means of increasing intelligence.

What accounts for this emergence of psychological conceptions? Here we admittedly shift to speculative ground to argue that the cognitive level of the child, the increase in peer interaction, and the cultural prototypes of intelligence contribute to these psychological conceptions. The development of psychological conceptions may be related to the development of the cognitive ability to decenter—that is, to refocus from what is perceptually salient to other covert or imagined possibilities of a stimulus. The focus on behavioral qualities suggests that the young child is centrated on the perceptual field. Decentration also involves the ability to refocus to another dimension—for example, the ability to take the perspective of others (Feffer, 1970) or to engage in self-reflection (Selman, 1980). These qualities of decentration may underlie the increasing concern of adolescents for social competence or social interaction in their conceptions of intelligence. (We shall return to this issue shortly.) Decentration is also reflected in the emphasis by older children and adolescents on the metacognitive qualities of intelligence, such as the specific intellectual skills underlying intelligence (e.g., mathematical or verbal reasoning) or the problem solving (or self-regulation) involved in intelligence. These metacognitive qualities suggest that the older child or adolescent may be able to refocus to another perspective outside the self and thereby reflect on the strategies of intellectual skill. The finding that psychological conceptions became more frequent during later childhood and adolescence supports other research on the development of conceptions of personality (Barenboim, 1981), social classes (Leahy, 1981b), and deviance (Coie & Pennington, 1976). These developmental trends argue for a common cognitive structure underlying social cognitive development.

DEVELOPMENT OF COMPARISONS OF INTELLIGENCE

We have proposed that the development of concrete operational thought will be reflected in the ability of the older child to find a basis of similarity of different groups and to compare individuals on the basis of test performance. The findings confirm these developmental expectations. In previous studies of children's conceptions of inequality, Leahy (1981b; Leahy & Shirk, in press) found that young children believe that social classes or genders have nothing in common. With increasing age and increasing classificatory flexibility, children recognize that groups have at least peripheral qualities in common (e.g., both are human). We suggest that conceptions of different groups first begin as stereotypical, but with increasing developmental level, the child becomes less stereotypical.

In his classic description of prejudice, Allport (1954) described the learning of racial prejudice as following different stages. Allport indicates that after the acquisition of a stereotype of *total rejection* (such that the child believes that the out-group is entirely characterized by negative qualities), there is *differentiation*, such that the stereotype allows for individual differences within the out-group. Although our findings are not precisely related to prejudice, they do indicate some empirical (and theoretical) support for Allport's observations, suggesting increasing differentiation with age in conceptions of stereotyped groups.

A second developmental change in comparisons is concerned with age changes in reference to test performance. We have proposed that test performance is a criterion for social comparison among children and that social comparison skill may entail decentration and seriation ability. Although we did not assess these nonsocial cognitive abilities, the findings of this study are supportive of the cognitive-developmental perspective. An interesting quality of some of the interviews of the older children and adolescents is their recognition that poor performance on a test may result in embarrassment and negative self-evaluations. This finding is consistent with our view that conceptions of intelligence may involve the ability to view intellectual skill within a social context of evaluating peers and adults.

FROM EXTERNAL SANCTIONS TO
INTERNAL CONTROL

Finally, the data from this study indicate that during adolescence there is an increasing emphasis on self-direction in intelligence. In fact, we might extend our concept of internal control to include motivation, study, and, of course, self-direction (plans and goals). The younger child's unilateral respect for adults is reflected in his or her belief that intelligence is under the control of the external sanctions typified by parental or school authority. Not all references to internal control are metacognitive in the sense that they refer to strictly cognitive processes. However, the development of these conceptions does suggest that the adolescent is considerably more aware of the manner by which a person intentionally controls his or her behavior to conform to the demands of the task.

ROLE THEORY AND INTELLIGENCE

Our proposal is that the developmental sequence is characterized by qualitative changes in the nature of social norms defining desirable behavior. For example, the younger child defines intellectual competence in terms of obedience, whereas the adolescent defines competence in terms of psychological qualities and social competence. These "higher" level conceptions are partly the consequence of the increased ability to recognize the internal states or perspectives of others, but they also reflect a change in the conception of rules.

Sociological theory of role (Sarbin, 1954) stresses three meanings of *roles*. These include continuity in behavior, expectation of others about the self, and the awareness of rules that guide behavior. Roles may also be described in terms of the inequality of power within relationships—for example, unilateral respect differs from mutuality with peers in the belief that individuals in the authoritarian relationship of unilateral respect may not make equal claims on one another. We propose that the development of conceptions of intelligence reflects (*a*) a shift in the power dimension of desired roles; and (*b*) an acquisition of the understanding of roles as behavior expected by others (social competence) and as rule following (self-regulation). The development of conceptions of intelligence is analogous to this wider meaning of role taking.

Power and equality

As the child's social interactions expand beyond the familial authority of the home, valued behavior (i.e., rewarded behavior) begins to encompass behavior that is independent of parental sanctions or guidelines. This individuation from the parent–child dyad results in an increasing emphasis on self-direction and self-control in that the self cannot rely entirely on the guidance of individuals with superior authority. The rule regulating child–adult relations at age 6 is externally imposed—that is, it is a *morality of constraint*. Young children are more likely than older children to value behavior conforming to adult commands or rewards (Leahy, 1979), suggesting that competence is viewed in terms of the consistency in behavior that is regulated by externally imposed sanctions. At this early level, it is stressed, behavioral not intentional consistency is the measure of competence. It is only at the later stage of psychological conceptions that intentional consistency (i.e., motivation) becomes an important factor defining competence. This is because behavioral consistency is supplemented by a new awareness of roles as self-guiding rules of behavior.

Acquisition of role concepts

We propose that between childhood and adolescence there is a shift from defining roles in terms of power orientation and behavioral consistencies to the recognition of roles as the expectations of others or the rule-following behavior of the individual. At the level of psychological conceptions the individual believes that intelligence reflects traits and motivation and the ability to engage in self-direction. We view these as components of rule following in that they refer to the individual's ability to direct his or her behavior by use of plans (i.e., self-direction) and the intention and capacity to perform (i.e., traits and motivation). These psychological conceptions are different from conceptions referring to peripheral–obedient aspects of intelligence in that psychological conceptions refer to *internal* determinants of intelligence, whereas peripheral–obedient conceptions stress the *external* or behavioral manifestations that are viewed as determined by or in conformity with the rules established by authority (e.g., teachers).

The second dimension of shift in role conceptions is the recognition that roles involve the expectations of others. Thus, during adolescence there is an increasing emphasis on social competence, association with others, and emotional support. Implicit in these conceptions of intelligence is the belief that the nature of intelligence (or competence more broadly defined) is found in the ability to interact effectively with others—that is, to be understood and respected by peers.

It is interesting to note that the development of conceptions of psychological deviance also involves a similar set of conceptions of role conformity (Coie & Pennington, 1976). Younger children emphasize behavioral infractions of rules, especially aggression, that presumably violate the sanctions imposed by adults. Adolescents, on the other hand, while mentioning behavioral rule infractions, also mention social isolation and distorted perspectives. We view these last two constructs as reflective of social interactionist and psychological conceptions, respectively. As suggested by the foregoing discussion, social isolation involves unresponsiveness to or lack of knowledge of the expectations of others, whereas distorted perspectives involves the inability to follow the rules of epistemology—that is, the rejection of the rules of perceiving a real world.

Lack of intelligence and roles

What conceptions of education are implied by the role conceptions described here? Our data on explanations of intelligence and conceptions of what schools, parents, or the self might do are relevant to this issue. We shall attempt to evaluate our findings within the framework of the role conceptions we have outlined. Our purpose is to describe whatever consistencies in logic are reflected by these conceptions.

The view that roles are defined by behavioral consistency and by power differences places little emphasis on the idea that nonconformity to a role is beyond the capability of the individual. The question of capacity, intention, motivation, or extenuating circumstances does not arise for the individual focused on behavior or power. Either the person engages in the subordinating behavior, or the person does not. At this level, conformity to the role can be enhanced either by increasing the salience of power or by simply practicing the desired behavior—that is, by acting in an appropriate manner. This is similar to the conceptions of the younger children in our study, who emphasize obedience, attendance at school or classes, and punishment as the primary means of education.

The view that roles are defined by the person's understanding of and compliance with rule following places considerable emphasis on the lack of capability of the unintelligent person. According to this view, lack of intelligence or deviance from a role is seen as reflective of the psychological qualities of the person: Some of these are within the control of the individual (e.g., effort, studying), whereas others are not (e.g., inherited differences, traits, general intelligence). The person who lacks motivation is seen as someone who chooses not to follow rules and, therefore, may be seen as morally reprehensible by these children. The enhancement of motivation and self-direction reflect the view that changes in the intentional and capacity aspects of rule following are expected to be effective in changing intelligence.

Related to these psychological conceptions of rule following is the view that roles are defined by the expectations of others. For the subjects ascribing to this view, inability to conform to a desired role reflects not only the lack of capacity and motivation of the individual but also the lack of supportive interactions with others. At this level, expectations of others may be seen as a determining factor for intellectual differences. Consequently, changing these expectations (stigmas?) to encouragement, understanding, special tutoring, or even association would be expected to alter the psychological qualities of the individual. At this level, "responsibility" for lack of intelligence is divided between the individual, who may lack motivation, and the social environment, which may be viewed as unsupportive.

To summarize our view on role taking and intelligence, we propose that the development of conceptions of intelligence entails developmental changes in conceptions of roles. First, the younger child defines roles as behavioral conformity to a power-assertive adult socializing agent. This is the level of unilateral respect. Second, role taking emerges in conceptions of intelligence at age 11 when emphasis is placed on the intentional qualities of people—that is, motivation. These psychological conceptions involve reference to the capacity and willingness of a person to perform the role of "being intelligent." Comparisons among people on the basis of test performance, motivation, or capacity are central at this level. Third, during adolescence the role-taking quality of intelligence is articulated as the ability of the person to anticipate the expectations and needs of others and to plan behavior. The transition between the first level and the last two levels is similar to the transitions in moral judgment described by Piaget and Kohlberg—that is, from heteronomous to autonomous morality or from preconventional to conventional morality.

EDUCATION AND SOCIAL INTERACTIONS

How do these developmental conceptions of intelligence affect the development of the child? In a discussion of effectance motivation, Harter (1976) suggests that competence may entail a number of components (e.g., physical, cognitive, social) and that one's self-esteem may depend not only on the perceived competence in a particular skill area but also on the importance of that skill during a particular period of development and the value placed on it by an individual or social group. The conceptions of intelligence that we have postulated, which may in a sense be viewed as conceptions of competence, provide a basis to delineate the skills emphasized by children at various developmental levels. The skills or traits favored at a particular developmental level thus become the important indexes of overall competence and ultimately of self-esteem.

Aside from the focus on reading, the younger child's emphasis on obedience to adult authority, along with the absence of any self-directed functioning, highlights the adult impact on individual views of intelligence at this age. Harter (1976) has noted that younger children are more sensitive to praise and approval from adults than are older children. For example, younger children evaluate their performance and expectancy of future success, not on objective indicators of present success, but rather on the social feedback given. Older children, by contrast, utilize both objective comparisons and social reinforcement from adults as well as peers. The adult orientation of the younger child requires that educators be fully aware of their important roles as feedback agents and behavioral commentators. A judgment of conduct may imply a judgment of ability (i.e., intelligence) in the relatively undifferentiated schemes of the Level I child.

As has been noted earlier, in older children, psychological and social interactionist conceptions of intelligence emerge (Levels II, III). The skills or traits emphasized at Level II are test performance ability and motivation and effort. Although children at this age distinguish outcome (test performance) from intentionality (motivation), they appear to use one to infer the other (e.g., low test performance implies low motivation), thereby yielding the moral evaluations that predominate at this stage. The child's understanding of motivation and effort, however, can be utilized in the classroom to emphasize the value of the learning process, while distinguishing it from product or outcome. The implication, then, is that children may profit from reinforcement of mastery attempts as well as from reinforcement of mastery achievements (Harter, 1976).

The social interactionist conceptions of adolescence are reflective of conventional level moral judgments (focus on conformity and peer mutuality), as well as an increasingly differentiated concept of intelligence. The skills emphasized during this period are social rather than strictly academic; the value placed on peer conformity implies that the specific skills emphasized in a particular group may depend on the values of that subgroup. In some cases, intellectual excellence may thus represent a point of conflict in groups that devalue academic achievement. We can see how at this age level the competence issues become much more individualized and even idiosyncratic. The possibilities with regard to valued, prescriptive behavior are more certain where obedience to adult authority is central; with the transition from adult constraint to peer conformity, the possibilities of valued behavior increase and become less clear.

As we have noted, the emphasis on peer conformity in Level III conceptions of intelligence alerts us to the fact that different skills may serve as indexes of competence (intelligence) and self-esteem, according to the values of the peer group. However, although emphasized content may vary across groups, the general transition from adult constraint to peer conformity suggests some educational implications. It may be, for example, that the educational role may be profitably shifted from adults to peers during this period. Alternatively, the emphasis on peer mutuality suggests that educational techniques may be most effective when they involve the student as a participant in the learning process, rather than as a mere recipient of information. Such an approach is in accord with the emphasis at this stage on mutual interchange and construction, rather than on submissive, passive intake.

In addition to paralleling moral development, the adolescent's emphasis on social competence, association with others, and self-directed functioning, as well as academic skill, implies a differentiation that rejects a narrow definition of intelligence (often termed *academic intelligence*) and asserts that adaptation to a wider environment requires attention to other important life skills. Thus, we argue that academic intelligence be distinguished from intelligence in general. Academic intelligence involves solving puzzles in an unemotional manner, using higher-order abstract skills, and leaving all motives aside except finding the correct answer. By contrast, a fuller view of intelligence takes into account the individual in his or her life situation, responding appropriately in reference to many motives and goals, some of which may be intrapersonal or interpersonal. It would appear that the adolescent conception of intelligence, as noted in this study, more closely corresponds to this latter view.

In terms of education, the implication of such a view is that, for these students, personal and social development are considered as important as academic development in contributing to adaptive intelligent behavior. Therefore, it would seem profitable that the goals and policies of an educational institution be relevant to these areas so that the nature of intervention matches the expectations and the concerns of the student. Specifically, this would involve addressing social competence as well as academic realms of functioning.

In addition to addressing the social component of intelligent behavior, we suggest that educators promote the further differentiation of conceptions of intelligence, so that distinct components would each be valued in its own right. Such a strategy would be directed toward fostering the proliferation of potential areas of mastery, which would provide a wider range of viable opportunities to a wider range of students. At present, for example, there appear to be fewer highly visible developmental markers of success for right-hemispheric skills (i.e., visual–spatial, intuitive, creative skills) than for verbal analytic abilities. This is no doubt due to the pervasive influence of language in the organization of culture, the requirements inherent in academic intelligence (e.g., convergent rather than divergent thinking), and the value placed on analytic academic intelligence in our culture. However, even if educators might follow such a suggestion and promote a truly differentiated view of intelligence, the fact remains that rich diversity cannot prevail while certain components of intelligence are differentially rewarded within the culture.

In the present educational context of the United States, it is clear that certain components of intelligence constitute the "major amplifying tools" of the culture. These tools give an individual control of resources, status, and power within a culture. This notion has been discussed by Cole and Bruner (1971), who suggest that verbal skills are important "cultural amplifiers." The dilemma for education is that it must promote in individuals the development of those amplifiers needed in the present society; however, in doing so, it may be constrained from functioning as an agent of change and promoting the emergence of other types of amplifiers. This may occur because dominant standards proclaim certain skills and behavior as the yardstick of success (Cole & Bruner, 1971). We agree with Cole and Bruner, who suggest that it is difficult to actually know, on the basis of our present knowledge of society, which cognitive skills and what kinds of situations are necessary to control and utilize resources. Obviously, as has been noted, verbal intelligence is important. However, the problem is undoubtedly more complex. We would contend, therefore, that the situations and skills of importance will derive from a much more differentiated conception of intelligence than the narrow view of academic intelligence promoted in education today.

In sum, we suggest that if education is to provide individuals with the full range of competencies that underlie performance and with access to the total range of resources within our culture, it may have to review and extend its mandate more vigorously. As indicated from the findings of this study, in doing so it would be following the adolescent's own lead.

SUMMARY AND CONCLUSIONS

We have proposed that the development of conceptions of intelligence reflects the development of moral judgment, concrete operations, and internal control of behavior. Our findings largely confirm the predictions derived from cognitive-developmental theory. First, the development of autonomous or conventional moral reasoning is reflected in several changes in conceptions of intelligence: Older subjects are less likely than younger subjects to emphasize obedience and punishment of unintelligent people and more likely to emphasize social competence and peer support. Second, the development of concrete operational thought is reflected in the increasing awareness with age of the internal states of people (e.g., traits and motivation), or increasing ability to find similarities between intelligent and unintelligent people, and an increasing tendency to compare the performances of people using test criteria. We view these changes as reflective of an increased ability to decenter, reclassify stimuli, and engage in seriation of social stimuli. Third, increased recognition of internal control of behavior is reflected in the greater emphasis by adolescents on self-direction (e.g., problem solving, setting goals, or planning) as a factor related to intelligence.

Each of these developmental trends is consistent with Piaget's and Kohlberg's theories of development. We have attempted to indicate how cognitive-developmental theory may be related to traditional role theory (Sarbin, 1954) and how the development of conceptions of intelligence may reflect changes in the conception of roles. In particular, we have argued that two general dimensions of changes in role conceptions are reflected in these data. First, the movement from power to equality conceptions of roles is indicated by the decrease with age in reference to obedience and the increase in reference to social conceptions and social support. Second, we have indicated that roles involve three qualities— behavioral consistency, reciprocity of expectations, and rule following. The conceptions of intelligence of the younger children reflect behavioral consistency (e.g., reading, actions, obedience), whereas the conceptions of the older children and adolescents reflect reciprocity of perspectives (e.g., social competence and social support) and rule following (e.g., self-direction). We speculate that these changes in conceptions may reflect the increasing emphasis on peer interaction as age increases with the opportunity to engage in conflicting opinions and to coconstruct rules for interaction.

Although we believe that our data provide support for the cognitive-developmental model, it is clear that many of the processes that we argue account for these age trends are not clearly demonstrated by our data. Many of these inferences may stand (and eventually fall) on tenuous speculative ground. However, the value of this cognitive-developmental model is that it links this area of research with a wide area of social cognitive data and helps provide some order to a complex set of data. In the absence of alternative theoretical models for the study of conceptions of intelligence, we suggest that future research in this area might contribute to our understanding of developmental processes by indicating the theoretical relevance of age trends rather than by simply indicating norms for different age groups.

REFERENCE NOTES

1. Shirk, S. R., & Leahy, R. L. *The development of trait conceptions in children: Use of covariation principles and knowledge of sex-trait stereotypes.* Unpublished manuscript, 1983. (Available from Department of Psychiatry, University of Pennsylvania, Phila., PA.)
2. Leahy, R. L. *The development of conceptions of intelligence.* Paper presented at International Society for the Study of Behavioral Development, Toronto, August 1981.
3. Leahy, R. L., & Hunt, T. *The development of explanations of intelligence.* Paper presented at Southeastern Conference on Human Development, Baltimore, April 1982.

REFERENCES

Achenbach, T., & Zigler, E. Social competence and self-image disparity in psychiatric and nonpsychiatric patients. *Journal of Abnormal and Social Psychology,* 1963, *67,* 197–205.

Achenbach, T., & Zigler, E. Cue-learning and problem-learning strategies in normal and retarded children. *Child Development,* 1968, *3,* 827–848.

Allport, G. W. *Personality: A psychological interpretation.* New York: Holt, 1954.

Barenboim, C. The development of person perception of childhood and adolescence: From behavioral comparisons to psychological constructs to psychological comparisons. *Child Development,* 1981, *52,* 129–144.

Cannell, C. F., & Kahn, R. L. Interviewing. In G. Lindzey & E. Aronson (Eds.), *The Handbook of Social Psychology* (Vol. 2). Reading, Mass.: Addison-Wesley, 1968.

Chandler, M., & Greenspan, S. Ersatz egocentrism: A reply to H. Borke. *Developmental Psychology*, 1972, *7*, 104–106.

Coie, J. D., & Pennington, B. F. Children's perception of deviance and disorder. *Child Development*, 1976, *47*, 407–413.

Cole, M., & Bruner, J. Cultural differences and inferences about psychological processes. *American Psychologist*, 1971, *26*, 867–876.

Damon, W. *The social world of the child.* San Francisco: Jossey-Bass, 1977.

Feffer, M. A developmental analysis of interpersonal behavior. *Psychological Review*, 1970, *77*, 197–214.

Festinger, L. Informal social communication. *Psychological Review*, 1950, *57*, 271–282.

Festinger, L. A theory of social comparison processes. *Human Relations*, 1954, *7*, 117–140.

Freud, S. *New introductory lectures on psychoanalysis.* New York: Norton, 1965. (Originally published, 1933.)

Glick, M., & Zigler, E. Self-image: A cognitive-developmental approach. In R. L. Leahy (Ed.), *The development of the self.* New York: Academic Press, forthcoming.

Harter, S. Effectance motivation reconsidered: Toward a developmental model. *Human Development*, 1976, *21*, 34–64.

Katz, P., & Zigler, E. Self-image disparity: A developmental approach. *Journal of Personality and Social Psychology*, 1967, *5*, 186–195.

Kohlberg, L. Stage and sequence: The cognitive-developmental approach to socialization. In D. A. Goslin (Ed.), *Handbook of socialization: Theory and research.* New York: Rand-McNally, 1969.

Kohlberg, L. The study of moral development. In T. Lickona (Ed.), *Moral development and behavior.* New York: Holt, 1976.

Leahy, R. L. The development of conceptions of prosocial behavior: Information affecting rewards given for altruism and kindness. *Developmental Psychology*, 1979, *15*, 34–37.

Leahy, R. L. Parental practices and the development of moral judgment and self-image disparity during adolescence. *Developmental Psychology*, 1981, *17*, 580–594. (a)

Leahy, R. L. The development of the conception of economic inequality. I. Descriptions and comparisons of rich and poor people. *Child Development*, 1981, *52*, 523–532. (b)

Leahy, R. L. The development of the conception of economic inequality. II. Explanations, justifications, and conceptions of social mobility and social change. *Developmental Psychology*, 1983, *19*, 111–125.

Leahy, R. L. The development of the self: Conclusions. In R. L. Leahy (Ed.), *The development of the self.* New York: Academic Press, forthcoming.

Leahy, R. L., & Eiter, M. Moral judgment and the development of real and ideal self-image during adolescence and young adulthood. *Developmental Psychology*, 1980, *16*, 362–370.

Leahy, R. L., & Shirk, S. The development of classificatory skills and sex-trait stereotypes in children. *Sex Roles*, in press.

Liben, L. S. Piagetian investigations of the development of memory. In R. V. Kail & J. W. Hagan (Eds.), *Memory in cognitive development.* Hillsdale, N.J.: Erlbaum, 1976.

Livesley, W., & Bromley, D. *Person perception in childhood and adolescence.* London: Wiley, 1973.

Luria, A. *The role of speech in the regulation of normal and abnormal behaviors.* New York: Liveright, 1961.

Maccoby, E., & Maccoby, N. The interview: A tool of social science. In G. Lindzey (Ed.), *The handbook of social psychology* (Vol. 1). Reading, Mass.: Addison-Wesley, 1954.

Mead, G. H. *Mind, self and society.* Chicago: Univ. of Chicago Press, 1934.

Meichenbaum, D. *Cognitive-behavior modification.* New York: Plenum, 1977.

Meichenbaum, D., & Asarnow, J. Cognitive-behavioral modification and metacognitive development: Implications for the classroom. In P. Kendall & S. D. Hollon (Eds.), *Cognitive-behavioral interventions: Theory, research, and procedures.* New York: Academic Press, 1979.

Peevers, B. H., & Secord, P. F. Developmental changes in attribution of descriptive concepts to persons. *Journal of Personality and Social Psychology,* 1973, *27,* 120–128.

Piaget, J. *The moral judgment of the child.* London: Kegan Paul, 1932.

Piaget, J. Piaget's theory. In P. H. Mussen (Ed.), *Carmichael's manual of child psychology* (3rd ed., Vol. 1). New York: Wiley, 1970.

Ruble, D. N., Feldman, N. S., & Boggiano, A. K. Social comparison between young children in achievement situations. *Developmental Psychology,* 1976, *12,* 192–197.

Ruble, D. N., Parsons, J. E., & Ross, J. Self-evaluative response of children in an achievement setting. *Child Development,* 1976, *47,* 990–997.

Sarbin, T. R. Role theory. In G. Lindzey (Ed.), *Handbook of social psychology* (Vol. 1). Reading, Mass.: Addison-Wesley, 1954.

Selman, R. L. Toward a structural-developmental analysis of interpersonal relationship concepts: Research with normal and disturbed preadolescent boys. *Tenth Annual Minnesota Symposium on Child Psychology.* Minneapolis: Univ. of Minnesota Press, 1976.

Selman, R. L. *The growth of interpersonal understanding.* New York: Academic Press, 1980.

Sternberg, R. J., Conway, B. E., Ketron, J. L., & Bernstein, M. People's conceptions of intelligence. *Journal of Personality and Social Psychology,* 1981, *41,* 37–55.

Vygotsky, L. S. *Mind in society.* Cambridge, Mass.: Harvard Univ. Press, 1978.

Walker, L., & Richards, B. S. Stimulating transitions in moral reasoning as a function of stage of cognitive development. *Developmental Psychology,* 1979, *15,* 95–103.

Williams, J., Bennett, S., & Best, D. Awareness and expression of sex stereotypes in young children. *Developmental Psychology,* 1975, *11,* 635–642.

Yando, S., Seitz, V., & Zigler, E. *Imitation: A developmental perspective.* Hillsdale, N.J.: Erlbaum, 1978.

Youniss, J. The nature of social cognition: A conceptual discussion of cognition. In H. McGurk (Ed.), *Issues in childhood social development.* London: Methuen, 1979.

Yussen, S. R., & Kane, P. Children's concept of intelligence. In S. R. Yussen (Ed.), *The growth of insight in children.* New York: Academic Press, forthcoming.

6 / Understanding differences within friendship[1]

JAMES YOUNISS

How do children come to accept themselves realistically, yet with respect? And how do children come to accept other persons with respect when they are seen realistically? Answers to these questions seem central to the study of individual differences insofar as that topic rests on the prior issue of individuation. Any person can be understood as an array of characteristics, some of which are strengths and are likable, others of which are weaknesses and may not be so likable. In any society, personal characteristics are associated with degrees of value and vary in their acceptability. It would seem easy to accept strong points that are highly valued whether they were claimed as one's own or respected in another. It may be more difficult, however, to claim or respect weaknesses and easier, when confronted with them, to react with such defenses as denial, rejection, or distortion. Unfortunately, defenses do not necessarily make these characteristics go away and thus, in the long run, work to the detriment of psychological adjustment.

The question of realism pertains to seeing oneself or others fully with their good and not so good points. If it were known how persons come to accept the full individual and how adjustments are made to full acceptance, we would have a better understanding of ways individual differences are recognized and dealt with. The present chapter offers an

[1]This work was supported in part by a grant from the W. T. Grant Foundation.

161

approach to the study of these issues from the point of view of children's friendships. The general thesis is that friendship provides a context for individuation that other relationships experienced during childhood do not. Because of its structural basis in reciprocity, friendship offers unique opportunities both to check the defenses of self-reflection and to encourage mutual respect grounded upon versions of self and others.

The present approach is based on two sources. One is the writings of H. S. Sullivan (1953), and the other is a set of data in which children gave accounts of their participation in friendships (Volpe, 1981; Youniss, 1980; Youniss & Volpe, 1978). Together they provide an interesting analysis of how children come to accept their whole selves, the good and not so good, and how children come to deal realistically with others in a continuing attitude of respect.

SULLIVAN'S THEORY

Although textbooks regularly cite Sullivan as representing "neo" or "social" psychoanalytic thinking, his work is not well known and has not been integrated into contemporary developmental theories. This omission is due in part to his posture toward the study of the individual. For Sullivan, the individual is understandable only from the perspective of the relationships in which the individual has membership. He goes so far as to suggest that development is not of the individual per se so much as "of relations and relational possibilities." As Sampson (1977) has noted, this starting point is obtuse to a psychology that is predicated on the irreducible unit of the individual as an entity. In such a psychology, self and self-interest need no supporting definition. For Sullivan, however, the fundamental unit is relationship, and through it, one sees clearly the self of relationship and the self whose interests are socially as much as individually oriented (Youniss, 1980).

Sullivan was concerned with the problem of psychiatric health and was aware of the prevailing notion that health stemmed from adjustment or balance within the individual's intrapsychic composition. He saw a weakness in psychoanalysis, where the means to health was based on the individual's powers of self-reflection. For example, persons were described as using self-reflective reasoning to judge their experiences and put them into sensible order. This was true of people in everyday settings as well as of individuals who presented themselves for formal, therapeutic analysis. Sullivan doubted the means, since he believed that self-reflection entailed the continuing risk of subjective error and illusion. He proposed that the way out of such traps was to seek and gain validation outside of the self. Therefore, he argued, the self's thoughts and feelings would have to be checked socially by being reflected in others who then would reject or verify them.

This led Sullivan to construe the individual's development within the context of social relations. This radical step put Sullivan with Mead in proposing that the self was a *social construction*, a product of interpersonal interactions. It further drove Sullivan to review relationships in which children lived and to reassess the structure of these relationships and the functions to which they gave rise. If his definition of relationship as the irreducible unit of analysis did not keep him out of the mainstream, then his appraisal of relational structures did. At a time when developmental theorists assumed en masse that the self or personality was shaped in the first years of life through the child's experiences with parents, Sullivan (1953) proposed:

> All of you who have children are sure that your children love you; when you say that you are expressing a pleasant illusion. If you will look closely at one of your children when he finally finds a chum—somewhere between eight-and-a-half and ten years—you will discover something very different in the relationship, namely, that your child begins to develop a real sensitivity to what matters to another person . . . not . . . "What should I do to get what I want" but instead "what should I do to contribute to the happiness or to support the prestige and feeling of worthwhileness of my chum" [p. 245].

Such quotations still seem unnecessarily contentious today. Although Sullivan's motives cannot be addressed, it is clear that his general position on relationship was coherent with a definite epistemological viewpoint (Youniss, 1980). The inherent fallibility of self-reflection forced Sullivan to situate the person in relationships where there was hope for objectivity. Fortunately, this epistemological position is no longer strange and without elaborate support. The self of relationship of whom Sullivan spoke is kin to the *self in communicative relations* whom one finds in a host of contemporary theories (e.g., Berger & Luckman, 1967; Habermas, 1975; Macmurray, 1961; Piaget, 1932, 1970; Ricoeur, 1978; Youniss, 1978, 1980). At least for these theorists, the self constructed through social means must face its assets and deficits directly in the arena of interpersonal interactions. In this context, the self either can or cannot meet the demands of reciprocity. While this does not guarantee honest self-appraisal, this form of reality testing provides the self with direct empirical evidence about its capabilities. The self need not accept the evidence, but failure to do so risks rejection by others whose participation forms part of the evidence. The fundamental role of the other person thus enhances the possibility of realism in a way that the self of private self-reflection cannot.

Working mainly with observations from psychiatric interviews, Sullivan (1953) suggested that children would be best understood through a differentiation between two types of relationships: with parents and with friends. He recognized the importance of the relationship with parents and caretakers and posited its primacy in getting development started. For Sullivan, this relationship served to help children realize that they were not isolated, self-sufficient individuals who had to invent reality on their own from point zero. Sullivan describes typical parents as quite ready to assist children in their task; they provide information, rules, and pictures of reality in terms designed to short-circuit what would otherwise be tedious trial-and-error learning (p. 153). The arrangement can be seen as a fit between needs (pp. 172–177). Children seek structure and parents want their offspring to be acceptable members of society. The result is that children turn to parents and work through them to achieve their goals.

In this analysis, Sullivan is in line with the general thinking of other developmental theorists. However, he consciously deviates from others in taking the further step of seeing the parent–child relationship as restricted in how far it carries the child forward in development. He contends that the relationship has a basic weakness because parents cannot clearly communicate their interpretation of reality to children and children cannot fully comprehend parents' interpretations (pp. 206–207). The communication process is faulty on several scores, including huge disparities in background experience as well as differences between parents' long-term goals and children's immediate needs. Sullivan admits that communication works to the extent that children understand standards set by parents and supported by overt acts of approval and disapproval. But underneath this seeming meeting of the minds, Sullivan sees parents and children each going in separate directions, effectively building different versions of reality.

Sullivan suggests that the problem lies in the small hand children take in actually setting standards (pp. 161–164). He agrees that parents may want to communicate the rationale behind standards and that they do in fact listen to children's side of them. But ultimately, communication remains *unilateral* in its direction, for to be otherwise, parents would have to be willing to negotiate seriously with children and honestly seek fresh compromise solutions through discourse with them. Sullivan doubts that adults can do this, even though they can modulate their views in light of children's ideas. The result is, then, that children do not fully grasp standards that they have not helped to construct and have not been able to tie specifically to experience. As a consequence, children end up adapting themselves to parental views and building a self shaped according to the question: What do adults ask of me? or What must I do to get what I want (p. 245)?

It is obvious that this question is not conducive to an unbiased realization of self. When adults hold the power to resources that children seek and have unilateral rights to approval (pp. 230–231), children are liable to shape themselves accordingly. Approved sides of the self are likely to be claimed in exaggerated fashion and nonapproved sides may be denied or rejected. It is here that Sullivan introduces a second form of communication that, in his mind, serves to remedy these weaknesses. This form begins in children's naive relationships with peers, who are equals from the point of view of the shared capacity for reciprocal contributions to interactions. It takes on new qualities and becomes an effective form when peer relations in general are differentiated into dyadic relations between chums or friends.

"Nothing remotely like that has happened before [p. 245]," says Sullivan, emphasizing that friends have joined in a novel enterprise of constructing reality together. What he means is that standards of acceptance are no longer prescriptions to be adopted but can be questioned, analyzed, and coconstructed by communicating partners. Specifically, any child is allowed to offer an interpretation that, by the rule of reciprocity, the other child must entertain. When taken literally, the means toward verification of standards becomes communicative procedures of discussion, negotiation, and compromise. The result is a novel kind of product: standards that are determined through *consensual validation* (p. 246). Instead of having reality come in already established packages, to which children must accede, children discover that their own views of reality are worthy of consideration and can be *verified* through the rules of discourse.

For Sullivan, friendship provides a whole new system for self-appraisal. The demands of reciprocity draw children out to take respective sides in communicative procedures. Personal thoughts and feelings are no longer prejudged but become parts to be inserted in the normal give-and-take that leads to consensus. Since neither friend has unilateral rights to control the evolving course of events, both friends can operate under the safeguard of at least having a hearing. The result is exposure of self by way of what it can and cannot contribute, what its interests really are, and how sensitive it can be toward other selves. In this context, the self as a whole becomes worthy of respect, even with its weaknesses and deficits. Its talents become understood as social responsibilities (p. 255), and its lack of talents becomes reciprocal to another's gifts. Consequently, friendship engenders mutual respect between persons who depend on one another, not as self-sufficient individuals, but as members of a relationship in which each can contribute to the other "in the pursuit of increasingly identical—that is, more and more nearly mutual—satisfactions [p. 246]." And thus, the self turns from the question: "What should I do to get what I want?" to the cooperative relationship where the issue is: "What should I do to contribute to the happiness or to support the prestige and feeling of worth-whileness of my chum [p. 245]?"

CHILDREN'S VIEWS OF FRIENDSHIP

Several investigators have begun to ask about children's conceptions of friendship (e.g., Bigelow, 1977; Bigelow & La Gaipa, 1975; La Gaipa, 1979; Selman & Jaquette, 1977). This seemingly obvious question lacked significance when friendship was construed simply as another independent variable in some large-scale array of conditions that elicited "pro-" and "antisocial behaviors." What marks the novelty of this work is the belief that friendship is a relationship with its own structure and, therefore, its own demands on behavior as well as requirements for self-management. Assessments of children's concepts of friendship are attempts to gain insight into this structure, functions that might follow from it, and implications for development that differ from those in different relationships.

The present discussion is focused on our own work (Volpe, 1981; Youniss, 1980; Volpe & Youniss, 1978) and centered on those findings that bear most directly on the topic of individual differences. We have now interviewed over 1200 subjects between ages 6 and 14 about their concepts of friendship. The methodology consists primarily of having children provide accounts of interactions between friends when the designated outcome of the exchange is specified. Various goals have been used across studies, including participating in activities that friends enjoy doing together, showing kindness, starting a conflict, resolving a conflict, showing unkindness, starting a friendship, ending a friendship, and so on. Selected results are now offered as illustrations of (*a*) how the self becomes differentiated within friendship; (*b*) how differences between selves are handled within friendship; and (*c*) how mutual respect becomes fundamental to the definition of friendship.

Specification of differences

Throughout the findings, the term *differences* has dual meaning. It refers to the array of characteristics that belong to the differentiated self, and it refers to comparisons of characteristics belonging to two friends. The former pertains to variations *within* and the latter to variations *between* persons. One further clarification is in order. The term *characteristics* is used loosely. It has multiple references in our data, including properties of the individual, such as traits; momentary states within the individual; talents; skills; feelings; thoughts; and values. Some of the characteristics appear to be identical with the individual, whereas others seem to be due to circumstances imposed on the individual.

To which domains do children look in differentiating characteristics within a self or between friends? Our findings show a long but obvious list.

Material resources. Children recognize that they differ from one another in the number of material things they possess. Specific reference was to toys, games, bicycles, books, records, money, and purchasing power for such activities as concerts, sporting events, clothes, and vacations.

Physical health. A number of references were made to physical well-being by way of illness, hospitalization, broken bones, and minor hurts such as would result from accidents mainly incurred while playing games.

School-related skills. Multiple references were made to school performance, with the implication that friends differed according to academic talents. Most references were to school subjects, including mathematics, spelling, and grammatical diagramming. Other instances referred to test taking, study habits, missing school, and liking school.

Special talents. Children also recognized that individuals differed in terms of talents for specialized activities. The predominant area was athletics, which included baseball, basketball, hockey, and soccer. Other areas, such as drama, were also mentioned, as were such generalized talents as running, catching, and physical coordination.

Social skills. Several children focused on the fact that individuals differed by way of social skills. These references were complex insofar as they intersected at times with personality traits. Instances were the ability to make friends, the inability to make friends, being popular or unpopular, being a student in school, speaking a foreign language, being an outcast, being a loner, being friendly or likable, being snobbish, being competitive, being jealous, being trustworthy, being considerate or consoling, being empathic or sympathetic, caring or sacrificing for another, being attentive, respecting others, being ready to help, being a good listener, and being a wise counselor.

Personality traits and states. Only a partial listing of all the items mentioned can be given: "kind," "nice," "responsive," "feels bad," "feels left out," "mean," "takes up for you," "depressed," "understanding," "treats you as an equal," "doesn't look down on you," "comforting," "homesick," "selfish," "pushy," "unkind," "not caring," "hateful," "helpful," "shy," "lonely," "unhappy," "dependable," "approachable," "faithful," and "believable." A subset of traits gave emphasis to intellectual status: "smart," "not smart," "good teacher," and "knows how to explain things."

Differences in context

The foregoing descriptions provide a picture of characteristics that children from 6 to 14 years spontaneously generated in their accounts of interactions between friends. There is face validity insofar as the descriptions pertain to domains that would be of obvious relevance to children. Most of them pertain to school, play and recreation, or interpersonal activities or situations. However, their deeper significance is not ascertainable outside the explicit context in which they were generated. The purpose of this section is to show the specific usage of these descriptions from children's viewpoints.

COMPLEMENTARY STRENGTHS AND WEAKNESSES

One of the clearest uses of differences occurred in response to the instructions when friends were to act in kindness to each other. A definite age-related result was obtained. Children from 6 to 8 years were nearly unanimous in saying that kindness was constituted in a symmetrical exchange of reciprocal acts of sharing and playing. After age 9, answers took a different form. The typical answer is illustrated in the following accounts: "Joe's dog died. John was his best friend. He takes time out to really understand him." And "[One boy] is smart in school and [the other boy] is not smart. One can help the other." This form begins with predication of a difference between friends. One is in a state of need—he's sad because his dog died—or has a traitlike deficit—he's not smart in school. The other is in a better position, such that he is able to improve the lot of the first. In the former example, understanding is offered, whereas in the latter example help is provided by way of teaching.

When children were asked to say what the recipient of kindness might do or say, subjects who used this form completed it as follows. They said, for example, "If he ever needs help, I'll do something for him." And "The one who's smart might not be a good athlete. Maybe he wants to learn to play soccer and the other one can help him." The second half of the form duplicates the earlier half, with one major change: The roles of actor and recipient are reversed. When the roles are viewed in terms of talents and deficits, a central point becomes clear. Children recognize that friends differ according to individual characteristics due to either inherent traits or momentary states. They also recognize that these characteristics may be distributed differently between the friends. The question, then, is how friends act in the face of these facts. The answer is that friends are persons who cooperate to use differences for the sake of mutual benefit. The key to this conclusion may be found in reciprocity that is based directly on the facts of difference. Their coupling results in the realization that anyone's position of advantage is momentary and relative to someone else's disadvantage. The relativity includes the possibility of disadvantage being switched between persons. With reciprocity added, the friend who acts to assist another gains a kind of guarantee of return and the friend who receives assistance realizes that there will come a time when the debt can be repaid (see Gouldner, 1960; Sahlins, 1965).

UNKINDNESS

The preceding data and conclusion gained support from other findings that were obtained in children's accounts of unkind interactions. The key result again pertained to accounts in children older than age 9. As with kindness, children began their accounts with spontaneous predication of a friend in a disadvantageous position or state of need. For example, children said "If they don't understand something in school and you understand . . . ."; or "If he's in trouble . . . ."; or "If a girl is not liked by anyone in class . . . ." In each case, what constituted unkindness was the *omission* of action. That is: ". . . you don't help him. Say you don't have time." ". . . you could help him get out of it. But you don't talk to him. Leave him there." And ". . . you make no effort to let them know you want to be friends."

The logical tie between these and the results on kindness is seen through the concepts of differences and reciprocity. First, differences that place friends in advantageous and disadvantageous positions are simply not attended to. This brings up the meaning of omission, which, of course, cannot constitute unkindness in and of itself. Failure to act could take on the meaning of unkindness only if it pertained to an obligation to act that was not met. It is plausible that the obligation implied by omission is that incurred through reciprocity that refers to past as well as future interactions between the friends.

CONFLICT-INDUCING EPISODES

Results obtained through a probe of conflict-inducing episodes were quite similar to those obtained in accounts of unkindness. State of need was predicated in one friend, and failure to take a remediating action was assigned to the other friend. As with unkindness, acts of omission in the face of need may be construed as violations of a reciprocal obligation. There was a subset of responses in which the differential between friends came out even more clearly. In these instances, differences were stated and then the friend in the better-off position actually took advantage of the other friend. Examples included: "Tease them about something they can't do." "Make fun of others' mistakes . . . ." "She was mean to everyone smaller than her." "We had a new student . . . he talked funny . . . . He was big and he was afraid of the people. We played keep away."

These data fit the results on kindness and unkindness, since they imply that violations of the rules of friendship cause conflict and put a breach in the relationship. They provide a look at the relationship's makeup from the reverse side by indicating rules through their violation. What these results specifically show is that friends should not take advantage of their respective differences. Children recognize that they are not equals in all ways. When differences are not respected, the relationship goes awry, and instead of getting along, friends find themselves in contending positions. While omission of action in time of need violates the rule of reciprocity, taking action that exacerbates individual differences and harms one person denies respect. The complementary case is seen in kindness, where sensitivity to difference affirms respect and calls forth continuation of positive reciprocity.

CONFLICT RESOLUTION

It is important to add that violations are not necessarily events that lead to termination of friendship. Of the several cases of conflict we have obtained, only a small percentage are said by children to be irreparable. What we have found is that children specify a variety of means by which friends can resolve conflict and correct the negative course that it caused the relationship to take. The means range from simple apology to long routines ending with the promise to conform to expectations in the future. These data indicate that children understand that there are rules for correcting violations and imply that violations are realistic parts of any friendship. Individual differences are probably responsible for this realism; persons do not always act according to the principles of their relationships. This fact, no doubt, makes it essential that children evolve rules to meet and correct violations. Were they not to do so, the rule of reciprocity would push friends apart once a negative act or omission were inserted in the relationship.

It is interesting, therefore, that in some instances of conflict resolution children found it appropriate to state the rule that had been breached and the rule that should have been followed. These clarifications were built into the repair process as definite notations on why the relationship went awry and how conflict could have been avoided.

> If they're outside playing a game and [one is] not too good at it. You want to be on the winning team, so you don't pick her. You would say, "I don't want her because she can't throw or she can't catch." . . . Later that night it would probably bother me. I would apologize and say, "You can't do things I can do and I can't do things you can do. I'm sorry. Next time you can be on my team because games are just for fun." [Then what does the other one say?] She would probably say, "Don't worry about it. We're still friends." And we would be friends [Youniss, 1980, p. 251].

And the second account is equally informative:

> There were two boys [who] help each other build go-carts. . . . One of them breaks. [The boy whose cart broke asked] "Should we build another one?" The boy who still has his said, "No we can just race in mine. . . ." The kid's really sad his friend won't help him build a new cart because he already has his. The boy builds his own cart and this one's really sharp. I mean this one's all out good. [They race and] the boy who had the old go-cart lost by really a lot. . . . [The winner] thinks he should tell him that he should have helped. So he tells him, "Maybe you should have helped me when mine broke, because then we could have shared the pleasure of having a good go-cart." So the boy with the old one said, "You know, I think you're right. Should we build another one out of my parts?" [Youniss, 1980, p. 242].

Communicating affect

One other set of results seems especially pertinent to the topic of individual differences in friendship. In the discussion so far, the kind of characteristics that children ascribe to friends pertain to traits or states that are closely connected to behavior. This may be due to the nature of instructions that were designed to elicit accounts of interactions. If, however, the present model of communicative relations has general applicability, it must be shown to apply to the more subtle aspects of individuated selves. By convention, psychologists have come to think of emotions, doubts, and personal problems as private events that are central in individuals' knowledge or awareness of themselves. It has yet to be shown in the examples presented that children deal with this deeper self.

The illustrations that follow are intended as demonstrations that even the private aspects of the self emerge as public phenomena within friendship and are open to consensual validation through communication. The illustrations are also designed to suggest why such communication can be undertaken in friendship despite the risk that full self-revealment entails. Most of the data for these points came, once again, from children over 9 years of age. The most evocative, but not the only, instruction in this regard was to "describe friendship" or "tell me how you know when someone is your friend." The examples are arbitrarily categorized according to the type of content that was the center of communication. All, however, illustrate the same general theme—that friends seek validation in purposeful exposure of self through discourse.

Informational knowledge. "When you have homework, and don't know the instructions, they tell you the instructions." "If they don't know certain problems with homework, you help them." "He reminds me of what we're supposed to do when we get back from gym."

Knowledge as understanding. "If the person is stuck, show them the answer but tell them why it's the answer." "They can tell you what's wrong and what's right in a way. You sort of think things out with them." "Someone messes up in diagramming. Instead of laughing, she helps out. Help him as an equal and don't look down at him."

Share feelings. "Joe's dog died. John was his best friend. He takes time out to really understand him." "Jane gets in trouble with her parents. Jill tries to comfort her . . . gives her advice." "When I had problems, he helped me. And when he had problems, I helped him." "A true friend is someone you can tell everything."

Analyze feelings together. "A friend helps you out in time of need and talks problems out with you." "If he had a problem, maybe the two of you could come to a conclusion on what you could do." "When you have a problem, you can tell that friend and talk it over with him." "She'll help you understand how you feel and give advice."

Communicative empathy. "If I have a problem, I can go to them. I would probably go to my friend more than I could go to my parents because they might understand it more than my parents." "Always listen when you have problems. . . . A friend always understands your problems because they go through the same experiences. Even if they can't help, they sympathize." "Well, if you're in trouble or if you need help, they can help you out. . . . They tell you their secrets and you tell them yours and you talk about things you wouldn't tell other people." "A person you can really tell your feelings to. When you're lonely, you'll always have a friend to tell your problems. . . . I know her so much that I can do anything with her."

It is worth reiterating that these representative examples of communication between friends deal with feelings that most psychological theorists have assumed to be private, hidden, and nonaccessible to others except through penetrating inferential probing. At least where friends are concerned, this assumption seems inapplicable. Friends express their feelings to one another. Friends present their feelings to each other for the sake of clarification. And friends talk out their respective feelings in order to gain validation for what would otherwise be a private burden they would have to carry alone, with all the hesitancy and self-doubt that would imply. In short, the self–other barrier usually assumed in theories, such as role taking, seems an arbitrary imposition when contrasted with what individuals actually do within communicative relations.

It would be incorrect to read these data as if children were simply naive in their opening of self to others in an idealistic fashion. Were naiveté actually the mode, children would be defenseless against the potentially competitive advantage others might take of self-exposure. The evidence indicates that children are quite aware of the liabilities entailed in communication. Some results bear directly on this point. They consist of statements that accompanied accounts of self-revealing interactions, such as those illustrated here. The majority of children who generated these accounts added spontaneously an important qualification to them. The core idea expressed by these qualifications was that friends could trust one another not to use the personal information to either person's disadvantage. The specific terms employed by children were "He won't embarrass you." "She won't laugh at you." "They'll treat you as an equal." "He won't put you down." "They'll try to understand." "They won't use it to get revenge on you when you get in a fight." To these should be added another set of qualifications that explicitly expressed the belief that personal exposure was held in confidence between the friends—that is, "They can trust you that you won't tell anybody."

Why, when they know the potential risk, do friends admit their differences and expose their feelings, problems, and doubts? According to our results, the answer lies within their understanding of the structure of friendship. In the first place, children seem to believe that they can control personal information insofar as they state that they tell things to friends that they would not tell to parents, siblings, or teachers. Second, children understand that there is reciprocity in the relationship and that its functioning depends wholly on each of the respective parties. Were one friend to break a confidence, the act would entitle the other friend to do the same. Likewise, if one friend respects personal information, the other is encouraged to do the same. Third, something like intimacy seems also to be implicated. Children clearly believe that they can achieve mutual understanding within friendship. The belief that one can be understood by another is probably a key link in the broader chain of reasoning for which intersubjective agreement is validation for what one feels and thinks. Obviously, children are discriminating in choosing others to whom to turn for validation. At least for our samples of children, friendship serves as a special relationship for this function, the implication being that open communication cannot be used indiscriminately but requires a context of mutual trust.

CONCLUSIONS

The aim of this chapter has been to show how friendship serves as a relationship in which the self is individuated realistically and individuated selves learn how to treat one another with respect. The analysis hinges on a model of the individual in communicative relations and on Sullivan's scheme for assessing relationships as structures from which particular functions logically follow. According to his thesis, friendship is grounded in reciprocity that, for communication purposes, permits friends to make identical contributions to interactive exchanges. Ironically, this practical equality allows friends to discover ways in which they differ as well as ways in which they are alike. Discovery seems to work through the individuation of self that comes from the demands of reciprocity and the juxtaposition of friends' capacities and incapacities.

Surely, parent–child relationships are also conducive to the discovery of differences. In Sullivan's analysis, however, several aspects of the relationship work against it. There is too great a distance between the parties. The focus of the relationship is on conformity, in which children try to become more like adults. And, most importantly, criteria for the acceptable self are preestablished in adults' minds and cannot easily be reformed in accommodation to children as they really are. The result is that children perceive parents as figures who are all-powerful and all-knowing rather than as individuals with strong and weak points. Simultaneously, perception of self is biased in terms of the criteria that are emphasized by the arrangement where approval is exchanged for conformity. The relationship allows only a limited insight into the self's capabilities and tends to block out an honest grasp of the self's weaker side.

It is important to recognize that Sullivan distinguishes friendship from what many psychologists have called peer relations. According to our data, this distinction is valuable. Both relationships operate through reciprocity, but friendship has the added dimension of cooperation in its use. This means that exchanges of tit for tat are replaced by a more advanced conception of reciprocity as a principle. The case is made by the numerous instances in which one friend found another in need and acted to relieve that need. Upon further analysis, it can be seen that friends realize that the individual in need would be unable to reciprocate in this current state. Moreover, the friend who helped is most probably not in a state of need at that moment. A third notation is that reciprocation depends on circumstances for which capacities for helping and the need to be helped occur and therefore waits upon appropriate situations that come up over time.

Given all these considerations, the form of reciprocity used by friends involves promises and commitment in a time-forward perspective. This changes reciprocity from a literal practice of immediate exchange of like for like to a principle for action that deals in equivalents within an indefinite time frame (Sahlins, 1965). Therein lies two fundamental elements of friendship, the foremost being cooperation for mutual benefit, and underlying it is children's understanding of individual differences. The two seem to be inextricably interwoven. Why would friends who know that they differ work to sustain their relationship? Part of the answer seems to be that their differences, when controlled by the principle of reciprocity, can be combined judiciously for one another's welfare. Across time, roles of helper and recipient switch back and forth as circumstances come up and consequently friends learn that each has need for the other as well as capacities to remediate the other's needs. In a very real sense, then, friends come to understand the value of interdependence. When the realization of the self's insufficiency, weaknesses, and fallibility is added, the purpose of cooperating for mutual benefit becomes even clearer.

The deeper question posed by Sullivan concerns realistic acceptance of oneself, a matter he considers simultaneous with mutual respect. It is now possible to discuss this issue with supporting data. Self-acceptance means first of all claiming the whole, which necessarily includes admission of incapacities. According to our data, friendship provides a context conducive to realism in self-claims. For any service one takes from a friend, there is some service that the person can contribute. More importantly, insofar as friends act sensitively to one another's differences, even personal weaknesses are found worthy of respect. That is, individuals are respected as wholes, as they are, and in this context, they do not have to deny parts of themselves in order to be accepted.

It is important to see this description of friendship in its full light. In stressing the structural properties and consequent functions, one may get the impression that children's accounts are terribly idealistic. Common observation says that children are competitive, seek self-advantage, and are notoriously mean to one another. According to our findings, children are quite aware of these facts, and their accounts of friendship are not distortions of reality. Children were readily able to generate instances of unkindness, conflict, and ways in which actions of friends caused the relationship to end. Participation in friendship is clearly diversifying in its exposure to interpersonal hurt as well as joy.

A full appraisal of friendship obviously requires a step into its dynamics where positive and negative aspects occur in interplay. Our data suggest at least one way to address the topic. Friends coexist in a communicative relation that takes its specialzed form in communicative procedures. Children appear to have command of a wide range of procedures that friends can use not only to produce positive results but also to correct negative states. The latter procedures cut through the aura of naive idealism and indicate that children's conceptions of friendship are attempts to deal with social life as it is, not just with ways they would like it to be. In this regard, Sullivan's analysis seems especially insightful in locating the origins of adult intimate relationships in friendship. Children's friendships are not identical to close relationships that are sustained throughout adulthood. Their common element, however, may be found in the procedures by which both function.

A case in point are those procedures children use to deal with individual differences while maintaining mutual respect. These include listening and giving advice, presenting problems and then talking them out, and criticizing and yet remaining sympathetically focused on reaching consensus. These procedures are transferable to other intimate relationships, even though they may apply to different content. One problem in seeing the connection that Sullivan has hypothesized may be due to the assumption that intimate relationships are defined by equality between their members. Equality has many meanings, and lack of agreement among theorists has tended to encourage distinctions among relationships according to interpersonal similarities, power differences, and the like. If children's conceptions of friendship are taken seriously, then they may help to clarify a valuable point. Recognizing individual differences between friends, children do not hopelessly seek to make the individuals identical. Instead, they evolve rules for the relationship that entitle each individual to make contributions through equal participation in communicative procedures. Through this means, the individuals' respective identities are honored while mutual respect maintains them in the relationship. Therein lies the key to self-validation and respect.

REFERENCES

Berger, P. L., & Luckman, T. *The social construction of reality.* Garden City, N.Y.: Doubleday, 1967.

Bigelow, B. J. Children's friendship expectations: A cognitive developmental study. *Child Development*, 1977, *48*, 246–253.

Bigelow, B. J., & La Gaipa, J. J. Children's written descriptions of friendship. *Developmental Psychology*, 1975, *11*, 857–858.

Gouldner, A. W. The norm of reciprocity: A preliminary statement. *American Sociological Review*, 1960, *25*, 161–178.

Habermas, J. *Legitimation crisis.* Boston: Beacon Press, 1975.

La Gaipa, J. J. A developmental study of the meaning of friendship in adolescence. *Journal of Adolescence*, 1979, *2*, 201–213.

Macmurray, J. *Persons in relation.* London: Farber & Farber, 1961.

Piaget, J. *The moral judgment of the child.* London: Routledge & Kegan Paul, 1932.

Piaget, J. Piaget's theory. In P. Mussen (Ed.), *Carmichael's manual of child psychology* (Vol. 1). New York: Wiley, 1970.

Ricoeur, P. The problem of the foundation of moral philosophy. *Philosophy Today*, 1978, *22*, 175–192.

Sahlins, M. D. On the sociology of primitive exchange. In M. Banton (Ed.), *Relevance of models of social anthropology.* New York: Praeger, 1965.

Sampson, E. E. Psychology and the American idea. *Journal of Personality and Social Psychology*, 1977, *35*, 767–782.

Selman, R. L., & Jaquette, D. Stability and oscillation in interpersonal awareness: A clinical-developmental analysis. In *Nebraska Symposium on Motivation* (Vol. 25). Lincoln: Univ. of Nebraska Press, 1977.

Sullivan, H. S. *The interpersonal theory of psychiatry.* New York: Norton, 1953.

Volpe, J. *The development of concepts of parent–child and friend relations and of self within these relations.* Unpublished doctoral dissertation, The Catholic University of America, 1981.

Youniss, J. Dialectical theory and Piaget on social knowledge. *Human Development*, 1978, *21*, 234–247.

Youniss, J. *Parents and peers in social development.* Chicago: Univ. of Chicago Press, 1980.

Youniss, J., & Volpe, J. A relational analysis of friendship. In W. Damon (Ed.), *Social Cognition.* San Francisco: Jossey-Bass, 1978.

7 / Inequalities in children's prosocial behavior: whom do children assist?

NANCY EISENBERG
JEANNETTE FLOM PASTERNACK

In the past decade there has been an exponential increase in research and theory regarding children's prosocial behavior (intentional, voluntary behavior that benefits another). In most of this research, however, only one of several topics has been examined—the characteristics of children who are prosocial, socialization practices that facilitate prosocial behavior, or situational variables that either enhance or inhibit children's prosocial functioning (Eisenberg, 1982; Mussen & Eisenberg-Berg, 1977; Rushton, 1976, 1980; Staub, 1979). Few researchers have explored another issue, the role of recipients' characteristics in children's prosocial responding—that is, the issue of *whom* children help. Indeed, in much of the research on prosocial behavior, experimenters seem to assume that, once children learn to act prosocially, they usually do not discriminate among various potential recipients.

The relative dearth of systematic research on whom children help is evidenced by the fact that discussion of this issue in volumes and reviews on children's prosocial behavior has been either very brief or nonexistent (Eisenberg, 1982; Mussen & Eisenberg-Berg, 1977; Rushton, 1976, 1980; Staub, 1979). The relative inattention of researchers to this matter is somewhat surprising given that social psychologists repeatedly have demonstrated that adults are very sensitive to differences among potential recipients and routinely assist some persons more than others

THE CHILD'S CONSTRUCTION
OF SOCIAL INEQUALITY

(Berkowitz, 1972; Fink, Rey, Johnson, Spenner, Morton, & Flores, 1975; Gruder, 1974; Macauley, 1975; Piliavin, Piliavin, & Rodin, 1975; Schaps, 1972; Schopler & Matthews, 1965; Staub, 1974, 1978). Apparently, the emphasis of developmentalists on socialization has diverted their attention from the fact that the expression of prosocial tendencies frequently varies depending on the specifics of a situation, including who the recipient might be. Nevertheless, there is a limited quantity of data in which the question of inequalities and biases in children's prosocial behavior is addressed, although many of the data are embedded in studies relating to other issues.

In this chapter, the research relevant to how children discriminate among potential recipients will be reviewed. The chapter is subdivided into sections corresponding to the different criteria on which people make (or could make) distinctions among potential recipients—the relationship of the potential recipient to the benefactor, physical and demographic characteristics of the potential recipient, role of the potential recipient in the ongoing social interaction, state of the potential recipient, personality of the potential recipient, and mode of presentation of the potential recipient.

RELATIONSHIP OF THE POTENTIAL RECIPIENT TO THE BENEFACTOR

A major factor influencing whom a child assists is the relationship of the potential recipient to the child. The nature of a child's relationship with a given individual can vary on a variety of dimensions. One important dimension concerns the role of the potential recipient in the child's life—whether the potential recipient is known or unknown, a friend or disliked, a family member or someone unrelated. Another dimension not entirely independent from the first is more dynamic and concerns the role of the potential recipient in the child's ongoing social interactions. This factor most frequently has been examined in the context of reciprocity in children's prosocial behavior. The focus of such research has been the relation of children's prosocial behavior to a potential recipient's prior or future prosocial behavior toward the benefactor. Finally, the third dimension of a child's relationship to another concerns the similarity or dissimilarity of an unknown potential recipient to the potential benefactor. These three dimensions will now be examined.

Status of the potential recipient

Even by the second year of life, children seem to direct more positive behavior toward some persons than others, depending on the other's relationship to the self. Lamb (1978a, 1978b) examined the behavior of 1-year-olds and their preschool siblings toward their parents and one another. The children directed significantly more "profers" (offers, shows, or points out toy for another) toward their parents than toward their siblings. This occurred despite the fact that infants and preschoolers engage in at least as many interactions involving the giving or getting of objects with peers as with adults (Holmberg, 1980). Along the same lines, Rheingold, Hay, and West (1976) found that 2-year-olds were more likely to give toys to their fathers than to an adult stranger. Given the importance of the parent–child attachment during the early years (Ainsworth, 1973; Ainsworth, Blehar, Waters, & Wall, 1978), it is not surprising that young children direct much positive behavior toward their parents.

There is some evidence to suggest that in adolescence, individuals do not direct more prosocial behaviors toward familiar adults than toward familiar peers and sometimes are more likely to assist peers. In studies with adolescents, Zeldin, Savin-Williams, and Small (1980) and Zeldin, Small, and Savin-Williams (1982) observed adolescents engaged in real-life activities (on bicycle or canoe trips). In the first study, involving males only (Zeldin et al., 1980), the adolescents helped peers, counselors, and the group as a whole about equally. However, in the second study, involving both adolescent males and females (Zeldin et al., 1982), more behavior was directed toward peers than counselors. The fact that adolescents are strongly influenced by peers as well as adults (Conger, 1977) may account for the relative frequency of peer-directed prosocial behaviors during adolescence.

Not only the quantity but the quality of children's prosocial behavior directed toward peers and adults may change with age. Youniss (1980) asked 6–14-year-olds to give examples of acts of kindness directed toward peer and adult recipients. The content areas of their examples for peers (in order of decreasing frequency) were giving–sharing, playing, physical assistance, understanding, and teaching. Examples of adult-directed acts of kindness (in order of decreasing frequency) were being good or polite, doing chores, obeying, and showing concern. With age, the children seemed slightly more likely to define kindness toward adults in ways similar to peer-directed kindness—as involving such prosocial acts as showing concern. Thus, the quality of kind acts directed toward adults versus peers seems to vary. Kindness toward adults is characterized by doing things that adults want children to do, whereas kindness toward peers is more characteristic of what we generally label "prosocial behavior."

Youniss's data are consistent with the hypothesis that school-aged children do not direct as many helping and sharing behaviors toward adults as toward peers. However, it is quite possible that children do direct as many prosocial behaviors toward adults but, for some reason, do not label these behaviors as "kind." At this time, researchers have not adequately determined whether school-aged children direct more prosocial acts toward familiar adults or familiar peers.

Friendship status

The friendship status of a potential recipient clearly influences children's prosocial proclivities, but in a complex manner. Children, especially older children, generally conceptualize friendships as including prosocial interchanges (Furman & Bierman, 1981; Furman & Childs, 1981; Sharabany, Gershoni, & Hofman, 1981; Youniss, 1980). Furthermore, children say that they expect more sharing from friends than from other peers (Berndt, 1978) and that they would share more with friends or liked persons than with strangers (girls only, Berndt, 1981b, 1981c; Furby, 1978). However, children do not always favor friends over less liked others in actual interactions. While Staub and Sherk (1970), Berndt (1981c), and Mann (1974) found more sharing and helpfulness between friends than nonfriends, other researchers have found that children share equally with friends and neutral others (Berndt, 1981b, for some tasks; Floyd, 1964; Staub & Noerenberg, 1981) or even help or share *less* with friends than with strangers or nonfriends (Berndt, 1981b, for boys but not girls on one task; Fincham, 1978; Sharabany & Hertz-Lazarowitz, 1981; Wright, 1942). Furthermore, although there are some data to suggest that older children occasionally favor friends more than do younger children, the data concerning this issue are somewhat inconsistent (Berndt, 1981a, 1981c).

It is likely that several factors account for the finding that children sometimes assist nonfriends more than friends. First, because children frequently compare themselves with their peers (Rubin, 1980), children (especially males) sometimes may choose to compete with their friends. This tendency may reduce differences in assisting friends versus other people (Berndt, 1981c). Furthermore, according to the reasoning of the 8-year-olds in Wright's (1942) research, children sometimes assist nonfriends more than friends to eliminate inequities between a stranger and a friend (57% of the children who favored a stranger gave this reason), to gain a friend or reduce the social distance between a nonfriend and the self, because a friend would understand favoring a stranger, or because "it is nice" or "polite" to assist a stranger. Wright found that greater generosity toward a friend was justified by loyalty considerations and reciprocity obligations.

It appears that children are more likely to favor nonfriends over friends if they feel secure rather than threatened in their relationships with their friends. If friendships are secure, children apparently feel freer to behave in a self-serving manner with friends than with nonfriends. In research with third and fourth graders, Staub and Noerenberg (1981) found that boys were more likely to be selfish with a friend (in comparison to a nonfriend, familiar peer) if their interaction with the friend had been unconflicted and had proceeded as expected. In contrast, when the interaction previously had not proceeded in a manner consistent with expectations (and the interaction probably had involved more conflict), the boys' sharing with friends and nonfriends did not differ. Furthermore, Morgan and Sawyer (1967) found that children were more accepting of self-serving behavior of a friend than of a nonfriend. Finally, Wright (1942) reported that children said that a friend (but not a stranger) would understand a decision not to behave generously. The fact that children seem to feel freer to act as they please with friends is consistent with findings demonstrating that friends' prosocial interactions are less characterized by strict, immediate reciprocity than are interactions with nonfriends (Floyd, 1964; Staub & Sherk, 1970). Children apparently feel that reciprocation with friends is more flexible and need not be immediate.

Despite Berndt's (1981a, 1981c) finding that older children are sometimes more likely than younger children to favor friends over nonfriends, the results of other research suggest that the tendency to favor liked individuals over less liked persons may decrease with age. Eisenberg (in press), in a study concerning prosocial behavior, asked second, fourth, sixth, ninth, eleventh, and twelfth graders to resolve a moral dilemma and then questioned the children regarding how the story protagonist should act toward a variety of different people in the same situations. The children's tendencies to discriminate in favor of particular groups of individuals were then coded from these data. Eisenberg found that older children were significantly less likely than younger children to say that they would make discriminations between friends or family members and others, or between liked and disliked individuals. While older children may merely have been more sensitive to the social repercussions for behaving in discriminatory ways, it is likely that some older children simply were attempting to maintain consistency between their moral principles (which might exclude discrimination based on the status of another) and their behavior (Eisenberg, 1977, in press). This conclusion is consistent with the moral judgment research demonstrating that children are less likely with age to make moral judgments based primarily on another relationship to the self (Kohlberg, 1969, 1971).

Similarity of the potential benefactor to the self

According to the social psychological literature, adults (Emswiller, Deaux, & Willits, 1971; Krebs, 1970; Pandey & Griffitt, 1974) are more likely to assist others similar to the self than those who are dissimilar. In general, the assumption is that individuals similar to the self are more attractive and, consequently, better liked.

Researchers seldom have investigated the role of similarity to a recipient in the elicitation of children's prosocial behavior. In a study with second graders, Panofsky (1976) found that similarity of interest (but not similarity of race) was positively related to the amount of sharing of peanuts with a recipient (but not to a measure of helping). The effect of similarity on sharing was significant for Jewish children, but not for Catholic children. Furthermore, in another study, 5–6- and 8- and 9-year-olds contributed more to a charity for individuals similar to the self (crippled children) than to a charity for dissimilar others (crippled adults) (Willis, Feldman, & Ruble, 1977).

It is possible that similarity to the recipient has somewhat less influence with age on the behavior of school-aged children. In the study with elementary and high school students mentioned previously, Eisenberg (in press) found that older children reported being significantly less likely to discriminate in their prosocial behavior in favor of individuals with some similarity or connection to the self (e.g., individuals from the same town or country, or of the same religion or ethnic group). However, the strength of the associations between age and the tendency to discriminate was not large. Thus, the age-related change in the tendency to help similar others more than dissimilar others may be relatively small.

In summary, children seem to be more inclined to help others similar to the self, and this tendency may decrease somewhat with age. Given the dearth of research, however, any conclusions relating to this issue must be considered as very tentative.

PHYSICAL AND DEMOGRAPHIC
CHARACTERISTICS OF
THE POTENTIAL RECIPIENT

Sex of the potential recipient

In comparison to the number of studies concerning the effect of a potential recipient's sex on adults' prosocial behavior, there are relatively few investigations regarding this issue with children. Generally speaking, however, researchers have found that preschool children tend to receive more prosocial and other positive behaviors from same-sex peers than from opposite-sex peers (Charlesworth & Hartup, 1967; Eisenberg-Berg & Hand, 1979; Marcus & Jenny, 1977; Walters, Pearce, & Dahms, 1957). Moreover, after age 4 or 5, the tendency to favor same-sex peers seems to diminish gradually. For example, Walters *et al.* (1957), in a study with 2–5-year-olds, found a decreasing tendency for children to favor same-sex peers when emitting affectional responses (including prosocial behaviors as well as physical affection and other positive behaviors). At 2 years of age, both girls and boys were more positive toward same-sex peers; at ages 3 and 4, only boys favored same-sex recipients; by age 5, the children did not respond more positively to either same-sex or opposite-sex individuals.

Other data also are consistent with the conclusion that the preference for same-sex recipients lessens with age. In a study with kindergarteners and first, third, and fourth graders, Ladd, Lange, and Stremmel (1981) found that younger children (kindergarteners and first graders) helped same-sex peers more than opposite-sex peers with a task; however, the older children (third and fourth graders) did not discriminate in favor of opposite-sex or same-sex recipients. Moreover, in a study of rivalrous and prosocial behavior, Skarin and Moely (1976) found that elementary school girls in their control group helped opposite-sex peers more than same-sex peers, whereas boys did not discriminate between recipients on the basis of sex (prosocial training for the children altered the pattern of data). They noted no change with age in this pattern; however, they reported only findings significant at the .01 probability level. Consequently, it is not clear if the three-way interaction of Sex of Benefactor × Sex of Subject × Age Group was significant at the .05 probability level. Thus, these data are not inconsistent with the hypothesis that preference for same-sex recipients decreases with age. Certainly, across all the studies discussed, the pattern is for older schoolchildren, in contrast to younger children, either to not differentiate between same-sex and opposite-sex peers or to discriminate in favor of opposite-sex peers.

There is very little research on the relation of sex of a recipient to adolescents' prosocial behaviors. In one study concerning this issue, Zeldin *et al.* (1982) found no significant interaction between sex of benefactor and sex of recipient for adolescent boys' and girls' (mean age was 15.6 years) assistance, support, and sharing. Boys did help girls almost twice as frequently as they helped boys; however, the number of subjects was so small that the interaction effect (between sex of benefactor and sex of subject) was not significant. Additional research is needed to determine if adolescents (especially males) are inclined to assist opposite-sex peers more than same-sex peers.

Race of a potential recipient

Relatively few researchers have investigated the influence of race of a potential recipient on children's prosocial behavior. However, there is evidence that children's social judgments about themselves and others are influenced by race, with Caucasians generally being viewed by both blacks and whites as superior (K. B. Clark & Clark, 1947; A. Clark, Hocevar, & Dembo, 1980; Katz, Sohn, & Zalk, 1975; Stephen, 1977; Turner & Forehand, 1976). According to research, white children's negative attitudes toward blacks seem to be relatively low before age $5\frac{1}{2}$, to peak from age $5\frac{1}{2}$ to 7, and to decrease during the early school years thereafter (A. Clark *et al.*, 1980). Thus, on the basis of research concerning children's racial attitudes, it would be reasonable to predict that children do discriminate among potential recipients of aid from varying racial backgrounds, especially during the early elementary school years.

Although there are data to support the conclusion that adult subjects frequently (but not always, Lerner & Frank, 1974a, 1974b; Thayer, 1973; Wispe & Freshley, 1971) discriminate against potential recipients of another race (Gaertner, 1973, 1975; Gaertner & Bickman, 1971; Graf & Riddell, 1972; Piliavin, Rodin, & Piliavin, 1969; Wegner & Crano, 1975; West, Whitney, & Schnedler, 1975; also see Crosby, Bromley, & Saxe, 1980), the data for children are inconsistent. In a study with Caucasian preschoolers and first and second graders, Zinser, Perry, Bailey, and Lydiatt (1976) asked children to donate candy to poor children who were either black, Caucasian, or Indian. While the preschool children did not differentiate among recipients, the school-aged children donated more to black and Indian recipients than to Caucasian recipients. Zinser *et al.* suggested that the bias in favor of minorities may have been due to the children's assumption that nonwhite children are more needy than Caucasian children.

In research with kindergarteners and fourth graders, Katz, Katz, and Cohen (1976) obtained very different results. In this study, the children were given the opportunity to assist a black or white adult who was either in a wheelchair or not. The children aided the white adult more than the black adult. Age of the child and handicapped status of the recipient did not interact with race of the recipient in determining the childrens helping behaviors.

Finally, in a third study, Panofsky (1976) gave white second graders the opportunity to share peanuts with either a white or black child and to help the same child with a task. Race of the stimulus child had no effect on the children's helping or sharing.

To summarize, in the three studies reviewed here, three different patterns of results were obtained. What could account for the differences? Age of the subject does not seem to be the relevant variable; in the various studies, first and second graders exhibited very different behaviors. However, mode of stimulus presentation could account, in part, for the divergent findings. In the one study in which children did discriminate against an individual of a different race, the potential recipient was a real person. In the studies in which the children either did not discriminate or assisted the person of another race more, the potential recipient was not a real-life person but was presented via visual media. It is possible that children react less negatively to hypothetical persons of a different race than to real individuals.

Socioeconomic status of the potential recipient

As with the variable of race, the relation of socioeconomic status of a potential recipient to children's benevolence has received relatively little attention from investigators. However, the limited research available is consistent with the conclusion that socioeconomic status of a recipient can, in some circumstances, influence how much adolescents help. In two studies on helping and reciprocity, Berkowitz (Berkowitz, 1968; Berkowitz & Friedman, 1967) investigated the amount of help rendered by adolescent boys to peers who had previously provided them with either much or little assistance. Berkowitz found that social class of a prior benefactor influenced the amount of help reciprocated both by American boys from middle-class entrepreneurial families (but not bureaucratic families) and by English adolescents from working-class and middle-class bureaucratic families. Among these boys, middle-class subjects were more likely to expend low effort on behalf of a peer who had previously provided little assistance to the subject only if the peer was from a working-class background. The working-class English boys followed a reciprocity principle primarily when dealing with middle-class peers: They worked harder for a middle-class person who previously had provided them with aid and expended the least energy for a middle-class peer who had given them little help previously.

Research concerning the influence of a recipient's socioeconomic status on preschoolers' and young children's helping is virtually nonexistent. Because socioeconomic status of an individual often is much less evident to an observer than is either race or ethnic group, one would not expect young children to be very reactive to this variable, especially in comparison to other more obvious demographic characteristics. Furthermore, a child's responses to someone from a different social class probably would depend on what information denoting an individual's class is available. For example, children may differentiate among potential recipients on the basis of relative wealth but not on the basis of linguistic accent. Socioeconomic status is a multifaceted characteristic, and it is unclear what aspects of this characteristic influence young children's prosocial behaviors.

ROLE OF THE POTENTIAL RECIPIENT IN THE ONGOING SOCIAL INTERACTION

Whether or not a child assists a particular recipient frequently is a function of reciprocity considerations. In many of the relevant studies, researchers have found that school-aged children (Dreman, 1976; Furby, 1978; Harris, 1970, 1971; Staub & Sherk, 1970) and adolescents (Berkowitz, 1968; Berkowitz & Friedman, 1967) frequently assist an individual more than other persons, or more than they would have otherwise, if that individual has previously helped or shared with them. Moreover, elementary school children frequently share or help a recipient more if that recipient can reciprocate in the future (Dreman & Greenbaum, 1973; Furby, 1978; Peterson, 1980). However, some individuals are more likely than others to respond in accordance with reciprocity considerations. Middle-class boys, especially those with fathers engaged in entrepreneurial occupations, seem to be especially attuned to reciprocity considerations (Dreman & Greenbaum, 1973; Berkowitz, 1968; Berkowitz & Friedman, 1967). Furthermore, among elementary school children, those who judge moral issues on the basis of an actor's intentions rather than on the basis of the consequences of an act (i.e., are morally subjective; Piaget, 1932/1965) are more likely to act in ways consistent with reciprocity considerations (Dreman, 1976).

Researchers also have found that children who assist others are themselves more likely to be recipients of peers' prosocial acts (to have their kindness reciprocated) than are other children. For example, in naturalistic observational studies, researchers have noted that children who give much positive reinforcement to peers (including affection, positive affect, prosocial behavior, and other positive social acts) are more likely than other children to be recipients of positive behaviors (Charlesworth & Hartup, 1967; Eisenberg, Cameron, Tryon, & Dodez, 1981; Kohn, 1966; Lamb, 1978b; Leiter, 1977). Moreover, reciprocity has been noted in preschoolers' exchange of explicitly prosocial behaviors. For example, Staub and Feinberg (1980) found that preschool boys' cooperation, sharing, and expression of positive emotion and humor were significantly related to the receipt of these and other types of positive behaviors. Similarly, girls' expression of positive emotions, humor, cooperation, and invitations to play (but not sharing) were associated with positive behaviors directed at them. Furthermore, Marcus and Jenny (1977) obtained high correlations between help given by preschoolers and help received from both teachers and peers. However, it is interesting to note that, in the Marcus and Jenny study, the reciprocity between help given and help received held only for help given voluntarily, not for help requested. Apparently involuntary helping was perceived as being less kind and thus less worthy of reciprocation than voluntary help.

Despite the bulk of research indicating that children prefer to assist others who can (or already have) helped them, it is important to emphasize that reciprocity considerations are not always salient in children's choices of recipients. Sometimes young children minimize or ignore reciprocity considerations when the potential recipient can no longer reciprocate help (Peterson, 1980). Furthermore, other facets of the ongoing interaction may overshadow reciprocity concerns when children decide who and how much to help. For example, although Staub and Noerenberg (1981) found that third- and fourth-grade boys sometimes exhibited negative reciprocity (were less likely to share with a peer who they believed previously had acted selfishly), they noted relatively little direct reciprocity in the boys' sharing of a drawing pencil with a peer who previously had had the opportunity to share candy with them. Because factors in the interactive situation besides the peer's prior generosity with candy (such as the subject's previous requests for the candy) influenced how much the peer originally shared with a subject, the boys' subsequent sharing with the peer was a function of much more than merely how much candy they previously received from the peer. In brief, the data from Staub and Noerenberg's study are consistent with the conclusion that children do not necessarily assist others who have assisted them. Rather, the transactional process (including such variables as why and how a potential recipient has assisted a potential benefactor in the past) is an important determinant of whether or not a child chooses to act in accordance with reciprocity considerations.

It is unclear if there is a developmental trend in the reliance of school-aged children on reciprocity considerations for choosing recipients. With age, children increasingly evaluate prosocial behavior that involves reciprocation less favorably than helping that does not involve reciprocation or other self-interested motives (C. P. Baldwin & Baldwin, 1970; A. L. Baldwin, Baldwin, Castillo-Vales, & Seegmiller, 1971; Peterson, Hartmann, & Gelfand, 1977; Suls, Witenberg, & Gutkin, 1981). For example, Peterson (1980) found that kindergarteners and third and sixth graders judged a donor who assisted a friend who had repeatedly helped the donor in the past as less meritorious than a child who helped a dependent (sick, poor) peer. Furthermore, preference for the reciprocating donor decreased with age.

One might conclude from such findings as these that with age reciprocation becomes a less powerful determinant of whom children help. However, children's evaluations of the merit of behaviors and how they actually behave are not necessarily equivalent. Furby (1978) noted that reciprocity considerations were very salient in fifth graders' reports of why they shared possessions. Reciprocity considerations were somewhat less evident among young and older individuals. Furthermore, Peterson (1980) found that the same group of grade school children who judged reciprocity-motivated prosocial behaviors as less worthy than helping a needy other were themselves somewhat more likely to help a recipient who could reciprocate (rather than a dependent other). This tendency to assist the individual who could reciprocate *increased* with age. When the recipient could no longer reciprocate, the children helped the dependent recipient and the recipient who had previously aided the subject approximately equally. Moreover, in another study, Peterson *et al.* (1977) found that with increasing age negative reciprocity (failure to help another who previously did not assist the self) became a *less* salient determinant of children's donating in comparison to need of the recipient. In sum, according to the limited data, it seems that elementary school children are increasingly likely with age to assist another if the other can reciprocate in the future. However, during elementary school, negative reciprocity seems to decrease with age, and giving to reciprocate past favors appears to be as important as assisting a dependent other. Researchers have yet to clearly delineate changes in responsiveness to reciprocity cues during the preschool and adolescent years.

STATE OF THE POTENTIAL RECIPIENT

Need state of the potential recipient

In general, children, even preschoolers, seem to prefer to assist dependent, needy others in comparison to nonneedy individuals. For example, Zinser and his colleagues (Zinser & Lydiatt, 1976; Zinser, Perry, & Edgar, 1975) found that preschoolers and kindergarteners, when given the opportunity to share with a rich recipient or a poor recipient, shared more candy with the poor recipient. Similarly, Liebert, Fernandez, and Gill (1969) found that elementary school boys (with mean ages of either 7 or 10) were more likely to donate to a friendless child than to a recipient who was not described as friendless. Preference for the friendless recipient did not increase with age. Furthermore, in a study with 10- and 11-year-olds, Fouts (1972) found that children were more likely to work to pull a lever if the proceeds (pennies) went to a charity for poor children than if the pennies simply remained in an unlabeled box.

Although Liebert *et al.* (1969) found no increase with age in children's preference for assisting a friendless individual, other researchers have obtained data consistent with the conclusion that older children are more likely than younger children to assist needy, dependent recipients. Ladd *et al.* (1981) provided first and fourth graders with the opportunity to assist one of two anonymous peers, one of whom needed help more than the other. Although both age groups displayed a strong tendency to help the peer in the greatest need, fourth graders were more consistent in doing so. In a second study, Ladd *et al.* (1981) allowed first and fourth graders to work for either a needy or a nonneedy peer. They found that the children worked hardest if assisting a needy peer. This tendency was more apparent for older subjects; however, the fourth-grade children also assisted the nonneedy subjects more than did the first graders so there was no Age × Neediness of recipient interaction. In this study, the children could not choose to assist *either* a needy or nonneedy peer (they were assigned to one condition or the other); thus, the results do not bear as directly on age differences in preference for needy recipients as do the results in Ladd *et al.*'s first study.

Although the data are scant in quantity, it is logical to assume that with age people increasingly prefer to assist needy, dependent individuals rather than nonneedy recipients. Presumably, one reason that people prefer to assist needy individuals is because benefactors empathize with individuals in need. While research regarding age-related increases in empathy is contradictory (Feshbach, 1978; Zahn-Waxler & Radke-Yarrow, 1979), with age children seem to attend increasingly to the need state of another when making moral judgments about prosocial behaviors (Eisenberg, Lennon, & Roth, in press; Eisenberg-Berg & Roth, 1980). Increased attention to the need state of another should enhance the individual's desire to assist a needy other. Furthermore, there is some evidence that with age children increasingly internalize norms related to social responsibility for dependent others. Children exhibit some prosocial behaviors more with age (Radke-Yarrow, Zahn-Waxler, & Chapman, in press; Underwood & Moore, 1982), and adolescents are much more likely than elementary school children to make moral judgments about prosocial behavior on the basis of internalized values relating to the importance of assisting persons in need (Eisenberg-Berg, 1979). As children internalize norms relating to assisting needy others, they should be increasingly likely to help needy rather than nonneedy individuals.

Children's helpfulness toward needy others apparently is influenced by the cause of the other's neediness. The role of deservedness of a recipient (how responsible individuals are for their neediness, and how much they merit help) will be discussed in the next section. Another distinction with regard to the basis of one's neediness concerns dispositional versus situational factors.

Children seem to prefer to assist another whose need is based on dispositional rather than circumstantial factors, but only in some situations. Ladd *et al.* (1981) asked kindergarteners, and first, third, and fourth graders whom they would rather help with school work in several different circumstances. In some scenarios, the potential recipient's relative need (high or low) was due to dispositional factors (the recipient was smart versus not so smart); in others, it was due to circumstantial factors (whether the child was on schedule or behind in schoolwork because of either an on-time or late school bus arrival). Sex of the potential recipient or cost of helping also was manipulated. Type of recipient need state (dispositional or circumstantial) influenced the decision to assist only if the recipient was of the opposite sex from the subject. If the potential recipient was of the opposite sex, children were more likely to decide to help when the recipient's need was based on dispositional factors. When cost of helping (but not sex of recipient) was manipulated, type of need state did not influence the children's helping decisions. Because children (particularly young children) were much more likely to assist same-sex than opposite-sex peers, Ladd *et al.* suggested that child benefactors respond to the dispositional versus circumstantial component of a recipient's need only when there are no other reasons (such as the recipient being of the same sex) that make them inclined to assist. In summary, these data suggest that children occasionally decide to help on the basis of source of neediness, but not when other, more salient criteria for a decision are available.

The fact that children frequently prefer to assist needy individuals does not nullify the fact that other characteristics of a potential recipient frequently are more powerful determinants of helping behavior than is neediness. Adults often do not act in accordance with social responsibility norms requiring that individuals assist needy others (Berkowitz, 1972); the same is true for children. For example, Peterson (1980) found that kindergarteners and third and sixth graders were more likely to help a child who might reciprocate than to assist a needy child and that this preference for the potential reciprocator increased with age. Thus, the hope of future benefits influenced whom the children assisted more than did neediness of a recipient. In the same vein, Eisenberg-Berg and Neal (1981), in a study of moral judgment about prosocial behavior, noted that children's reasoning was more self-oriented and less oriented toward the needs of a potential recipient when the cost of a prosocial behavior was high rather than low. According to these data, children use need as a criterion for helping primarily when cost of assistance is not too high. Furthermore, it is likely that a number of other criteria, such as how well a recipient is liked, sex of a recipient, and personality of a recipient, frequently are more significant determinants of a child's helping than is a potential recipient's neediness.

Deservedness of the potential recipient and social comparison processes

It is clear that how much a child deserves a commodity frequently influences both the child's allocation of rewards (at least after age 6; Hook & Cook, 1979) and the child's tendency to assist or share with others (Barnett, 1975; Long & Lerner, 1974; Staub & Noerenberg, 1981). However, researchers seldom have examined the effects of deservedness of a potential recipient on children's prosocial behavior.

According to research conducted with adults, people will help potential recipients less if the recipients are perceived as responsible for their state (deserving of their neediness) than if they are seen as not responsible for their neediness (Berkowitz, 1972; Horowitz, 1968; Schopler & Matthews, 1965). With some exceptions (Leung & Foster, 1981), the same general pattern has been noted in the scant literature involving children.

In a study conducted by Barnett (1975), fourth- and fifth-grade boys were given the opportunity to share tokens with one of two groups of children: children who had no tokens because they had not had an opportunity to win them or children who had no tokens because they had lost in a competitive game and had won no tokens. The boys were more charitable toward peers who had no tokens as a result of chance than toward peers who had not won any tokens. Furthermore, the children judged it fairer for the losers in the competition not to receive any tokens. The more fair the children perceived it to be for a potential recipient not to receive any tokens, the fewer tokens they donated. In another study with elementary school children (fourth and fifth graders), Braband and Lerner (1975) obtained a similar pattern of findings but the results were not statistically significant. However, a child was significantly more likely to help a peer if that peer was not responsible for his or her needy state *and* if the child (the benefactor) was not deserving of the free playtime that would be lost if he or she assisted the needy other. Finally, in a third study, Miller and Smith (1977) found that fifth graders donated more money to other children who had no money because the experimenter had run out of funds (deserving condition) than to children who had been careless and lost their money (nondeserving condition). However, this finding was significant only when the subjects (the benefactors) had been paid properly for previous work or if they had been underpaid; when the children had been overpaid, they donated equally to deserving and undeserving peers.

Deservedness of a potential recipient apparently can influence children's generosity in another, more subtle way—in interaction with deservedness of the benefactor and through social comparison processes. Sometimes, especially in clearly competitive situations, children seem to compare their own performance with another's, and if they do not measure up (if they are less deserving than the other), subsequent prosocial behavior toward the other person may be reduced. For example, McGuire and Thomas (1975) found that fourth- and fifth-grade boys (but not girls) who had won chips good for prizes in a competitive game were especially unlikely to donate their chips to a peer recipient when they themselves had done worse at the game than the potential recipient. If the boys had done as well or better than the potential recipient or if they had been awarded the chips in a noncompetitive (rather than competitive) game situation, donations to the recipient were relatively generous. According to McGuire and Thomas's data, when children are induced to think in comparative terms, males are relatively unwilling to share if they appear less competent than the potential recipient. Under these conditions, males may feel threatened by or negative toward the recipient because of the role the recipient plays in the comparison process. In another study with fourth graders, the effects for sharing were not replicated; however, boys who lost in a competitive situation were especially likely to take a toy from the peer who won the competition (Crockenberg, Bryant, & Wilce, 1976). (See Masters, 1971, for more data related to this general issue.)

To summarize, by school age, children apparently prefer to assist individuals who deserve assistance—that is, individuals who are needy because of factors beyond their control. However, if the needy other's performance is contrasted with the children's own performance so that the potential recipient appears to be more worthy or more deserving, children sometimes are less likely to assist the competent recipient. At this time, the age at which children first discriminate along the dimension of deservedness of recipient is unknown. Furthermore, it is unclear when social comparison processes first influence children's helping behavior. However, because children infrequently use social comparison information to evaluate their own accomplishments before age 7 or 8 (Ruble, Boggiano, Feldman, & Loebl, 1980), it is likely that the role of social comparison processes in shaping children's reactions to deserving others is relatively minor until the middle elementary school years.

PERSONALITY OF THE POTENTIAL RECIPIENT

It is common knowledge that our interactions with others vary greatly as a function of personality characteristics of other persons. People differ in attitudes, values, habits, and modes of social interaction, and these variations elicit different reactions from others. Thus, it should not be surprising that personality characteristics of a potential recipient influence his or her chance of being assisted by a child.

Although it is not entirely clear how someone becomes popular with children, popular children and well-liked adults do seem more likely than less popular individuals to be helped by children, especially if the amount of help received is compared to the amount of help given to others. In an interview study, Raviv, Bar-Tal, Ayalon, and Raviv (1980) found that sixth-grade pupils perceived popular peers as both giving and receiving more help than unpopular peers. Furthermore, popular students were viewed as receiving more help than they gave, and both popular and unpopular peers preferred both to give and to receive help from popular peers. Similarly, in another study (Furby, 1978), elementary school children, high school students, and adults reported that the likelihood of their sharing possessions depended on their evaluation of a potential recipient as nice, friendly, or likable. Furthermore, while Marcus and Jenny (1977) found no correlation between sociometric status and help received in the preschool class, high-status, popular children received more help than they gave, whereas less popular children gave more help than they received. Finally, in a study with fifth and sixth graders, children pledged to donate more to elderly persons who were described as having attractive personalities than to elderly persons who were described as less understanding and accepting (Leung & Foster, 1981).

In studies concerning the receipt of social reinforcers in general (including prosocial behavior as well as other positive behaviors), similar results have been obtained. Masters and Furman (1981), in a naturalistic study with preschoolers, found that popular children received more positive reinforcement (including gift giving, reassurances, protection, and help, as well as such positive behaviors as invitations to play, cooperative play, smiling, praise, affection, and greetings) than did either disliked peers or peers who were neither popular nor disliked. Gottman, Gonso, and Rasmussen (1975) obtained similar results. Moreover, Charlesworth and Hartup (1967) noted that preschoolers who were warm and positive toward peers were recipients of many positive reinforcements from others.

Researchers also have examined the relationship between the receipt of aid and several other aspects of children's social interaction styles and personalities besides popularity. In a study involving 18–24-month-olds, children with a secure attachment to their mothers (Ainsworth, 1973) received no more offers of objects or social interaction from peers than did less securely attached toddlers (Pastor, 1981). Because in other research securely attached children have been found to be more competent in peer interactions (Waters, Wippman, & Sroufe, 1979), it would be interesting to learn if older securely attached children receive more positive reinforcement, including prosocial behaviors, from peers.

In another study, the relation of receiving aid to a number of different individual characteristics was examined. Eisenberg *et al.* (1981) observed 33 4- and 5-year-olds over a 9-week period during free playtime at their preschool. Instances of prosocial behaviors (helping and sharing), the children's reactions to peers' prosocial behaviors, and a number of other social behaviors were noted. According to correlational analyses (unpublished data), children who received relatively many *unsolicited* prosocial behaviors were those who were significantly more social with peers, were more likely to take objects from others, and were likely to react positively rather than passively to others' solicited prosocial behaviors (prosocial behaviors that the subject requested from a peer).

These children also tended ($p < .10$) to help and share with others without being asked, tended to defend objects in their possession, and were relatively unlikely to react passively to peers' spontaneous prosocial behaviors. In comparison to those low in receipt of solicited prosocial behavior, children who received more *solicited* behaviors were those who frequently asked teachers and peers for assistance, were social with teachers, and responded passively rather than positively to solicited behaviors directed toward them. They also tended ($p < .10$) to score low on a test of internal locus of control and to emit relatively few spontaneous prosocial behaviors themselves. Thus, the children who received spontaneous prosocial behaviors were relatively social, emotionally reactive, and assertive (tended to take and defend possessions), whereas those who asked for and received solicited prosocial actions frequently asked for help (perhaps they could be called dependent) and were relatively nonreactive in their emotional responses to others. Apparently, those children who asked for aid received it when they asked, but unrequested assistance was rendered to those who were social with peers and frequently reacted positively to the receipt of aid.

At the present time, the limited research is consistent with the conclusion that children are more likely to assist certain types of children than others. However, exactly which personal characteristics are related to the receipt of aid and the strength of these relations are currently unclear.

MODE OF PRESENTATION OF THE POTENTIAL RECIPIENT

Occasionally (especially in research situations), children have an opportunity to help a person who is not present. In such situations, mode of presentation of the potential recipient seems to influence the likelihood of an individual receiving assistance. In general, the more vividly and concretely a potential recipient is represented, the more likely children are to help. For example, Zinser and Lydiatt (1976) found that 4- and 5-year-olds were more likely to donate to a recipient whose plight was presented visually as well as verbally (with pictures and description) than to a recipient whose need was presented only visually or only verbally. Similarly, Presbie and Kanareff (1970) noted that providing photographs of potential recipients enhanced children's donating behavior. Furthermore, Coward (1975) found that first and second graders assisted a recipient presented in concrete terms more than one presented abstractly. These findings are to be expected given the concrete nature of young children's thinking (Piaget & Inhelder, 1958) and children's limited role-taking abilities (Shantz, 1975).

CONCLUSIONS AND FUTURE DIRECTIONS

According to the research reviewed in this chapter, children, like adults, do not help all individuals equally. However, many recipient characteristics that may influence children's helping, such as ethnicity and mental or physical status of an individual, seldom have been studied. Furthermore, many issues relating to how children discriminate among recipients have yet to be addressed adequately.

One such issue concerns the identification of hierarchies of criteria used by children at various ages to discriminate among potential recipients. Even as early as the preschool years, it is clear that children can use more than one criterion in deciding whom to help. With few exceptions (e.g., Peterson, 1980), researchers seldom have attempted to determine the relative strength of one criterion versus others in children's choices of recipients.

According to the limited data base, the relative importance of a potential recipient's characteristics to a benefactor seems to change with age (Furby, 1978; Peterson, 1980; Peterson et al., 1977). Thus, just because a given characteristic of a recipient has a strong influence on the decision making of benefactors at one age does not mean that the same characteristic will be important to benefactors at a different age. To trace age-related changes in the importance of various recipient characteristics to a benefactor, longitudinal or cross-sectional research is needed.

A related issue is that, in any given situation, more than a single characteristic of a recipient may influence whether or not a child assists a specific individual. The effect of one or more recipient characteristics may interact with other aspects of both the situation and the potential benefactor's own background and personality in determining whether or not a benefactor assists an individual. To rephrase this idea, we know relatively little about when (in which situations) characteristics of the potential recipient are important determinants of the child's choices regarding whom to assist, which other variables influence whether or not a potential benefactor attends to characteristics of the recipient in a given situation, and how other aspects of a situation modify the influence of a potential recipient's characteristics. These are complex issues, and multifaceted research designs are needed to address them.

Another issue not yet adequately considered is the fact that benefactors assist for a variety of reasons (Eisenberg-Berg, 1979; Eisenberg-Berg

& Neal, 1979) and a child's motives for helping probably are related to whom he or she assists. When children help for one type of reason (e.g., to gain approval), they may assist different people than when they help for another reason (e.g., because of empathic responding). Thus, in order to accurately determine how recipient characteristics influence children's prosocial behavior, prosocial behaviors engendered by different motives must be differentiated. As was discussed previously, receipt of solicited and unsolicited behaviors is associated with different recipient characteristics (Eisenberg *et al.*, 1981; unpublished data; see also Marcus & Jenny, 1977). There are many other distinctions that also should be attended to, including the differences among prosocial behaviors motivated by self-gain, by cues of a potential recipient's need, or by the desire to enhance the quality of the relationship between recipient and benefactor. Furthermore, it is logical to assume that at times the child's a priori motive for assisting another will determine whom he or she assists, whereas at other times, who the potential recipient is will influence the motives behind a benefactor's helping actions. Consequently, until we know more about the range of motives that may engender children's prosocial behavior in different situations, it will be difficult to determine when and why children discriminate among various potential recipients of aid.

One final issue concerning how children discriminate among potential recipients should be raised. Should we consider the fact that children help some persons more than others as positive or negative? On one hand, it may be adaptive and realistic for children to be discriminating when dispensing their time and resources. Children who help everyone may have a difficult time surviving in our world. On the other hand, can some of the discriminations made by children be considered repugnant or immoral? These are philosophical issues that someday may need to be considered if we are to develop the means to enhance more effectively children's prosocial responding.

REFERENCES

Ainsworth, M. D. S. The development of infant–mother attachment. In B. M. Caldwell & H. N. Ricciuti (Eds.), *Review of child development research* (Vol. 3). Chicago: Univ. of Chicago Press, 1973.

Ainsworth, M. D., Blehar, M. C., Waters, E., & Wall, S. *Patterns of attachment: A psychological study of the strange situation.* Hillsdale, N.J.: Erlbaum, 1978.

Baldwin, A. L., Baldwin, C. P., Castillo-Vales, V., & Seegmiller, B. Cross-cultural similarities in the development of the concept of kindness. In W. W. Lambert & K. Weisbrod (Eds.), *Comparative perspectives in social psychology.* Boston: Little, Brown, 1971.

Baldwin, C. P., & Baldwin, A. L. Children's judgments of kindness. *Child Development,* 1970, *41,* 29–47.

Barnett, M. A. Effects of competition and relative deservedness of the other's fate on children's generosity. *Developmental Psychology,* 1975, *11,* 665–666.

Berkowitz, L. Responsibility, reciprocity, and social distance in help-giving: An experimental investigation of English social class differences. *Journal of Experimental Social Psychology,* 1968, *4,* 46–63.

Berkowitz, L. Social norms, feelings, and other factors affecting helping and altruism. In L. Berkowitz (Ed.), *Advances in experimental social psychology* (Vol. 6). New York: Academic Press, 1972.

Berkowitz, L., & Friedman, P. Some social class differences in helping behavior. *Journal of Personality and Social Psychology,* 1967, *5,* 217–225.

Berndt, T. J. *Children's conceptions of friendship and the behavior expected of friends.* Paper presented at the Annual Meeting of the American Psychological Association, Toronto, Canada, August 1978.

Berndt, T. J. Age changes and changes over time in prosocial intentions and behavior between friends. *Developmental Psychology,* 1981, *17,* 408–416. (a)

Berndt, T. J. Effects of friendship on prosocial intentions and behavior. *Child Development,* 1981, *52,* 636–643. (b)

Berndt, T. J. Generosity and helpfulness between friends in early adolescence. *Child Development,* 1981, *52,* 636–643. (c)

Braband, J., & Lerner, M. J. "A little time and effort" . . . Who deserves what from whom. *Personality and Social Psychology Bulletin,* 1975, *1,* 177–179.

Charlesworth, R., & Hartup, W. W. Positive social reinforcement in the nursery school peer group. *Child Development,* 1967, *38,* 993–1002.

Clark, A., Hocevar, D., & Dembo, M. H. The role of cognitive development in children's explanations and preferences of skin color. *Developmental Psychology,* 1980, *16,* 332–339.

Clark, K. B., & Clark, M. P. Racial identification and preference in Negro children. In M. M. Newcomb & E. L. Hartley (Eds.), *Readings in social psychology.* New York: Holt, 1947.

Conger, J. J. *Adolescence and youth: Psychological development in a changing world* (2nd ed.). New York: Harper, 1977.

Coward, R. T. Cognitive and affective dimensions of children's sharing behavior (Doctoral dissertation, Purdue University, 1974). *Dissertation Abstracts International,* 1975, *35,* 5612B–5613B. (University Microfilms No. 75-10, 861)

Crockenberg, S. B., Bryant, B. K., & Wilce, L. S. The effects of cooperatively and competitively structured learning environments on inter- and intra-personal behavior. *Child Development,* 1976, *47,* 386–396.

Crosby, F., Bromley, S., & Saxe, L. Recent unobtrusive studies of black and white discrimination and prejudice: A literature review. *Psychological Bulletin,* 1980, *87,* 546–563.

Dreman, S. B. Sharing behavior in Israeli school children: Cognitive and social learning factors. *Child Development,* 1976, *47,* 186–194.

Dreman, S. B., & Greenbaum, C. W. Altruism or reciprocity: Sharing behavior in Israeli kindergarten children. *Child Development,* 1973, *44,* 61–68.

Eisenberg, N. The development of prosocial moral judgment and its correlates (Doctoral dissertation, University of California, Berkeley, 1976). *Dissertation Abstracts International,* 1977, *37,* 4753B. (University Microfilms No. 77-4444)

Eisenberg, N. (Ed.), *The development of prosocial behavior.* New York: Academic Press, 1982.

Eisenberg, N. Children's differentiations among potential recipients of aid. *Child Development,* in press.

Eisenberg, N., Cameron, E., Tryon, K., & Dodez, R. Socialization of prosocial behavior in the preschool classroom. *Developmental Psychology*, 1981, *17*, 773–782.

Eisenberg, N., Lennon, R., & Roth, K. Prosocial development: A longitudinal study. *Developmental Psychology*, in press.

Eisenberg-Berg, N. The development of children's prosocial moral judgment. *Developmental Psychology*, 1979, *15*, 128–137.

Eisenberg-Berg, N., & Hand, M. The relationship of preschoolers' reasoning about prosocial moral conflicts to prosocial behavior. *Child Development*, 1979, *50*, 356–363.

Eisenberg-Berg, N., & Neal, C. Children's moral reasoning about their spontaneous prosocial behavior. *Developmental Psychology*, 1979, *15*, 228–229.

Eisenberg-Berg, N., & Neal, C. The effects of person of the protagonist and costs of helping on children's moral judgment. *Personality and Social Psychology Bulletin*, 1981, *7*, 17–23.

Eisenberg-Berg, N., & Roth, K. The development of children's prosocial moral judgment: A longitudinal follow-up. *Developmental Psychology*, 1980, *16*, 375–376.

Emswiller, T., Deaux, K., & Willits, J. E. Similarity, sex and requests for small favors. *Journal of Applied Social Psychology*, 1971, *1*, 284–291.

Feshbach, N. D. Studies of empathic behavior in children. In B. A. Maher (Ed.), *Progress in experimental personality research* (Vol. 8). New York: Academic Press, 1978.

Fincham, F. Recipient characteristics and sharing behavior in the learning disabled. *Journal of Genetic Psychology*, 1978, *133*, 143–144.

Fink, E. L., Rey, L. D., Johnson, K. W., Spenner, K. I., Morton, D. R., & Flores, E. T. The effects of family occupational type, sex, and appeal style on helping behavior. *Journal of Experimental Social Psychology*, 1975, *11*, 43–52.

Floyd, J. M. K. *Effects of amount of reward and friendship status of the other on the frequency of sharing in children.* Unpublished doctoral dissertation, University of Minnesota, 1964.

Fouts, G. T. Charity in children: The influence of "charity" stimuli and an audience. *Journal of Experimental Child Psychology*, 1972, *13*, 303–309.

Furby, L. Sharing: Decisions and moral judgments about letting others use one's possessions. *Psychological Reports*, 1978, *43*, 595–609.

Furman, W., & Bierman, K. L. *A feature's model theory of children's conceptions of friendship.* Paper presented at the Biennial Meeting of the Society for Research in Child Development, Boston, April 1981.

Furman, W., & Childs, M. L. *A temporal perspective on children's friendships.* Paper presented at the Biennial Meeting of the Society for Research in Child Development, Boston, April 1981.

Gaertner, S. Helping behavior and racial discrimination among liberals and conservatives. *Journal of Personality and Social Psychology*, 1973, *25*, 335–341.

Gaertner, S. The role of racial attitudes in helping behavior. *Journal of Social Psychology*, 1975, *97*, 95–101.

Gaertner, S. L., & Bickman, L. Effects of race on the elicitation of helping behavior: The wrong number technique. *Journal of Personality and Social Psychology*, 1971, *20*, 218–222.

Gottman, J., Gonso, J., & Rasmussen, B. Social interaction, social competence and friendship in children. *Child Development*, 1975, *46*, 709–718.

Graf, R. G., & Riddell, J. C. Helping behavior and a function of interpersonal perception. *Journal of Social Psychology*, 1972, *86*, 227–231.

Gruder, C. L. Cost and dependency as determinants of helping and exploitation. *Journal of Conflict Resolution*, 1974, *18*, 473–485.

Harris, M. B. Reciprocity and generosity: Some determinants of sharing in children. *Child Development*, 1970, *41*, 313–328.

Harris, M. B. Models, norms and sharing. *Psychological Reports*, 1971, *29*, 147–153.

Holmberg, M. C. The development of social interchange patterns from 12 to 42 months. *Child Development*, 1980, *51*, 448–456.

Hook, J. G., & Cook, T. D. Equity theory and the cognitive ability of children. *Psychological Bulletin*, 1979, *86*, 429–455.

Horowitz, I. A. Effect of choice and locus of independence on helping behavior. *Journal of Personality and Social Psychology*, 1968, *8*, 373–376.

Katz, P. A., Katz, I., & Cohen, S. White children's attitudes toward blacks and the physically handicapped: A developmental study. *Journal of Educational Psychology*, 1976, *68*, 20–24.

Katz, P. A., Sohn, M., & Zalk, S. R. Perceptual concomitants of racial attitudes in urban grade-school children. *Developmental Psychology*, 1975, *11*, 135–144.

Kohlberg, L. Stage and sequence: The cognitive-developmental approach to socialization. In D. A. Goslin (Ed.), *Handbook of socialization theory and research*. New York: Rand McNally, 1969.

Kohlberg, L. From is to ought: How to commit the naturalistic fallacy and get away with it in the study of moral development. In T. Mischel (Ed.), *Cognitive development and genetic epistemology*. New York: Academic Press, 1971.

Kohn, M. The child as a determinant of his peers' approach to him. *Journal of Genetic Psychology*, 1966, *109*, 91–100.

Krebs, D. Altruism: An examination of the concept and a review of the literature. *Psychological Bulletin*, 1970, *73*, 258–302.

Ladd, G. W., Lange, G., & Stremmel, A. *Personal and situational determinants of children's helping decisions and persistence.* Paper presented at the Biennial Meeting of the Society for Research in Child Development, Boston, April 1981.

Lamb, M. E. Interactions between eighteen-month-olds and their preschool-aged siblings. *Child Development*, 1978, *49*, 51–59. (a)

Lamb, M. E. The development of sibling relationships in infancy: A short-term longitudinal study. *Child Development*, 1978, *49*, 1189–1196. (b)

Leiter, M. P. A study of reciprocity in preschool play groups. *Child Development*, 1977, *48*, 1288–1295.

Lerner, R. M., & Frank, P. Laboratory analogue of field helping behavior. *Psychological Reports*, 1974, *35*, 557–558. (a)

Lerner, R. M., & Frank, P. Relation of race and sex to supermarket helping behavior. *Journal of Social Psychology*, 1974, *94*, 201–203. (b)

Leung, J. J., & Foster, S. F. *Induction, recipient deservedness, and personality attractiveness: Effects on children's helping behavior.* Paper presented at the Annual Meeting of the American Educational Research Association, Los Angeles, April 1981.

Liebert, R. M., Fernandez, L. E., & Gill, L. Effects of a "friendless" model on imitation and prosocial behavior. *Psychonomic Science*, 1969, *16*, 81–82.

Long, G. T., & Lerner, M. J. Deserving, the "personal contract," and altruistic behavior by children. *Journal of Personality and Social Psychology*, 1974, *29*, 551–556.

Macaulay, J. Familiarity, attraction, and charity. *Journal of Social Psychology*, 1975, *95*, 27–37.

McGuire, J. M., & Thomas, M.H. Effects of sex, competence, and competition on sharing behavior in children. *Journal of Personality and Social Psychology*, 1975, *32*, 490–494.

Mann, S. A. Sharing in kindergarten children as a function of friendship status and socioeconomic status. *Dissertation Abstracts International*, 1974, *34*, 4050.

Marcus, R. F., & Jenny, B. A naturalistic study of reciprocity in the helping behavior of young children. *The Alberta Journal of Educational Research*, 1977, *23*, 195–206.

Masters, J. C. Effects of social comparison upon children's self-reinforcement and altruism toward competitors and friends. *Developmental Psychology,* 1971, *5,* 64–72.

Masters, J. C., & Furman, W. Popularity, individual friendship selection, and specific peer interaction among children. *Developmental Psychology,* 1981, *17,* 344–350.

Miller, D. T., & Smith, J. The effect of own deservingness and deservingness of others on children's helping behavior. *Child Development,* 1977, *48,* 617–620.

Morgan, W. R., & Sawyer, J. Bargaining, expectations, and the preference for equality over equity. *Journal of Personality and Social Psychology,* 1967, *6,* 139–149.

Mussen, P., & Eisenberg-Berg, N. *Roots of caring, sharing, and helping: The development of prosocial behavior in children.* San Francisco: Freeman, 1977.

Pandey, J., & Griffitt, W. Attraction and helping. *Bulletin of the Psychonomic Society,* 1974, *3,* 123–124.

Panofsky, A. D. The effect of similarity/dissimilarity of race and personal interests on empathy and altruism in second graders (Doctoral dissertation, University of California, Los Angeles, 1976). *Dissertation Abstracts International,* 1976, *37,* 200A. (University Microfilms, No. 76-16, 659)

Pastor, D. L. The quality of mother–infant attachment and its relationship to toddlers' initial sociability with peers. *Developmental Psychology,* 1981, *17,* 326–335.

Peterson, L. Developmental changes in verbal and behavioral sensitivity to cues of social norms of altruism. *Child Development,* 1980, *51,* 830–838.

Peterson, L., Hartmann, D. P., & Gelfand, D. M. Developmental changes in the effects of dependency and reciprocity cues on children's moral judgments and donation rates. *Child Development,* 1977, *48,* 1331–1339.

Piaget, J. *The moral judgment of the child.* New York: Free Press, 1965. (Originally published, 1932.)

Piaget, J., & Inhelder, B. *The growth of logical thinking from childhood to adolescence.* New York: Basic Books, 1958.

Piliavin, I. M., Piliavin, J. A., & Rodin, J. Good samaritanism: An underground phenomenon? *Journal of Personality and Social Psychology,* 1969, *13,* 289–299.

Piliavin, I. M., Piliavin, J. A., & Rodin, J. Costs, diffusion, and the stigmatized victim. *Journal of Personality and Social Psychology,* 1975, *32,* 429–438.

Presbie, R. J., & Kanareff, V. T. Sharing in children as a function of the number of shares and reciprocity. *Journal of Genetic Psychology,* 1970, *116,* 31–44.

Radke-Yarrow, M., Zahn-Waxler, C., & Chapman, M. Prosocial dispositions and behavior. In P. Mussen (Ed.), *Manual of child psychology.* New York: Wiley, in press.

Raviv, A., Bar-Tal, D., Ayalon, H., & Raviv, A. Perception of giving and receiving help by group members. *Representative Research in Social Psychology,* 1980, *11,* 140–151.

Rheingold, H. L., Hay, D. F., & West, M. J. Sharing in the second year of life. *Child Development,* 1976, *47,* 1148–1158.

Rubin, Z. *Children's friendships.* Cambridge, Mass.: Harvard Univ. Press, 1980.

Ruble, D. N., Boggiano, A. K., Feldman, N. S., & Loebl, J. H. Developmental analyses of the role of social comparison in self-evaluation. *Developmental Psychology,* 1980, *16,* 105–115.

Rushton, J. P. Socialization and the altruistic behavior of children. *Psychological Bulletin,* 1976, *83,* 898–913.

Rushton, J. P. *Altruism, socialization, and society.* Englewood Cliffs, N.J.: Prentice-Hall, 1980.

Schaps, E. Cost, dependency, and helping. *Journal of Personality and Social Psychology,* 1972, *21,* 74–48.

Schopler, J., & Matthews, M. W. The influence of the perceived causal locus of partner's dependence on the use of interpersonal power. *Journal of Personality and Social Psychology,* 1965, *2,* 609–612.

Shantz, C. U. The development of social cognition. In E. M. Hetherington (Ed.), *Review of child development research* (Vol. 5). Chicago: Univ. of Chicago Press, 1975.

Sharabany, R., Gershoni, R., & Hofman, J. E. Age and sex differences in the development of adolescent intimate-friendships. *Developmental Psychology*, 1981, *17*, 800–808.

Sharabany, R., & Hertz-Lazarowitz, R. Do friends share and communicate more than nonfriends? *International Journal of Behavior Development*, 1981, *4*, 45–59.

Simon, W. E. Helping behavior in the absence of visual contact as a function of sex of person asking for help and sex of person being asked for help. *Psychological Reports*, 1971, *28*, 609–610.

Skarin, K., & Moely, B. E. Altruistic behavior: An analysis of age and sex differences. *Child Development*, 1976, *47*, 1159–1165.

Staub, E. Helping a distressed person: Social, personality and stimulus determinants. In L. Berkowitz (Ed.), *Advances in experimental social psychology* (Vol. 7). New York: Academic Press, 1974.

Staub, E. *Positive social behavior and morality: Social and personal influences* (Vol. 1). New York: Academic Press, 1978.

Staub, E. *Positive social behavior and morality: Socialization and development* (Vol. 2). New York: Academic Press, 1979.

Staub, E., & Feinberg, H. K. *Regularities in peer interaction, empathy, and sensitivity to others.* Paper presented at the Annual Meeting of the American Psychological Association, Montreal, September 1980.

Staub, E., & Noerenberg, H. Property rights, deservingness, reciprocity, friendship: The transactional character of children's sharing behavior. *Journal of Personality and Social Psychology*, 1981, *40*, 271–289.

Staub, E., & Sherk, L. Need for approval, children's sharing behavior, and reciprocity in sharing. *Child Development*, 1970, *41*, 243–252.

Stephen, W. G. Cognitive differentiation in intergroup perception. *Sociometry*, 1977, *40*, 50–58.

Suls, J., Witenberg, S., & Gutkin, D. Evaluating reciprocal and nonreciprocal prosocial behavior: Developmental changes. *Personality and Social Psychology Bulletin*, 1981, *7*, 25–31.

Thayer, S. Lend me your ears: Facial and sexual factors in helping the deaf. *Journal of Personality and Social Psychology*, 1973, *28*, 8–11.

Turner, S. M., & Forehand, R. Imitative behaviors as a function of success–failure and racial–socioeconomic factors. *Journal of Applied Social Psychology*, 1976, *6*, 40–47.

Underwood, B., & Moore, B. S. The generality of altruism in children. In N. Eisenberg (Ed.), *The development of prosocial behavior.* New York: Academic Press, 1982.

Walters, J., Pearce, D., & Dahms, L. Affectional and aggressive behavior of preschool children. *Child Development*, 1957, *28*, 15–26.

Waters, S., Wippman, J., & Sroufe, L. A. Attachment, positive affect, and competence in the peer group: Two studies in construct validation. *Child Development*, 1979, *50*, 821–829.

Wegner, D. M., & Crano, W. D. Racial factors in helping behavior: An unobtrusive field experiment. *Journal of Personality and Social Psychology*, 1975, *32*(5), 901–905.

West, S. G., Whitney, G., & Schnedler, R. Helping a motorist in distress: The effects of sex, race, and neighborhood. *Journal of Personality and Social Psychology*, 1975, *31*, 691–698.

Willis, J. B., Feldman, N. S., & Ruble, D. N. Children's generosity as influenced by deservedness of reward and type of recipient. *Journal of Educational Psychology*, 1977, *69*(1), 33–35.

Wispe, L. G., & Freshley, H. G. Race, sex, and the sympathetic helping behavior: The broken bag caper. *Journal of Personality and Social Psychology*, 1971, *17*, 59–65.

Wright, B. A. Altruism in children and the perceived conduct of others. *Journal of Abnormal and Social Psychology*, 1942, *37*, 218–233.

Youniss, J. *Parents and peers in social development: A Sullivan-Piaget perspective.* Chicago: Univ. of Chicago Press, 1980.

Zahn-Waxler, C., & Radke-Yarrow, M. *A developmental analysis of children's responses to emotions in others.* Paper presented at the Biennial Meeting of the Society for Research in Child Development, San Francisco, March 1979.

Zeldin, R. S., Savin-Williams, R. C., & Small, S. A. *A naturalistic study of prosocial and dominance behavior in two groups of adolescent boys.* Paper presented at the American Psychological Association, Montreal, September 1980.

Zeldin, R. S., Small, S. A., & Savin-Williams, R. C. Prosocial interactions in two mixed-sex adolescent groups. *Child Development*, 1982, *53*, 1492–1498.

Zinser, O., & Lydiatt, E. W. Mode of recipient definition, affluence of the recipient, and sharing behavior in preschool children. *Journal of Genetic Psychology*, 1976, *129*, 261–266.

Zinser, O., Perry, J. S., Bailey, R. C., & Lydiatt, E. W. Racial recipients, value of donations, and sharing behavior in children. *Journal of Genetic Psychology*, 1976, *129*, 29–35.

Zinser, O., Perry, J. S., & Edgar, R. M. Affluence of the recipient, value of donations, and sharing behavior in preschool children. *Journal of Psychology*, 1975, *89*, 301–305.

8 / The development of children's equity judgments

JAY G. HOOK

Equity is one of those words that is both useful and useless. It can be applied in almost any circumstance, but it is insufferably vague as to particulars. For youth, it offers appealing vistas of uprightness and fairness. For older folk, it refers to that downright unfairly small part of the mortgage payment that actually reduces the debt—and should not have been deducted on the taxes. In the law schools, equity is a whole course, more palatable than federal income taxation, about those appealing doctrines that rescue litigants from the jaws of laws that have failed to adapt to changing times; yet, it includes those injurious cases in which the defendant is denied a jury of his peers and the plaintiff can win even though he or she has no cause of action in law. In social psychology, the word refers to a general theory of cognition and motivation, embracing every social thought any subject could have, from subjective inputs—"I loved him"—to objective outcomes—"He owes me $100." Because of its all-embracing generality, and consequent failure to make singular predictions in specific cases, the theory has not been generally embraced by psychologists. It has received some play, however, in distributive justice research, perhaps because that area concerns the fair allocation of "things," which are usually limited by norm to the objective and measurable. Thus, although she may think it unfair that he is paid as much as she for joint labor, when he enjoys it so much more, norms dictate that such job satisfaction criteria are too ill defined to be included as inputs in the fairness (equity) equation.

This chapter, then, concerns the formal, social psychological version of equity theory (Adams, 1965; Walster, Berscheid, & Walster, 1976) as it predicts the judgments of children about the resolution of distributive justice dilemmas. The pièce de résistance of the chapter, to foreshadow a bit, is a four-step model, called NOIR, of the development of mediating cognitions of distributive justice judgment during the school years, together with a summary of the evidence for the model, and a proposed methodology to shed further light on NOIR. Before NOIR, however, the chapter includes descriptions of the typical distributive justice–equity dilemma, the equity theory predictions about evaluations of that dilemma, and the problems with those predictions as applied to children, who, it will be argued, typically generate different mediating cognitions than do adults. The task is a daunting one, and even the very first section will require divine guidance.

As reported in Matthew 20:1–16, Jesus told his disciples the parable of a householder who hired laborers to work his vineyards. At the beginning of the 12-hour day, he agreed with the first set of laborers (Y) that they would be paid a penny each. Since the Roman penny of that day was worth one-eighth ounce of gold, the reader should not despair for them. Subsequent cohorts of laborers were hired throughout the day, at the third, sixth, ninth, and finally, the eleventh hour (X) for the agreed pay, "whatsoever is right." At the end of the day, the householder paid every laborer the same amount—one penny. In equity theory terms, then, the workers had rather different inputs, but the same outcomes. For example, members of cohort Y labored 12 hours, whereas members of cohort X labored a mere 1 hour; the equity ratios for Y and X, of outcomes over inputs, were 1/12 and 1/1, respectively. Since the two ratios are not equal—that is, not proportional—equity theory states that persons cognizant of the nonproportionality should have felt some form of dissonance that should have motivated them to act, or alter their cognitions, so as to restore proportionality. In this case, the Y laborers "murmured against the goodman of the house." Matthew does not describe the response of the X eleventh-hour laborers, although it is easy to imagine their smug silence. Despite the murmurous mood of the workers, the householder did not yield, pointing to the contract with the Y's and saying: "Is it not lawful for me to do what I will with mine own?"

What did Jesus make of this? He seems to have been in his master politican mode this time, uttering the rather cryptic moral: "So the last shall be first, and the first last." Although this is in itself of little help, it is clear that Jesus approved of the outcome. Thus, the cognitive psychologist's task of exegesis is to discern what interpretation rule He used to reach His positive evaluation. Jesus seems to have been, rather characteristically, of three minds on this issue. First, He could have used an *equality* rule. After all, why should relative work matter? Second, He could have had an *authority* rule in mind. The fair distribution is whatever distribution a power figure orders. This is the distributive justice morality Piaget (1932/1965) attributed to young children under the hierarchical influence of their families. Third, he could have had a *contractarian* rule in mind. The appropriate distribution rule is the one that the participants negotiate and bind themselves to in advance. This approach is similar to Piaget's morality of peer interaction.

Each of these three textual interpretations implies an allocation rule alternative to the equity rule (Adams, 1965). Thus, the same allocation may have different rationales or cognitive sources. If, on the other hand, several different persons are all using the equity rule, will they all make the same allocation? The answer is no. Another messianic figure provides an example.

In *Capital* (1906), Marx described an equity theory of value. Such disparate items as a hat, house, and locomotive all have value in that they fetch a price on the market. Marx argued that, although every item is imbued with value in a unique way, all item values share a common denominator—labor. Every marketable item contains labor. But what is the measure of labor? If one hat is made by a slow-working novice, the other by a speedy expert, is the former hat more valuable than the latter? No. Although labor is the relevant input, which is proportional to value, it could be measured by time, or skill, or effort. Thus, labor may be expressed as different inputs—of time, and skill, and effort, and many others. It is not clear, of course, that Marx thought rewards, or outcomes, should correspond to value created—in fact, he probably did not. If he had, however, his system would have involved an equity rule with no clear specification that input is relevant. Should the novice hatter be paid more, for fewer hats? Would that make the expert hatter mad?

Between Marx and Jesus, then, there seem to be two interpretations of individual differences in preferred outcome allocations. On the one hand, disagreeing allocators could have entirely different allocation rules in mind, such as equity versus equality. On the other hand, the allocators could all be following an equity rule but be using different inputs, such as time versus quantity of production. The cognitive psychologist interested in a full explanation of allocation behaviors must be concerned, in the first place, with which interpretation or combination of interpretations is correct. The proper methodology for such discovery is the concern of a later section of this chapter. A second question for the cognitive psychologist is: Why do people prefer different rules or different inputs within the equity rule? Although many explanations of different rule or input preference spring to mind, they can probably be placed in groups labeled "situation" and "person." The situation in which the allocation is made may command or reinforce certain allocation rules, as when a third-party observer makes the socially normative allocation salient, or it may constrain the information available for various rules, as when the allocator thinks effort is the key input but has no information about relative effort. Certain personal attributes of the allocator may influence allocations in the same two ways. The values and reinforcement history of the allocator may cause him or her to prefer certain rules or inputs, and the cognitive capacity of the allocator may constrain his or her ability to acquire or process relevant information. The next section of the chapter, beginning with Table 8.1, summarizes what little is known of the factors that influence rule or input selection in children's allocations.

CAUSES OF INDIVIDUAL DIFFERENCES IN OUTCOME ALLOCATIONS

Table 8.1 is a two-by-two matrix defined by the "situation–person" dimension (rows) and the "values–information" dimension (columns). Each cell in the table defines a set of factors that might influence the rule of allocation chosen (equity, equality, authority, self-interest, etc.) or the particular inputs chosen within the equity rule (time, effort, quantity, etc.). For example, the upper-left cell, at the confluence of "situation" and "values," defines a set of values that are triggered or made salient by the situation in which the allocation occurs. The word *values* is used in a broad sense. A child may have learned that it is best to

Table 8.1. Factors that Influence Outcome Allocation Behavior

	Values	Information
Situation	Observers, future interaction, incentives, etc.	How richly specified is the independent variable? Task complexity, etc.
Person	Genetic and learned attributes: Age, race, sex, etc.	Allocator capacity to receive information and transform into proper rule-based allocation

please authority figures. When asked to allocate the partridges in pear trees, say, the child may allocate in the way he or she thinks the authority wants them allocated. This is situational in that children may allocate differently in the presence and absence of authorities (Kidder, Bellettirie, & Cohn, 1977; Leventhal, Popp, & Sawyer, 1973; Reis & Gruzen, 1976). If the child is likely to interact with one of the allocation recipients in the future, it might cause a different allocation than if no interaction is anticipated (Grumbkow, Deen, Steensma, & Wilke, 1976; Morgan & Sawyer, 1967). If the allocation is purely hypothetical, involving pretend characters, it may be different than if it has real implications (Dreman, 1976; Lerner, 1974). If the allocation recipients are team members or cooperating, the allocation may be different than if they are competitive (Crockenberg, Bryant, & Wilce, 1976; Lerner, 1974). If the rewards being allocated are very valuable (e.g., turtle doves), the allocation may be different than if the rewards are trivial. Many such variables have been studied, but they have rarely been studied in more than one study with commensurable designs. Thus, the only conclusion is to suggest that these are primarily methodological studies, addressing less the theoretical interpretations of allocations than the problems of internal validity.

The upper-right cell, at the confluence of "situation" and "information," has a similar methodological flavor. If a child as asked to divide 12 French hens between two workers but is not told how much work each performed, then he or she does not have sufficient information to make an equitable allocation but does have sufficient information to make an equal allocation. If that child is asked to divide 12 calling birds between two workers who did 2 and 4 hours of work, respectively, the child has sufficient information to make an equitable allocation based on labor time inputs, but not based on labor effort inputs. The form of information given the allocator does not constrain the range of possible allocations, but it does constrain the range of possible cognitive mediations, or rules linking the inputs to the outcome allocations. Substantively, this means that the allocation rule or preferred input the psychologist seeks to discover must have been anticipated in the design of the stimuli. Methodologically, the problem is both a boon and a bane. Manipulations that are far less rich in information than are real-life situations make it possible to identify whether individual factors (e.g., an input), in isolation, affect allocations. Such single-factor manipulations, however, do not allow the experimenter to discover which of several inputs have priority over, or cancel out, others. The orthogonal manipulation of two or more inputs at once ostensibly allows estimates of the extent to which each input and input interactions influence allocation variability; however, such manipulations imply, as does equity theory, that persons can hold in mind and calculate several inputs at once—a dubious assumption (cf. Anderson & Butzin, 1978; Hook & Cook, 1979).

The lower-left cell of Table 8.1, at the confluence of "person" and "values," defines a set of reasons for preferred rules of allocation or relevant inputs that reside in the head of the allocator transsituationally. Traditional theories of attitude and value formation seem to apply here. When asked to divide 12 geese a-laying between two butchers who worked 2 and 4 hours, respectively, to catch them, one child might divide 6 and 6 because he was once punished for not sharing equally, because a revered uncle once divided a gift equally between the allocator and his brother, or because he had read Kohlberg. Another child might divide the geese 8 and 4 for somewhat different experiential reasons. In addition, the geese might be cleaved differently between the butchers as a consequence of static person variables of the allocators, such as race or sex. As might be expected, a fairly large literature exists on sex differences in allocations (Kidder, Bellettirie, & Cohn, 1977; Lerner, 1974; Leventhal & Anderson, 1970; Leventhal et al., 1973; Uesugi & Vinacke, 1963). Although a couple of studies suggest that females prefer equality and males prefer equity, methodological problems render this interpretation dubious. Several studies show socioeconomic status to be related to differences in distributive justice judgments, such that higher-class children attend to inputs higher on the Damon (1975, 1980) hierarchy than do lower-class children (Enright, Enright, Manheim, & Harris, 1980; Enright, Franklin, & Manheim, 1980; Enright & Sutterfield, 1980). Race has not been included as an independent variable. Consideration of the ultimate developmental person variable, age, begins in the next paragraph.

The lower-right cell, at the confluence of "person" and "information," defines a set of explanations of differences in rule and input preferences based on the capacity of the allocators to acquire and manipulate the information necessary for the implementation of different rules and input types. If a child is asked to allocate 12 swans a-swimming to two farmers who worked 2 and 4 hours, respectively, to earn them, equity theory says the child should create two ratios, Farmer X swans/2 and Farmer Y swans/4, then sift through various combinations of ($X + Y = 12$), such as 10 and 2, 9 and 3, 8 and 4 (eureka), until the two ratios are proportional. If, however, the child does not know fractions, what will she do? She is not capable of an equitable allocation, but she is capable of an equal allocation (e.g., by one-to-one correspondence of hens). Will she adopt a different allocation rule because it is what she knows how to do? This capacity-based changing of rules is one interpretation of Piaget's (1932/1965) three-stage description of negative justice development, from authority to equality to equity (equality tempered by other considerations). On the other hand, this information-capacity interpretation could focus on changing inputs within an equity framework. If the farmers produced the same amount of work despite disparate time worked, because X tried harder, the child might want to give X and Y the same number of swans. If the equal work resulted because X had more ability, however, the child might want to give Y more hens than X. But what if the child's capacity for inferring effort (requiring knowledge of subjectivity) or ability (requiring memory of past performance) is not adequately developed? Again, there is a collateral literature that documents age-related development of such inferential capacities (Sedlak & Kurtz, 1981).

This last cell is the principal concern of the present chapter, not because it is more important than the other cells, but because the present literature on the normal cognitive development of children seems more relevant and easily transported to the allocation situation within this cell. The next section, then, contains a developmental analysis of the equity problem and literature in terms of the ''person'' and ''information'' cell of Table 8.1. The NOIR model proposed therein implies that there are equity problems that children confront, perform, talk about, and probably think about within each age range but that the essential quality of the equity problem changes from time to time, in rough synchrony with similar changes in thinking about a wide range of similar problems. The model focuses on development as a process of rule changes, as in the Piaget three-step description, rather than as a process of input substitutions, primarily because the latter approach assumes some kind of adult equity processing throughout the age span—an unlikely assumption.

THE NOIR MODEL

In the typical equity judgment study, the child subject learns of the work of two persons, say A and B, by means of actual observation, videotape, or perhaps a story reading. For example, say A and B have done 2 and 4 hours of work, respectively. Next, the child subject is asked to decide what part of a reward, or outcome, A and B should each receive. These reward shares are here labeled X (A's share) and Y (B's share). For example, if the experimenter asks the child to divide 12 golden rings between A and B, then the principal dependent measure, say the outcomes to the superior, B worker, could range from 0 to 12 golden rings.

Equity theory (Adams, 1965) states that the allocator will create two ratios, one for each worker, of golden rings per hours of work, if work is
the relevant input, and compare the two ratios for proportionality. In
other words, the child will search for an allocation of rings such that
$X/A = Y/B$, or in this case, $4/2 = 8/4$. Before swallowing the equity
interpretation, however, it will be useful to step back and examine the
ways in which the four elements in this dyadic relationship—two of work
(A and B), and two of reward (X and Y)—can be related to each other
and what the intellectual demands of such relating are.

The following table displays the four elements as the vertex of a
square.

Outcomes	X	Y
Inputs	A	B

The very simplest relationship of elements is both *nominal* and *unidimensional*. In order to graph the nominal relationship, the reader should
draw one arrow from B to Y, in his or her mind's eye, and one arrow
from A to X. At this step, the child who thinks about the relationships
merely has to notice the co-occurrence or association, within one person, of an input and an outcome. When certain classes of actions (work,
good works, being good) are performed by an individual, certain positive outcomes normally follow. When they are not performed, the outcomes do not follow. This relationship is, of course, a special case of
good old stimulus–response. It is special in that the child is noticing or
thinking about the association rather than merely behaving within its
constraints, and in that the $A \leftrightarrow X$ and $B \leftrightarrow Y$ links are part of that
special class of events whose relationship can be thought to be "fair"
or "deserved" (beyond a law of nature, a law of society). These relations
are also unidimensional in that they refer to single individuals—their
acts and outcomes—and are not yet *social* in the sense of comparing
individuals. Their social dimension is probably of the adult giver–child
receiver type. The child notices that his or her act, rewarded by the parent the last time, is not rewarded this time. In such a case, does the
child's observation of failed regularity provoke feelings of injustice? Or
does the sense of injustice follow from the adult's recognition that the
failed regularity was wrong?

Now if the reader will erase the arrows from A to X and from B to Y
on her mental blackboard, and draw new arrows from A to B and from
X to Y, she will be ready for the other unidimensional relationships. At
some point, the child may notice that a valuable object or rewarding
outcome denied her is given to another child—maybe a brother or sister,

or a day-care peer. Probably later, the same child might notice that she received a reward that another child did not receive. These are nominal, $X \leftrightarrow Y$ relations. Later still, the $A \leftrightarrow B$ relations, the selective presence and absence of various input-like acts and attributes in various children, may also be noticed. These are all unidimensional relations in that, although they involve interindividual social comparisons, they are *within* the outcome and input domains. Just as the child noticed inconsistencies in the parent's rewarding behavior, so the child may notice inconsistencies between outcomes for different individuals, independent of input, that may provoke a sense of failed regularity. This observation may then be transformed into a sense of injustice, given the appropriate response by authority to the child's notification of the inconsistency.

The children who are neophyte noticers of these unidimensional relations are young preschoolers. At this age, it seems reasonable to tie the nominal and unidimensional ideas together. At an older age, these children will notice that one of their peers got more reward than another, an ordinal notion. By then, however, they will also be comparing relationships on different dimensions, the next step in the NOIR model. It should be noted that a major class of models of justice cognitions, the relative deprivation theories (cf. Crosby, 1976), are mixtures of nominal and ordinal principles. These theories assume that people make ordinal comparisons on the outcome dimension ($X \leftrightarrow Y$) between those persons who are appropriate for comparison (a nominal idea, since A is either comparable or not comparable to B). Unlike equity theory, relative deprivation theory has stirred little interest among researchers in child development (Stephenson & Barker, 1972; Stephenson & White, 1968), although it may be appropriate. A second point about these preschool, nominal, unidimensional cognitions bears mentioning. Children of this capacity should be able to make equal or self-interested allocations, even if not equitable ones. Thus, evidence of such allocations in this age range suggests cognitive limitations as much as preference for alternative rules.

Just as the child should experience more cognitive strain with the *ordinal* problem than the nominal problem, so should the explanation of the former require more mental gymnastics of the reader, who should now erase the arrows connecting the elements $X \leftrightarrow Y$ and $A \leftrightarrow B$ and place relational signs between X and Y (e.g., $X < Y$) and between A and B (e.g., $A < B$). In the initial example, B's 4 hours of work is greater than A's 2 hours. The ordinal relationship between B and A is not so sophisticated as "twice" as much, or even "two more than." It is merely "more than." At this step, the simple equity rule is that B must be allocated more golden rings than A (i.e., $X < Y$), such that the sign relating A and B is the same as the sign relating X and Y. Thus, the reader's mental arrow should point from one relational sign to another ($<$ $\leftrightarrow$ $<$). At this stage, any allocation of golden rings between and including 7 and 12 to B serves equity. As simple as this seems, it is quite sophisticated for, a 7-year-old, who is mastering the capacity to hold a relationship—an abstraction—in mind for comparison to another relationship —another abstraction. A rather more simple case, a transition from nominal to ordinal, would involve the child's realization that a reward for work given to one child was not given to another child who had also done some work.

Several lines of research with children's social comparisons seem to imply this type of ordinal relationship process. Homans's (1961) sociological theory of justice is an ordinal theory, and many child development researchers who claim they are equity theorists employ data analyses that test only the ordinal form (cf. Hook & Cook, 1979). Work by Ruble and her associates (e.g., Ruble, Boggiano, Feldman, & Loebl, 1980), in which academic performance information is ordinally manipulated across children to cause ordinal differences in self-esteem among the same children, posits a similar cognitive process. Generally, this type of theory does not successfully predict children's judgments until about 7 years.

An added complication characterizes the *interval* stage. The reader should subtract the lesser input value from the greater input value to yield a value called P, and subtract the lesser outcome value from the greater outcome value to yield a value called Q. In the golden rings example, $B - A = P$; that is, $4 - 2 = 2$. Also, $Y - X = Q$; that is, $8 - 4 = 4$. As children begin to mind their P's and Q's, probably around age 10 years, they notice not only that greater work corresponds with greater reward but also that "much greater" work corresponds with "much greater" reward.

Of course, the whole story began with the last stage, the *ratio* stage. The reason ratio proportionality in equity judgments is so hard for preadolescents is that the comparison being made is between two formal abstractions, the ratios. It seems clear that such proportional thought, across a wide variety of contents, is not acquired before adolescence (cf. Hook & Cook, 1979). It is also doubtful that even adults, although they perhaps arrive at the equity prediction, actually employ the problem solving strategy suggested by equity theory. Informal reports by graduate students of their introspections while solving the golden rings example suggest that they do not set up the $X/A = Y/B$ proportionality, but rather they search out either a satisfactory $Y/(X + Y) = B/(B + A)$ relationship or a satisfactory $Y/X = A/B$ relationship. Equity theory also states that, when multiple inputs are available and considered relevant, they will be added together in the denominators. For example, if workers *A* and *B* worked 2 and 4 hours, respectively, but produced, say, four and two quantities of product, respectively, equity theory suggests that allocators will set up the ratios $X/(4 + 2) = Y/(2 + 4)$. The graduate student reports suggest that allocators first calculate for *Y* alone, $Y1/(X + Y1) = B/(A + B)$ for input one, $Y2/(X + Y2) = B/(A + B)$ for input two, then $(Y1 + Y2)/2 = Y$ for the allocation. Although there is some research on multiple inputs with adults and children (Anderson, 1976; Anderson & Butzin, 1978; Anderson & Farkas, 1975), this topic is too unstudied and complex to justify any conclusions just now.

DARK VICTORY: SUPPORT FOR
THE NOIR MODEL

The NOIR model is based on the assumption that various classes of behaviors that seem to require structurally similar supporting cognitions will develop in a similar sequence. It is certainly possible, however, to imagine circumstances in which this assumption would be false. Consider the golden rings example from the last section. If *A* and *B* worked 2 and 4 hours, respectively, in a nail factory, and at the end of the day they had finished 12 barrels of nails and were to receive 12 golden rings as payment, the mathematical problem of how many nail barrels did each fill and the allocation problem of how many golden rings should each receive are fundamentally different. An adolescent who learned an equality rule way back in the nominal stage, and was continuously taught and reinforced for equality allocations, might divide the golden rings 6 and 6, even while accurately calculating the 4 and 8 relationship in barrels filled. Yet, what little information is available seems to support the assumption of parallel development.

First, the NOIR model, generalized to a wide variety of contents involving mathematical proportionality, such as speed and time, space, probability, and balance arms, seems consistent with observations of the development of behavior and explanation in those content areas (cf. Hook & Cook, 1979). Second, there is some evidence to the effect that proportional thinking does not occur until adolescence in content areas outside (as well as within) the traditional mathematics and physics examples cited earlier. For example, in a study of metaphor comprehension, Billow (1975) found no evidence for such comprehension before adolescence. The metaphor, of course, has a nonmetric proportional form. The statement "Anna roared" can be analyzed Anna–lion as Anna's voice–roar. Green (1979) found that children did not attain consistency in their evaluation of the speakers of linguistic modals (e.g., "may" or "could") until adolescence and until they achieved proportionality on the Piagetian probability problems. The modal is the linguistic ratio term, and consistent use of modals is like proportionality (to say "I will help you" implies a different probability than "I may help you."). Third, a secondary analysis of equity studies done before the NOIR model was proposed was consistent with the model (cf. Hook & Cook, 1979). Finally, the one study based on the model (Hook, 1982) supported it.

In this study, children aged 7–13 years old were told stories in which two characters had cooperatively done eight units of work. The work units, in the three independent conditions, were divided 8/0, 6/2, and 4/4 between the workers, A and B. The children were then asked to divide 16 rewards between A and B. The design allowed for separate allocation predictions, depending on whether the children were using the nominal, ordinal, or ratio rules. The author had not yet thought of the interval stage. At the nominal stage, workers who did two or four units of work should have received the same rewards, more than the zero-unit worker, because they had both done *some* work, whereas he had done *none*. At the ordinal stage, the four-unit worker should have received more than the two- and zero-unit workers, because, whereas she had done as much work as her dyad mate (4/4), the two- and zero-unit workers had done *less* work than their dyad mate (4/4), the two- and zero-unit workers had done *less* work than their dyad mates (6/2, 8/0). At the ratio stage, the four-unit worker should have recieved more rewards than the two-unit worker, who in turn should have received more rewards than the zero-unit worker, because each worker had done a different proportion of the total work. The results supported the predictions. The 7-year-olds made nominal allocations, the 9- and 11-year-olds made ordinal allocations, and the 13-year-olds made ratio allocations.

FUTURE RESEARCH: A DESIGN

There is a modest amount of support for NOIR in the literature—modest in that it is indirect and inferential. This last section is a modest proposal for a direct test of NOIR—modest in that it includes just one research design through which NOIR could be falsified and a few measures designed to rule out the most obvious rival interpretations.

The reader will not be surprised to learn that the design involves telling children stories in which two characters A and B have worked, say to make nails in a factory. The ratios of their work periods, B/A, form one independent variable with four levels, 3/1, 2/1, 3/3, and 2/2. The children are also told how much reward worker A received. This reward for A, labeled X, is the second independent variable, with two levels, three and five golden rings. In each case, there are two dependent measures—one mathematical and one allocational. These two measures tap structurally identical problems. For example, the mathematical problem might be: "If A, who worked 1 hour, filled three big barrels with nails, how many big barrels did B, who worked 3 hours, fill?" The parallel allocation problem would be: "Since A, who worked 1 hour, was paid three golden rings, how many golden rings do you think B, who worked 3 hours, should be paid?" The amount attributed to worker B, be it barrels filled or golden rings received, is labeled Y. Thus, the design is a four (work ratios) by two (rewards for X) factorial manipulation, and Y is the dependent measure.

The principal value of this design is that it yields a different pattern of predicted allocations (or mathematical, barrels filled, solutions) for each of the NOIR steps and the major alternative allocation rules as well. If children follow egalitarian rules, then there should be a monotonic relationship between X and Y, with no main effect for work ratio. The *nominal* step implies no main effect at all, since under all ratios both workers did some work. The *ordinal* step demands two main effects, for X reward and for work ratio, such that B should receive more rewards (Y) when she has done more work than A (3/1 and 2/1) than when she has done the same work (3/3 and 2/2). The *interval* step requires, further, that allocations be greater to Y under the 3/1 work ratio than the 2/1 work ratio. Finally, the formal *ratio* rule of equity theory demands two main effects and an interaction. The differences between levels of Y for various work ratios should be larger in the five golden ring level of X than the three golden ring level. This final pattern would be displayed by the correct solution to the mathematical (barrels filled) problem.

Now consider the implications of data generated within this design. If the patterns of data predicted by the various NOIR steps cannot be located within different age groups, in chronological sequence, the model is falsified. This falsification would be particularly resounding if children's mathematical solutions, with appropriate incentives, did follow the model. In the extreme case, a child's allocations would be entered into the empirical evaluation of a particular NOIR step only if that child had demonstrated capacity by solving all the mathematical analogue items at that level. In that case, it would be difficult to attribute disconfirmatory data to mathematical incapacity.

With the capacity interpretation ruled out, failure of the model could be attributed more directly to failure of the equity ideas as a description of social norms of judgment. The ideal study would include process and follow-up measures concerning each child's stated rationale for allocations and his or her assessment of alternative allocation rules. This ideal study would also include probes relevant to an alternative inputs interpretation. For example, the child might be asked whether he or she decided to give more to *B* than *A* because *B* worked longer, or because "*B* wanted golden rings more? *B* is more handsome or bigger or older? *B* did more work quantity? *B* needed the rewards more?" This directed probe, following some theoretical rationale (the example follows Damon's theory), would not prove that an alternative inputs sequence characterized development, but it would infuse more useful information into the equation.

The critical reader's response to this elaborate analysis might go something like this: "So what?" This particular reader might be wondering about the wisdom of lavishing great resources on a problem so narrow and artificial. Is fair distribution really a psychological issue, or is it a political issue? How often do real children actually confront allocation situations involving exactly two persons doing numerically defined work and receiving numerically defined rewards? The defense is familiar to the laboratory, basic-research-oriented psychologist. The allocation problem, though not inherently psychological or especially salient for the child, is a valuable tool for the study of truly psychological, pervasive constructs. Proportionality, once pinned down methodologically in a bed of problems that are all formally analogous across a range of contents (physics to justice), will increase understanding of such significant issues as the relationship between thought and action, and the priority of formal, instructed, or informal osmosed knowledge. The fact that the mathematical structure of equity is shared with a large slice of the child's cognitive world makes equity a candidate for elegant experiments of much utility.

REFERENCES

Adams, J. Inequity in social exchange. In L. Berkowitz (Ed.), *Advances in experimental social psychology* (Vol. 2). New York: Academic Press, 1965.

Anderson, N. Equity judgments as information integration. *Journal of Personality and Social Psychology*, 1976, 33, 291–299.

Anderson, N., & Butzin, C. Integration theory applied to children's judgments of equity. *Developmental Psychology*, 1978, 14, 593–606.

Anderson, N., & Farkas, A. Integration theory applied to models of inequity. *Personality and Social Psychology Bulletin*, 1975, 1, 588–591.

Billow, R. A cognitive-developmental study of metaphor comprehension. *Developmental Psychology*, 1975, *11*, 415–423.

Crockenberg, S., Bryant, B., & Wilce, L. The effects of cooperatively and competitively structured learning environments on inter- and intra-personal behavior. *Child Development*, 1976, *47*, 386–396.

Crosby, F. A model of egoistical relative deprivation. *Psychological Review*, 1976, *83*, 85–113.

Damon, W. Early conceptions of positive justice as related to the development of logical operations. *Child Development*, 1975, *46*, 301–312.

Damon, W. Patterns of change in children's social reasoning: A two-year longitudinal study. *Child Development*, 1980, *51*, 1010–1017.

Dreman, S. Sharing behavior in Israeli school children: Cognitive and social learning factors. *Child Development*, 1976, *47*, 186–194.

Enright, R., Enright, W., Manheim, L., & Harris, E. Distributive justice development and social class. *Developmental Psychology*, 1980, *16*, 555–563.

Enright, R., Franklin, C., & Manheim, L. Children's distributive justice reasoning: A standardized and objective scale. *Developmental Psychology*, 1980, *16*, 193–202.

Enright, R., & Sutterfield, S. An ecological validation of social cognitive development. *Child Development*, 1980, *51*, 156–161.

Green, M. The developmental relation between cognitive stage and the comprehension of speaker uncertainty. *Child Development*, 1979, *50*, 666–674.

Grumbkow, J., Deen, E., Steensma, H., & Wilke, H. The effects of future interaction on the distribution of reward. *European Journal of Social Psychology*, 1976, *6*, 119–123.

Homans, G. *Social behavior: Its elementary forms.* New York: Harcourt, 1961.

Hook, J. The development of equity and altruism in judgments of positive and negative justice. *Developmental Psychology*, 1982, *18*(6), 825–834.

Hook, J., & Cook, T. Equity theory and the cognitive ability of children. *Psychological Bulletin*, 1979, *86*, 429–445.

Kidder, L., Bellettirie, G., & Cohn, E. Secret ambitions and public performances: The effects of anonymity on reward allocations made by men and women. *Journal of Experimental Social Psychology*, 1977, *13*, 70–80.

Lerner, M. The justice motive: "Equity" and "parity" among children. *Journal of Personality and Social Psychology*, 1974, *29*, 539–550.

Leventhal, G., & Anderson, D. Self-interest and maintenance of equity. *Journal of Personality and Social Psychology*, 1970, *15*, 57–62.

Leventhal, G., Popp, A., & Sawyer, L. Equity or equality in children's allocation of reward to other persons? *Child Development*, 1973, *44*, 753–763.

Marx, K. *Capital.* Chicago: Charles Kerr, 1906.

Morgan, W., & Sawyer, J. Bargaining, expectation, and the preference for equity. *Journal of Personality and Social Psychology*, 1967, *6*, 139–149.

Piaget, J. *The moral judgment of the child.* New York: Free Press, 1965. (Originally published, 1932.)

Reis, H., & Gruzen, J. On mediating equity, equality, and self-interest: The role of self-presentation in social exchange. *Journal of Experimental Social Psychology*, 1976, *12*, 487–503.

Ruble, D., Boggiano, A., Feldman, N., & Loebl, J. Developmental analysis of the role of social comparison in self-evaluation. *Developmental Psychology*, 1980, *16*, 105–115.

Sedlak, A., & Kurtz, S. A review of children's use of causal inference principles. *Child Development*, 1981, *52*(3), 759–784.

Stephenson, G., & Barker, J. Personality and the pursuit of distributive justice: An experimental study of children's moral behavior. *British Journal of Social and Clinical Psychology*, 1972, *11*, 207–219.

Stephenson, G., & White, J. An experimental study of the effects of injustice on children's moral behaviors. *Journal of Experimental Social Psychology*, 1968, *4*, 460–469.

Uesugi, T., & Vinacke, W. Strategy in a feminine game. *Sociometry*, 1963, *26*, 75–88.

Walster, E., Berscheid, E., & Walster, G. New directions in equity research. In L. Berkowitz & E. Walster (Eds.), *Advances in experimental social psychology* (Vol. 9). New York: Academic Press, 1976.

9 / Conceptions of deviance and disorder

KATHERINE FROME PAGET

Understanding when and by what means children come to appreciate the variations in human social behavior, particularly extreme deviations from social norms, is critical for both practical and theoretical reasons. Persons responsible for setting policy concerning the mainstreaming of atypical children in normal settings require evidence from which to make informed decisions. This line of inquiry has theoretical significance as well, since it occupies an intersect between the routes of developmental and clinical child psychology by its concern with the development of cognitive awareness of affectively laden behavior.

Two serious obstacles immediately arise in attempting to review the empirical literature on the development of conceptions of deviance and disorder. First, the protean quality of adult conceptualizations and definitions leave the developmentalist out in deep water when attempting to chart a linear course toward an end state. One marker is clear, however, although it is a bit of a truism. We conceptualize deviance by its contrast to normalcy. The relational nature of deviance raises the second obstacle to this endeavor. We have a limited data base concerning the development of conceptions of normal human behavior since social cognition as an area of empirical inquiry has been in existence for less than two decades.

Nevertheless, a small provocative group of developmental studies have been done in the last several years that directly or indirectly ad-

THE CHILD'S CONSTRUCTION
OF SOCIAL INEQUALITY

223

dress the question of how children come to recognize and process psychological deviance and disorder in others. The purpose of this chapter is to review the developmental empirical literature on this topic, with particular attention given to the methods of inquiry used by various investigators. An attempt will be made to integrate the confluence of results of major studies and recommendations will be made for future research in the area.

These studies fall under three major headings:

1. Studies that explicitly address the development of understanding of psychological deviance and disorder
2. Studies concerned with how children come to understand psychological defense mechanisms
3. Studies of social judgment of aggression, attribution of responsibility, and social comparison

Each of these groups of studies will be dealt with in turn.

DEVELOPMENTAL STUDIES OF DEVIANCE
AND DISORDER

Five studies have appeared in the last several years that have directly addressed the development of children's understanding of deviance and disorder (Barenboim, 1981; Coie & Pennington, 1976; Maas, Maracek, & Travers, 1978; Marsden & Kalter, 1976; Budoff & Conant, Note 1). Four of these cross-sectional studies, all of which address age-related changes in how children come to understand adult categories of abnormal behavior, employ similar procedures. A set of hypothetical stories portraying child characters enacting deviant behavior as defined by adult standards is verbally presented to an individual child. Each child is then asked a series of questions concerning the central character's behavior. The content of these questions varies according to the research question of the investigator.

Coie and Pennington (1976) administered a two-part interview to first-through eleventh-grade children with the aim of delineating age-related changes in awareness of behavior considered irrational by adults. In Part I of the interview, each subject was asked to describe other children whom they believed were different from themselves and then asked why these children acted differently. The second part of the task involved verbal presentation of two hypothetical stories: One depicted a character who lost control of himself; the other involved a character with a distorted sense of reality. Part II was scored for recognition of the disorder or normalization of the behavior. In Part I, first-grade children most often used self-referent attributions, while fourth, seventh, and eleventh graders referred to adult rule violations. Only seventh and eleventh graders spontaneously referred to incidents of distorted perspective or being "crazy." Eleventh graders alone referred to incidents of social withdrawal. In response to the hypothetical stories of Part II, effects for age were accompanied by effects for disorder type. For the distorted-perspective story, there was a linear trend with age for attributed deviance, but for the loss-of-control story, there was no clear pattern of findings. The authors argue that their particular story combined loss of control with aggression and that children at different grade levels were probably responding to different meanings in this story. Since the youngest group did not make normative evaluations in Part I of the task, Coie and Pennington focus on the age differences in the responses of the remaining fourth, seventh, and eleventh graders to the hypothetical stories. Fourth and seventh graders made normative statements in terms of violations of concrete behavioral rules and observable behavior, in contrast to eleventh graders, whose judgments were primarily in terms of nonnormative internal states and psychological perspectives. The major age effect in this study occurred between seventh and eleventh grade, with the youngest group (first graders) unable to use a normative framework whatsoever.

Marsden and Kalter (1976) posed much the same research question in their cross-sectional study. Although more limited age range was included, a more expanded range of disorder types was used. These investigators created stories with central male characters who exhibited (a) incipient school phobia; (b) antisocial character disorder; (c) passive–aggressive character disorder; and (d) psychotic behavior plus a normal control. In order to ensure that these stories indeed represented the nosological categories intended, the authors requested that seven clinicians rate the stories in terms of both diagnostic category and severity. Reasonable agreement was obtained.

Fourth- and sixth-grade children were asked to describe each central character, react to him, explain why he came to behave the way he did, and predict the prospects for his future. These interviews were scored for the extent to which the central character was thought to be emotionally disturbed, and evaluated according to a five-point scale that was then reduced to a dichotomous score. A significant main effect for disorder type showed that both the normal character and the psychotic character were judged to be significantly different from the three intermediate types. The psychotic character was seen to be most disturbed, and the passive–aggressive type was judged to be significantly less disturbed than the antisocial character disorder. Although no overall main effect for sex was obtained in the recognition of emotional disturbance, boys were more likely than girls to see the psychotic character as having clear emotional problems. Girls who did not recognize that the psychotic character was disturbed tended to judge him as intelligent, preoccupied, and imaginative. Of the total 16% of subjects who did not judge this character as being emotionally disturbed, most argued that he was feigning belief in space fantasies in order to get attention. This normalization of behavior is quite similar to the modal response Coie and Pennington (1976) found in comparably aged children. Sixth graders saw more emotional disturbance than did fourth graders. In their more qualitative analyses of the protocols, the investigators point out that 40% of the children saw neither the passive–aggressive nor the school-phobic character as being disturbed. Girls who judged the passive–aggressive character as emotionally disturbed tended to feel empathic to his feelings of loneliness and inadequacy, whereas the boys were more likely to characterize him as a "goof-off" and did not consider his behavior to be evidence of psychological problems.

Interestingly, over 20% of the girls saw the normal character (described as having a hard time in class because his friends were in another classroom) as disturbed, but this was not true of any boys. These sex differences are suggestive, but without data on males' views of female behavior, we cannot generalize to cross-sex differences. It may be that girls tolerate less acting-out behavior than do boys, and boys tolerate less withdrawn behavior than do girls. A more elaborate research design including cross-sex comparisons is clearly needed in order to support this interpretation.

Marsden and Kalter's inclusion of a normal character for comparison with the four disturbed characters is a definite methodological advantage, yet their restriction of stimulus characters to one gender limits the generalizability of their findings. The authors conclude that fourth- and sixth-grade normal children do perceive as emotionally disturbed the behavior that mental health professionals characterize as psychopathological. Specific behaviors are perceived differently by boys and girls, but an integrated interpretation of these findings is still forthcoming.

Barenboim (1981) has presented the Coie and Pennington loss-of-control and distorted-perspective stories to college students (mean age 19.8). Same-sex stimulus characters were rated for "how different is this person compared to most people" on a five-point scale ranging from "not at all different" to "extremely different." Barenboim's interest was in the relationship of the deviance ratings to subjects' use of psychological comparisons. His findings indicated that subjects rated the distorted-perspective character as more deviant than the loss-of-control character. The deviance ratings of the distorted-perspective character were significantly and positively correlated to subjects' use of psychological comparisons, whereas ratings of the loss-of-control character were not. Barenboim argues that responsibility for this may be due to the different nature of the two disorders. The distorted-perspective story, in contrast to the loss-of-control story, contains fewer overt manifestations and may require more psychological comparisons.

Maas, Maracek, and Travers (1978) included second, fourth, and sixth grade male and female subjects and three types of disorder in their cross-sectionally designed study. Ten male and 10 female subjects at each grade level were read stories depicting a withdrawn character, an antisocial character, and a self-punitive character. The task was administered in two parts: First, each subject was asked in open-ended format (a) the reasons the story character behaved the way he or she did; then (b) whether the character was born that way, or whether things happened to make him or her behave that way; (c) whether the character wanted to behave the way he or she did; and (d) whether the character could change, and if so, how? In the second part, subjects were asked to rate each story character according to 19 bipolar adjectives along a four-point scale.

With increasing age, children were more likely to locate the causes of deviant behavior in the social environment. Younger children, in contrast, saw internal factors as predominantly responsible for disordered behavior. In addition, older children believed that change could be effected by altering the social environment and generated more reasons for deviant behavior. The socially withdrawn character was most often perceived as having been "born that way." The self-punitive character was primarily seen as not wanting to behave that way, and the antisocial character as wanting to behave that way. This last finding was more true for the sixth graders than the two groups of younger children.

The majority of children at all age levels believed that behavior could be changed, especially self-punitive behavior. There were pronounced developmental trends in the ways children believed that change could be effected. Second graders all believed that personal effort would bring about change; the majority of fourth graders agreed that personal effort would work, but the rest opted for social support or both. In contrast, most sixth graders believed that social support would bring about change, but 30% felt both personal effort and social support were necessary. When the results of the adjectival ratings were factor analyzed, four factors emerged: social desirability, assertiveness, well-being, and social assets. The antisocial character, according to both the factor analyses and the analyses of variance, was viewed differently from both the self-punitive character and the socially withdrawn character. The antisocial character was seen as healthy, happy, and wanting to behave that way; persistence of behavior was seen as due to lack of effort to change. Clearly, antisocial deviance was understood within a different causal framework than were the other forms of disorder.

The second-grade subjects in the Maas *et al.* study interpreted causes for interpersonal behavior in terms of dispositions rather than as situationally determined. These results are not at all consistent with the findings of other studies. A close look at the stimulus materials may help to explain the conflicting results. In most studies, children are asked to interpret a slice-of-life situation devoid of historical context, but in the Maas *et al.* study, the characters were portrayed as behaving in certain ways over time. Clearly, this type of stimulus contains very different information. The enduring quality of the character's behavior is made particularly salient, and the situational determinants pale in comparison. It is not unexpected that young children, when presented with information in this form, focus their attention on the most salient aspect of the stimulus. As Chandler, Greenspan, and Barenboim (1973) have demonstrated within the moral judgment paradigm, children younger than 8 or so have difficulty with the simultaneous coordination of intention and consequence, and will center their attention on one dimension or another, depending on which is made salient. In the present study, scoring for internal or external causes yields certain information, but the developmentally more mature response, which unfortunately was not included in the scoring system, might very well be the joint consideration of the interaction of these two factors. The last question, which asked if the story character could change his or her behavior, and if so, how, was the only one that was conceived along this complexity dimension. The results indicated that only the sixth-grade subjects saw change as effected by both personal and situational causes simultaneously with any degree of frequency (30%).

The tendency of adult observers to attribute the causes of behavior to dispositions rather than to situational factors was described by Heider over 20 years ago. "It seems that behavior . . ." he wrote in *The Psychology of Interpersonal Relations* "has such salient properties that it tends to engulf the field rather than be confined to its proper position as a local stimulus whose interpretation requires the additional data of a surrounding field—the situation in social perception [1958, p. 54]." E. E. Jones and Nisbett (1971) have demonstrated that the tendency to attribute to aspects of the person rather than to the situation is intimately tied to the role the attributor plays in the interaction. If indeed it is the case that there is a bias on the part of the adult observer to make dispositional attributions, a natural question for the developmentalist to ask is whether children exhibit this bias. While this question has not been directly addressed in the empirical literature, research on developmental person perception has demonstrated that young children typically describe others in terms of more physical rather than psychological descriptions (Livesley & Bromley, 1973) and do not possess the implicit trait-implicative personality theory characteristic of older children and adults (Honess, 1978, 1979). In order to attribute causal status to dispositions, it would appear to be necessary to think along those conceptual lines, and it is not surprising that young children do not make such attributions.

It is not at all clear that attributions of responsibility follow in any systematic developmental fashion from situational to personal. In a cross-sectional study of recursive thinking, when 60 8-, 12-, and 16-year-old children we asked to attribute reasons for the enigmatic behavior of characters in Hans Christian Andersen fairy tales (Paget, 1979), no age differences emerged in attributions to personal or situational causes for behavior. Rather, the pattern of results was determined by the particular content of the story and the specific behaviors of the story character. When responses were scored for complexity—that is, for multidetermined outcomes—clear developmental differences emerged. Only the 16-year-olds used multidetermined explanations with any frequency at all, and even then the frequency was just over 20%. According to the results of this study, not until middle adolescence does the spontaneous use of multidetermination begin to appear. Support for the contention may be found in a study by Erwin and Kuhn (1979). Kindergarten through twelfth-grade children were presented with stories that had either two possible motives or two possible external events as causes. These motives were presented, and then each subject was directly asked whether both could be correct and how that could be. The major developmental shift occurred between fourth and eighth grade, but only twelfth graders *spontaneously* indicated with any real frequency (28%) that multiple determination was possible. Both of these studies suggest that developmental changes in attribution of causes for human behavior may be best charted according to a trajectory of complexity ranging from simple main effects, either personal or situational, to more complex interaction effects.

Budoff and Conant (Note 1) interviewed subjects ranging from preschoolers to adults with respect to issues of blindness, deafness, orthopedic handicaps, mental retardation, and psychological disturbance. Questions concerning awareness of the existence of the handicapping condition, understanding its causes, views on curability, coping and adaptation, and attitudes toward handicapping conditions as well as responses to hypothetical dilemmas were scored with respect to the content of belief systems. Scalogram analyses indicated that psychological disturbance was the most difficult condition for subjects to understand, and mental retardation the second. This effect is supported by the findings of other studies (Brightman, 1977; Budoff, Siperstein, & Conant, 1979), which suggest that even young adolescents have little knowledge of mental disabilities in general.

Confusion between various kinds of handicaps was most frequent between mental retardation and psychological disturbance. Among the high school students, who were at least minimally aware of psychological disturbance, few spontaneously mentioned that there are different degrees of this handicap, in contrast to the bulk of the adult sample, who expressed awareness of degree of impairment. Reference to extreme psychological disturbance (e.g., psychosis, bizarre behavior, hysteria, and multiple personalities) revealed some interesting comparisons. It was not apparent in the spontaneous repertoires of subjects until junior high school, and it increased monotonically from there on, but percentages of subjects who discussed only extreme cases reflected a U-shaped curve rather than a linear function. The clinical impression of Budoff and Conant (Note 1) is that high school students seemed to be ''enthusiastic consumers of popularized accounts of mental illness and of dramas featuring people with extreme disturbance [p. 137].''

In contrast to these adolescents who seemed to conceptualize psychological disturbance as something outside one's ordinary experience, adults tended to integrate such concepts into ordinary life events, and not only expressed awareness of a continuum of disturbance, but portrayed themselves as occupying a position along this continuum.

Explanations for psychological disturbances also varied with age. While adolescents primarily referred to personality traits and several referred to emotional maltreatment, only adults mentioned organic causes for psychological disturbance. There was a progressive increase with age in mention of psychotherapy. High school students primarily referred to factors in the interpersonal milieu, while adults mentioned drugs as intervention.

In response to the hypothetical dilemma concerning mainstreaming, no group was overwhelmingly in favor of mainstreaming, and decisions were based on the social–emotional good of the ''special child'' rather than on principled reasons. Adolescents normalized the behavior of the protagonist, whereas none of the older or younger subjects did so. The authors suggest that normalization of aberrant behavior should not be equated with the expression of positive attitudes but rather that it reflects a transition prior to more mature understanding, when such differences are both recognized and accepted. The Budoff and Conant data suggest that recognition and understanding of handicapping conditions are most problematic when conditions are covert and psychological.

Several attitudinal studies (Novak, 1974, 1975) have indicated that middle years children (Novak, 1974, 1975) and undergraduates (Yamamoto & Dizney, 1967) express more negative attitudes toward aggressive than toward more clinically symptomatic but withdrawn peers. The overt effects of behavior on others rather than the clinical severity determine evaluations. Coie, Costanzo, and Cox (1975) report that conceptions of mental illness held by adults in the "gatekeeper" professions vary. Police were particularly aware of overt and antisocial behavior, whereas physicians and nurses were more attuned to internal disruption. The tendency of children to base their evaluations of deviance an overt effects may not be best characterized in developmental terms. Cross-sectional studies are clearly needed to address this issue.

Certain behavioral dimensions carry different meanings for children than for adults. Aggression does not seem to be categorized as deviant behavior by children. Rather it is seen as self-serving and more within the normative framework than other forms of clinically defined psychopathology. Contrasting instrumentally aggressive and passive–aggressive behavior yields several points of comparison. The instrumentally aggressive character's goals, motives, and outward behavior dovetail nicely with each other, whereas the passive–aggressive character's goals and outward behavior contradict one another. These behaviors differ along the dimension of outwardness–inwardness as well. The acting-out, aggressive character requires less social inference than does the passive–aggressive character, because the surface behavior corresponds to the intentions. One does not need to go beyond the information given for the instrumentally aggressive character, but for the passive–aggressive character, one must read between the lines.

The preceding discussion should highlight the fact that our criteria as psychologists for judging whether certain behavior is deviant may be irrelevant to the social judgment of the child. The problem of how to characterize deviance (i.e., what kind of typology to use) has been dealt with in a rather logical fashion by a small set of research studies that explore the ways in which children decode psychological defense mechanisms. Both the methodological benefits and the findings of this group of studies constitute the substance of the next section.

DEVELOPMENTAL STUDIES OF
PSYCHOLOGICAL DEFENSE MECHANISMS

In a series of three studies (Whiteman, 1967, 1970; Whiteman, Luboff, & Breining, Note 2), Whiteman and his colleagues examined how well children understand mechanisms of adjustment. It was predicted that with increasing age children would more fully understand these mechanisms, but these expectations were based rather globally on the development of physical causality notions and the wane of animistic thinking.

In the first study, Whiteman (1967) presented children 5–6 and 8–9 years old with a series of hypothetical stories about a same-sex character who in turn engaged in repression, regression, displacement, rationalization, denial, wishful dreaming, and projection. Comprehension scores indicated that very few of the younger children understood any of the mechanisms of adjustment, but if any were comprehended, repression was the most likely and projection the least. In a second study, Whiteman assessed older children (8–11) on the adjustment stories, but the projection story was dropped because of its lack of relation to the other stories. Only the 11-year-olds were likely to achieve the highest level comprehension scores, and there was a significant relationship between these comprehension scores and conservation ability. Unfortunately, Whiteman chose to abandon the projection story rather than explore the possible explanations for its greater level of difficulty.

This unexplained result proved to be one of the stimuli for our program of research in which we sought to look at psychological defense in terms of cognitive complexity dimensions and logic rather than clinical diagnostic categories. In a series of three studies, we have attempted to look at the complexity dimensions of a set of behaviors termed *psychological defenses* and predict along the lines of a logical analysis which defenses would be too complex for which children to process.

We have argued that three forms of negation characterize many examples of defensive behavior. For a behavior to be labeled as defensive, an affective relationship between a subject and an object is experienced as personally unacceptable and anxiety producing. The most straightforward and logically simple way of transforming the unacceptable subject–affect–object relationship is to simply eliminate one of the three elements by applying the logical operator called the inverse, notated by the symbol $\bar{x}$. The inverse may be applied to the affect term—for example, "I don't feel anger" (repression $= \bar{A}$); or it may be applied to the object term—"My anger is not directed at you" (denial $= \bar{O}$). Second, any single element in the subject–affect–object complex could be trans-

formed by substituting for that term its reciprocal. Applying the reciprocal operator involves neutralization of a variable by substitution, not
outright elimination. The elements in the subject–affect–object complex
retain their existence and relationship to one another, but their meaning
is altered. Continuing with the example of anger, this transformation
either would substitute for the subject some alter, intentionally defined
as "not me by any present definition," replace anger with affection, or
substitute for the target of the anger an alternative (e.g., "not you but
someone substantially different"). Finally, a subject–affect–object complex could be transformed by an operation that focuses, not on individual elements per se, but on more encompassing joint propositional
statements that combine into a single superordinate unit the separate
elements previously considered. The negation of such a joint propositional statement embeds the separate features of both inverse and reciprocal operations transforming a statement such as "I am angry at
you" to the alternative "You are angry at me."

These three possible alternative means of negating in whole or part
various subject–affect–object complexes proved to be quite comprehensive for classifying many commonly described mechanisms of
psychological defense. In terms of this provisional descriptive model,
repression and denial were grouped together as involving the application of a simple inverse to either the affect or the object term. Mechanisms of psychological defense that were judged to involve negations
that transformed elements in the subject–affect–object complex through
the application of reciprocals were rationalization, displacement, and
turning against the self. All may be characterized by a substitution of a
more acceptable alternative for the original object term. Reaction formation substitutes a more supportive reciprocal affective alternative for
the unacceptable affect. Two defense mechanisms, projection and introjection, operate on joint propositional statements involving two or
more elements from subject–affect–object complexes. In the case of projection, "I am angry at you" becomes "You are angry at me." Introjection is the mirror image of this operation, and accordingly, "You are
angry with me" is transformed into "I am angry at you." According to
this structural analysis, two defense mechanisms were categorized as
involving simple inverses (repression and denial), four as involving simple reciprocals (rationalization, reaction formation, displacement, turning against the self), and two as involving negations of propositional
statements (projection and introjection).

In our first study of defense decoding (Chandler, Paget, & Koch, 1978),
one example of each type of defense was employed. Each child was
presented with eight different defenses grouped at three levels of logical

complexity and interviewed for his or her comprehension of the target character's behavior. Since a scheme that permitted the joint characterization of the structural features of both children's cognitive operations and the demand characteristics of mechanisms of psychological defense was established, a set of specific hypotheses became possible. First, since all defense mechanisms appear to hinge upon transformations involving either or both inverse or reciprocal operations, preoperational children said not to possess these cognitive operations should not be able to understand defensive strategies of any logical order. Second, although inverse and reciprocal operations are both achieved during the concrete operational stage, Inhelder and Piaget (1958) provide both empirical and theoretical arguments to indicate that children employ inverse before reciprocal operations. It was our expectation that comprehension of psychological defense mechanisms would follow a similar pattern. Finally, formal operational children who possess all the requisite cognitive operations were expected to understand defense mechanisms of any sort.

The subjects in this study were 30 kindergarten through sixth-grade students selected from a total of 50 children on the basis of their performance on our cognitive level screening procedures. The mean age and age range for the preoperational group was 6.3 (5.3–9.0), for the concrete operational group 9.7 (8.5–11.0), and for the formal operational group 11.4 (9.5–12.3). The assessment procedures employed included Form C of the Goldschmidt-Bentler Concept Assessment Kit—Conservation (Goldschmidt & Bentler, 1968) and a measure of combinatorial reasoning closely patterned after a procedure designed by Elkind, Barocas, and Rosenthal (1968).

All children were individually presented a randomized series of eight tape-recorded stories, each depicting a mechanism of psychological defense. Each story, matched for length and linguistic complexity, contained two distinct segments. In the first, a story character of the same sex as the child subject was portrayed in an interpersonal context that required an affective response of anger, fear, or sadness. For example, the story concerning rationalization described an episode in which "a boy was excited because he and his friends had tickets to the circus. On the day he was supposed to go he woke up with the measles and had to stay in bed all day and couldn't watch T.V." In a similar fashion, other stories involved characters who were afraid of a particular dental procedure, were angry with a younger sibling, or were frightened at the prospect of walking through a spooky graveyard. The tape was interrupted at the completion of the first segment, and the child was asked to infer "How did the boy (girl) feel?" and "How would you finish the story?" After the child had conveyed an affective judgment and proposed an ending to the story, the defensive resolution to each tape was played. For example, the story portraying the defense of rationalization was concluded when "his friend called to say what a good time he had, the boy said staying in bed was okay with him because circuses weren't fun and he didn't want to go anyway." Similarly, the target characters of the seven other stories were depicted as engaging in reaction formation, denying, displacing, repressing, projecting, introjecting, or self-inflicting their feelings. Children were then asked to explain why the story ended as it had and to discuss the difference between these endings and their own. The same procedure was then repeated for each of the remaining seven tape-recorded stories.

It is important to note here that this procedure of interrupting the tape and asking the child to supply an ending was deliberately orchestrated in order to ensure that the defensive ending was indeed a problem in need of a solution. For each and every subject, a "normal expectable ending" was supplied for all stories. Continuing with the rationalization example, a typical ending supplied by the child was "He got better and was able to go the circus the next week." We found it essential to the procedure that a conflict exist between the child's ending and the defensive ending. Without the existence of such a discrepancy, there would be no problem with which to wrestle. In addition to this deliberate inconsistency between a normal expectable ending and a defensive ending, a conflict exists between the antecedent and consequent parts of the story. In some cases, a transformation of affect occurs; in others, the subject or object is transformed. Successful decoding of the defensive maneuver involves identifying the invariance of the causal agent or affect despite its defensive transformation, much in the way a conservation task demands we remain loyal to our belief in the invariance of substance, weight, or volume despite the perceptual illusion created. In order to understand the defense of displacement, one must know who the actual target of the aggression should be. In order to understand the defense of reaction formation, one must know that whistling in the dark is really a camouflage. The ability to logically deduce what must be so, despite what appears to be, is a hallmark of concrete operational reasoning. Analogously, the concrete operational child's newly acquired strengths at logical deduction prevent him or her from being taken in by interpersonal cover stories of others.

All interviews were scored for comprehension of defense, according to two criteria. The first scoring procedure consisted of dichotomously rating the eight explanatory accounts offered by each child as to whether or not they reflected an understanding of the defense portrayed. For example, successful decoding of the defense of rationalization involves understanding, not only that the target character was truly unhappy in the consequent part of the story when he said circuses were not fun and he did not want to go anyway, but that he could not admit his bad feelings to his friends and so argued that circuses were not desirable entertainment. The second scoring procedure focused on responses that were judged not to reflect an adequate understanding of the defense in question. Correct responses necessarily located the causal locus for the outcome in the antecedent event; that is, the target character's defensive behavior was seen as a response to the distal interpersonal situation and affect in the first tape segment. Some children did not demonstrate an adequate understanding of particular defenses but appreciated that the story endings were a response to earlier antecedent events. Others made no such distal interpretation and located the cause for the defensive behavior on the proximal turf on which it occurred. Children who offered such proximal interpretations imagined, for example, that the story character who came down with the measles and could not go to the circus found some other recreation he liked better (e.g., was allowed to watch television). All responses initially scored as reflecting a failure to understand the defenses portrayed were dichotomously categorized as offering either proximal or distal interpretations. This proximal–distal distinction has been successfully employed by Berndt and Berndt (1975) and indicates that although young children are aware that motives and intentions underlie interpersonal behavior, they have difficulty in following the causal connectedness of events where the relevant motives are located in a context that is different from the behaviors to be explained. Proximal explanations for behavioral outcomes are conceptually analogous to "normalization" of behavior according to the Coie and Pennington approach. In each of these types of responses, children justify the behavior in terms of an explanatory event that they construct in order to level the apparent contradiction encountered.

Results showed significant main effects for both cognitive ability and defense complexity. As predicted, formal operational children were better able than concrete operational children to understand defenses at all levels of complexity. Complexity of defense also significantly influenced understanding, with inverses being easier to understand than reciprocals, and defenses that incorporated both inverse and reciprocal operations being the most difficult of all.

The design of this study reflected Piaget's interactionist position; that is, the hypotheses hinged upon the match between the cognitive complexity of the child and the structural complexity of the psychological defense. Therefore, a contrast between two groups was in order. First, all subjects classified as preoperational and all concrete operational children when struggling with the third most complex level of defense, were compared with all formal operational subjects and concrete operational children confronting instances of defense hinging upon the application of simple inverses or reciprocals. The differences in defense comprehension between these two groups were quite substantial.

The results of our second scoring procedure, designed to take a more microscopic look at the kinds of errors made, yielded a significant effect for cognitive level. Preoperational children invoked distal explanations 40% of the time; formal operational children used distal explanations 89% of the time even when they failed to understand the particular defense portrayed. Concrete operational subjects fell in between these two extreme groups.

In a second study, Koch (1981) replicated the defense paradigm using three examples of one defense from each level of formal complexity: repression (inverse), displacement (reciprocal), and projection (joint propositional statements). Her research attempted to integrate the individual difference dimension of cognitive style (Santostefano, 1978) with the developmental dimension of cognitive stage. Although integration was the major thrust of this research effort, by using three examples of each defense, Koch was able to repair the methodological flaw of the first study, in which defense story and defense were confounded. The pattern of findings was similar to the 1978 study; $10\frac{1}{2}$–12-year-olds were more successful at decoding repression and displacement than they were at projection. While the repression scores were higher than the displacement scores, this difference did not reach conventional levels of statistical significance. Given the age range of her subjects, one would expect high concrete operational skills, including the use of reciprocal negations. Koch's introduction of the cognitive style dimension into the predictive equation enabled her to account for a higher percentage of the variance than the use of cognitive stage alone as the independent variable would have allowed. Counter to expectation, however, children who scored higher on the leveling end of the leveling–sharpening continuum were more successful at understanding defenses than were children classified as "sharpeners" on the Leveling–Sharpening House Test designed by Santostefano (1978). Koch interprets these findings in terms of a psychoanalytic framework wherein levelers are viewed as both more attuned to their own affective lives and more socially sensitive to others than are sharpeners. Although no data concerning the affective arousal level of the subjects classified as levelers were obtained, it is suggested that their leveler status influenced their greater sensitivity to and comprehension of the affective content in the defense stories.

In a third study (Koch, Harder, Chandler, & Paget, 1982), we expanded the scope of our research paradigm and looked at the impact of parental defense complexity on children's social competence in actual families. A number of researchers (Bandura & Walters, 1959; Becker, Peterson, Luria, Shoemaker, & Hellmer, 1962; Schaefer, 1959) have reported that various kinds of parental environments exert a differential effect on the social and cognitive development of children. Our work on defense complexity suggested that, within families where a parent has been hospitalized for a psychiatric disorder, social competence of children would be jointly dependent on the major defensive modes of the disturbed parent and the cognitive maturity level of the child. The interactionist hypotheses of the first two studies was finally applied to a sample of families where the environment for the child could be characterized by defense complexity.

Fifty families, selected from a total of 145 families who participated in the University of Rochester Child and Family Study, were the subjects of this study. Families chosen were those for whom three kinds of information were available: the child's level of cognitive maturity, a personality assessment of the hospitalized parent, and measures of social competence of the child.

Cognitive maturity of the children was evaluated by means of Form A of the Goldschmidt-Bentler Concept Assessment Kit—Conservation (Goldschmidt & Bentler, 1968). Three measures of social competence based on parental reports were obtained for all children. These included the Rochester Adaptive Behavior Inventory (F. H. Jones, 1977) and the Missouri Children's Check-List (Sines, Parker, Sines, & Owens, 1969) scored separately for mother and father reports. Data from a teacher rating scale and a peer rating scale of school behaviors and social competence (Fisher, 1980) were available for the 40 children attending school. Parental defensive style was assessed through an item analysis (Haan, 1965) of the Minnesota Multiphasic Personality Inventory (MMPI) scales. The MMPI profiles for each of the previously hospitalized parents were scored according to the scales reflecting the five defense mechanisms of repression, denial, displacement, intellectualization, and projection. According to our structural model, repression and denial represent Level 1, involving simple inverses; displacement and intellectualization are Level 2 defenses, involving reciprocal operations; and projection is a Level 3 defense, employing features of both inverse and reciprocal operations. Parents were assigned to the highest level of defense complexity they employed significantly. This procedure is detailed in Koch et al., 1982. Parents who did not score significantly high on any of the five defense mechanisms are grouped in a nonprimary defense category.

Combinations of parental defensive style and child cognitive maturity were scored as "matched" or "mismatched." Matched combinations were those in which the major defensive style exhibited by the parent was logically resolvable for the child's cognitive level. Mismatched combinations were those in which the parent's defensive style was too complex for the child to decipher. Thus, all significantly defensive parents (Levels 1, 2, and 3) with preoperational children were categorized as mismatched. Level 2 parents were classified as mismatched if they had preoperational or transitional children, and matched if they had concrete operational children. All parents at Level 3 were categorized as mismatched, since none of the children were formal operational.

A second scoring procedure was employed post hoc that subdivided the mismatched group of parent–child combinations into "small-mismatch" and "large-mismatch" groups. The small-mismatch group was composed of slightly incongruent combinations—that is, those where the child's cognitive level was one notch below the parent's modal defensive style. Families in the large-mismatch group were those where the parental defensive style far exceeded the child's cognitive ability.

The hypothesis that children of mismatched parent–child groups would be judged as less competent than children of matched groups was supported by data from peer ratings and father ratings on the Missouri checklist. Results of the other three measures were in the predicted direction but did not reach conventional levels of statistical significance. These results are consistent with the present view that joint consideration of parental defense style and child cognitive competence are necessary for predicting child outcomes. Post hoc analyses indicated that children in the large-mismatch group were more competent than children in the small-mismatch group yet less competent than children in the matched group, as measured by peer and father ratings.

This third study has both theoretical and practical implications. On the theoretical level, the methodological strategy of joint consideration of child variables and adult variables enhanced the predictive power. While cognitive-developmentalists often refer to the interactionist position, our research program translated the interactionist position into a match–mismatch research design. On the more practical level, implications for psychotherapeutic treatment of children are suggested. We believe that it might serve the therapist well to consider the defensive style of the parent and cognitive level of the child when attempting mediation. Some children may be relatively insulated from the psychopathology of their parents because of the mismatch between their own cognitive immaturity and the parental defensive strategy and would not benefit from attempts at intervention. At a later point in time, however, when the mismatch becomes less pronounced, such intervention efforts might be quite beneficial.

This last recommendation for intervention brings into sharp relief the difference between the approach of the studies of deviance and disorder and the approach of the studies of psychological defense mechanisms. The former studies all use diagnostic categories as the way of organizing information for children. They attempt to chart the developmental progression of children's successive approximations of adult understanding. But these adult categories have been clinically and empirically derived, and although they may serve as useful ways for diagnosing and treating disturbed persons, they may not reflect the categories used by children in their understanding of behavior. Our logical analyses may provide a closer match with children's cognitive categorization.

A study by Dollinger, Staley, and McGuire (1981) has examined children's evaluations of defenses in others. These investigators anticipated that their fifth- and sixth-grade subjects would evaluate characters exhibiting various defensive behaviors more positively if the defenses were internalizing (self-blame or denial) and more negatively if they were externalizing (projection). Of interest as well were attributions to personal or situational causes and the perceived sex of the defensive character. Results indicated that the internalizing character was evaluated more positively than the externalizing character and was typically viewed as feminine, whereas the projecting character was viewed as masculine. The authors suggest that, since use of particular defense styles becomes sex-typed prior to adolescence, cross-sex use of defense (e.g., boys using an internalizing defense such as self-blame) may exacerbate peer relation difficulties.

This tendency on the part of adolescents toward sex-typed use of defenses has been documented by Cramer (1979). Using the Gleser Defense Mechanism Inventory (Gleser & Ihelevich, 1969), Cramer assessed 80 younger and older adolescents for their choice of externalizing and internalizing defenses. Results indicated that, although sex-related choices of defense mechanisms are operative in early adolescence, these preferences become stronger during the adolescent years.

The relationship between understanding psychological defense mechanisms in others and defense use is theoretically problematic and empirically uncharted. Developmental theory pays more than lip service to the role of experience in the developmental process, but it is difficult to predict how defense use may affect defense understanding because of the very definition of psychological defenses as unconscious mechanisms. Evidence for sex-typed preferences may prove to be a starting point for such efforts.

DEVELOPMENTAL STUDIES OF AGGRESSIVE BEHAVIOR, ATTRIBUTION OF RESPONSIBILITY, AND SOCIAL COMPARISON

Aggression appears to have a different meaning for children than it does for adults and is the topic of a handful of developmental studies. Rule, Nesdale, and McAra (1974) examined the ability of kindergarten through sixth-grade children to distinguish among different bases for aggression. The moral evaluations of same-sex story characters who aggressed for personal hostile, personal instrumental, or prosocial reasons indicated that even 5- or six-year-olds are capable of distinguishing among different bases for aggression. Whether such information is used by young children is unclear.

Two investigations directly address this important issue. Dodge (1980), in a two-part report, examined the relationship between aggressive status in second-, fourth-, and sixth-grade boys and their interpretation of behavior characterized by hostile, benign, or ambiguous intent. All boys responded with more behavioral aggression to the hostile condition than to the benign condition, but the aggressive boys, in contrast to the nonaggressive boys, responded to the ambiguous condition in much the same manner as they responded to the hostile condition. In a second study, the aggressive status of the actors was manipulated in order to ascertain whether the predetermined attributes of the person would affect interpretations of the behavior. Four hypothetical stories with negative outcomes about peers and three levels of intent were presented to second- through sixth-grade boys. In the ambiguous circumstance, aggressive boys were more likely than nonaggressive boys to attribute hostile intent to a peer. However, the aggressive status of the peer had an even greater impact than did subject status on the attribution of hostility. Developmental differences emerged for this last effect, with fourth and sixth graders supplying more hostile attributions than did second graders. In the ambiguous intent condition, older children were likely to say that peers with a strong reputation for aggression were more likely to continue to aggress and less likely to be trusted. It appears that by 9 years or so, children no longer forgive and forget, and one's reputation, once made, continues to affect the expectations others have for one's future behavior.

Nasby, Hayden, and De Paulo (1980) report complementary findings in a clinical sample. Thirty-two emotionally disturbed boys, ages 10–16, were assigned to the categories of aggressive or nonaggressive, according to their scores on a behavior problem checklist, and were presented with the Profile of Nonverbal Sensitivity (PONS) test, which depicts interpersonal problems through still photographs (Rosenthal, Hall, DiMatteo, Rogers, & Archer, 1979). Results of the first study indicated that subjects' aggressive status correlated positively and significantly with the percentage of negative-dominant response choices. The authors concluded that this correlation may reflect a bias to attribute hostility on the part of aggressive boys. In a second study, the same investigators used a more open-ended procedure with the PONS test with 40 boys from the same population. The sorting categories spontaneously supplied in this study reflected a tendency on the part of the more aggressive boys to use labels that expressed negative-dominant affective status. These results complemented the findings of the procedurally more structured first study.

Both the Dodge and Nasby *et al.* studies are unique in their inclusion of personal attributes (e.g., aggressive status) among the independent variables. This advantage, however, unfortunately occurs in tandem with a distinct disadvantage. Even though the subjects in the study by Nasby *et al.* ranged in age from 10 to 16 years, differences in developmental level were not of obvious interest to the researchers. The Dodge study does take a more developmental perspective, and effects for age are reported, but since second through sixth graders served as subjects of this study, it is quite possible that several cognitive stage levels were included for each age group. More convincing explanations for the developmental differences found among second-, fourth-, and sixth-grade subjects would be possible if information about their cognitive level status as well as their chronological age was considered.

The clinical focus of the Nasby *et al.* study would be well offset by inclusion of a noninstitutionalized control group in the design of future research. A coordinated methodology building on the strengths of the clinical focus in tandem with the developmental focus would provide us with the kinds of data that would fill out our rather sketchy picture of how and why children understand aggressive behavior.

Aggressive behavior has served as stimulus content in a developmental study of differences in the attribution of responsibility by Harris (1977). Heider's (1958) levels of responsibility were tested, ranging from local or superficial attributions to dispositional attributions that were intentionally based. A videotaped story of damage-creating behavior, varied across levels of internal causation, was shown to five groups of young people, ranging from first graders through college students. After watching each videotape, subjects were interviewed concerning the protagonist's responsibility for the outcome and her moral culpability. The pattern of results revealed that first- and third-grade subjects attributed more responsibility to the actor than did sixth or eighth graders or college students. Between eighth graders and college students, there was a significant increase in attributed causality between Level 4 (compliance with authority figure's request) and Level 5 (free will). The data structure for perceived naughtiness was quite different. As expected, first graders attributed more naughtiness to Nancy than did older subjects. The most dramatic differences for the effect of age occurred at Level 4 (compliance), with first and third graders attributing significantly more naughtiness to Nancy than did their older counterparts, who in turn saw her as more culpable when the action was a result of her own free will. Harris concludes that younger children's attributions are relatively undifferentiated across stimulus levels, whereas older subjects show increasing attributions to the person as the behavior becomes more internally directed.

Both the Dodge and Nasby *et al.* studies on aggression and the Harris study on attribution of responsibility signal that before age 7 or 8 children have a tendency toward syncretism in their social judgments. Often intentionality is erroneously attributed to behavior, and behavior that is the joint product of situational constraints, as well as intentions, is thought to be the result of purely personal motivation. These findings are suggestive of the reaction of young children to behavior that is hurtful but not under the control of the subject. On the other hand, since children of this age tend to normalize behavior, situational explanations will probably be constructed and the self-fulfilling prophecy characteristic of adult's social judgments will not operate. This would not necessarily be true when specific personality tendencies work against it, according to the work of Dodge and Nasby *et al.*

Research is clearly needed in order to determine the complexity limitations of causal judgments children at various developmental levels experience. Two studies of social comparison have addressed the question of the impact of causal judgment on children's self-evaluations. Nicholls (1978) hypothesized a positive relationship between the development of self-concept attainment and attribution of success to ability. Children between ages 5 and 13 were shown a film and asked to infer ability when achievement was held constant and when effort was varied. Nicholls, using the semiclinical interview method, found age-related changes in the ability to reason about effort and ability. The 5–6-year-olds did not distinguish effort, ability, and outcome; the 7–9-

year-olds considered effort but not ability; the 9–10-year-olds partially considered ability; and the 12–13-year-olds did so fully.

These results supported the Piagetian inspired hypothesis that the development of effort and ability causal schemes is structurally isomorphic to the coordination of proportional relations. Children younger than 12 years of age were not expected to succeed on this problem. Nicholls was interested in the development of self-concept of attainment as well, and he expected that children with a high self-concept of attainment would expect success and attribute it to ability. The opposite effect was anticipated for children with a low self-concept of attainment. Self-concept of attainment was measured by asking the children to rate themselves in comparison to their classmates on reading performance. Teachers were also asked to rate their pupils' reading performance. Self-rankings produced an interesting pattern of data. The youngest subjects' self-rankings were very high, but by 9 years of age, children's self-rankings approached the mean and correlated positively and significantly with teacher rankings. It seems that with developing cognitive maturity children become capable of both attributing success to ability when it is appropriate and considering their own achievements in a realistic light.

Ruble, Boggiano, Feldman, and Loebl (1980) examined age-related changes in the role of peers in children's self-evaluations in an achievement context. First- and second-grade children were asked to perform a task in the presence of three peers, and each child was given two types of concrete information: how well they had done (outcome information) and how well their peers had done (social comparison information). Results showed that only the second graders made any use of social comparison information in their judgments of their own performances, whereas younger children evaluated their own performance in terms of outcome information alone. In a second study, kindergarten and second- and fourth-grade children performed a task with an ambiguous outcome and were asked, "Can you beat the other children," in three social conditions: (*a*) relative success; (*b*) relative failure; and (*c*) no information. Only the fourth graders made systematic use of social comparison information in their judgments.

The results of both the Nicholls and Ruble *et al.* studies suggest that, before age 9, children rarely make use of social comparison information in their judgments and tend to have unrealistic yet inflated images of their own competence. These two studies provide indirect evidence for possible outcomes for atypical children in normal settings. Children younger than 8 or 9 will probably attribute failure of their peers to lack of effort rather than lack of ability, but this does not mean that the nonachieving child will not acquire a stigma for his lack of success. The stigma, however, may be based on incorrect assumptions.

Children who are not successful will probably not internalize and react with depression toward this failure until at least third grade, when their awareness of social comparison information affects them negatively. Elkind (1979) has suggested that the onset of depression in early adolescence for handicapped persons who, until then, have been "happy children" partially derives from a cognitive base. Of importance, of course, is not only the child's self-awareness but also the awareness of others' awareness of him or her.

CONCLUSIONS AND IMPLICATIONS

Our understanding of when and by what means children both become aware and make sense of deviance and disorder in others is as yet in its own early stages of development. In light of this brief history, a short summary of major developmental trends will be attempted, and several methodological recommendations made.

In his information processing model of social perspective taking, Flavell (1974) articulates the multifaceted quality of the process of understanding the position of the other. This five-part model is partially developmental, in that certain aspects must be accomplished before it becomes possible for others to operate. These five aspects include: existence (knowing that other perspectives exist); relevance (knowing that adopting the perspective of the other would be useful in this situation); ability (the competence of making a veridical inference); performance (the ability to maintain this perspective despite the press of one's own perspective); and application (the use in behavior or verbal communication).

The development of understanding deviant behavior and psychological disorder involves three aspects of this model: existence, ability, and application. Awareness that deviant behavior exists is based on some rudimentary expectation that persons behave in particular ways in given circumstances. Although preschoolers can predict happiness for a child at a birthday party and unhappiness for the same in a dental chair, they tend to be confused when presented with affect that is incongruent with the situation (Burns & Cavey, 1957; Greenspan & Chandler, Note 3). This difficulty with processing conflicting affective cues resembles the well-documented tendency for preoperational children to focus on the perceptual characteristics of a task and experience difficulty with the compensating nature of logical relationships (Elkind, 1969). Young children's confusion with respect to behavior that does not conform to these rather unidimensional expectations appears to take the form of normalization of "deviant" behavior to previously constructed expectations. At this early point in development, deviance is not yet defined as a problem to be grappled with, since its very existence is barely recognized. Psychological disorder, in contrast to other handicapping conditions, appears to await recognition of its very existence until middle childhood. This is likely a result of its partially covert and often multiple cued nature.

The ability to execute a veridical inference is characterized by dramatic transformations from early childhood to late adolescence. Elementary-school-aged children, in contrast to their younger counterparts, are capable of making inferences about concrete behavior and will compare and contrast these kinds of data when required to do so (Harris, 1977; Ruble *et al.*, 1980; Rule *et al.*, 1974). It is not until early adolescence, however, that social inferential strategies are characterized by comparisons based on covert psychological attributes (Barenboim, 1981; Nicholls, 1978). Behavior that is fraught with contradictions (i.e., when the underlying affect is not directly expressed in behavior), such as defensive behavior (Chandler *et al.*, 1978; Koch, 1981; Whiteman, 1967, 1970), passive–aggressive behavior (Marsden & Kalter, 1976), and delusional or psychotic behavior (Barenboim, 1981; Coie & Pennington, 1976; Marsden & Kalter, 1976), poses serious problems for children prior to early adolescence. Both the nature and complexity of the behavior to be explained are intimately involved in its comprehensibility, according to the results of the various studies reviewed in this chapter. Issues of visibility and familiarity with the behavior are critical as well when attempting to predict a developmental trajectory of recognition and comprehension.

The familiarity issue involves a discrepency with respect not only to normal expectable behavior but to children's actual experience with psychologically disordered persons. An overwhelming commonality among these various studies reviewed is that children's understanding of deviance and disorder is indexed by their responses to the behavior of hypothetical others. Three studies (Coie & Pennington, 1976; Dodge, 1980; Nicholls, 1978) are exceptions to this trend, since they include procedures that require children to consider the behavior of their actual peers. Coie and Pennington use the results of this procedure to evaluate responses to behavior disorders of hypothetical characters. Responses to hypothetical others, however, yield the basic data for their study. Nicholls includes children's rankings of their own achievement status relative to actual classmates, and he correlated these findings with teacher rankings and success at understanding the schemes of ability and effort. The basic data for his study, however, were children's responses to the performance of hypothetical others.

In the second part of his study, Dodge (1980) uses the aggressive status of actual others as an independent variable. Interestingly, results indicated that the aggressive status of the stimulus character made a more powerful contribution to the subject's bias to infer hostility from ambiguous content than the subject's own aggressive status. The design of Dodge's study is commendably elegant. Age as well as individual difference variables are included in the assessment of subjects, and persons actually known to his subjects serve as stimulus figures. Dodge's attention to stimulus as well as to subject dimensions is welcome, since as Chandler (1976), has suggested, research in the development of social cognition has focused more on delineating the complexity dimensions of the child's cognitive processing apparatus than on the impact exerted by the environment.

With the exception of these three studies, the evidence concerning children's understanding of deviance and disorder is based on responses to hypothetical characters. Consequently, the relationship between developmental competencies indexed under controlled laboratory conditions and real-life understanding remains unclear. It may be the case that these controlled studies yield a conservative estimate of children's abilities, since the portrayals of deviant behavior in these studies are relatively devoid of context. In real life, various contextual cues may provide other kinds of information that would aid social judgment. Conversely, the procedures used in these studies may highlight the salient features of a problem and ease the inferential burden of the subject. In the study of psychological defense (Chandler *et al.*, 1978), for example, our procedure of providing the antecedent causal event and the subsequent defensive outcome collapsed dimensions of real time for the subject. In real life, a defensive behavior is often witnessed by an observer who has no direct information about the antecedent causal event. In order to both recognize and make sense of such a defensive maneuver, the observer must select a potential motivating event from a large sample of antecedent behaviors or must supply a possible causal event to explain the defensive outcome. Our experimental procedure may have reduced the difficulty of the task, or it may have rendered it more difficult. We must also entertain the possibility that our controlled conditions yield a completely different problem that bears little resemblance to the meaning extracted from real-life events. We have no available data concerning the relationship between comprehension of hypothetical and real-life deviant behavior. Such a study is critical in order for us to understand this relationship, as well as to provide us with a means of evaluating the evidence we already have.

Only the two clinically oriented studies of Dodge and Nasby *et al.* and the research of Koch have included individual difference variables in their research designs. Since the very content of this line of inquiry is individual differences, viewing our subjects through this lens would provide much needed information. The major issue raised by our psychodynamically oriented colleagues in response to our work on defense decoding has concerned the effect of use of particular defenses on understanding defense mechanisms. This query holds more than academic interest. According to the genetic epistemology of Piaget (1970), the interdependence of the subject and object in the construction of knowledge is primary. Integration of personality dimensions and experiential factors into our normative developmental research designs would enable us to sight this multivariate research problem through an appropriately multidimensional lens.

We have to date no information concerning the ways in which children apply their social knowledge of psychological deviance to their social interaction with disordered peers. The utilization of such competence in performance is uncharted research territory of first-order importance. Persons who bear the responsibility for setting policy concerning the integration of atypical children with their more normal peers require more than attitudinal and anecdotal information. Children's conceptions and definitions of psychological deviance and disorder are most certainly related to dimensions of tolerance and acceptance. The social responsibility for explicating this relationship is ours.

REFERENCE NOTES

1. Budoff, M., & Conant, S. *The development of concepts of handicaps: A preliminary study* (RIEP-Print No. 117). Cambridge, Mass.: Research Institute for Educational Problems, 1980.
2. Whiteman, M., Luboff, J. R., & Breining, K. *Development of conceptions of psychological causality.* Paper presented at the meetings of the Eastern Psychological Association, Washington, D.C., April 1968.
3. Greenspan, S., & Chandler, M. J. *Empathy and pseudo-empathy: The affective judgments of first and third graders.* Unpublished manuscript, 1975. (Available from the Department of Psychology, University of Rochester, Rochester, New York.)

REFERENCES

Bandura, A., & Walters, R. H. *Adolescent aggression: A study of the influence of child training practices and family inter-relationships.* New York: Ronald Press, 1959.

Barenboim, C. The development of person perception in childhood and adolescence: From behavioral comparisons to psychological constructs to psychological comparisons. *Child Development*, 1981, *52*(1), 129–144.

Becker, W. C., Peterson, D. R., Luria, Z., Shoemaker, D. J., & Hellmer, L. A. Relations of factors derived from parent-interview ratings to behavior problems of 5 year olds. *Child Development*, 1962, *33*(1), 509–535.

Berndt, T. J., & Berndt, E. G. Children's use of motives and intentionality in person perception and moral judgment. *Child Development*, 1975, *46*, 904–912.

Brightman, A. But their brain is broken: Young children's conceptions of retardation. In H. Harmonay (Ed.), *Promise and performance: Children with special needs; ACT's guide to TV programming for children* (Vol. 1). Cambridge, Mass.: Ballinger, 1977.

Budoff, M., Siperstein, G., & Conant, S. Children's knowledge of mental retardation. *Education and training of the mentally retarded*, 1979, *14*(4).

Burns, N., & Cavey, L. Age differences in empathic ability among children. *Canadian Journal of Psychology*, 1957, *11*, 227–230.

Chandler, M. J. Social cognition: A selective review of current research. In W. Overton & J. Gallagher (Eds.), *Knowledge and development* (Vol. 1). New York: Plenum, 1976.

Chandler, M. J., Greenspan, S., & Barenboim, C. Judgments of intentionality in response to videotaped and verbally presented moral dilemmas: The medium is the message. *Child Development*, 1973, *44*, 311–320.

Chandler, M. J., Paget, K. F., & Koch, D. The child's demystification of psychological defense mechanisms: A structural and developmental analysis. *Developmental Psychology*, 1978, *14*(3), 197–205.

Coie, J., Costanzo, P., & Cox, G. Behavioral determinants of mental illness concerns: A comparison of ''gatekeeper professionals.'' *Journal of Consulting and Clinical Psychology*, 1975, *43*, 626–636.

Coie, J. D., & Pennington, B. F. Children's perceptions of deviance and disorder. *Child Development*, 1976, *47*, 407–413.

Cramer, P. Defense mechanisms in adolescence. *Developmental Psychology*, 1979, *15*(4), 476–477.

Dodge, K. Social cognition and children's aggressive behavior. *Child Development*, 1980, *51*, 162–170.

Dollinger, S. J., Staley, A., & McGuire, B. The child as psychologist: Attributions and evaluations of defensive strategies. *Child Development*, 1981, *52*, 1084–1086.

Elkind, D. Conservation and concept formation. In D. Elkind & J. Flavell (Eds.), *Studies in cognitive development*. New York: Oxford Univ. Press, 1969.

Elkind, D. *The child and society*. New York: Oxford Univ. Press, 1979.

Elkind, D., Barocas, R., & Rosenthal, B. Combinatorial thinking in adolescents from graded and ungraded classrooms. *Perceptual and Motor Skills*, 1968, *27*, 1015–1018.

Erwin, J., & Kuhn, D. The development of children's understanding of the multiple determination underlying human behavior. *Developmental Psychology*, 1979, *15*(3), 352–353.

Fisher, L. Child competence and psychiatric risk: I. Model and method. *Journal of Nervous and Mental Disease*, 1980, *168*, 323–331.

Flavell, J. The development of inferences about others. In T. Mischel (Ed.), *Understanding other persons*. Oxford, England: Blackwell, 1974.

Gleser, G., & Ihelevich, D. An objective instrument for measuring defense mechanisms. *Journal of Consulting and Clinical Psychology*, 1969, *33*, 51–60.

Goldschmidt, M. L. T., & Bentler, P. M. *Concept assessment kit—conservation*. San Diego, Calif.: Educational Testing Service, 1968.

Haan, N. Coping and defense mechanisms related to personality inventories. *Journal of Consulting Psychology*, 1965, *29*(4), 373–378.

Harris, F. Developmental differences in the attribution of responsibility. *Developmental Psychology*, 1977, *13*(3), 257–265.

Heider, F. *The psychology of interpersonal relations*. New York: Wiley, 1958.

Honess, T. A comparison of the implication and repertory grid techniques. *British Journal of Psychology*, 1978, *68*, 305–314.

Honess, T. Children's implicit theories of their peers: A developmental analysis. *British Journal of Psychology*, 1979, *70*, 417–424.

Inhelder, B., & Piaget, J. *The growth of logical thinking from childhood to adolescence*. New York: Basic Books, 1958.

Jones, E. E., & Nisbett, R. E. The actor and the observer: Divergent perceptions of the causes of behavior. In E. Jones, D. Kanouse, H. H. Kelley, R. E. Nisbett, S. Valins, & B. Weiner (Eds.), *Attribution: Perceiving the causes of behavior*. Morristown, N.J.: General Learning Press, 1971.

Jones, F. H. The Rochester Adaptive Behavior Inventory: A parallel series of instruments for assessing social competence during early and middle childhood and adolescence. In J. S. Strauss, H. M. Babigian, & M. Ross (Eds.), *The origins and course of psychopathology*. New York: Plenum, 1977.

Koch, D. A. *Stage and style in social cognition*. Unpublished doctoral dissertation, University of Rochester, 1981.

Koch, D. A., Harder, D., Chandler, M. J., & Paget, K. F. Parental defense style and child competence: A match–mismatch hypothesis. *Journal of Applied Developmental Psychology*, 1982, *3*, 11–21.

Livesley, W. J., & Bromley, D. B. *Person perception in children and adolescents*. New York: Wiley, 1973.

Maas, E., Maracek, J., & Travers, J. Children's conceptions of disordered behavior. *Child Development*, 1978, *49*, 146–154.

Marsden, G., & Kalter, N. Children's understanding of their emotionally disturbed peers. *Psychiatry*, 1976, *39*, 227–238.

Nasby, W., Hayden, B., & De Paulo, B. Attributional bias among aggressive boys to interpret unambiguous social stimuli as displays of hostility. *Journal of Abnormal Psychology*, 1980, *89*(3), 459–468.

Nicholls, J. G. The development of concepts of effort and ability, perception of academic attainment, and the understanding that difficult tasks require more ability. *Child Development*, 1978, *49*, 800–814.

Novak, D. W. Children's reactions to emotional disturbance in imaginary peers. *Journal of Consulting and Clinical Psychology*, 1974, *42*, 462.

Novak, D. W. Children's responses to imaginary peers labeled as emotionally disturbed. *Psychology in the Schools*, 1975, *12*, 103–106.

Paget, K. F. *Egocentrism, social inference and assumptive psychologies: A developmental study*. Unpublished doctoral dissertation, University of Rochester, 1979.

Piaget, J. Piaget's theory. In P. Mussen (Ed.), *Carmichael's manual of child psychology* (Vol. 1). New York: Wiley, 1970.

Rosenthal, R., Hall, J. A., DiMatteo, M. R., Rogers, P. L., & Archer, D. *Sensitivity to nonverbal communication: The PONS Test*. Baltimore, Md.: Johns Hopkins Press, 1979.

Ruble, D., Boggiano, A., Feldman, N., & Loebl, J. Analysis of the role of social comparison in self-evaluation. *Developmental Psychology*, 1980, *16*(2), 105–115.

Rule, B. G., Nesdale, A. R., & McAra, M. J. Children's reactions to information about the intention underlying an aggressive act. *Child Development*, 1974, *45*, 794–798.

Santostefano, S. *A biodevelopmental approach to clinical child psychology: Cognitive controls and cognitive control therapy*. New York: Wiley, 1978.

Schaefer, E. S. A circumplex model for maternal behavior. *Journal of Abnormal and Social Psychology*, 1959, *59*, 226–235.

Sines, J. O., Parker, J. D., Sines, L. K., & Omen, D. R. Identification of clinically relevant dimensions of children's behavior. *Journal of Consulting and Clinical Psychology*, 1969, *33*, 728–734.

Whiteman, M. Children's conceptions of psychological causality. *Child Development*, 1967, *38*, 143–156.

Whiteman, M. The development of conceptions of psychological causality. In J. Hellmuth (Ed.), *Cognitive studies* (Vol. 1). New York: Brunner/Mazel, 1970.

Yamamoto, K., & Dizney, H. Rejection of the mentally ill: A study of attitudes of student teachers. *Journal of Counseling Psychology*, 1967, *14*, 264–268.

10 / Cultural effects on the development of equality and inequality

WILLIAM S. HALL
PAUL E. JOSE

I pledge allegiance to the flag of the United States of America and to the republic for which it stands, one nation under God, indivisible, with liberty and justice for all.

Children who have attended schools in the United States should know the Pledge of Allegiance very well. Although the idea of equality is strongly implied in the phrase "liberty and justice for all," children eventually learn that people are not treated equally in our society. The understanding that certain groups of people do not enjoy the same resources or opportunities for advancement that other groups do is achieved by children at different rates for a number of reasons. For instance, a child may not encounter clear and convincing evidence of inequality in his or her environment. And even if the child does, he or she may lack the knowledge or cognitive sophistication to interpret it accurately. Also, conceptions of inequality are not always abstracted naturally in an inductive fashion; often these beliefs are explicitly communicated to children by adults. Cultural continuity requires that values, roles, and expectations be communicated by the old to the young.

M. Mead (1970) has described three forms by which this transmission process may be organized: *postfigurative* (in which persons—both children and adults—learn primarily from their forebears); *cofigurative* (in

THE CHILD'S CONSTRUCTION
OF SOCIAL INEQUALITY

which both children and adults learn from their peers); and *prefigurative* (in which adults learn from their children). The continuity of a culture, then, depends on the living presence of at least three generations.

The traditional postfigurative culture depends on the actual presence of three generations—thus, it is especially generational. As Mead (1970) notes:

> It depends for continuity upon the expectations of the old, and upon the almost ineradicable imprint of those expectations upon the young. It depends upon the adults being able to see the parents who reared them, as they rear their children in the way they themselves were reared [p. 4].

Postfigurative cultures are defined by the fact that a group of people consisting of at least three generations take the culture for granted, so that as the children grow older they accept unquestioningly whatever is inculcated in those around them. However, our modern technological society has vitiated the old mode of enculturation to some extent. Attitudes, beliefs, and systems of knowledge are now transmitted from the young and one's peers more often than they once were. The role of the youth culture in the development of beliefs about equality has not yet been well understood in the research literature; we still persist in viewing this process as directed by parents, adults, and society at large. Mead's formulation raises the useful question in this context of whether a child's peers corroborate, oppose, or exert little influence on the acquisition of a coherent belief system about equality from the adult culture. It is not obvious, however, how the postfigurative forces work.

Either by learning about inequality in the abstract sense or by personally experiencing it, children over time acquire beliefs about how our society differentially treats various ethnic and social class groups, and in particular how it will treat them as individual members in those groups. On the one hand, our prevailing national ethos proudly proclaims liberty and equality for all, but on the other hand, cultural forces and our experiences may contradict this view. How does a developing child make sense of these conflicting interpretations? What are the mechanisms by which a child learns about equality and inequality? Figure 10.1 presents a general schematic model of how conceptions of equality derive from a child's developing cognitive capabilities and are shaped by the enculturation process. General labels for complex concepts in the model will serve a heuristic function at this point in the discussion. Explication of the terms will follow a general treatment of the main concepts.

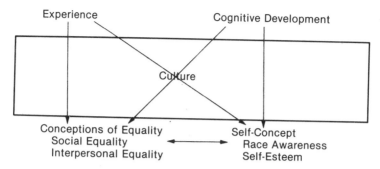

Figure 10.1. A general schematic model.

OVERVIEW OF SCHEMATIC MODEL

The outline in Figure 10.1 is our attempt to summarize several of the most important influences on the development of conceptions of equality. The "primitives" in this system are real-world experience and cognitive development. They are fundamental since they provide the basis of development for the individual. Socialization of an individual then occurs through the filtering influence of culture. Thus, culture effectively provides an explanatory mechanism for the developing child's interpretation of the environment. Although culture is represented by a single box in the model, we do not intend to connote that it is a simple unitary entity. The box includes all enculturation pressures, both intentional and accidental, manifested by the wide variety of its agents (i.e., parents, peers, television, schools, etc.).

Development of the self, one of the two derivative phenomena, is seen as dependent on social experience, cultural beliefs, cultural interpretations of social experience, and the level of cognitive ability achieved at any given age. Two aspects of the self particularly important in the present context are race awareness and self-esteem. Implicit in this development of the self is the process of social comparison (Festinger, 1954). Since acquisition of race identification and self-esteem is to a large extent shaped by significant others in a child's early life, it is important to ask who those significant others are and how they transmit crucial cultural beliefs and attitudes.

The last component of the model is the development of conceptions of equality. We feel it is crucial to distinguish between two aspects of this concept. The first one, which we call social equality, can be thought of as referring to society-wide or sociological aspects of equality. The second aspect, interpersonal equality, is concerned with the distribution of resources between individuals in direct interaction. The former deals with the understanding of political and economic forces that have caused one's socioeconomic or cultural group to prosper or struggle. The main components of this process involve acquisition of identification with a particular racial, ethnic, or social class group; an appreciation of how this group has fared in the past; and an expectation of how it will do in the future. Interpersonal equality focuses on fairness of exchange between individuals in face-to-face interactions regardless of race, sex, or other individual differences. The research on this topic strives to tie cognitive development to the sequence of successive sets of rules acquired by children in their determination of fairness in resource allocation. Little attention has been paid so far to whether culture might affect the progression through the sequence, although there is some work on how the rules of interpersonal equality may affect judgments of the social equality type.

We think there should be significant interconnections between concepts described in the preceding outline. One of the most pressing questions, it seems to us, is the one just enunciated: How do developmental trends in distributive justice decisions affect perceptions of social equality? We take the position that the psychological level is more basic than the sociological, which is to say that advances in the development of equity allocation should enable the child to perceive aspects of the sociological environment with greater sophistication. This is, of course, arguable. There may be little interaction between these two systems of thought. And one could argue that the direction of influence is from social equality to interpersonal equality. For instance, if a poor child is convinced that his poverty is unjust, he may favor an equalitarian approach in distributing resources. However, the equality allocation mode is the earliest and most primitive type of distributive rule that a child expresses in the interpersonal domain. If the child is older—in sixth grade, for example—he will presumably possess an equity rule of distribution that may contradict his political belief that everyone should receive equal shares of available resources. How is this possible? The two systems seem to impinge on one another. How precisely does this occur, and how are discrepancies resolved?

The other major consideration inherent in the schematic outline is the role of a child's self-concept in judgments of equality and inequality. Whether children identify themselves as members of a particular ethnic or social class involves a difference in how they interpret the environment and, resultantly, what their expectations are for advancement in society. Categorical self-concept should pertain more to issues relevant to social equality than interpersonal equality, although it can be seen that social factors can intrude there also.

The puzzle has been laid out earlier in Figure 10.1 in one large piece. We now will disassemble the whole to inspect the pieces more closely. Once the literature has been examined in detail, we will indicate certain lacunae in the existing fabric of research that need to be filled in order to understand how socialization processes, and in particular cultural forces, cause differential beliefs about equity. We will consider first the formation of the self-concept, with particular attention to race awareness, social status awareness, and self-esteem. These interact to affect conceptions about the second variable, beliefs about equality. As suggested earlier, equality has been studied in two discrete ways by two separate disciplines: interpersonal equality by psychologists, and social equality by sociologists. There are, nevertheless, a number of overlapping points of view that we will focus on while comparing the assumptions of the two domains.

SELF–CONCEPT

The development of the concept of inequality in children permits the implication of both cognitive and social functioning. As we indicated earlier, we are especially interested in examining the role of the self-concept and its related concepts, racial awareness and self-esteem, in children's development of the concept of inequality. Porter and Washington (1979) point out:

> Self-concept is in large part a social product, determined by the attitudes and behavior of others toward the individual. Since many American ethnic groups have been the victims of prejudice, it has been assumed that low self-esteem may result from minority status [p. 53].

We are in agreement with Porter and Washington's formulation in that we are concerned with trying to understand possible connections between a group's status in the socioeconomic system, a group member's concept and self-esteem, and his or her perception of equality.

What people think about themselves is exceedingly complex and is determined by a multitude of factors, such as real-world experience, cultural interpretations of that experience, and cognitive development. The symbolic interactionists (Cooley, 1902; Mead, 1934) suggested that a substantial part of one's self-concept is derived from perceptions of how one affects other people. This so-called looking-glass self (Cooley, 1902) is only possible when a person is sufficiently cognitively developed to transcend an egocentric point of view (Leahy, 1981; Leahy & Huard, 1976). The development of the self-concept is irrevocably tied to the development of a child's cognitive capacities in several ways. The child must understand that other people do not necessarily agree with his or her perspectives on reality, learn how to interpret the other's behavior that communicates these divergent views, and integrate his or her own conceptions with other people's.

Of the various aspects of the self-concept, three seem particularly relevant in understanding how a child's developing self might affect ideas about equity: race awareness, social class awareness, and self-esteem. Each will be discussed with particular emphasis on how cognitive development underlies them and how cultural forces may or may not shape them.

ACQUISITION OF RACIAL AWARENESS

Clark and Clark's (1939, 1940, 1947) studies of racial identification and preference in black children was the stimulus for a large body of work concerned with how children learn that they are a member of a particular race. Using a doll-choice methodology, they found that black children indicated a high preference for white dolls even when racial identification was demonstrated. In one study (1947) of 3–7-year-old children, they found that 66% of the children correctly identified themselves with the black doll, although levels of preference for the white doll ("nice doll," "like to play with," and "nice color") averaged around 60%. The authors argued that these results indicated that the ambient white culture exerts a strong, pernicious effect on the development of the black child's self-concept. The impact of the Clark's work was twofold: It was used in testimony for the landmark 1954 *Brown* v. *Board of Education of Topeka, Kansas* Supreme Court decision, and it sparked considerable interest in studying racial self-concept. The Clark and Clark work highlights the early awareness of racial differences displayed by the children in their experiments. One implication of this early racial understanding coupled with black children's preference for white dolls is that these children are developing a schema that categorizes people as "good" and "bad" on the dimension of skin color.

Developmental factors can only be inferred from the Clark and Clark work since they are not specifically addressed. Other researchers have been curious about how the racial self-concept develops and have proposed several stage theories. Goodman's (1952) work was one of the first. She found racial awareness to be present as early as age 3; this is in addition to incipient prowhite preference in black children. These mild preferences intensify over the next year of development to the point that one-fourth of the 4-year-olds express deeply internalized racial attitudes. Her theoretical model states that ethnic awareness occurs at age 3–4 years, ethnic orientation occurs between 4 and 7, and ethnic attitudes that began to form as early as 3 years are made concrete and solid (i.e., less easily changeable) after 7 years.

While supporting the basic findings of the Clarks and Goodman, the more sociologically oriented investigations of Porter (1971) extend their generalization by covering a wide range of subjects as well as employing a variety of stimulus materials and methodologies. Unlike the Clarks' and Goodman's work, however, Porter is more explicit about when each aspect of race awareness appears. Porter maintains that 3-year-olds have only an incipient notion of color differences (i.e., white dolls are better than brown ones) and they are not able to identify their own race. By 4 years, they understand that some colors have evaluative labels, and they begin to apply these distinctions to people. At age 5 years, racial identification is largely accomplished and the evaluative component of color differences is apparently integrated into conceptions of race. Thus, a 5-year-old black child is likely to understand that he is a black, or a Negro and that being so is not as good as being white. Thus, the seed is present at this time for developing ideas about social inequality.

Both Goodman and Porter proffer stages of development, but they are somewhat general. Katz (1976; see also Chapter 2, this volume) has presented the most detailed developmental stage theory yet concerning race concepts. Her sequence includes eight steps, some of which overlap:

1. Early observation of racial cues; no internalization (before age 3)
2. Formulation of rudimentary concepts; evaluative component is implicated ($2\frac{1}{2}$–4 years)
3. Conceptual differentiation; elaboration of basic concepts about race (4 years on)
4. Recognition of the irrevocability of cues; race is permanent, as is gender (after 4 years)
5. Consolidation of group concept; integration of disparate aspects of racial concepts (age 5 through grade school)
6. Perceptual elaboration; sharpening of "us" versus "them" distinctions through further contact (grade school)

7. Cognitive elaboration; racial concepts become more sophisticated and form attitudes (grade school and middle childhood)
8. Attitude crystallization; attitude becomes rigid (later grade school)

In developing these stages, Katz drew upon the principal studies in the development of racial attitudes. It has not yet been exactly determined when some stages occur. This would appear to be a formidable task, since certain factors, such as one's own race and contact with other races, seem to affect the timing. Another point of interest is that the emphasis is on racial attitude broadly defined; there is little attention paid to the distinction between self and others. It is assumed that when children are able to identify the race of others, they will be capable of identifying their own also. This may not necessarily be so.

When children learn about race, they seem to be highly dependent on the type of experiences and information they are exposed to in the process of developing feelings about themselves vis-à-vis an ethnic identity. As Proshansky and Newton (1968) have noted, children learn about race both directly and indirectly—at home, at school, in the streets, and from parents and peers. For this reason an inviolable timetable of racial attitudes is unlikely. Also, it would seem to be susceptible to the winds of cultural change. For example, Ward and Braun (1972) report findings of children growing up since 1963 that indicate that the older finding of the studies of children's racial preference conducted in the 1950s and early 1960s—namely, that black children chose white models and rejected black ones—has now reversed itself. Fox and Jordan (1973) and Cross (Note 1) report similar results. Fox and Jordan (1973) studied 360 black, 360 Chinese, and 654 white children who ranged in age from 5 through 7 in either integrated or segregated schools in New York City. They found that a majority of the black children preferred and identified with their own racial group—indeed, all the children showed a preference for their own group.

Another line of thought emphasizes the invariant sequence of cognitive development that underlies acquisition of race awareness and racial beliefs. Semaj (1980) became dissatisfied with the lack of a firm foundation for the stage theories proposed by Goodman (1952), Porter (1971), and Katz (1976). He believes that it is possible to take advantage of Kohlberg's (1969) cognitive-developmental approach to construct a theory based soundly on cognitive milestones. He predicted that Piagetian impersonal cognition (i.e., conservation) would underlie and motivate changes in social development about race knowledge and race attitudes.

Semaj's findings showed three discrete age stages:

1. *4–5 years*—Children understand that people can be categorized into various ethnoracial groups, but they do not yet understand the bases for these groupings, neither do they appreciate the permanence of these classifications. While they are beginning to learn some evaluative connotations of race, these are merely reflective of values of their social environment.
2. *6–9 years*—Acquisition of conservation facilitates development of racial constancy. Appreciation of self in regard to own racial group begins; thus, positive in-group evaluations are possible.
3. *8–11 years*—Previous egocentric stance is ameliorated by increased impersonal and social cognitive development and other experiential factors. At this age, blacks are more unwilling to say that blacks are better than whites; instead they are seen as the same.

Progress in the study of the self-concept as it relates to the development of children's conceptions of equality seems to be moving forward on two grounds: Attention is being paid to cognitive development, and the traditional doll-choice experiments are being placed in historical perspective. Future work concentrating on the following topics still needs to be done: (*a*) development of measures of self-esteem from the perspective of comparative cognitive theory; (*b*) investigation of other ethnic groups besides blacks; and (*c*) clearer understanding of who serves as a comparison group for a particular respondent. We will return to a discussion of these later.

CONCEPTIONS OF EQUALITY

As noted before, the following section will differentiate between two types of equality that have been studied by social scientists. The first one, interpersonal equality, has been investigated primarily by developmental and social psychologists and is the description of the heuristic strategies people use in allocating rewards or resources. The second type, social equality, has been studied largely by sociologists and concerns judgments of fairness for social groups (e.g., Do blacks receive a disproportionately small share of the production of our economy?). There are common threads of theoretical concerns between the two areas, since similar processes seem to underlie both (see Brickman, Folger, Goode, & Schul, 1981). Also, we will attempt at the end of the following section to incorporate some of the disparate lines of thought on these two topics with the former section on self-concept.

Interpersonal equality

The concept of justice has been a major focus of developmental research since the early 1970s. Piaget's *The Moral Judgment of the Child* (1932) laid the foundation for the resultant explosion of work in moral development, and Kohlberg's (1969, 1976; see also Kurtines and Greif, 1974) elaboration of the Piagetian model has ensured continued interest in the area. One of the more robust areas of investigation is concerned with the child's understanding of intentionality in judgments of an actor's blameworthiness (e.g., Karniol, 1978, 1980; Keasey, 1977). Other subareas include role-taking ability (Hoffman, 1977a), prosocial behavior (Blasi, 1980), and distributional justice.

The last, also referred to as resource or reward allocation, is the subarea in which existing research most closely touches on issues of equality. The essential question has been: What types of distributional strategies do children use to divide rewards or resources between several individuals? The first testable theory of distributive justice was equity theory proposed by Homans (1961), a prominent sociologist; soon after, it was followed by elaborations by Adams (1965) and Walster, Walster, and Berscheid (1978), which were more psychologically based. A relationship is determined to be equitable between two individuals, *A* and *B*, if the following equation results in an equality, not an inequality:

$$\frac{A\text{'s Outcomes}}{A\text{'s Inputs}} = \frac{B\text{'s Outcomes}}{B\text{'s Inputs}}$$

(For the complete mathematical formula see Walster, Walster, & Berscheid, 1978, pp. 262–266; see also Hook, Chapter 8, this volume.)

A crucial point to note is that determination of outcomes and inputs is performed by a fallible perceiver—or "scrutineer," to use Walster *et al.*'s name—so what may be relevant inputs for one person may be irrelevant to another. Thus, it is entirely possible that two co-workers could disagree strongly as to whether one enjoys a better situation than the other. Generally, however, people tend to agree that certain outcomes and inputs are relevant to their situation and others are not; otherwise, conflict and dissension would disrupt the social fabric of society (Adams, 1965).

The importance of equity theory to the development of distributive justice lies in the capacity of the theory to incorporate differences of opinion about what constitutes a proper input or outcome. In fact, the cognitively maturing child progresses through several stages marked by use of different inputs in the equity equation (Damon, 1975, 1977). In particular, Lerner (1974) has posed three possibilities: (*a*) parity, or equality (i.e., resources are distributed equally); (*b*) need (i.e., to each according to his or her need); and (*c*) equity (i.e., to each according to his or her contribution). If relative contribution to the task varies, do children allocate resources equitably or equally?

There is no clear consensus for an answer to this question. Despite some work that suggests that young children begin with an equity heuristic and gradually shift to an equality strategy (Streater & Chertkoff, 1976), most research indicates that the developmental progression is the opposite—that is, equality (or parity) first, then equality (Hook & Cook, 1979; Leventhal, Popp, & Sawyer, 1973; Peterson, Note 2). Usually the interpretation is that younger children (before 6 years of age) are not sufficiently cognitively mature to understand the importance of such internal personal variables as intention, ability, and effort, which mediate successful performance, whereas older children are. Thus, the reasoning goes, children initially allocate on the basis of equal shares for everyone because they have no other criteria to use. When they are cognitively able to perceive and integrate more subtle factors, then they begin to use an equity rule.

There are some flaws to this simple cognitive-developmental progression theory. The most telling is that the child is probably not beginning with an innocent, Rousseauian philosophy of egalitarianism. Piaget's description of the egocentric child does not support the idea that he or she would use an equality allocation strategy. Rather, the egocentric child is likely to allocate ''selfishly.'' Since children are ignorant of countervailing norms, children's behavior cannot be morally condemned (use of the adjective *selfish* is inappropriate since it connotes such a meaning); instead, children should be understood to be pursuing self-interested strategies. Thus, the original position should be thought of as self-centered: If children want something, they take or keep it, and if they do not want it, they may keep it or give it away largely on idiosyncratic grounds. Giving of an object is not understood to be dependent on other's needs, so there is no systematic variation due to deservedness or equality.

However, as Lerner and his colleagues have pointed out (Lerner, Miller, & Holmes, 1976), the child learns that delay of gratification is instrumental in ''earning'' greater future outcomes. With the concept of earning or understanding the legitimacy of owning or possessing and with the loss of an egocentric point of view comes the appreciation of deservedness. In the phrases of Lerner *et al.* (1976), children form ''personal contracts'' with themselves to obey. Children understand at this stage that there are many desirable objects that may be possessed only by "earning" or "deserving" them. Motivated by the desire to have an object, children seek to decode the set of laws communicated by adults and peers. The ability to understand and internalize these rules is dependent on cognitive level. Thus, one should consider the development of the child's distributional justice ability to be jointly caused by the child's current cognitive ability and the history of distributional social norms that have been taught to the child.

It is not accurate to state that cognitive ability alone determines distributive justice rules. Acknowledgment that taught social norms may become seriously distorted when a particular allocation rule appears in a child's repertoire is not common among researchers in this area. Most prefer to assume that they are uncovering an invariant sequence of distribution rules that are intimately and solely tied to cognitive development. For instance, the inconsistent finding on the appearance of equality and equity rules noted earlier may be due to the fact that parents and adults stress sharing, or equality, as a desirable allocation rule early on. Thus, children understand that the socially desirable rule to use is equality, even though they may privately prefer another rule (e.g., equity). Some researchers (e.g., Peterson, Note 2) have used a private or secret allocation methodology to avoid the contamination of social desirability, but this still does not disentangle the socialization history from cognitive ability. It seems desirable, if not necessary, to gather data on explicit and implicit instruction in allocation rule use before one can convincingly argue that the equality–equity sequence is invariant.

A potentially influential series of studies by Enright and his colleagues (Enright, Enright, Manheim, & Harris, 1980; Enright, Franklin, & Manheim, 1980; Enright & Sutterfield, 1980) present data relevant to this concern. Using Damon's stage model of distributive justice development (Damon, 1975, 1977), they derived a test, the Distributive Justice Scale (DJS), to assess children's standing on the continuum of distributive justice development (Enright, Franklin, & Manheim, 1980). Damon's (1975) model has five stages:

0–A: The child believes that whoever wants the most money or goods should have it.
0–B: The child bases distributive decisions on external characteristics. The oldest one, for example, should get more than the others.
1–A: The child believes everyone should receive the same amount regardless of other characteristics.
1–B: The child bases distributive decisions on behavioral reciprocity. The child believes that those who work harder or do more than the others should get more.
2–A: The child bases distributive decisions on psychological reciprocity. The child believes that those who are most in need should receive more than others [p. 303].

It is necessary to interpret the stages in the light of previous discussion of distributive rules before progressing. Stage 1–A is the equality rule; stage 1–B is the "contributions" rule (Leventhal, 1976), which is the archetypal equity rule; and stage 2–A is the "needs" rule, as described by Lerner (1974). However, all but stage 1–A are specific instances of the general equity rule, including 0–A and 0–B. As will be shown later, any input will serve in an equity equation, whether it is wanting the outcomes the most (0–A), some external characteristic (0–B), contribution to the task (1–B), or need (2–A). Most researchers are referring only to the contributions rule, 1–B, when they use the label "equity rule," although that is not technically correct. Obviously, confusion may arise if one is expecting a simple equality–equity progression because Damon's model stipulates some equity decisions before the equality rule is used, and then instantiation of different equity rules after that.

Enright *et al.* do not fall prey to this terminological pitfall, but on the other hand, their use of Damon's stage model is perhaps too uncritical. In one study (Enright, Enright, Manheim, & Harris, 1980), they tested black and white kindergarteners and third graders of lower- and middle-class backgrounds on the DJS. They found lower DJS scores for younger children and lower-class children; scores did not differ significantly by race. Thus, they concluded that children of low socioeconomic status (SES) enter school with a developmental delay in at least this one aspect of moral growth and that it is probably exacerbated by poor peer relations.

It is then an easy step of logic, which to their credit they do not take, to assert that the low-SES children suffer a cognitive developmental delay. In fact, they point out that verbal vocabulary scores do not differ between the two SES groups, so they do not propose 1–B as a causative factor. Instead, they suggest that since lower-SES children do not enjoy reciprocal peer relations with higher-SES children then (*a*) their less developed conceptions of distributive justice remain isolated; and (*b*) the lack of reciprocity in peer relations between SES groups prevents the child from progressing to high stages in the DJS scale. These arguments explicitly depend on the assumption that the development of school-aged children is significantly affected by the nature of peer interactions in addition to cognitive maturation. We would basically agree with this view, but there are potential problems with the approach taken earlier.

One potential problem is the artifact of social desirability. Certainly, children are frequently instructed as to how they should divide candy and other rewards, usually by the equality rule, so the higher means of middle-class children on the DJS may simply reflect a greater inclination to demonstrate the sharing norm to an adult rather than another, less acceptable rule. Thus, the difference in scores between the SES groups would be more a test of sensitivity to and knowledge of mainstream social norms than a pure test of cognitive strategies in resource allocation. It is impossible to tell at present how great a factor social desirability is, but the scale should eventually be tested alongside a more unobtrusive measure (i.e., private allocations) in order to rule out that interfering factor.

A second problem with the DJS as a measurement tool of distributive strategies is that there is no accurate assessment of combined responses. In other words, the DJS is not sensitive to subjects who prefer to combine several allocation rules simultaneously. Using a repeated pairwise comparison procedure (e.g., stage 0–A versus 0–B, 0–A versus 1–A), Enright *et al.* determine which of the five stage solutions is preferred, and the subject is given a single score corresponding to the preferred stage. Thus, the DJS does not permit the possibility of using two or more strategies at once.

Leventhal (1976) has previously explained in convincing detail the necessity of measuring allocation rules by a method that assesses the relative strength of two or more strategies simultaneously. He proposed the following equation:

Deserved outcomes $= W_c D$ by contributions $+ W_n D$ by needs $+ W_e D$ by equality $+ W_o D$ by other rules.

Outcomes is the numerator of the Walster *et al.* (1978) equity equation presented earlier and stands for the overall estimate of the outcomes deserved by a person. *D* signifies deservedness; so "*D* by needs," for example, indicates the deservedness by neediness. *W* denotes the weight the perceiver gives to a particular allocation rule. According to Leventhal (1976), estimation of fairness is then computed by following a complicated four-step process. Even more involved algorithms have been proposed by Anderson's cognitive algebra approach (Anderson & Butzin, 1978; Farkas & Anderson, 1979), which also provides a sophisticated method for assessing the temporal order of the cognitive processing of the four steps. Although these methods have largely been used for adult populations (except for Anderson & Butzin, 1978), it is clear that developmental psychologists could profit from these theoretical and methodological advances.

In sum, then, the question of which distributive justice rule is used at a particular age has not yet been answered satisfactorily. Damon (1975, 1977) has proposed a provocative stage model that has provided the foundation for the DJS created by Enright and his colleagues (Enright, Enright, Manheim, & Harris, 1980; Enright, Franklin, & Manheim, 1980; Enright & Sutterfield, 1980). Damon's proposal to take one of the justice concepts embedded in Kohlberg's 1976 moral development model, isolate it, and test it on children younger than Kohlberg normally studied is a good one, and he has certainly furthered our understanding of preschoolers' (and grade schoolers') use of distributive justice. Both Damon and Enright, however, have thus far failed to allow in their assessment procedure for the possibility that children may combine several sources of information in their distributive decision. Anderson and Butzin (1978) provide evidence that they do. Although the problems of eliminating social desirability and of obtaining meaningful and reliable responses from young children have not yet been solved, there is good reason to think that they can be handled satisfactorily.

It is important that researchers move beyond asking the simple question "Which comes first, equality or equity?" and consider the whole continuum of possibilities proposed by Damon and by the equity theorists, such as Walster and Berscheid. Although Damon (1975) and Hook and Cook (1979) have shown that the progression of distributive justice stages is correlated with age, we are still unsure how big a factor social learning is. Answers to the equality–equity question do not form a uniform chorus, which suggests that enculturation may have a significant effect on when stages appear. Useful research at this point would be ethnographic or naturalistic laboratory studies designed to answer the question of whether parents and peers exert significant pressure on young children to adopt certain strategies (i.e., sharing or equality) and not others. Ability to describe the form and strength of socialization pressures will enable a more informed description of the cognitive invariants in distributive justice development.

Social equality

The distinction posed earlier between interpersonal equality and social equality requires elaboration at this point. By the latter term, we mean the set of organized beliefs, attitudes, and concepts that people use to interpret and understand equality at the societal level.

An excellent example is the progressive income tax schedule used in the United States. Is it fair and equitable to tax higher income brackets at a higher percentage than lower ones? The reasons for such a schedule are several and complex. One is the belief that poor people should not be hurt by taxes as much as the more wealthy. What sort of distributive justice strategy is operating here? Several are probably working at once; the most obvious are (a) almost everyone pays some tax—equality; (b) the poor are asked to pay less—the needs rule of the equity equation; and (c) the rich are given tax breaks for investment—the contributions rule of the equity equation.

The tax schedule is perhaps the clearest instance of how justice rules operate at a societal level, as opposed to at the microlevel of interpersonal equality dynamics discussed earlier. It is nevertheless very unrepresentative in several ways. The tax schedule is quantified, concrete, and very public, whereas most social equality mechanisms exert pressure in a subtle fashion. For example, the cycle of poverty experienced by a sizable proportion of the population is probably misunderstood by the victims. The following quote from *The Grapes of Wrath* (1939) by John Steinbeck is a poignant portrayal of how the causes of economic hardship are often indistinctly perceived by the victim. In this scene, a sharecropper confronts a man hired to bulldoze the farmer's house down to make room for more mechanized farming.

> ". . . It's mine. I built it. You bump it down—I'll be in the window with a rifle. You even come too close and I'll pot you like a rabbit."
>
> "It's not me. There's nothing I can do. I'll lose my job if I don't do it. And look—suppose you kill me? They'll just hang you, but long before you're hung there'll be another guy on the tractor, and he'll bump the house down. You're not killing the right guy."
>
> "That's so," the tenant said. "Who gave you orders? I'll go after him. He's the one to kill."
>
> "You're wrong. He got his orders from the bank. The bank told him, 'Clear those people out or it's your job.'"
>
> "Well, there's a president of the bank. There's a board of directors. I'll fill up the magazine of the rifle and go into the bank."
>
> The driver said, "Fellow was telling me the bank gets orders from the East. The orders were, 'Make the land show profit or we'll close you up.'"
>
> "But where does it stop? Who can we shoot? I don't aim to starve to death before I kill the man that's starving me [From *The Grapes of Wrath* by John Steinbeck. New York: Viking Press, 1939, pp. 51–52. Copyright © 1939 by John Steinbeck. Copyright renewed 1967 by John Steinbeck. Reprinted by permission of Viking Penguin Inc.]."

Given that the relationship between action and consequence in a social system may often be very tenuous, as in the preceding example, how do individuals perceive injustice? Also, given our society's economic and social stratification, how are individuals socialized to accept their roles in the hierarchy? Why do individuals not rebel against the forces that have caused the large inequalities in our society? These questions will be answered in the following sections, and the relevance of each to developmental issues of social justice will be discussed.

PERCEPTION OF SOCIAL JUSTICE—
RELATIVE DEPRIVATION THEORY

The workhorse theory of determining social inequality has been equity theory (Adams, 1965; Walster *et al.*, 1978), as described in the previous section. Its roots are primarily in Homans's (1961) distributive justice theory; they also derive from the ideas proposed in the concept of relative deprivation.

Relative deprivation was first described in Stouffer's studies of the American soldier during World War II (Stouffer, Suchman, DeVinney, Star, & Williams, 1949). They explained differential dissatisfaction between two Army units by referring to the discrepancy between expectations and actual reality. Since expectations are based on social comparison and choice of the comparison group is often idiosyncratic, then judgments of inequality may be surprising to someone with a different perspective. The most useful insight provided by the notion of relative deprivation is that it is relative—that is, dependent on a particular comparison group, not an abstract comparison group or one thought more appropriate by an outside observer.

Since the earliest formulation of the concept, four writers (Crosby, 1976; J. A. Davis, 1959; Gurr, 1970; Runciman, 1966) have offered formal definitions to clarify the rather general description presented by Stouffer *et al.* Of the four, Crosby (1976; Bernstein & Crosby, 1980; Cook, Crosby, & Hennigan, 1977) offers the most detailed model. She states that five conditions must exist before a feeling of injustice or deprivation may occur (Crosby, 1976, p. 85). Assume that person *A* lacks object *X*.

1. *A* wants *X*.
2. *A* perceives that another possesses *X*.
3. *A* feels entitled to *X*.
4. *A* thinks it is feasible to attain *X*.
5. *A* does not think current failure to possess *X* is his own fault.

The "entitlement" referred to in Number 3 seems to be determined almost entirely by whether the "other" in Number 2 is considered to be similar or not. Similarity is computed by selecting among available inputs, as in the equity formulation, descriptive of oneself and another. Obviously, there can be great differences in choice of comparison characteristics between individuals and even for individuals over time, so entitlement can vary considerably.

One helpful aspect of the relative deprivation notion has been in understanding that, as a result of these comparison processes, objectively nondeprived groups act as if they are deprived. For instance, Pettigrew

(1967, 1971) has profitably used the approach to explain why blacks expressed rage and discontent during the 1960s when by comparison to their previous standing and in relation to other people's their living situation was improving dramatically. Pettigrew (1971) cited a claim by Bell (1963) that blacks in the United States at that time had a consumer buying power comparable to a similarly populated Canada and that a larger percentage of blacks than of residents of the British Isles attended college. Bell went on to add that an objective judgment of standard of living is not possible: Blacks compared themselves to those they were most familiar with, in this case white Americans who were doing even better than they were.

Rechecking Crosby's five criteria, one should note that all five were true. Again, the choice of the comparison "other" is crucial. If the other is fellow blacks rather than whites, then the comparison is not as galling because the gap is not as large. We will return to the problem of choosing a comparison other later when we consider the literature on children's awareness of stratification.

PERCEPTION OF SOCIAL JUSTICE—EQUITY THEORY

Let us consider again the role of equity theory in distributive justice, in this case with respect to social equality. Its generalizability to different settings and contexts is extremely good. Just as it can be used to describe and predict allocation of candies earned by performing an experimental task, it is as easily applied to issues of minority and women's rights, intimate relationships, employer–employee relationships, liability and restitution in law, altruism, and many other social concerns (Walster *et al.*, 1978). As long as inputs and outcomes can be determined and a known distribution rule is used, the general equation seems to hold.

In order for equity or inequity to be perceived, one must insert certain values into the equity equation to see if the two resultant quantities are relatively equal or not. Where those values come from has not been investigated—they are usually taken as a given. The Piagetian cognitive-developmental approach typical in the interpersonal equality literature presumes that cognitive capacity "selects" the type of inputs at any given time, but this ideology begs the question: After a person has achieved the formal operations stage, what determines type of inputs chosen? Our belief, stated earlier, is that cognition does not completely dominate input selection strategies; rather, there is a complex interplay between cognitive ability and culturally taught heuristics. (Also see Major and Deaux, 1981, for discussion of individual differences.) The latter is most obvious after an individual has reached the "age of reason." There are literally hundreds of ways to solve the equity equation, and current evidence indicates that after adolescence it is more constrained by cultural beliefs than intelligence.

Another example of this is the development of beliefs concerning social and economic stratification. After the next section, the stratification problem will be examined in depth.

PERCEPTION OF SOCIAL JUSTICE—
STATUS ATTRIBUTION THEORY

Della Fave (1980) points out that in addition to equity theory another mechanism may function in the process of determining whether a situation is fair or not. Status attribution theory (Berger, Zelditch, Anderson, & Cohen, 1972) predicts that when incomplete information is used to characterize another person the person's unknown status-relevant characteristics are presumed to be consistent with the known ones. Thus, if a particular person is known to be wealthy, it is usually also assumed to be true, in the absence of other information, that he or she is highly intelligent and knowledgeable about economic or business matters. This inclination to attribute other inputs on the basis of knowing one, or only a few, is similar to the stereotyping process (Hamilton, 1979) and implicit personality theory (Bruner, 1973) wherein other attributes are assumed to be true if a certain attribute is true. Although stereotyping is sometimes inaccurate, it is frequently accurate, and it serves a useful function in helping an individual predict into unknown areas.

Della Fave (1980) used status attribution theory to partially explain why gross inequalities in a society are tolerated. He suggests that perceivers often think "backwards" in the following manner: Since a person is powerful and rich he must possess superior contributions or inputs to deserve such rewards and since I am not rich or powerful, I must not possess such inputs. Thus, legitimation of wealth and power discrepancies are "explained" in the absence of any real evidence, and the individual is prevented from feeling that the arrangement is inequitable. The willingness to believe that people who possess power and wealth are duly rewarded for presumed valuable characteristics, such as expertise and hard work, is socialized, and it constitutes an important part of the legitimation of inequality. We will use and amplify Della Fave's (1980) ideas concerning legitimation and self-concept in the following section on social and economic stratification.

ACQUISITION OF THE CONCEPT OF STRATIFICATION

At the beginning of this chapter, it was claimed that children learn early that, contrary to our national rhetoric embodied in the Pledge of Allegiance, the American Creed, and elsewhere, all people are *not* created equal. Simmons and Rosenberg (1971) found in a sample of Baltimore youth that, in answer to the question "Do all kids in America have the same chance to grow up and get the good things in life [p. 239]?" 48% of grade schoolers, 63% of junior high students, and 70% of high school students answered no. Although the stratification system is perceived indistinctly at first, it is obvious that children learn early that it exists and that it has consequences for them and others.

This section will be presented in three parts. The first will detail the research that describes how children become aware of the stratification system. The second part shows how this affects the child's self-concept and particularly self-esteem. The last part pulls this work together in an explanation of how legitimation of stratification occurs.

Development of awareness of stratification. Children learn of the inequalities in our society gradually through the preteen and adolescent years. Two approaches have been used to study this acquisition process: the sociological and the psychological. The latter is well represented by the work of Leahy (see Chapter 3) and will not be discussed here.

The second one seeks to understand how groups develop certain attitudes as a result of demographic, social, and cultural forces. Simmons and Rosenberg (1971) studied almost 2000 students from Grade 3 to Grade 12 in a cross-sectional design to assess how age, race (black or white), and social class would impinge upon their growing appreciation of the stratification system. They measured (*a*) recognition of differential occupational statuses; (*b*) comprehension of the term *social class*, (*c*) personal awareness of poorer and richer peers; and (*d*) recognition of barriers to equal opportunity. The results can be summarized by saying that at younger ages (grade school) race and social class of respondent makes little difference, whereas as the child grows older differences begin to emerge. Specifically, it is the advantaged groups (white and high social class) that become aware of social class and its ramifications earlier than disadvantaged groups (black and lower social class).

In elementary school, children are relatively ignorant of stratificational reality; this is demonstrated by overestimating prestige of father's occupation and underestimating how constraining societal forces are on economic advancement. They inflate the prestige rating of their father's occupation and are more likely to believe that their parents have done "very well" in life. They predominantly (85%) answer no to the question, "Do you know what the word *social class* means?" And they identify their social class standing as higher than that of comparable junior high or senior high students. In addition, they are less likely to say that they know children from richer or poorer families.

Awareness of stratification does not appear fully developed at any particular age; the Simmons and Rosenberg data indicate that it is a gradual process. Even the high school students express unrealistic beliefs about the likelihood of their doing better than their fathers economically. The general outlook is one of optimism—97% of the children sampled believed that they have "as good" or "better" chance to rise in the world than most people—and it apparently survives until the first attempts are made to get a job or prepare for a particular occupation. Simmons and Rosenberg note the lack of appropriate data to detail this presumed loss of optimism.

In sum, then, Leahy (1981, Chapter 3, this volume), Furby (1979), and the other more psychologically oriented researchers who have been studying the development of children's knowledge of the stratification system emphasize the role of intelligence or cognitive development in this acquisition process, but the sociological approach tends to focus more on potentially causative social variables, such as one's own social class, amount of contact with other social classes, and other cultural belief systems. At younger ages, preschool and elementary school, it is probably true that cognitive ability mediates understanding of the abstract social world, but it loses its power as a predictor as the child grows older. However, this has not been demonstrated empirically and would be useful to do. There might be a greater rapprochement between the two existing paradigms if (*a*) it is important to know the relative contributions of cognitive ability and socialization for different ages; and (*b*) one would like to interleave the existing data so as to construct a developmental progression over the entire age span.

Effect of awareness of stratification on self-esteem. Phillips and Zigler (1980) have indicated that a child's social class may affect his or her self-esteem to some degree. The literature is not conclusive as to the direction or intensity of the effect, however. For instance, St. John (1971) and Yancey, Rigsby, and McCarthy (1972) have found no consistent effect of race on self-esteem; Soares and Soares (1969) and Rosenberg and Simmons (1971) found a small effect favoring blacks, and others (e.g., Rosenberg, 1965) have found a weak effect favoring whites. Rosenberg and Pearlin (1978) have attempted to clarify this muddled situation by examining self-esteem over the life span (8 years to adult). They found that self-esteem of children (8–16 years) is not affected significantly by their social class, but adults do evidence a moderate relationship.

Rosenberg and Pearlin suggest four mechanisms for how one's social standing in the stratification hierarchy will affect self-esteem formation: (*a*) social comparison of self and family to others; (*b*) reflected appraisals from significant others, such as teachers, peers, and relatives; (c) self-perception of one's own accomplishments; and (d) psychological centrality of given attributes or characteristics of the individual in his or her self-concept. They make the point that children's perceptions of their families' social standing is largely the fathers' doing and, although children will experience differential feedback as a result of their fathers' social class, children will largely discount such an evaluation since they are not responsible for it. Rosenberg and Pearlin maintain that all four principles operate continuously from a very early age, so social class would only make a significant difference when the individual has personally failed or succeeded in society as a young adult.

However, the Rosenberg and Pearlin data are not simple. The data show an increase in the correlation between social class and self-esteem over the three ages of the children. It is possible to argue (with Simmons & Rosenberg's, 1971, findings) that these children are only just realizing by about junior high age the true position of their families' status in the class hierarchy and that this perception correspondingly affects their self-esteem. Unfortunately, one cannot disentangle these hypothesized effects in the present data for several reasons. First, data on stratification awareness and self-esteem have apparently not been collected from the same sample of subjects. Second, even if these data become available, it would be essential that a longitudinal design be used to collect the data because it permits stronger conclusions about causality. Third, the method of measurement of self-esteem is a crucial one also. Zigler and his colleagues (Katz & Zigler, 1967; Phillips & Zigler, 1980; Zigler, Balla, & Watson, 1972) have demonstrated the usefulness of real–ideal self-image disparity in measuring self-esteem and of tying it to cognitive development of the child. A few researchers in this area have used this method (e.g., Soares & Soares, 1969), but unfortunately the idea of using multiple measures of self-esteem does not seem to have wide acceptance.

In sum, then, awareness of social class may affect self-esteem development, but the precise mechanisms are not clear. Rosenberg and Pearlin suggest four ways in which social class may affect self-esteem, but empirical support is thus far lacking.

Legitimation of stratification. As children learn of the existing inequalities in our social system, what prevents them from rejecting a system where certain people are going to do well partly at the expense of other people? This inclination should be particularly strong among those children who realize that their family falls within the latter category and that they run a sizable risk of ending up as an adult in that group too.

However, the overwhelming majority of children from all social strata are convinced that they personally can succeed in a system where everyone cannot succeed. The question of how a child can be socialized to see a social system as legitimate is crucial to our understanding of how children perceive social justice in general, because stratification is an institutionalized and culturally agreed upon form of inequality. In other words, the appropriateness of inputs used to determine access to the higher rungs of the social system should be widely shared by the majority of our populate.

Sociologists speak of two types of theories that explain how people perceive the stratification of society: functionalist theories and conflict theories. The functionalist approach (K. Davis & Moore, 1945; Parsons, 1949, 1951) proposes that the reward system inherent to the stratification structure of society is essentially accepted by the majority of people affected by it, and thus it remains relatively stable even though a significant portion suffer from it. Citizens are socialized to believe that certain occupations should be paid better and accorded higher prestige than others. This is functional, they say, because society will benefit from attracting the most able people to those occupations consensually deemed the most important. For instance, it is necessary to reward medical doctors (in terms of pay and prestige) more than garbage collectors because it is more important to society to have the most able doctors rather than the most able garbage collectors. It is expected, then, that occupations would vary in pay and prestige largely as a function of their utility to society. The stability of the system supposedly derives from two shared belief systems: (*a*) agreement on the prestige value of all occupations; and (*b*) belief in equal opportunity in gaining admittance to any occupation. Insofar as people believe that they have (or had in the case of adults) an equal chance to succeed, then they will continue to view the stratification system as legitimate.

The conflict theorists (e.g., Habermas, 1973; Marx, 1936; Mosca, 1939) oppose the idea that stratification is necessarily functional in providing the greatest good for the greatest number of people. They argue that the system may be, and probably is, subverted by the wealthy and powerful to protect both their unequal share of the society's resources and their preferential treatment in pursuing the choice occupations. Instead of existing to reward able persons who struggle to attain the appropriate education and training necessary for occupational advancement, the system exerts a conservative influence in preventing upward movement of lower classes. Equal opportunity may *seem* to exist, they allege, but in reality, powerful elitist mechanisms seriously undermine its effectiveness. The appearance of an avenue for upward mobility seduces the average person into thinking the social structure is just and reduces their dissatisfaction with the status quo. Marx, of course, argued that development of class consciousness by the working class would reverse this trend and prepare it for the more egalitarian philosophy of socialism.

Both views see legitimation of stratification as very important, but most of the theoretical descriptions thus far have not effectively incorporated theories of psychological development. Della Fave (1980), however, combines several psychological perspectives in constructing a theory of how people internalize acceptance of stratification. He begins with George Herbert Mead's (1934) concept of the self. Mead's position was that development of the self and the concomitant level of self-evaluation are derived from reflected self-appraisals by others (i.e., from the generalized other). Della Fave extends this self-evaluation to include evaluation of self based on social class that reflects success or failure within the social hierarchy. As noted earlier, Rosenberg and Pearlin (1978) also considered this idea in regard to self-esteem and aspirations for upward mobility.

Another aspect of Della Fave's formulation involves the role of equity theory and status attribution theory in explaining the propensity of people to view inequality as just. He stresses the tendency of people to seek cognitive balance and consistency (Festinger, 1957; Heider, 1958), an idea that is inherent in equity theory. This is well exemplified by Lerner's (Lerner & Matthews, 1967) "just world" theory, which shows the extent to which people will distort an equity equation in order to restore balance. Della Fave concludes that, since people in power are remote from the average person, the latter can very easily attribute to the former superior status characteristics, or *inputs* in equity terms, that will maintain a justification of the existing inequality between the two. This mechanism of overestimating a superior's contributions coupled with reflected self-appraisals constitutes a powerful legitimizing force according to Della Fave.

The data relevant to his propositions do not confirm them in a simple way, but they do not disconfirm them either. Rosenberg and Pearlin's (1978) findings on the relation between social class and self-esteem show that it is weak for children under 18 years of age. The paucity of findings indicating low self-esteem among blacks also tends to weaken the contention that reflected self-appraisal of the lower classes leads to lessened self-esteem. It is not clear, however, that self-esteem is the most sensitive measure of self-evaluation; perhaps aspiration more directly tests people's evaluations of how they will perform in the social hierarchy. Again, Simmons and Rosenberg's (1971) data show that lower-class children markedly overestimate their chances of succeeding. As the children got older, they became more accurate, and the relationship of self-esteem to social class grew stronger. So it seems that Della Fave's ideas are more relevant for adolescents and young adults.

Whether children overestimate the status attributes of the rich and powerful in comparison to the self is not clear. Leahy (1981, Chapter 3, this volume) discusses at length elsewhere the development of explanations given for being rich or poor and for social mobility. Generally, class and race of subject do not substantially affect the types of reasons given. Still, it is clear that the rich are described as being quite different from the poor, and among these characteristics are having more ability and working harder (Furby, 1979).

Della Fave's theoretical description of stratification legitimation is as yet the only comprehensive theory that specifically incorporates psychological processes. It is very unclear, however, how reflected self-appraisals and biased status attributions change to reflect developing awareness of the stratification system. Also, work by Furby and Leahy demonstrates that cognitive development underlies these more differentiated phenomena, so a child's standing on the cognitive dimension needs to be taken into account also.

MISSING LINKS: SUGGESTIONS FOR FUTURE RESEARCH

It has been our observation that the various research areas that purport to study how people arrive at judgments of equality have not shown much cognizance of each other. By stepping back to take a larger view, we have hopefully clarified the ways in which these research areas are related. The gaps that still remain will be pointed out as areas in which research could profitably be done.

Cognition, culture, and conceptions of equality

As already noted, there seems to exist in the literature two kinds of equality judgments: social equality and interpersonal equality. The former is largely studied by sociologists, the latter by psychologists; and the overlap between the two seems minimal. Psychologists (e.g., Damon, 1975, 1977; Enright, Franklin, & Manheim, 1980) have invested considerable time and effort into trying to uncover an invariant developmental sequence of how children allocate resources since it seems likely that this cognitive process follows the Piagetian theory of cognitive development. At the other extreme, sociologists have been pursuing the causes for various social attitudes or beliefs, such as occupational aspiration and perceptions of social class. The primary interest is in detailing the effect of experience on the formation of these attitudes; thus, such variables as race, chronological age, and contact with other races and social classes in integrated schools are studied.

Referring back to Figure 10.1 one can notice that the two paradigms correspond roughly to the two elements, cognitive development (interpersonal equality) and real-world experience (social equality). Our intention was to employ this schematic diagram to clarify the distinction between the two types of justice. We claim that they should be treated separately, since researchers explain their phenomena by referring to two different causative factors.

However, we mean by "separate treatment" only that they use a clear and unambiguous demarcation of whether a study attempts to tie judgments of equality to cognitive development or experience factors. When researchers employ chronological age as an independent variable, it may not be clear which they intend to study. Efforts to relate justice judgment to cognitive development should include a test of Piagetian reasoning (e.g., a test of conservation ability) or else a test already normed on Piagetian levels (Damon, 1977; Enright, Franklin, & Manheim, 1980). Otherwise, age is just a gross measure of the child's developing cognitive abilities.

Also, we would urge a more considered estimation of how cognitive development and cultural forces together affect justice evaluations. They obviously interactively determine a child's response, and it makes little sense to measure one and ignore the other. One of Enright's studies (Enright, Enright, Manheim, & Harris, 1980) is a good example of how both can be studied at once. They obtained scores on their DJS from white and black middle- and lower-class kindergarten and third-grade children. They argued that by controlling for vocabulary ability any resulting difference between race and class should result from cultural dynamics. They concluded that culture affected the rate of progress along the presumably fixed DJS scale.

A significant problem with this suggestion is that Piagetian levels for adolescent children and young adults are gross or nonexistent. Since much sociological work is aimed at adolescents and young adults, it is perhaps unfeasible to ask for measures of cognitive ability for them. Intelligence test scores could be used, but since they are flawed by cultural bias, they would give misleading results in cultural group comparisons.

Two other pressing concerns in the comparison of the two types of equality are method and topic. Interpersonal equality is primarily a question of distributional justice. Social equality is a mixture of equity considerations (of which distributive justice is a part), attribution of status characteristics, and assorted attitudes and beliefs that are used in equity decisions. Thus, research on equality runs the gamut from allocating pennies earned doing an experimental task to rating the social class to which one's family belongs. It seems important to relate the work on children's allocation strategies to the work on children's and adults' social justice attitudes so as to construct a life-span description of justice decision making. The observation we would like to make is that it would probably be helpful to use a multimethod approach, particularly for younger children, in order to see how the various justice phenomena interrelate. Specifically, gathering data of the three main types given in the next section on the same set of children (preferably longitudinally) would permit conclusions about how interpersonal justice decision-making rules are, or are not, carried over into the large societal domain of equity decisions and social justice attitudes.

Experience, culture, and conceptions of equality

One of the likeliest reasons why the three subareas of equality research may not develop interactively is that culture and personal experience may strongly push individuals' conceptions of justice in diverging directions. Enright, Franklin, and Manheim (1980) suggest that disadvantaged social groups evidence a retardation in progression through the cognitively determined DJS scale. It is unclear what may be causing these lower DJS scores: slower cognitive development or culturally learned behavior patterns advantageous in their social environment.

We suggest that culture and the child's set of experiences strongly mold social justice attitudes and beliefs and weakly affect distributive justice decision making (which is determined more by cognitive development). Therefore, it is imperative to study systematically the likely events and forces that shape social equality judgments. Race, social class, school integration, and geographic area have all received attention thus far. The data indicate that race and social class are not particularly meaningful in themselves, but in interaction with other variables (e.g., integrated school settings), they give very informative results.

The question of how children learn about inequalities in our society is still unanswered. Rosenberg and Simmons's (1971) work on black and white children's self-esteem in segregated and integrated schools indicates that the progress of gaining information about others and comparing one's own standing to that of others' is a subtle and complicated process. We urge researchers to become more aware of the ways in which such social comparison information is transmitted (television, teachers, peer groups, relatives, etc.) and to study it in context with cultural background variables.

Self-concept and conceptions of self-esteem

Lewis (Lewis & Brooks, 1974, 1975) and his colleagues have identified two kinds of self relevant to the development of the self-concept: (*a*) the *existential* (the basic awareness of an existing and continuing consciousness); and (*b*) the *categorical* (coming to see oneself in terms of relevant categories (e.g., boy–girl, child–teenager, black–white). Within the context of this chapter, the categorical self in Lewis *et al.*'s schema is perhaps the most relevant. According to Lewis and Brooks, an early dimension of self noticed by children is age, occurring between 3 and 5 years. A second dimension, growing independence, typified by the ''I can do it'' kind of statement, also emerges as a part of the categorical self's differentiation. The best available evidence suggests that by the fifth year, the categorical self seems well developed and all that remains to be developed is the further complexity of the self-concept. At the core of this complex development is the child's movement from seeing him- or herself largely in terms of external, visible categories (e.g., size, age), to more subtle, abstract characterizations. This shift, from external to abstract characterizations of self, parallels the one in cognitive development from concrete to formal operations. It is not precisely known how the shift in development interacts with the developing child's conception of equality and inequality. The possible intersection between this shift and the development of conceptions of equality and inequality is not clear. This statement might be most appropriately thought of in the context of the findings of Simmons and Rosenberg (1971) to which we referred earlier in this chapter. Recall that they found a progressive increase in children's tendency to respond no to the question: ''Do all kids in America have the same chance to grow up and get the good things in life?'' Just how pervasive responses like the one observed by Simmons and Rosenberg might be among children is an area worthy of investigation. Investigations in this area might involve children from a variety of cultural and geographic contexts.

SUMMARY

In this chapter, we have explored some theoretical underpinnings for the observation by social scientists that children eventually learn that people are not treated equally in our society. We have argued that the understanding that certain groups of people do not enjoy the same resources or opportunities for advancement that other groups do is achieved by children at different rates for a number of reasons. An explication of some of the reasons for this differential rate of achievement of the concept of inequality by children is an area that should be investigated.

We have emphasized the possible relationship between children's acquisition of the concept of equality and cultural continuity. Invoking M. Mead's (1970) formulation of cultural transmission as postfigurative, cofigurative, or prefigurative, we have proffered that cultural continuity requires that values, roles, and expectations be communicated by the old to the young. The role of the concept of equality in this formulation is unclear and should be tested empirically.

We have offered a model of the important influences on the development of conceptions of equality. Our model links culture (real-world experience) and cognitive development in an intimate interaction as major and fundamental categories influencing the child's acquisition of conceptions of equality. In our view, the child is socialized to develop conceptions of equality and inequality through the filtering influence of culture. In this way, culture effectively provides an explanatory mechanism for the developing child's interpretation of aspects of the environment, such as equality and inequality in the treatment of persons.

The development of conceptions of equality and inequality is largely a sociocognitive phenomenon. The culture affects the cognitive development of the individual through his or her self-concept. Development of the self depends, in part, on social experience and the level of cognitive ability achieved at any given age. We have argued that the relationship between social experience, cognitive development, and conceptions of self perhaps relates most directly to the interpersonal aspect of conceptions of equality that focuses on the distribution of resources between individuals in direct interaction.

REFERENCE NOTES

1. Cross, W. *Black identity: Rediscovering the distinction between personal identity and reference group orientation.* Unpublished manuscript, 80 (Available from Department of Human Development and Family Studies, Cornell University).
2. Peterson, L. *Understanding of ratioproportionality rules and equality vs. equity in children's sharing.* Paper presented at the biennial meeting of the Society for Research in Child Development, Boston, Massachusetts, April 1981.

REFERENCES

Adams, J. S. Inequity in social exchange. In L. Berkowitz (Ed.), *Advances in experimental social psychology* (Vol. 2). New York: Academic Press, 1965.
Anderson, N. H., & Butzin, C. A. Integration theory applied to children's judgments of equity. *Developmental Psychology*, 1978, *14*, 593–606.

282   *William S. Hall and Paul E. Jose*

Bell, D. (Ed.). *The radical right.* Garden City, N.Y.: Doubleday, 1963.
Berger, J., Zelditch, M., Anderson, B., & Cohen, B. P. Structural aspects of distributive justice: A status value formulation. In J. Berger, M. Zelditch, & B. Anderson (Eds.), *Sociological theories in progress* (Vol. 2). Boston: Houghton Mifflin, 1972.
Bernstein, M., & Crosby, F. An empirical examination of relative deprivation theory. *Journal of Experimental Social Psychology,* 1980, *16,* 442–456.
Blasi, A. Bridging moral cognition and moral action: A critical view of the literature. *Psychological Bulletin,* 1980, *88,* 1–45.
Brickman, P., Folger, R., Goode, E., & Shul, Y. Microjustice and macrojustice. In M. J. Lerner & S. C. Lerner (Eds.), *The justice motive in social behavior.* New York: Plenum, 1981.
Bruner, J. S. *Beyond the information given: Studies in the psychology of knowing.* New York: Norton, 1973.
Clark, K. B., & Clark, M. P. The development of consciousness of self and the emergence of racial identification in Negro preschool children. *Journal of Social Psychology,* 1939, *10,* 591–599.
Clark, K. B., & Clark, M. P. Skin color as a factor in racial identification of Negro preschool children. *Journal of Social Psychology,* 1940, *11,* 159–169.
Clark, K. B., & Clark, M. P. Social identification and preference in Negro children. In T. M. Newcomb & E. L. Hartley (Eds.), *Readings in social psychology.* New York: Holt, 1947.
Cook, T. D., Crosby, F., & Hennigan, K. M. The construct validity of relative deprivation. In J. M. Suls & R. L. Miller (Eds.), *Social comparison processes: Theoretical and empirical perspectives.* New York: Wiley, 1977.
Cooley, C. H. *Human nature and the social order.* New York: Scribner's, 1902.
Crosby, F. A model of egoistical relative deprivation. *Psychological Review,* 1976, *83,* 85–113.
Damon, W. Early conceptions of positive justice as related to the development of logical operations. *Child Development,* 1975, *46,* 301–312.
Damon, W. *The social world of the child.* San Francisco: Jossey-Bass, 1977.
Davis, J. A. A formal interpretation of the theory of relative deprivation. *Sociometry,* 1959, *22,* 280–296.
Davis, K., & Moore, W. E. Some principles of stratification. *American Sociological Review,* 1945, *10,* 242–249.
Della Fave, L. R. The meek shall not inherit the earth: Self-evaluation and the legitimacy of stratification. *American Sociological Review,* 1980, *45,* 955–971.
Enright, R. D., Enright, W. F., Manheim, L. A., & Harris, B. E. Distributive justice development and social class. *Developmental Psychology,* 1980, *16,* 555–563.
Enright, R. D., Franklin, C., & Manheim, L. A. Children's distributive justice reasoning: A standardized and objective scale. *Developmental Psychology,* 1980, *16,* 193–202.
Enright, R. D., & Sutterfield, S. An ecological validation of social cognitive development. *Child Development,* 1980, *51,* 156–161.
Farkas, A. J., & Anderson, N. H. Multidimensional input in equity theory. *Journal of Personality and Social Psychology,* 1979, *37,* 879–896.
Festinger, L. A theory of social comparison processes. *Human Relations,* 1954, *7,* 117–140.
Festinger, L. *A theory of cognitive dissonance.* Stanford: Stanford Univ. Press, 1957.
Fox, D. J., & Jordan, V. B. Racial preference and identification of black, American Chinese, and white children. *Genetic Psychology Monographs,* 1973, *88,* 229–286.
Furby, L. Inequalities in personal possessions: Explanations for and judgments about unequal distribution. *Human Development,* 1979, *22,* 180–202.

Goodman, M. E. *Race awareness in young children.* Cambridge, Mass.: Addison-Wesley, 1952.

Gurr, T. R. *Why men rebel.* Princeton, N.J.: Princeton Univ. Press, 1970.

Habermas, J. *Legitimation crisis.* Boston: Beacon Press, 1973.

Hamilton, D. L. A cognitive-attributional analysis of stereotyping. In L. Berkowitz (Ed.). *Advances in experimental social psychology* (Vol. 12). New York: Academic Press, 1979.

Heider, F. *The psychology of interpersonal relations.* New York: Wiley, 1958.

Hoffman, M. L. Moral internalization: Current theory and research. In L. Berkowitz (Ed.), *Advances in experimental social psychology* (Vol. 10). New York: Academic Press, 1977. (a)

Hoffman, M. L. Personality and social development. *Annual Review of Psychology, 1977, 28,* 295–321. (b)

Homans, G. C. *Social behavior: Its elementary forms.* New York: Harcourt, 1961.

Hook, J. G., & Cook, T. D. Equity theory and the cognitive ability of children. *Psychological Bulletin, 1979, 86,* 429–445.

Karniol, R. Children's use of intentional cues in evaluating behavior. *Psychological Bulletin, 1978, 85,* 76–85.

Karniol, R. A conceptual analysis of immanent justice responses in children. *Child Development, 1980, 51,* 118–130.

Katz, P. A. The acquisition of racial attitudes in children. In P. A. Katz (Ed.), *Towards the elimination of racism.* New York: Pergamon, 1976.

Katz, P. A., & Zigler, E. Self-image disparity: A developmental approach. *Journal of Personality and Social Psychology, 1967, 5,* 186–195.

Keasey, C. B. Children's developing awareness and usage of intentionality and motives. In H. E. Howe, Jr. (Ed.), *Nebraska Symposium on Motivation.* Lincoln: Univ. of Nebraska Press, 1977.

Kohlberg, L. Stage and sequence: The cognitive-developmental approach to socialization. In D. A. Goslin (Ed.), *Handbook of socialization theory and research.* New York: Rand McNally, 1969.

Kohlberg, L. Moral stages and moralization: The cognitive-developmental approach. In T. Likona (Ed.), *Moral development and behavior.* New York: Holt, 1976.

Kurtines, W., & Greif, E. B. The development of moral thought: Review and evaluation of Kohlberg's approach. *Psychological Bulletin, 1974, 81,* 453–470.

Leahy, R. L. The development of the conception of economic inequality. 1. Descriptions and comparisons of rich and poor people. *Child Development, 1981, 52,* 523–532.

Leahy, R., & Huard, C. Role-taking and self-image in children. *Developmental Psychology, 1976, 12,* 504–508.

Lerner, M. J. The justice motive: "Equity" and "parity" among children. *Journal of Personality and Social Psychology, 1974, 29,* 551–556.

Lerner, M. J., & Matthews, G. Reactions to the suffering of others under conditions of indirect responsibility. *Journal of Personality and Social Psychology, 1967, 5,* 319–325.

Lerner, M. J., Miller, D. T., & Holmes, J. G. Deserving and the emergence of forms of justice. In L. Berkowitz & E. Walster (Eds.), *Advances in experimental social psychology* (Vol. 9). New York: Academic Press, 1976.

Leventhal, G. S. Fairness in social relationships. In J. W. Thibaut, J. T. Spence, & R. C. Carson (Eds.), *Contemporary topics in social psychology.* Morristown, N.J.: General Learning Press, 1976.

Leventhal, G. S., Popp, A. L., & Sawyer, L. Equity or equality in children's allocation of reward to other persons? *Child Development, 1973, 44,* 753–763.

Lewis, M., & Brooks, J. Self, other, and fear: Infants' reactions to people. In M. Lewis & L. Rosenblum (Eds.), *Fear: The origins of behavior* (Vol. II). New York: Wiley, 1974.

Lewis, M., & Brooks, J. Infants' social perception: A constructivist view. In L. B. Cohen & P. Salapatek (Eds.), *Infant perception: From sensation to cognition.* New York: Academic Press, 1975.

Major, B., & Deaux, K. Individual differences in justice behavior. In J. Greenberg & R. L. Cohen (Eds.), *Equity and justice in social behavior.* New York: Academic Press, 1981.

Marx, K. *Capital: A critique of political economy.* New York: Modern Library, 1936.

Mead, G. H. *Mind, self, and society.* Chicago: Univ. of Chicago Press, 1934.

Mead, M. *Culture and commitment.* New York: Doubleday, 1970.

Mosca, G. *The ruling class.* New York: McGraw-Hill, 1939.

Parsons, T. An analytical approach to the theory of social stratification. In T. Parsons (Ed.), *Essays in sociological theory.* New York: Free Press, 1949.

Parsons, T. *The social system.* New York: Free Press, 1951.

Pettigrew, T. Social evaluation theory. In D. Levine (Ed.), *Nebraska Symposium on Motivation* (Vol. 15). Lincoln: Univ. of Nebraska Press, 1967.

Pettigrew, T. F. *Racially separate or together?* New York: McGraw-Hill, 1971.

Phillips, D. A., & Zigler, E. Children's self-image disparity: Effects of age, socioeconomic status, ethnicity, and gender. *Journal of Personality and Social Psychology,* 1980, *39,* 689–700.

Piaget, J. *The moral judgment of the child.* London: Kegan Paul, 1932.

Porter, J. R. *Black child, white child: The development of racial attitudes.* Cambridge, Mass.: Harvard Univ. Press, 1971.

Porter, J. R., & Washington, R. E. Black identity and self-esteem: A review of studies of black self-concept, 1968–1978. *Annual Review of Sociology,* 1979, *5,* 53–74.

Proshansky, H., & Newton, P. The nature and meaning of Negro self-identity. In M. Deutsch, I. Katz, & A. B. Jensen (Eds.), *Social class, race, and psychological development.* New York: Holt, 1968.

Rosenberg, M. *Society and the adolescent self-image.* Princeton: Princeton Univ. Press, 1965.

Rosenberg, M., & Pearlin, L. I. Social class and self-esteem among children and adults. *American Journal of Sociology,* 1978, *84,* 53–77.

Rosenberg, M., & Simmons, R. *Black and white self-esteem: The urban school child.* Washington, D.C.: American Sociological Association, 1971.

Runciman, W. G. *Relative deprivation and social justice: A study of attitudes to social inequality in twentieth century England.* Berkeley: Univ. of California Press, 1966.

St. John, N. The elementary classroom as a frog pond: Self-concept, sense of control and social context. *Social Forces,* 1971, *49,* 581–595.

Semaj, L. The development of racial evaluation and preference: A cognitive approach. *The Journal of Black Psychology,* 1980, *6,* 59–79.

Simmons, R. G., & Rosenberg, M. Functions of children's perceptions of the stratification system. *American Sociological Review,* 1971, *36,* 235–249.

Soares, A. T., & Soares, L. M. Self-perceptions of culturally disadvantaged children. *American Educational Research Journal,* 1969, *6,* 31–45.

Steinbeck, J. *The Grapes of Wrath.* New York: Viking Press, 1939.

Stouffer, S. A., Suchman, E. A., DeVinney, L. C., Star, S. A., & Williams, R. M., Jr. *The American soldier: Adjustment during Army life* (Vol. 1). Princeton, N.J.: Princeton Univ. Press, 1949.

Streater, A. L., & Chertkoff, J. M. Distribution of rewards in a triad: A developmental test of equity theory. *Child Development,* 1976, *47,* 800–805.

Walster, E., Walster, G. W., & Berscheid, E. *Equity: Theory and research.* Boston: Allyn & Bacon, 1978.

Ward, S. H., & Braun, J. Self-esteem and racial preference in Black children. *American Journal of Orthopsychiatry,* 1972, *42,* 644–647.

Yancey, W. L., Rigsby, L., & McCarthy, J. D. Social position and self-evaluation: The relative importance of race. *American Journal of Sociology,* 1972, *78,* 338–359.

Zigler, E., Balla, D., & Watson, N. Developmental and experimental determinants of self-image disparity in institutionalized and noninstitutionalized retarded and normal children. *Journal of Personality and Social Psychology,* 1972, *23,* 81–87.

11 / The development of views about the role of social institutions in redressing inequality and promoting human rights

JUDITH TORNEY-PURTA

For many centuries, theologians have proposed that the inevitable injustices of this world will be redressed in another; philosophers, meanwhile, have debated ways in which a just society might be established in this world. Psychologists are latecomers to this discussion. Only a little more than a half-century ago, developmental and social psychologists began to conduct research on the development of morality and social attitudes. The study of sequential, organized, and progressive change has been an approach frequently taken. The majority of this work has dealt with familiar or face-to-face situations in which the child is asked to identify just action and reason about it. It will be argued here that to understand the development of ideas about injustice and inequality requires a somewhat more complex approach. In particular, an adequate characterization of the process by which children acquire an understanding of inequality requires a consideration of their awareness of ways of preventing or ameliorating its concrete results. Understanding remedies for injustice is part of understanding injustice, in other words. Furthermore, these remedies often involve situations that are not familiar and dilemmas where the child does not directly control the necessary resources—where redress depends on other individuals or societal institutions.

Two questions are related to the approaches taken by developmental psychologists in recent studies of social cognition. The first is: What kind of parallelism exists between the recognition of inequality or injustice (its distribution and causes) and the construction of prescriptions for its amelioration? In situations of physical causality, understanding the source of the problem and its solution are closely related. Given the fragmentation of the child's social world, it cannot be assumed that such close parallelism exists. In the face-to-face social world of children, this may be responsible for part of the gap between verbal expression and behavior in situations involving inequality or injustice. The child may understand that another pupil is economically deprived or less intellectually able, but not try to convince classmates to treat this child with basic respect because of the absence of a parallel understanding of the problem and of its solution. With respect to more distant problems, parallelism is even more doubtful.

The second question is: How does the child's construction of the social world extend beyond his or her face-to-face experience? How does the young person come to understand either the source or solution of injustice mediated by other individuals (usually adults) occupying roles within social institutions or by the institutions themselves (e.g., laws, social policy)? Leventhal, Karuza, and Fry (1980) note that there has been extensive macrostudy of allocation in large social aggregates by sociologists but that social psychologists have studied a single individual's allocation within a "decomposed" model of the environment, ignoring the social structure in which the allocation is embedded. They are referring to studies of adults; the criticism is even more appropriately applied to studies of children.

Some developmental psychologists explicitly place the question of social institutions outside their realm of concern:

> Children's early construction of justice principles in their own social world prepares them for the later reorganization and amplification of the justice principles necessary for functioning in the adult social world. But it would be a mistake to expect, for example, an eight-year-old child demonstrating benevolence to construct a benevolent solution to a problem in adult social welfare [Damon, 1977, p. 77].

It will be argued in this chapter that a conception of the social welfare system, for example, is being constructed at least in a fragmentary way by children. Understanding the links between face-to-face methods of redressing injustice and constructed notions about institutions can give valuable clues concerning sources of political ideology. This involves understanding how the child comes to view social policies that attempt to deal with injustice.

One could choose several themes around which to discuss the existence of parallelism between understanding problems of injustice and their solutions and the relation of the developing organism to social institutions beyond face-to-face groups. At several points in this chapter, human rights will be used as such a theme. The distinction is often made between basic rights (e.g., life and integrity of person), social–economic–cultural rights (e.g., an adequate standard of living), and civil–political rights (e.g., participation in one's government). One way to make the negative phrase ''redressing injustice'' more positive is to speak of the enhancement and promotion of human rights. These rights are to be found in the Constitution and law of the United States and are also recognized in international law (the Charter of the United Nations and the Universal Declaration of Human Rights passed unanimously by the United Nations in 1948). Every year sees expanding concern at the international and regional levels and among nongovernmental organizations for enhanced protection recognized for human rights. This reflects the rising aspiration of human beings all over the world to live free from fear of arbitrary arrest or torture, with an adequate standard of health and nutrition for themselves and their families, and with the opportunity to participate in the government of their nation without discrimination.

The purpose of this chapter is to consider the development of structures of social order that include the recognition of injustice as well as face-to-face modes of promoting justice and human rights, and the construction of judgments regarding social institutions or policies that are related to redressing injustice.

RESEARCH ON
THE YOUNG PERSON'S CONSTRUCTION OF
THE SOCIAL–POLITICAL ORDER

Research on children's and adolescents' construction of the social or political order has devoted only passing attention to remedies for injustice (or to children's concepts of human rights). Two studies in this research area stand out, nevertheless.

Furth's (1979, 1980) work is the most recent attempt to consider the growth of understanding that results from the child's exploration of ''theories of society'' derived from interaction, culminating in a construction of the social and economic order. English children aged 5–11 were interviewed using a free response format to elicit thought about social and economic institutions (especially money). Although a concern for justice and human rights was not an explicit part of the interview, the results are important because they present evidence for developmental factors resulting in progressively more adequate social constructions. The following evidence for developmental process was presented: Children in the course of talking about a social event with an adult interviewer (who was being nonjudgmental) spontaneously corrected previously inadequate conceptions or related unconnected pieces of information. Furthermore, original interpretations of social events by children showed that they apprehended reality differently than did adults, not merely that they lacked factual knowledge. Social institutions lie between physical phenomena (where the laws of nature operate) and personal relations such as friendship (where the almost unknowable laws of human nature operate), Furth concludes.

Some of the characteristics of young children's views of social institutions are important in understanding their approaches to policy dealing with injustice. First, the young child is egotypic (believing that all bus drivers, for example, are like those he knows) and insensitive to individual differences. It is not surprising that children growing up in American suburbs have little understanding that others live in poorer circumstances or that those in other countries may experience certain violations of their rights. The young child also fails to recognize conflict, according to Furth; this leads to difficulties in understanding alternative solutions to problems of inequality, which so frequently involve conflict. The stages Furth identified in progressive development begin with the playful approach to social institutions—experimenting with ideas about social reality from an egocentric basis. The second stage is described as functional (with some notions of money as payment but with substantial playful characteristics). At the third stage, children come to terms with the difference between a personal and a societal point of view; however, business profits and money controlled by the government are still poorly understood (making it not surprising that various policies that might be adopted for the redress of economic or political injustice are not well comprehended). At the fourth stage, major inconsistencies are dealt with, while at the fifth stage, there is a relatively clear conception of government, community, and law. Only one-third of the 12-year-olds whom Furth tested had reached the fourth stage.

Furth's work does not explicitly consider the redress of injustice, but it gives important clues to the process by which notions about social institutions and policy are constructed in a developmental framework.

The second research on construction of the social order is that of Connell (1971), who interviewed Australian young people aged 5–16. Like Furth, he describes the extent to which the child is constrained in acquiring knowledge of the social political world by the lack of opportunity to operate on it and see its reactions. Children tend to absorb scraps or bits of information, not blocks or packages of it; thus, many inconsistencies and misconceptions persist. Connell does not explicitly deal with justice and injustice. However, the inability of the child before about age 10 to understand policy and political conflict is clearly illustrated. Children may perceive that an individual in a political role has a particular intention (e.g., stopping the Vietnam War). However, they often do not perceive that different individuals have different intents or that different courses of policy action would follow from those intents. The adolescent is often able to comprehend that political issues have two sides (each of which disagrees with the other about alternative policies) and to comprehend social institutions, such as political parties, that serve to mobilize conflict in line with their own particular interests. This depends to a considerable extent on the achievement of formal operations. To move beyond understanding issue conflict to a coherent ideology, according to Connell, is relatively rare in adolescence and occurred (in his sample) only in a few students whose working-class origins included politically active leftist families.

These two studies, focused on the younger age periods, have dealt with the way in which the child constructs a view of political institutions. They suggest that both English and Australian children acquire, through what would be called developmental processes, progressively more complex notions about the economic and social system. We may assume that this construction forms the basis on which other educational processes build. Neither study, however, deals explicitly with injustice or its redress.

MORAL DEVELOPMENT RESEARCH

Studies of moral development have extensively addressed the problem of justice but not its relation to social institutions. The situation most frequently used by Kohlberg—Heinz, who must decide whether to steal a drug to cure his terminally ill wife—may be viewed as posing the problem of balancing the value of human life against property rights (Kohlberg, 1976). This type of dilemma does reflect one aspect of situations of injustice and inequality—a conflict between two (or more) conflicting or competing sets of demands. The dilemma, however, has little in it to enlighten us about respondents' views of social institutions that have responsibilities for promoting justice. They are not asked whether there should be a law or agency that would allow individuals needing medicine for life-threatening illnesses to obtain it or how the financial obligations created by such a law or agency should be handled. Although adolescents and adults responding to these moral dilemmas certainly know about the existence of hospitals where patients are treated (sometimes at very low cost) as well as about laws concerning stealing, these notions are not thought to be relevant to judging respondents' levels of reasoning about justice and morality. They are asked instead to judge an individual's choice in a single situation, without considering how the creation of an institutionalized arrangement by some group (voluntary organization or government) might result in greater morality and justice for this individual (and others as well).

Montada (1980) notes the relation of Kohlberg's description of the fifth stage of moral development to human rights. At this level, a social contract exists, and the individual gives up certain rights to the partner in the contract, whether it be the nation or the community. "The protection of basic human rights is one of the guarantees often mentioned in connection with the state's duties as a contract partner. . . . In conflicts between basic human rights and codified statute law, human rights are preeminent [Montada, 1980, p. 275]." Yet this interpretation of Kohlberg's position has not been tested with moral dilemmas concerning the social contract or human rights.

Tapp and Kohlberg's research (1977) moves in the direction of greater concern with a model of the political system than does other moral development work. The questions they asked of their kindergarten through college sample in the United States (and also in a cross-national study) were phrased in relatively general terms: What is a rule? What is a law? What if there were no rules? Why should people follow rules? Can rules be changed? Are there times when it might be right to break a rule? With the exception of the one question about laws, the remainder used the term *rules.* However, even a sizable proportion of the elementary school group phrased their answers in terms of laws—dealing directly with a social institution and not merely face-to-face groups. Older individuals dealt much more with the importance of rules in system maintenance than did younger respondents.

In other words, responses were oriented toward broader issues of law, sometimes in the absence of questions that prompted such an approach. Justice was discussed most often in response to a question about when it would be right to break a rule. Among the college sample, it was not the hardship of compliance that justified breaking a law or rule, but its morality.

Similar results from interviews and a survey are reported in the same volume by Torney (1977). There was a tendency for children to prescribe institutionalized legal responses when asked about social problems.

They seemed to be seeking a kind of personal protection from the institution against the threat of social disorder.

Turiel (1978) has approached the problem of understanding justice by separating the domains of conventional and moral. He distinguishes trangressions violating justice (threat to life, physical or psychological harm to others, violations of rights, and deprivations of something to which the person is entitled) from trangressions violating social conventions (uniformities in social interactions that result from the observation of behavioral uniformities among those with whom one is participating in a given social system). Whereas social conventions have an arbitrary basis in a given social organization, issues of justice and morality have an intrinsic prescriptive basis, he argues. One of the questions Turiel asks young people in order to categorize issues as moral or social conventional is directly related to the institution of law: "Suppose there was a country where there was no law against stealing, would it be right to steal in that country?" Moral transgressions are those that young people believe would be wrong regardless of whether there were laws prohibiting them or not. Social conventional transgressions are those that would depend on knowledge of social organization and its associated rules and laws before one could judge rightness or wrongness.

Distinguishing issues of justice from issues of convention is an important step. What is ironic about this approach to defining justice issues is that it seems to remove them from any kind of relationship to or action by social institutions. Turiel elaborates at length on the way in which the young person constructs a notion of society, social structure, and the social order and then considers only social conventions within those conceptions.

The possible role of the social structure or social order in relation to issues of justice is not discussed by Turiel. Even if one accepts the notion that moral transgressions are wrong by definition (apart from particular social institutions), it does not necessarily follow that social structures or institutions play no role in preventing injustice or ameliorating its consequences. In fact, a large proportion of the laws in all societies deal with preventing stealing, murder, and deprivations of things to which a person is entitled (to use Turiel's examples of transgressions that are clearly moral).

Turiel's work has taken us part of the way. It is encouraging that cases of true injustice are judged as "wrong" by young people regardless of the existence of laws or rules that prohibit them. They are of a different nature than social conventions, which are dependent on agreements among members of a social group, often exemplified in rules or laws. However, it is unfortunate that none of the work using this distinction has considered ways in which ideas about social institutions influence preferred ways of redressing moral transgressions.

This may be because Turiel and Kohlberg have not anchored their formulations in any analysis of social–political reality. The moral issues studied have not been chosen as exemplifications of any particular conception of the good society or the basic rights and needs of the human being.

An attempt has been made, although only at the pilot level, to explore in somewhat more depth what Turiel has called moral or justice issues but defined in relation to the framework of international human rights (Torney & Brice, 1979). Forty-five white, lower-middle class children aged 9–13 (from Grades 4, 6, and 8) were asked questions taken directly from the Universal Declaration of Human Rights. Without identifying the source of the questions, interviewers asked children whether the transgressions should be categorized as matters of morality and justice or of social convention (using Turiel's categorization and questions). One of the aims of the study was to ascertain whether, at least among American children, there was consensus about basic rights that all human beings ought to enjoy by virtue of their humanity.

The children were asked a question relating to slavery (whose prohibition is one of the basic rights in the Universal Declaration): "If people in another country decided it was all right to buy and sell people like slaves, and they had no rules or laws against that, would it be right?" All the students said that it would not be right—one-third of them citing equality of people and another third mentioning freedom as reasons for laws prohibiting slavery. A few respondents referred to the inhumanity of treating people as objects—"they aren't products to sell." When asked how people got rights like these, one child answered, "They get them by being alive." The right not to be held in slavery, applying Turiel's criterion to these data, is an issue of morality or justice. However, an interesting kind of response was observed when a follow-up question was asked, "What if that country passed a law saying slavery was right, would it be right then?" Some children appeared to reason as follows: "I have been told there are reasons for the laws I know. If there is a law somewhere else allowing slavery, there must be a reason for it. It must be my job to think up what that reason might be." In response, some gave a personalized and authority-based view of laws: "We have to listen to the head of the country." Many of the fourth graders and some of the sixth graders responded to the follow-up in this way: "A law saying slavery was OK would have to have another law saying slaves are equal—that they'd get the same food and clothes," or "You'd have to pay your slaves something." In other words, injustice could be overlooked by younger children if it were compensated for by equitable distribution to meet concrete needs.

The older children's responses differed. They dealt with this basic injustice by referring to some notion of the social order and institutions as a source for both preserving justice and dealing with injustice. Typical of their answers to the question of whether slavery would be right if a country passed a law saying that slavery is right were:

> It depends on the situation in the country and how the people would think about it.

> It depends on if you have any say in the government; if not, you can't do anything about it.

They responded to a question about rightness with an answer dealing with the individual as a participant in social and political institutions, which are sources for both preserving justice and dealing with injustice. Children seem to be ready to perceive law and policy as closely associated with justice dilemmas.

A number of the eighth graders were adamant that no law could make slavery right, whereas some referred the problem not only to the national but to the international order.

INTERVIEWER: *What if they made a law saying slavery was right?*
STUDENT: *They wouldn't get along with other countries.*
INTERVIEWER: *What if the leader of the country said it was OK?*
STUDENT: *He wouldn't be a good leader.*

Even in the absence of references in the question to any institution other than law, these young people refer to social and political institutions when they are asked to deal with blatant examples of injustice.

Let us examine another example. In many countries where apartheid and other forms of racial restriction are practiced, there are laws that limit citizens' freedom of movement. The Universal Declaration declares that everyone has the right to freedom of residence and movement. The children in this study were asked the following question: "If a government in another country passed a law that said that people had to live in the same place all the time and never move to or visit any other part of the country, would that be right?" Of the respondents, 100% said it would be wrong. The large majority referred to "freedom" in their justification. Younger children tended to reason from the perspective of the individual (wanting to be with one's family). At the eighth-grade level, justifications were provided for some conditions under which the government might "plead with individuals (such as doctors) to stay in a place where they were needed." In general, the older students referred to some concept of the public good in justifying exceptions to freedom of residence.

Another set of questions dealt with civil and political rights. "What if the law said that a small group of people in the country would make all the decisions for the people there, but they never asked them what they thought or let them vote; would that be right?" Only 1 student out of 39 thought it would be. The fourth graders seemed to focus on voting for the leader as a necessary process for its own sake. The older students considered the long-range consequences of a small group in control.

Two other questions dealing with social and economic rights were asked of a part of the sample. "What should be done when people get too old to work and don't have any money saved up?" And "What should be done if a person cannot make enough money to feed his family no matter how hard he works?" All fourth graders thought that something should be done about such problems and that the government should be the agency to act. Two of the eighth graders (out of nine questioned) believed that the people should have saved their money and should not expect help from social or governmental institutions.

The results indicate that children view slavery, enforced residence, unfair trial, and lack of opportunity to participate in government as wrong no matter what laws may be put forth to justify them. These are basic human rights. When one raises the question of how these rights are woven into laws and what to do when the general welfare of the public conflicts with these rights, children have greater difficulties. But the majority of eighth graders see issues of injustice embedded in a social order that has some responsibility to promote justice.

These respondents believed that rights are more secure in the United States than in many other countries of the world; some equated human rights (which in fact are guaranteed in many other constitutions in the world) with the rights in the United States Constitution. Some, for example, said that other countries should compare their laws to the ones we have to see if they were fair. These young people are raising important questions about the redress of injustice and the interconnection of civil–political rights with economic–social rights. Faced with human rights issues, young people refer them to the social institutions. Moral justice issues appear to be closely tied to policy in the minds of young people.

RESEARCH RELATING TO HUMAN RIGHTS IN
THE SOCIAL CONSTRUCTIONIST PERSPECTIVE

A few studies have considered the development of concepts of civil–political and social–economic–cultural rights and ideology. Patterson (1979) conducted an interview study attempting to establish a stage sequence for political reasoning using fourth and sixth graders. The source of his original concern was the discrepancy frequently reported in the literature between the verbal agreement with abstract statements in support of civil and political human rights (especially freedom of speech) and answers to questions about specific instances where Communists or others with unpopular causes want to exercise such freedoms (Zellman & Sears, 1977). Patterson's study is of special interest because the major dilemma involved a group of individuals who obtain a permit from a city for a protest against bad treatment of poor people (a form of social injustice and deprivation of economic rights). Another group demands that the city's mayor revoke the permit because of fear of violence. Respondents were asked what the mayor would do, whether that is the right or wrong thing to do, and what they would do if they were the mayor. Then an additional condition was introduced: The mayor allowed the permit to stand but later found that the protest leaders were Communist.

The author concluded that understanding the right of freedom of speech (a civil and political right) develops through four stages. It is interesting to note that the criteria for scoring specified that students who focused on the effectiveness (or lack of effectiveness) of the protest in meeting the needs of poor people would receive a scale score of 2; in contrast, a higher level of reasoning was scored for responses that referred to the right of free speech abstractly without reference to redressing economic inequality.

Two of the other findings of the study are of considerable interest. There was a positive correlation (tau = .30) between level of political–moral reasoning and amount of time spent working for a candidate or other political activity (interpreted as an index of opportunity to take on the role of others). Furthermore, there was greater consistency between support for free speech in abstract and in concrete situations among those at high political–moral reasoning levels.

This study asks fundamental questions about the process of constructing notions of justice and the redress of injustice. It deals with deprivation of two types of human rights—economic and social (poverty) and civil and political (freedom of speech). It could have gone further by considering the promotion of these rights by various policy alternatives. For example, how do these children believe that poverty has arisen? If the protest were to be successful, what outcomes in the form of changed policy should be expected?

Adelson studied 120 11-, 13-, 15-, and 18-year-olds in the United States and comparable groups in England and Germany (Adelson, Green, & O'Neil, 1969; Adelson & 0'Neil, 1966; Gallatin & Adelson, 1977). A set of dilemmas was constructed in which subjects were asked about the establishment of policies where there was potential conflict between the good of the community and violations of individual rights on a newly settled Pacific island. Rapid developmental progress was noted between ages 13 and 15. The older subjects were much more capable than the younger subjects of seeing collective consequences and communal needs rather than personal consequences and individual needs. For example, when asked whether universal smallpox vaccination should be required even of those who objected to it, the older subjects stressed protecting the public health rather than the health or preferences of individuals. Likewise, income tax was seen as providing for public needs or the support of the government as a whole by the older students, whereas the younger ones concentrated on concrete (often local) services.

The authors noted that, once the sense of a political community had been established, ideas about laws and rights tended to become more consistent. Younger subjects expressed judgments about laws without much concern for the needs they served or for the feasibility of carrying a given policy into effect. Older subjects expressed high levels of general respect for the institution of law, but specific laws were to be scrutinized according to their service to various competing interests and short-term versus long-term benefit. Some of the 15- and 18-year-olds even traced out long-range consequences of laws and seemed to calculate the cost-effectiveness of one decision compared with another. In a sense, the older adolescent has become policy critical.

Of special interest for conceptions of policy relating to human rights is the tendency for many young people to place special importance on civil and political rights (Gallatin & Adelson, 1977). Although older subjects argued more than younger subjects that laws in general should be considered amendable, they believed that laws guaranteeing such rights as freedom of speech should never be changed. Special protection for this civil right in the hierarchy of rights corresponds to views of legal specialists—that the guarantee of freedom of speech and participation in government can serve as a bulwark against violations of other rights.

Many of the older adolescents formulated a general principle that stressed communal welfare. Some individuals applied a particular right across situations. For example, one young person would stress the sanctity of property rights, whereas another paid attention to the individual's right to privacy, whatever the dilemma. These principles are the root of what Adelson calls an ideology.

Adelson stressed the explanatory power of the achievement of formal operations during the adolescent period. In the cross-national study, it was noted that differences across age were more striking than differences between the British, German, and American students' views of community and rule of law. However, it was possible to characterize the German students as somewhat authoritarian and the British as particularly concerned with social welfare. These studies dealing with the substance of policies relating to civil and political rights are of special importance. Although there are implications for justice and injustice, these are not spelled out.

Leahy (1981) has studied the development of conceptions of inequality, especially in the economic realm. He was interested in determining whether the concept of poverty included a construction of class structure (which encompasses life chances and conflict). Especially important was whether race or social class (presumably as indexes of experience with the system) were associated with individual differences in these concepts. He found general decreases between ages 6 and 17 in references to peripheral characteristics in defining the poor and the rich, and increases in central and sociocentric references. Dialectical models of class consciousness were not substantiated.

Steinitz (1976) looked less at developmental and more at individual differences in judgments of upward mobility, using interviews with 60 adolescents from three working-class New England towns. Perceptions of life chances were especially important. She found considerable coherence between notions of how American society works and explanations for wealth, poverty, success, and failure. Subjects felt sympathetic to welfare recipients but ambivalent about possible abuses of this particular structure for dealing with injustice. They expressed difficulty in resolving their recognition that some need special help with fears that unscrupulous individuals would take advantage (but could only be rooted out with policies representing invasions of privacy). Conflicts of rights are recognized by these subjects, and they try to balance civil and political rights with social and economic rights.

These subjects expressed considerable faith in education as a road to mobility. They were cautious, however, about blanket approval of policies that would provide free post-high school education to all. A number of potential policies that could lead to more equal distribution of income were rejected by these teenagers as placing unfair limits on individual freedom. Individual responsibility was important to them, and the possibility of freeloaders was a concern. There were some individual differences associated with the subjects' backgrounds. Those who were intent on their own mobility but concerned that they might not achieve it were less compassionate and more concerned about individuals who would take advantage of welfare or free education.

Research on perceptions of the just world suggest possible roots for ambivalence, such as that expressed in the preceding study. Lerner (1980) argues that when viewing injustice people of all ages engage in a certain amount of cognitive distortion. Individuals have a stake in maintaining the belief that the world is just—that people get what they deserve. When confronted with a victim of blatant injustice, the observer will often minimize the amount of suffering being experienced or distort the perception of the victim to emphasize how suffering was deserved. Victims of human rights violations—poor people in this country or hungry people in other nations, political prisoners, racial groups that are discriminated against—may be perceived in an ambivalent fashion because of this cognitive distortion. Individuals engage in this distortion, according to Lerner, because then they can believe that as long as they are "good people" they will not suffer bad results. There are some conditions in which individuals are less likely to derogate and more likely to help. These include times when the help is to be given to a single suffering victim or when the help is temporary (when no long-range policy decisions are involved).

In conclusion, these studies deal imaginatively with the recognition of injustice and some notions about how it might be redressed. Some reference is made to implications for social institutions and policy, though they are not always carefully spelled out. Although civil and political rights are clearly perceived as essential in a just society, situations where social or economic justice is involved or where rights come into conflict are considerably more problematic for young people. The existence of individual differences in ideology is perhaps the most interesting dimension highlighted.

CROSS-SECTIONAL STUDIES OF AGE CHANGE IN IMAGES OF SOCIAL INSTITUTIONS

Previous sections have focused on the developmental-constructive process as it shapes the understanding of social and political institutions and their role in the redress of injustice. The largest volume of research on concepts of social institutions has been performed with surveys of political socialization using a cross-sectional model. In addition to differences between age groups, other individual differences have been described. Data related to the topics previously covered in this chapter will be briefly summarized from one study of elementary school children, one study of 14- and 17–18-year-olds, and one study of college freshmen and seniors.

The elementary school survey (Hess & Torney, 1967), in which approximately 12,000 students in eight United States cities were surveyed, concluded that, over the grades from two through eight, children increasingly perceive political power as institutionalized rather than personalized (a trend extended by Adelson's work previously cited). Elementary school pupils generally believe that all laws are fair and see little political conflict. Although studies done since Watergate have picked up some variations in these patterns, the broad outline of these findings is still widely accepted.

Subjects saw few differences in policy orientations between the political parties. Up through the seventh grade, equal percentages chose the Republicans and the Democrats when asked "Who does most to help the rich?" Up through the fifth grade, equal proportions chose each party when asked "Who does most to help the unemployed?" (It should be noted that many responded "don't know" or "both about equally" to these questions.) Analyses were done controlling for IQ to examine the effect of social class and controlling for social class to examine the effect of IQ. Over a large number of attitudinal variables, social class was a less substantial source of variance in attitudes than was IQ.

The Civic Education survey conducted by the International Association for the Evaluation of Educational Achievement (IEA) will be described in more detail (Torney, Oppenheim, & Farnen, 1975). Questionnaire data were collected from more than 30,000 students in 10 countries. Although 10-year-olds were tested in some countries, in the United States only 14-year-olds and seniors in high school participated. Comparable age groups also participated in the Federal Republic of Germany, Finland, Ireland, Netherlands, and New Zealand; so that set of countries will be compared here. A two-stage probability sample (school and students within schools) was drawn in each country, so the data are quite representative of national patterns. This was intended as a broad-based political socialization study, and not a study of human rights. When the IEA attitudinal questionnaires were factor analyzed, however, a strong factor emerged with scales relating to discrimination on the basis of race and religion, beliefs concerning the importance of treating different social groups equally, issues of civil and political rights concerned with citizens' freedom to criticize the government, and support for the rights of women.

Mean scores for racial and religious tolerance showed some between-country differences, in the direction of higher scores in the Netherlands, the Federal Republic of Germany, and Finland. However, the between-country differences for the women's rights items were considerably more pronounced. Students in the United States (and also in New Zealand) were considerably less supportive of political rights for women than were students in the Federal Republic of Germany and Finland. Although more than 50% of the respondents in these countries strongly agreed that "women should run for political office and take part in the government much the same as men do," only 27% of the 14-year-olds in the United States did so.

An analysis of variance on matched samples in the United States, Finland, and New Zealand showed the following significant differences. Higher scores in support of several types of rights were found among older students, those from higher social class origins, and those from urban residence areas. Girls were more supportive of equality and women's rights; boys tended to be more supportive of civil liberties in the form of the citizen's right to criticize.

Some more detailed analysis was conducted to determine the effect of socioeconomic status and different aspects of schooling on a scale of antiauthoritarianism. A regression analysis indicated that socioeconomic home background factors were more important for the 14-year-olds than for the older students in predicting antiauthoritarianism. If the variance accounted for by the two categories of school variables measured (type of school and specific learning conditions) is summed, it appears that home background is more influential than school factors in shaping these attitudes only in the United States. The most consistent positive predictor of antiauthoritarianism in all countries was the extent to which teachers were reported to encourage the expression of opinion by students in the classroom. The extent to which patriotic ritual was practiced was a negative predictor in all countries at both levels.

There are other items in the IEA survey that bear on civil and political rights because they deal with the perception of the power structure in which policy is formulated. Ratings were made of the perceived impact of 10 individuals and groups on the laws made in the country. There was a remarkable similarity in the perceptions of the structure of power by the 14-year-olds in these countries. The president (prime minister) and members of Congress (Parliament) were the most influential, followed by union leaders and rich people. Big companies were seen as more influential by students in the Netherlands and the Federal Republic of Germany than in Ireland or the United States. Only in Ireland were church leaders thought to have substantial policy influence. Newspaper editors and radio and television commentators were rated quite low in their amount of influence on laws and policy—ninth or tenth of

10 in all the countries. Variation between nations was greatest in the rating given "the average person." He or she was seen as moderately influential in New Zealand, Ireland, and the United States and lacking in influence in the Federal Republic of Germany.

Among those in the last year of secondary school before university entrance, the scores in different countries diverged in interesting ways. In Germany, for example, rich people were seen as equal in influence to the prime minister; big companies were seen as equal in influence to members of the Bundestag. The average person ranked last. This was an indication of general cynicism among the youth in Germany.

In certain other countries (Ireland, Netherlands, and New Zealand), union leaders were seen as nearly equal in policy influence to members of Parliament. In general, the older students ranked newspaper editors higher and the average person lower than did the younger students. The perception of influence on policy in countries that share basic traditions of civil and political rights shows that for younger adolescents the formal political structure is primary, whereas for older students the economic interest group structure (and the role of media) are clearer.

Another part of this instrument included ratings of 10 institutions according to 12 values they might promote. One of the values was "Makes sure there are fair shares for everyone" and another was "Gives help to rich people." Table 11.1 indicates the rankings of 7 institutions (elections, laws, Congress, political parties, welfare agencies, labor unions, and large business organizations) according to their relation to these values, by the 14-year-olds in five countries. One might consider "Gives help to rich people" as loaded more with the creation of inequality than its redress; "Makes sure there are fair shares for everyone" is closer to the redress of inequality. In general, the adolescents were more likely to see these institutions promoting fairness than they were to see them favoring the rich.

Three of these institutions were perceived relatively unequivocally by the 14-year-olds. Large business organizations were rated as the most likely (of these seven institutions) to help rich people and the least likely to ensure fair shares for everyone. In contrast, labor unions were perceived in every country except the Netherlands as considerably more likely to ensure fair shares than to help the rich. However, an examination of these data and those for the older group suggests that in several countries (including the United States and New Zealand) the image of unions is ambivalent, including the attributes "shows who is stronger," "creates disagreements," and "makes prices go up."

"'Welfare agencies" was variously ranked in the different nations. In the Netherlands, New Zealand, and the United States, these agencies were thought of as contributing to "making sure there are fair shares,"

Table 11.1. Rankings within Country of Seven Institutions according to Degree to Which They Realize Selected Values (14-Year-Olds)[a]

Institution	Federal Republic of Germany	Finland	Netherlands	New Zealand	United States
Makes sure there are fair shares for everyone:					
Elections	6.5	1	5	4.5	2
Laws	2	5	3	2	1
Congress	3	3.5	3	4.5	5
Political parties	4.5	3.5	6	6	6
Welfare agencies	4.5	6	1	2	3.5
Unions	1	2	3	2	3.5
Large business organizations	6.5	7	7	7	7
Gives help to rich people:					
Elections	3	4.5	3.5	7	4.5
Laws	3	3	6	2	2.5
Congress	5	4.5	6	3	4.5
Political parties	3	2	2	5	2.5
Welfare agencies	6.5	6	6	5	7
Unions	6.5	7	3.5	5	6
Large business organizations	1	1	1	1	1

[a] Data are from IEA Civic Education survey. Total numbers of 14-year-olds tested in the Federal Republic of Germany was 1317; Finland, 2401; the Netherlands, 1696; New Zealand, 2010, and the United States, 3207. A misprint in the Irish questionnaire led to the omission of this data table for that country. Mean ratings given to each of the seven institutions on the value were ranked within country to give a pattern of institutional perceptions for realizing that value. Tied ranks are indicated. See Torney, Oppenheim, and Farnen (1975) for further information.

and not "giving help to rich people." In some of the other countries, this was less clear. The image of the extent to which the other political institutions—elections, laws, Congress, political parties—serve either to create or redress injustice varied greatly by country. There does seem to be some parallelism in the perception of institutions as both creating justice and redressing injustice (and not performing contradictory functions).

An analysis of variance was also conducted on a summed index of the perception of political conflict using items from the institution–value instrument just discussed. Older students in the United States, Finland, and New Zealand perceived more political conflict than did younger students. In the United States only, those of high socioeconomic status perceived more conflict than did those of low status, and boys perceived more conflict than did girls. There were no urban–rural differences in any of the nations.

In summary, selected results from the IEA survey have indicated certain cross-national differences and similarities, as well as age and socio-economic status differences in perceptions of human rights, of the structure of social institutions that influence policy, and of institutions seen as promoting the redress of injustice (at least economic injustice). Even 14-year-olds have reasonably well-defined perceptions of these issues, although too few questions were asked concerning support for specific policy to redress injustice for a strong statement on that point.

The Council on Learning and the Educational Testing Service conducted a survey of 3000 American college freshmen, college seniors, and students in 2-year colleges (Barrows, 1981). Some items measuring human rights attitudes were included. Of the freshmen, 75–80% agreed with such items as the following: "Political freedom is a basic human right, and no government should be permitted to abridge it." "No government should deny access to basic education to any of its citizens." In contrast, fewer than 20% agreed with the following statement: "It is none of our business if other governments restrict the personal freedom of their citizens."

These same freshmen ranked the denial of basic human rights as fourth in importance out of 10 global issues. It was seen as less important than malnutrition and inadequate health care, but as more important than overpopulation, for example. These students were also asked to rate 8 global problems on several scales, including whether they were "solvable or unsolvable" and whether they were "avoidable or unavoidable." The denial of basic human rights, malnutrition and inadequate health care, and environmental pollution were the three problems that freshmen rated as the most solvable and avoidable. These ratings contrasted considerably with the rating for inflation, for example. Again some parallelism seems to exist. It is also interesting to note that these students, somewhat naively perhaps, believed that the American government could do a lot to solve these problems. On a five-point scale measuring that dimension, the following justice issues were all rated 3.5 or above: intergroup conflict, denial of basic human rights, malnutrition, and inadequate health care. This is one example of a general tendency for students to simplify the role, power, and position of the United States and its government in solving problems through policy action.

CONCLUSIONS

Several principles appear to be important in understanding the process by which young people arrive at conceptions of ways to remedy injustice and the role of the policies of social institutions in promoting human rights. The first principle is that such understanding grows from and is based on psychological characteristics, some of which may change ontogenetically and some of which may not. For example, there appears to be a certain deep structure of respect for human rights, human dignity, and justice that can be found even in relatively young children as well as young adults (as demonstrated by the studies of Barrows, 1981; Damon, 1977; Torney & Brice, 1979; Turiel, 1978). The sense of injustice is strong and seems to be stimulated by basic issues of justice regardless of the respondent's age. Second, cognitive ability (which certainly varies across age) is important; Connell and Adelson present evidence that the achievement of formal operations is important for adolescents' understanding of society and of the social contract. Third, there appears to be a basic egocentrism (characteristic of children and adults), which is also recognized by Lerner when he concludes that preserving one's own sense of deserving good outcomes is important. Furth points to a particular deficiency among young children in the ability to see social roles from another's perspective. Fourth, there appears to be a general tendency (perhaps on the part of researchers as well as respondents) to see civil and political rights as more important than social or economic rights. Poverty and social inequality are of secondary concern as long as freedom of speech is preserved, for example. Several authors (especially Steinitz) note the ambivalence that many students express about policies designed to right economic inequality. Fifth, there appears to be a tendency for young children to prescribe laws and policy as ways of protecting themselves from the chaos they believe is the basic state of society. On their own initiative, they move from seeing a social problem to prescribing an institutionalized (often legal) solution (see Connell, 1971; Tapp & Kohlberg, 1977; Torney, 1977). Several of these five basic psychological characteristics have developmental aspects; individuals differences (not associated with development) are also observed.

Given these basic psychological principles as a framework, two processes appear to be at work in the changes observed in concepts of remedies for injustice and inequality; the developmental–constructive process and the socialization–transmission process. The developmental–constructive process with respect to the recognition of inequality is well described in other chapters of this volume. Furth and Connell both provide useful data regarding the construction of notions about social institutions, though they pay limited attention to inequality. Kohlberg and Turiel consider justice and morality from a constructive perspective but pay limited attention to the role of social institutions in redressing injustice. Adelson, Leahy, and Steinitz consider both development and individual differences in views of issues that relate closely to human rights and inequality. We might summarize these studies by noting that all these researchers have studied the construction of concepts related to the function of law and policy in society.

There are several implications of the developmental–constructive position for psychologists and educators. First, it suggests a reflective and conflict-driven model of change. In the ideal situation, the individual would be able to "play with" or "manipulate" institutions and justice structures much as he or she would manipulate clay or other physical materials. In reality, young people have very little of this kind of experience, though they may (as Furth suggests) play with ideas about the social or political system. The presentation of political life in social studies textbooks has been described in several studies (Hess, 1972). They conclude that many young people are not exposed to the conflictual nature of the political process or to the clash of interest group opinions about policies for redressing inequality. This poorly prepares young people to deal with human rights problems that frequently involve a conflict between rights. Leahy also looked at the role of conflict—in this case, class conflict—in shaping children's notions of wealth and poverty. He found few class differences but speculated that more would be found in a culture with more obvious class conflict. The IEA study found increases in the perception of political conflict by older students in several countries, but it was those from higher not lower classes who perceived conflict most clearly. Another finding of the IEA study suggests the importance of opinion diversity; in classes where the teacher encouraged the conflict of ideas, students were more supportive of human rights.

In addition to prescribing a certain amount of conflict experience, the developmental–constructive model sensitizes the practitioner to the issue of timing and sequence in children's understanding of justice and its remedies. This means more than simply classifying the young person as "in formal operations" or "not in formal operations." It means being sensitive to other developmental–constructive processes and to the unique structures already developed by the child for understanding the world.

The socialization–transmission process, to which political socialization research since the mid-1960s has contributed, is also important in understanding young people's ideas about remedies for inequality. It is ironic that the developmental–constructive model and the socialization–transmission model have operated in such isolation. It is probably the case that the information transmitted by agents of socialization is the raw material on which much of the constructive process operates. Likewise, the misunderstandings in what the young child takes away from a civics lesson because of cognitive limitations are probably more striking than many socialization researchers realize.

Those who have studied the socialization–transmission process have considered attitudes toward social or political institutions and the laws or policies they put forth rather than the rule of law. Some criticisms have recently been lodged against socialization studies for focusing too much on the reproductive function of socialization and failing to give young people the skills to criticize the institution as well as comply.

Up to this point, we have considered the second question to which this chapter was addressed: How do children move from understanding face-to-face situations in which inequality exists to understanding institutions and their policies? More research that combines the developmental–constructive with the socialization–transmission approach is clearly needed.

Let us move to the other question: What evidence is there that parallelism exists in the child's recognition of injustice or inequality and the construction of prescriptions for its amelioration (taking primarily the developmental–constructive model)? Some evidence for parallelism can be drawn indirectly from the work of Tapp and Kohlberg and the IEA study. However, there is also strong ambivalence and naiveté in the young person's attitude toward the redress of social inequality. The political socialization literature is full of responses that suggest that young children expect the government to pay for all kinds of programs without understanding the source of that money. This naiveté about financing of government policy is similar to that of Furth's respondents who were vague about the storekeeper's monetary sources. There is little evidence that understanding of remedies for inequality or injustice progresses in a parallel fashion to (or as rapidly as) awareness of injustice or inequality.

The problem of lack of parallelism is not merely academic. Studies of desegregated schools, for example, often show that the recognition of injustice is not matched by support for efforts to remedy it. Even on the basis of fragmentary research, it may be useful to describe several steps in the development of understanding of remedies for injustice. At each step, recognition of the existence of injustice comes before understanding of remedies of either a personal or an institutionalized nature. The first step is lack of awareness of inequality (well documented by many researchers). At a second step, the individual becomes aware but prescribes rather vague laws or poorly articulated actions by other persons (often a political leader such as the president) to help the people in need. At a third step, the child begins to see the operation of social and political institutions in providing remedies for injustice or inequality. At a final step (achieved perhaps by only a few adolescents), the individual is aware of conflicts of policy, is policy critical, and becomes capable of evaluating actions that would redress inequality. These steps are proposed as a framework for further research integrating the developmental–constructive and the socialization–transmission models for understanding the acquisition of ideas about remedies for injustice.

REFERENCES

Adelson, J., Green, B., & O'Neil, R. Growth of the idea of law in adolescence. *Developmental Psychology*, 1969, *1*, 327–332.

Adelson, J., & O'Neil, R. The growth of political ideas in adolescence: The sense of community. *Journal of Personality and Social Psychology*, 1966, *4*, 295–306.

Barrows, T. (with contributions by S. Ager, M. Bennett, H. Braun, J. Clark, L. Harris, & S. Klein). *College students' knowledge and beliefs; A survey of global understanding.* New Rochelle, N.Y.: Change Magazine Press, 1981.

Connell, R. W. *The child's construction of politics.* Melbourne, Australia: Melbourne Univ. Press, 1971.

Damon, W. *The social world of the child.* San Francisco: Jossey-Bass, 1977.

Furth, H. Young children's understanding of society. In H. McGurk (Ed.), *Issues in childhood social development.* New York: Methuen, 1979.

Furth, H. *The world of grown-ups: Children's conceptions of society.* New York: Elsevier, 1980.

Gallatin, J., & Adelson, J. Legal guarantees of individual freedom. In J. L. Tapp & F. J. Levine (Eds.), *Law, justice, and the individual in society.* New York: Holt, 1977.

Hess, R. D. The systems maintenance function of social development in the schools. *Proceedings of 1971 Invitational Conference.* Princeton, N.J.: Educational Testing Service, 1972.

Hess, R. D., & Torney, J. V. *The development of political attitudes in children.* Chicago: Aldine, 1967.

Kohlberg, L. Moral stages and moralization. In T. Lickona (Ed.), *Moral development and behavior.* New York: Holt, 1976.

Leahy, R. The development of the conception of economic inequality. I. Descriptions and comparisons of rich and poor people. *Child Development*, 1981, *52*, 523–532.

Lerner, M. J. *The belief in a just world.* New York: Plenum, 1980.

Leventhal, G. S., Karuza, J., & Fry, W. R. Beyond fairness: A theory of allocation preferences. In G. Mikula (Ed.), *Justice and social interaction.* New York: Springer-Verlag, 1980.

Montada, L. Developmental changes in concepts of justice. In G. Mikula (Ed.), *Justice and social interaction.* New York: Springer-Verlag, 1980.

Patterson, J. W. Moral development and political thinking: The case of freedom of speech. *Western Political Quarterly*, 1979, *32*, 7–20.

Steinitz, V. People need help, but people take advantage: The dilemma of social responsibility for upwardly mobile youth. *Youth and Society*, 1976, *4*, 399–437.

Tapp, J., & Kohlberg, L. Developing senses of law and legal justice. In J. Tapp & F. Levine (Eds.), *Law, justice, and the individual in society.* New York: Holt, 1977.

Torney, J. Socialization of attitudes toward the legal system. In J. Tapp & F. Levine (Eds.), *Law, justice, and the individual in society.* New York: Holt, 1977.

Torney, J., & Brice, P. *Children's concepts of human rights and social cognition.* Paper presented at the meeting of the American Psychological Association, New York, September 1979.

Torney, J., Oppenheim, A. N., & Farnen, R. *Civic education in ten nations: An empirical study.* New York: Wiley, 1975.

Turiel, E. Social regulations and domains of social concepts. In W. Damon (Ed.), *Social cognition.* San Francisco: Jossey-Bass, 1978.

Zellman, G., & Sears, D. Childhood origins of tolerance for dissent. In J. Tapp & F. Levine (Eds.) *Law, justice, and the individual in society.* New York: Holt, 1977.

12 / The child's construction of social inequality: conclusions

ROBERT L. LEAHY

The contributions to this volume span a wide variety of conceptions of social and nonsocial inequality. Obviously, as the title of the book indicates, it was the editor's assumption that many of the developmental trends in this area are generally consistent with a cognitive-developmental perspective—specifically, with the major theoretical models advanced by Piaget (1932, 1970) and Kohlberg (1966, 1969). Such a theoretical predisposition, of course, is not shared by many of the contributors to this volume. Consequently, this final chapter is written with the caveat that there is not a unilateral perspective represented in this area.

COGNITIVE DEVELOPMENT AND INEQUALITY

What are the major tenets of a cognitive-developmental model of conceptions of social inequality? First, we should expect to find qualitative changes with age in the conception of social inequality. That is, development is described not as a simple continuous acquisition of factual information (as one obtains from an almanac), but rather as a discontinuous trend such that there are new ways in which information is processed, including changes in the kinds of information viewed by the child as relevant to a judgmental process. Second, we should find that the development of conceptions of social and nonsocial inequality should be parallel. Third, although some critics of cognitive-developmental theory (Shweder, 1981) argue that such a theory places undue emphasis on the "rational" qualities of social cognition, both Piaget (1932) and Kohlberg (1969) have indicated that changes in social interaction contribute to the development of social cognition. Consequently, we should examine the relevance of these interpersonal relationships to the development of conceptions of social inequality. The purpose of this chapter is to propose a model of levels of conceptions of social inequality, review evidence indicating changes in explanations of inequality, and examine the view that conceptions of social inequality are based on impersonal cognition and on social interaction. Finally, I shall briefly indicate some of the negative consequences of the development of stratification concepts.

LEVELS OF CONCEPTIONS OF SOCIAL INEQUALITY

The general description of levels of conceptions of social inequality that I shall propose is derived both from a review of the research in this area and from a consideration of related developmental trends in social cognition and moral judgment. This model is a *proposal* of general trends—it is not presented as a finished product validated by longitudinal or cross-cultural data.

Peripheral and authority-dependency conceptions

Several of these reviews and the work of others suggest that the young child's view of social inequality is focused on the observable or external appearances or behaviors of groups, a belief in the desirability of deference to authority, and a belief in the benevolence of adult authority figures.

The emphasis on peripheral or behavioral qualities appears to pervade the view of the young child. For example, the first dimensions of gender or race awareness are physical cues, which are learned quite early (by age 3). Research by Williams, Bennett, and Best (1975) indicates that the first sex-role stereotypes that are learned are descriptions of observable behaviors, whereas personality trait descriptions are learned in later childhood. In describing individual differences or psychological deviance, the first emphasis is on appearances and behaviors (e.g., aggression for deviance) (Coie & Pennington, 1976; Livesley & Bromley, 1973).

Similarly, rich and poor people are described in terms of possessions, behaviors, and appearances (Leahy, 1981).

Early stereotypes of groups are rigid: The young child believes that groups that differ cannot have other qualities in common. This is true for descriptions of social classes, genders, and groups differing in intelligence (Leahy, 1981; Leahy & Shirk, in press; Leahy, Note 1). The rigidity of early stereotypes also reflects an evaluative component such that out-groups (e.g., races) are attributed negative qualities and in-groups are attributed positive qualities.

The importance of deference to adult authority is another hallmark of early conceptions of social inequality. For example, Damon's (1977) study of early sex-role conceptions suggests that young children view conformity to adult sanctions as a major criterion for "appropriate" behaviors. In describing and explaining intelligence, younger children emphasize obedience and punishment contingencies (Leahy and Hunt, Chapter 5, this volume). Deviance is defined by indicating how some children disobey the adult-imposed rules of school settings. Even prosocial behavior for the young child is justified by reference to adult rules, and distributive justice judgments by young children are sometimes based on the dictates of adults.

Adult authority, however, is not viewed as an ogre of uncaring unilateral power. Young children often claim that economic inequality can be changed by asking others for money (Leahy, 1983) or that shopkeepers, bus drivers, and teachers are motivated by a desire to help others, especially children, with profit or wage incentives taking a backseat to unmitigated altruism (Furth, 1979).

Psychological conceptions

At about age 10 or 11 (and throughout adolescence for many), there is a substantial change in the child's view of social inequality. Rather than viewing people mainly in terms of their observable behaviors or appearances, the older child begins to attribute psychological qualities to others—for example, traits, motivations, attitudes, and values.

Friends, other peers, and the self are increasingly described in terms of these inferred qualities (Barenboim, 1981; Livesley & Bromley, 1973). These psychological comparisons are also the focus of psychological explanations and implicit personality theories (Barenboim, 1981). Conceptions of intelligence are increasingly linked to motivation, and the rich and poor are described by references to ability, personality traits, and motivation. Friendships are also understood in terms of the ways in which children may respect and, in some cases, give mutual advantages to their individual differences. Finally, older children are more likely than younger children to understand the nature of some psychological defenses, with this ability increasing during adolescence.

These descriptions of stratified groups in terms of their inferred psychological qualities parallel the concern with individual differences in distributive justice concepts. The need state of the recipient of kindness becomes more important as children mature (Eisenberg-Berg & Roth, 1980; Youniss, 1979), and the question of the recipient's deservedness of deprivation also becomes more salient for older children. Although many children advocate greater equalization of wealth, equity concepts become increasingly more popular with increasing age in justifying wealth and poverty (Furby, 1979; Leahy, 1983). Furthermore, the question of merit accumulating through work production is an important factor in the older child's ordinal equity conceptions and in explanations of wealth (Hook & Cook, 1979; Leahy, 1983).

Although these stereotypes do gain salience, they do not preclude the older child from applying a more flexible categorization to people. Older children are more likely to see the similarities between groups—for example, gender, class, and intellectual level. Their views of other races are less egotypic—that is, they understand that both blacks and whites share similar positive and negative qualities. Finally, another development of importance is the increasing tendency to engage in social comparisons. Older children are likely to request information about others' performances in order to evaluate their own performance (Ruble, Boggiano, Feldman, & Loebl, 1976). Similarly, older children place greater emphasis on test performance as a criterion of intelligence.

Social interaction and social structure conceptions

During adolescence, there is an increase in the reference to the importance of peer groups and social interaction in general in defining inequality. For example, deviance is understood in terms of "distorted perspectives" or not belonging to the group (Coie & Pennington, 1976), suggesting that some adolescents believe it is essential to share in a veridical interpretation of reality. Maas, Maracek, and Travers (1978) found that sixth graders were more likely than second graders to refer to distal rather than proximal causes of deviance and to suggest that changing the social environment would change disturbances. Similarly, as Paget (Chapter 9, this volume) indicates, social interactionist conceptions advocating interpersonal factors and psychotherapy increased during adolescence. The research by Chandler, Paget, and Koch (1978) indicates that references to distal (or unobservable and distant) causes is related not only to age but also to impersonal cognitive level (especially formal operational thinking), offering some support to the view that these stages of conceptions of social inequality are structurally ordered. Similarly, intelligence is understood as the competence to interact with others.

The importance of social institutions in maintaining or changing inequalities is also recognized during adolescence. As both Furth (1980) and Connell (1971) have shown, the adolescent is more aware of the conflicting perspectives of social, economic, and legal issues. The findings of Torney, Oppenheim, and Farnen (1975) indicate general similarities among adolescents in industrialized countries in their view that certain groups (e.g., business or labor) reflect specific, competing interests. Finally, in the conception of social class, some adolescents do propose that economic inequality may be changed by altering social structure.

EXPLAINING INEQUALITY

The one model of distributive justice that has gained the greatest attention is the equity model. As Hook's and Hall and Jose's reviews indicate, there are a number of possible equity models to which one might refer. In this section, I shall attempt to raise some questions about the relevance of equity models for the study of conceptions of social inequality and examine some of the developmental evidence pertaining to equity.

Although the NOIR model advanced by Hook may account for descriptions of the cognitive capacities of allocators, it need not describe the actual, or real-life, judgments made by children or adolescents confronted by various situational factors, such as competition or self-interest (Hall and Jose, Chapter 10, this volume). Thus, it may be that adolescents choose equality as a basis of distribution while simultaneously possessing the formal operations necessary for ratio-proportional equity. In the case of their conceptions of economic class, however, it appears that adolescents subscribe overwhelmingly to equity theory in their explanations and justifications of economic stratification.

Although the NOIR model does receive some support in the literature on age trends and nonsocial cognitive parallels (Hook & Cook, 1979), it does not address the question of what factors not entering into the experimenter's equation of work input and work outcome might be considered by the individual allocating or justifying rewards. For example, as the research on person descriptions (Barenboim, 1981) and social class (Leahy, 1981, 1983) demonstrates, there is an increasing recognition of individual differences in capacity (e.g., effort, intelligence, and person-ality) between early and later childhood. It may very well be that in attributing psychological (capacity) differences to people, the older child or adolescent is also making a corresponding attribution of work output differences—that is, "hard-working, smart, and well-mannered people produce more."

One of the shortcomings of applying equity theory directly to concep-tions of social class (or national differences in rewards or rights) is that when we talk about differences among occupations (or nationalities) we do not have a simple equation or metric of work input and output. For example, it is not easy to imagine how we might compare the metric of work of picking five bushels of apples with selling five houses in South-ern California. It does not seem likely that people judging the income differences of these two workers are thinking about the work output variable. Rather, they may be thinking of other factors that enter into a more complex equity equation that includes education, effort, intelli-gence, and even personality. And finally, it does not seem probable to me that in explaining class differences people are using the more ad-vanced calculations of interval or ratio-proportional models in compar-ing psychological qualities of workers. At best, it would seem, they might say that an ordinal comparison is appropriate—that is, one person has "more" of these qualities than the other. When equity theory begins to consider these psychological dimensions, it will come closer to de-scribing some of the significant bases of class and race conceptions.

The research on distributive justice has also produced somewhat mixed findings regarding age trends. Hook's model, NOIR, stresses the formal aspects of Adams's (1965) equity equation, which proposes that equity is based on a ratio-proportional analysis of outcomes (or inputs) and rewards. NOIR is a developmental sequence model: Nominal eq-uity states that people differ in outcomes; ordinal equity states that one should get more than another; interval equity states that a great deal more work deserves a great deal more pay; and ratio-proportional eq-uity ("true" equity in the Adams sense) is based on comparing ratios of inputs and outputs. The research by Hook does suggest a develop-mental progression conforming to the NOIR model, with some empir-ical support for the view that impersonal cognitive operations are related to these various solutions.

This interesting and promising structural analysis advanced by Hook, however, does not preclude other kinds of distribution rules not men-tioned in his model. For example, Damon (1977) has advanced a se-quential model based on interview data that indicate that, at first, children do allocate rewards differentially but that these rewards are not contingent on "relevant" work input. (They may be based, for instance, on the target person's desires or external qualities, i.e., appearance.) This "inequitous" distribution gives way to equality, which later is replaced by, at least, some kind of ordinal equity. Other support for the Damon model is provided by Enright, Franklin, and Manheim (1980). Hall and Jose suggest that even these data are limited because the Damon model does not provide for combining decision rules at different levels. Furthermore, as Torney-Purta (Chapter 11, this volume) demonstrates, young children and adolescents tend to agree that certain human rights are inalienable and constitute fundamental dimensions of equality. However, one must conclude that the research in this area does not entirely support a Piagetian view that equality always precedes equity (in the ordinal sense). What is in keeping with the Piagetian view, though, is that the belief in rewards contingent on behavior does seem to develop during later childhood.

The view that equalization of wealth is desirable or is a means of reducing inequality *increases* during later childhood. The idea that ending poverty by taking money from the wealthy is structurally analogous to simple conservation problems: A transformation on one dimension is compensated by a transformation on another dimension—in this case, conserving societal wealth. This age trend is again not entirely consistent with Piaget's (1932) earlier studies of moral judgment, although the structural analysis is consistent with his later theory of cognitive stages (Piaget, 1970).

Equity in a society that is economically stratified involves concerns other than cognitive level. It is entirely possible to be concrete or formal operational (as I would suppose Marx was) but not subscribe to a belief that distribution of wealth should be based on work productivity. (In fact, one might argue that Marx's claim "each according to his needs" is somewhat similar to Damon's earliest stage. However, Marx and others from different persuasions [Rawls, 1971] argue distributive claims from a societal perspective—and obtain different conclusions.) The question of equity is a question of legitimation of what exists (Della Fave, 1980) and, for the child, represents the postfigurative transmission rules of adults handing down stratification to the young. Although inequalities in friendship may be coconstructed or redressed by rules of reciprocal respect, as Youniss (Chapter 6, this volume) maintains, there is considerable import to the agrument advanced by Shweder (1981). According to Shweder many conventions, rules, or principles are "constituted" or given in the acculturation process by previous generations. Thus, the outcome of socialization may, for some, be adherence to rules constituted and not up for negotiation by the child and his or her peers.

However, there are limits to this constituted or postfigurative model. First, children go through developmental changes—perhaps, stages—in their conceptions of social inequality. They do not form "inaccurate" imitations of constituted rules of stratification. Their early rationales are either focused on the desires or external qualities of people who have less or, in contrast to stratification concepts, they advocate equality. Thus, one cannot explain early concepts by a theory of socialization that relies solely on imitation of values. This is certainly true for children's conceptions of similarities of groups (e.g., classes or groups differing in intelligence). It is doubtful that the young child hears an adult say that groups have absolutely nothing in common. A second factor raising questions for a constituted rule approach is that some adolescents or adults question the conventional order of things. For example, some adolescents and adults advocate postconventional morality, question traditional sex-role values, challenge the inevitability of class differences, and even engage in political action against the state (Bem, 1977; Keniston, 1968; Kohlberg, 1969; Leahy, 1983; Leahy & Eiter, 1980). In fact, even the conception of rules of convention does not follow a simple continuous acquisition curve: At succeeding levels of conception, children and adolescents affirm, negate, and then again affirm conventions—each time for a different reason (Turiel, 1978). A theory that relies entirely on imitation of values seems to lack the flexibility to handle these memorable exceptions to the rules.

In summary, the research on equity theory does not necessarily address the question of what criteria children and adolescents do use in deciding on unequal distributions. Second, young children may advocate unequal distributions before changing to equality norms. Third, some inequalities of rights are viewed at an early age as unjustifiable regardless of laws allowing for inequalities. Fourth, with increasing age adolescents are more likely than children to believe that inequalities may be redressed by changes in social structure (e.g., government or the economy). Finally, models of cultural transmission emphasizing social learning of inequalities are limited in that they do not account for qualitative age changes in conceptions of inequality nor do they account for conceptions that may be antagonistic to the values of the dominant culture.

NONSOCIAL AND SOCIAL INEQUALITY

What is the relationship between understanding nonsocial and social inequality? It is not surprising to learn that cognitive developmentalists stress the similarities of these two domains of thought. However, it would be quite myopic of psychologists to reduce social inequality to nonsocial inequality. Let us consider the development of the understanding of social class—that is, the child's conception of whether people should be rich or poor. Is this "problem" reducible to the understanding of cognitive rules for comparing proportions (e.g., John produced twice the amount that Tom produced, therefore John should get twice as much money)? The key word here is *reducible*, because what I wish to stress is the excess meaning involved in judging people within one's own society.

How are social and nonsocial cognition different from one another in this example? First, we do not make judgments regarding the ethics or morality of physical objects: It would be quite unusual to claim that it is unfair for one beaker or pile of chips to be fuller or larger than another. Related to this is our emotional response to the perception of inequalities in these domains: People do not wage revolutions to rectify the imbalance of ratios.

Second, as Youniss (Chapter 6, this volume) implies, we are capable of relationships of personal reciprocity with people occupying different social strata—the poor person may be our friend. In fact, we may not know what our own eventual position in society may be. An implication of this for the prudent person is that the rules of stratification may be applied against our favor at a future time—for example, we may fail an exam, lose a job, encounter a more prestigious ethnic group in power, or be less successful at something than our friends. This "modified veil of ignorance" (Rawls, 1971) about our future standing in a recurrent race for status may suggest to us that the "stratification that men do lives after them," perhaps boomeranging in an unsavory manner at a later date. Quite simply, social rules of stratification apply to the self as well as to others and have implications for continued relationships. Such reciprocity and implications are rare for nonsocial inequality.

Third, there are often substantial consequences to an individual in rejecting or accepting rules of stratification. We are fortunate to be living in a time when many of these rules of stratification are widely challenged. But imagine if in an earlier time in history—say, 1900—a black demanded equal treatment, or a woman claimed that her rights should not be abridged because of her gender, or a laborer claimed that incomes should be distributed equally. Rejecting rules for social stratification might lead to ostracism; certainly, rejecting rules for subitizing items does not lead to one's exclusion from physical reality. Similarly, acceptance of stratification may center on the lower-status person's ambition and lower self-esteem; in contrast, acceptance of concrete operations does not place one above or below the objects of the physical realm.

Notwithstanding these comments, a recurrent theme of cognitive-developmental theory is the relevance of nonsocial cognition in the development of social cognition. There are four perspectives on this issue. The first view—the *prerequisite* model—advocated by Kohlberg (1969, 1976), is that certain cognitive skills are necessary but not sufficient conditions for the development of social cognitive skills. The second view argues that the development of social and nonsocial cognition are *parallel* developments such that correlations of abilities across domains would be expected. The third view, which is an extension of the position advocated (but later somewhat modified) by Flavell (1982, forthcoming), would be that there are conceptually *distinct domains* of cognition: Thus, performance on one set of problems need not imply similar performance on another (presumably similar) set of problems. The fourth position is what I would call the *similar sequence* model, which makes no claims about sequential priority of performance in one domain compared to another, or even of an empirical relationship of skills across different domains. Rather, this model proposes that our research strategies on social cognition may be informed by examining the apparent "gross" qualitative changes in impersonal cognition that occur with increasing age.

What is the relevance of these models for the study of social inequality? What empirical data support or refute the predictions derived from each position mentioned?

The first level of conceptions of social inequality reflects the preoperational child's limitations in cognition. Shultz's review of conceptions of nonsocial inequality suggests that the young child is capable of a number of simple manipulations of information. First, there is the recognition at age 3 of simple inequalities (e.g., X is "more than" Y). Second, young children are capable of classification of objects according to their most salient features (e.g., color). Third, there is some evidence that at $4\frac{1}{2}$ years of age children understand one-to-one correspondence of different physical arrays. Furthermore, the young child focuses on perceptually salient features and has difficulty recognizing possible transformations of these dimensions (Nelson, Zelniker, & Jeffrey, 1969). The most noted case of this is the lack of conservation of volume or quantity.

The understanding of *more* and *less* suggests that very young children are able to recognize differences in rewards among people. Their perceptual categorization of objects is also reflected in the ability to classify genders and races and to distinguish other groups (e.g., peers or social classes) in terms of their observable qualities. The fact that $4\frac{1}{2}$-year-old children understand one-to-one correspondence suggests that this ability is manifested earlier in impersonal cognition and later in the understanding of ordinal and interval equity. Furthermore, the research on comprehension of functions ($Y = F(X)$) indicates that by later childhood (ages 9–11) there is an increasing ability to redress differences between distributions of tokens (Shultz, Chapter 1, this volume), a factor that resembles equity conceptions in social cognition. This ability to understand multipliers as functions may be an essential cognitive factor in the understanding of ratio-proportional equity. Thus, the understanding that twice as much output yields twice as much reward entails the understanding that multiplying one side of the equation of $Y = X$ must require similar multiplication of the other side: $2Y = 2X$. Likewise, doubling the output of work would correspond to doubling the allocation of rewards for equity judgments.

Hook's description of the NOIR developmental model of equity assists greatly in understanding some of the inconsistencies in age trends in equity. Using Adams's (1965) ratio-proportional model of equity, we can see that the ability to employ multiplying functions (for both direct and inverse proportions) is an essential component of advanced equity judgments. Simpler equity models (e.g., ordinal equity) do not require a systematic algebraic solution: Thus, for ordinal equity, increases in Y are associated with variable increases in X (e.g., "He did more; he should get more").

Although Piagetian theory and research on equity has generally relegated equality judgments to a lower developmental level, the research on class conceptions suggests some increase in these conceptions at age 11 (Leahy, 1983). A factor possibly accounting for this is the understanding of reciprocal transformations necessary for equalization of wealth: Simply, the money you give to the poor must come from somewhere—possibly the rich. Thus, conservation ability is reflected in the recognition of conservation of wealth.

Although some strict structuralists might argue for isomorphism between impersonal and social cognition, the data reported in this volume and the research in other areas of social cognition (Berndt, 1981) do not support such a view. Some studies do suggest a relationship between gender constancy, sex-role stereotypes, race awareness, and equity with impersonal cognition. However, the magnitudes of these relationships are generally not very impressive and certainly suggest that somewhat distinct domains are being assessed. Furthermore, we do not have data indicating a strong relationship across different conceptions of social inequality—data that would be essential in arguing common structural properties.

However, impersonal cognition is not entirely irrelevant in the study of conceptions of social inequality. The sequential quality of cognitive stages—and the nature of these sequences—may be roughly paralleled in social cognition. Thus, in the study of conceptions of differences between social groups, we find similar age trends in impersonal and social cognition, indicating increasing flexibility in categorization with increasing age (Leahy & Shirk, in press). Similar approaches that consider social categories as somewhat analogous to categories with impersonal content might be a possible direction for future study in this area.

SOCIAL AND CULTURAL TRANSMISSION

Where do these dimensions of stratification come from? The transmission model advanced by Della Fave (1980) indicates that either forebears or peers may be the source of cultural values. Thus, the "content" of the dimensions of stratification may be that blacks, women, the mentally ill, and the retarded will be the groups occupying less power or prestige in a stratification system; but these contents are quite arbitrary, and we could easily imagine societies in which whites, men, the "rational" (like Socrates), or the intellectuals might be the objects of discrimination. These contents of stratification I would place within the constituted or established "social realities" that are handed down to new generations.

The "constructivist" perspective does not necessarily deny the importance of constituted rules or conventions. (Indeed, Piaget, 1932, studied children's attitudes toward marbles—a constituted game handed down to new generations.) What is of significance to cognitive-developmentalists is how these already constituted conventions are understood by children. Oddly, Shweder (1981) claims that Kohlberg's and Piaget's view is that the child or adolescent is simply self-reflective. Although self-reflection may be important (especially during later adolescence), Piaget and Kohlberg give considerable emphasis to role-taking opportunities or, what Youniss (1981) calls "communicative acts." This is why social cognition is not reducible to impersonal, or totally rational, cognition in its etiology—that is, social cognition has a large "social" component.

An early source of this social interaction and social construction is the unilateral authority of the parents over children. These generational boundaries serve to enhance the belief that rules or conventions are given by powerful figures and are not open to negotiation. Thus, stratifications other than familial roles are based on simple allegiance to authority figures—to be intelligent or sane implies obeying in school and not fighting and to get rich you should ask others for money. With the movement to the peer group and the general mutuality and discourse available there, children do not abandon the constitutive conventions of authorities. In fact, each of them who is imbued with the parental voice of sanctions will share those sanctions with others in the group. What has changed is not the content of sanctions (e.g., "It is wrong to steal"), but rather the audience to which one's reflection is given: Rather than thinking of parental punishments, the child now considers the importance of his or her reputation with peers. Thus, the generalized other has changed from a particular pair of individuals (i.e., mother and father) to a consideration of the views of age peers. The child essentially attempts to solve the problem: "Given these conventions or dimensions of stratification, how can I make sense out of what exists?"

The solution to this problem is partly found through peer interaction. Cognitive-developmental theory proposes that an important factor in peer interaction is the opportunity for the expression of individual perspective—that is, peer interaction allows for the kinds of communicative acts in which participants become aware of differences among themselves and the desirability to resolve those differences. Thus, decentering—the ability to refocus on two or more dimensions and coordinate them—is seen as a consequence of peer interaction and conflict.

The ability to refocus and to coordinate perspectives (i.e., decentering) is structurally analogous to several aspects of psychological, social interactionist, and sociocentric conceptions. This decentering presumably arises from peer interaction and has implications for conceptions of social inequality. First, the ability to refocus from one's own perspective allows the child to recognize the inferred, or internal, qualities of others—such as feelings, thoughts, and traits—and the child is able to disengage from perceptual or behavioral qualities of people. Second, the group of peers demands some cohesion and compromise. Thus, inequalities among members of a group will not be as great a focus of disparagement, as members (or friends) attempt to provide some reciprocal benefits to one another. A possible implication of this coordinating function of the group is that out-group differences might be maximized. Third, social interaction may enhance the view that role conformity is highly desirable. With increased ability to refocus to the perspectives of others, the child's reputation will become a major concern for the self—that is, children will view norm compliance in terms of how others evaluate norms, not simply in terms of the threat of punishment or the promise of rewards from adults.

Fourth, refocusing also allows for social comparison. Thus, older children will evaluate their performances by comparing them with those of others, and they will begin to view ordinal scaling of individuals, using test performance, as informative of their own worth and the worth of others. Fifth, because the group seeks consensus through dialogues, the members of a group may insist on a general set of values to which all adhere. Thus, the idea that there is a veridical perspective of reality will be reflected in the view that very different interpretations of reality are deviant and possibly threatening. In contrast, egocentric younger children are not particularly concerned with a legitimate or veridical perspective. Deviance, for them, implies behavioral differences. Sixth, because consensus with groups is the hallmark of sanity, according to these children, social interactions (e.g., psychological support or changing relationships) will be viewed as corrective interventions. Younger children, in contrast, are not concerned with this: They will advocate punishment. Seventh, the value of the group will also demand that, in tasks involving coordination of members' skills (e.g., baseball games), effort will be taken as a sign of group loyalty. Imagine 10-year-olds playing baseball on the same team and one player claims that he or she does not really care who wins. The younger child, more engaged in solitary and noncompetitive play, will not suffer many interpersonal consequences because of lack of effort.

Ninth, the ability to refocus does not end with the awareness of the views of peers. It extends to the recognition of the different groups in society (e.g., business and labor unions) and how these perspectives may or may not be coordinated by the social structure (e.g., the law). Furthermore, the conventions of the society that provide for stratification may also become the object of the adolescent's consideration. Refocusing on these conventions—possibly because of interactions with people or knowledge of cultures with different conventions—may lead to a rejection of some stratification concepts. Finally, tenth, with increased interaction with a variety of people, the older child's stereotypes become less rigid. Thus, the child understands that both males and females have common qualities and that rich and poor are both people. Stereotypes, once formed, subsequently become less stereotypic.

THE COSTS OF
SOCIAL INEQUALITY CONCEPTIONS

Cognitive-developmental theorists, fascinated with the idea of progress in the individual, may raise some arguments with the view that "man is born free but everywhere he is in chains." Many of us have internalized Piaget's view of development as adaptation, pointing with satisfaction to the adolescent who has mastered the difficult matrices of formal operational thought. I would like to offer a different side to the coin of development, deflating its growth potential by suggesting that there are costs to development. What are some of these negative consequences in the development of conceptions of social inequality?

First, the development of psychological conceptions in which individual differences are attributed to stratified groups may be likened to the formation of a cognitive schema. For example, Martin and Halverson (1981) and others (Cantor & Mischel, 1977; Taylor & Fiske, 1978) have described the effects on information processing and retrieval that are consequences of cognitive schemas about individuals. Cognitive schemas may underlie stereotypes and may help to simplify one's perception of reality such that one may use these schemas to regulate behavior, organize and attend to information consistent with the stereotype, and to perceive characteristics in common (illusory correlations) that are not objectively associated with one another (Martin & Halverson, 1981). The interesting possibility is that, once stereotypes are formed, they may impede the recognition of disconfirming evidence. They may accentuate the perception of group differences and lead one to believe that there is more consistency in a person's behavior than is evident in objective reality.

Although this kind of cognitive model has been of interest mostly to nondevelopmentalists, it does have some relevance to the research discussed in this volume. A possible line of research interfacing the schematic processing model with developmental changes in concepts of inequality is to determine if the formation of stereotypes about groups (e.g., classes or intellectual groups) is related to the selective recall of information about members of those groups.

A second cost of these developments is that psychological conceptions are notoriously difficult to disconfirm (Mischel, 1968). If I believe that Carol is generally narcissistic, I may have a difficult time finding evidence to disconfirm this attribution, since behavioral exceptions do not logically negate the general quality of the trait. Thus, Carol may be generous in some circumstances, but I might discount this as an exception to her narcissism. A third cost of these psychological conceptions of inequality is that they may be applied to the self, resulting in some negative consequences for self-esteem. If I am lower class and I attribute psychological differences to classes, I may end up feeling depressed. Certainly lack of self-esteem will not necessarily follow from the simple observation that I dress differently from a wealthy person. The negative consequences for the self are enhanced by the attribution of psychological attributions that are difficult to disconfirm and that imply evaluation.

Finally, there are social costs to the development of conceptions of social inequality. As elusive a concept as alienation may be necessary to describe the tension, conflict, and loss experienced by individuals who perceive themselves at the lower end of the stratification system. And, although generally not considered as aversive, we should not forget the cost for those at the upper end who may feel compelled to enact traditional roles that, for some, deprive them of a fuller range of experience and may isolate them from individuals in other strata.

SUMMARY

The data reported in this volume are suggestive of three general levels of conceptions of social inequality—peripheral–obedient, psychological, and social interactionist–social structural conceptions. This proposed model needs further empirical support to provide the information necessary for a cognitive-developmental theory of conceptions of social inequality. Such theories as equity theory and postfigurative theories emphasizing handed-down ideas of stratification are not fully adequate in describing the kinds of criteria children and adolescents use in explaining or justifying inequality, nor do these theories adequately describe the apparent qualitative differences between adults and children in their conceptions of social inequality. The construction of social inequality may have some parallels with impersonal cognition, but the social interaction with peers may be an important source of conceptions of individual and social differences. Finally, the development of these conceptions reflects the fact that there are costs to development in that the formation of stereotypes impedes veridical perception of people and events and provides an illusion of group differences that may be difficult to disconfirm.

REFERENCE NOTE

1. Leahy, R. L. *The development of conceptions of intelligence.* Paper presented at the meeting of the International Society for the Study of Behavioral Development, Toronto, August 1981.

REFERENCES

Adams, J. Inequity in social exchanges. In L. Berkowitz (Ed.), *Advances in Experimental Social Psychology* (Vol. 2). New York: Academic Press, 1965.

Barenboim, C. The development of person perception in childhood and adolescence: From behavioral comparisons to psychological constructs to psychological comparisons. *Child Development*, 1981, *52*, 129–144.

Bem, S. On the utility of alternative procedures for assessing psychological androgyny. *Journal of Consulting and Clinical Psychology*, 1977, *45*, 196–205.

Berndt, T. Relations between social cognition, nonsocial cognition, and social behavior: The case of friendship. In J. Flavell & L. Ross (Eds.), *Social cognitive development*. New York: Cambridge Univ. Press, 1981.

Cantor, N., & Mischel, W. Traits as prototypes: Effects on recognition memory. *Journal of Personality and Social Psychology*, 1977, *35*, 38–48.

Chandler, M., Paget, K., & Koch, D. The child's demystification of psychological defense mechanisms: A structural and developmental analysis. *Developmental Psychology*, 1978, *14*, 197–205.

Coie, J. D., & Pennington, B. F. Children's perception of deviance and disorder. *Child Development*, 1976, *47*, 407–413.

Connell, R. W. The child's construction of politics. Melbourne: Melbourne Univ. Press, 1971.

Damon, W. *The social world of the child*. San Francisco: Jossey-Bass, 1977.

Della Fave, L. R. The meek shall not inherit the earth: Self-evaluation and the legitimacy of stratification. *American Sociological Review*, 1980, *45*, 955–971.

Eisenberg-Berg, N., & Roth, K. The development of children's prosocial moral judgment: A longitudinal follow-up. *Developmental Psychology*, 1980, *16*, 375–376.

Enright, R. D., Franklin, C., & Manheim, L. A. Children's distributive justice reasoning: A standardized and objective scale. *Developmental Psychology*, 1980, *16*, 193–202.

Flavell, J. On cognitive development. *Child Development*, 1982, *53*, 1–10.

Flavell, J. Structures, stages, and sequences in cognitive development. In A. Collins (Ed.), *Minnesota Symposia on Child Psychology* (Vol. 15). Hillsdale, N.J.: Erlbaum, forthcoming.

Furby, L. Inequalities in personal possessions: Explanations for and judgments about unequal distribution. *Human Development*, 1979, *22*, 180–202.

Furth, H. Young children's understanding of society. In H. McGurk (Ed.), *Issues in childhood social development*. London: Methuen, 1979.

Furth, H. *The world of grown-ups: Children's conception of society*. New York: Elsevier, 1980.

Hook, J., & Cook, T. D. Equity theory and the cognitive ability of children. *Psychological Bulletin*, 1979, *86*, 429–445.

Keniston, K. *Young radicals: Notes on committed youth*. New York: Harcourt, 1968.

Kohlberg, L. A cognitive-developmental analysis of children's sex-role concepts and attitudes. In E. Maccoby (Ed.), *The development of sex differences*. Stanford: Stanford Univ. Press, 1966.

Kohlberg, L. Stage and sequence: The cognitive-developmental approach to socialization. In D. Goslin (Ed.), *Handbook of socialization theory and research*. New York: Rand McNally, 1969.

Kohlberg, L. The study of moral development. In T. Lickona (Ed.), *Moral development and behavior*. New York: Holt, 1976.

Leahy, R. L. The development of the conception of economic inequality. I. Descriptions and comparisons of rich and poor people. *Child Development*, 1981, *52*, 523–532.

Leahy, R. L. The development of the conception of economic inequality. II. Explanations, justifications, and conceptions of social mobility and social change. *Developmental Psychology*, 1983, *19*, 111–125.

Leahy, R. L., & Eiter, M. Moral judgment and the development of real and ideal self-image during adolescence and young adulthood. *Developmental Psychology*, 1980, *16*, 362–370.

Leahy, R. L., & Shirk, S. The development of classificatory skills and sex-trait stereotypes in children. *Sex Roles*, in press.

Livesley, W., & Bromley, D. *Person perception in childhood and adolescence*. London: Wiley, 1973.

Maas, E., Maracek, J., & Travers, J. Children's conceptions of disordered behavior. *Child Development*, 1978, *49*, 146–154.

Martin, C. L., & Halverson, C. F. A schematic processing model of sex typing and stereotyping in children. *Child Development*, 1981, *52*, 1119–1134.

Mischel, W. *Personality and assessment*. New York: Wiley, 1968.

Nelson, K., Zelniker, T., & Jeffrey, W. E. The child's concept of proportionality: A reexamination. *Journal of Experimental Child Psychology*, 1969, *8*, 256–262.

Piaget, J. *The moral judgment of the child*. London: Kegan Paul, 1932.

Piaget, J. Piaget's theory. In P. H. Mussen (Ed.), *Carmichael's manual of child psychology* (3rd ed., Vol. 1). New York: Wiley, 1970.

Rawls, J. *A theory of justice*. Cambridge, Mass.: Harvard Univ. Press, 1971.

Ruble, D., Boggiano, A., Feldman, N., & Loebl, J. Analysis of the role of social comparison in self-evaluation. *Developmental Psychology*, 1980, *16*, 105–115.

Shweder, R. Discussion: What's there to negotiate? Some questions for Youniss. *Merrill-Palmer Quarterly*, 1981, *27*, 405–412.

Taylor, S., & Fiske, S. Salience, attention, and attribution: Top of the head phenomena. In L. Berkowitz (Ed.), *Advances in experimental social psychology* (Vol. 11). New York: Academic Press, 1978.

Torney, J., Oppenheim, A. N., & Farnen, R. *Civic education in ten nations: An empirical study*. New York: Wiley, 1975.

Turiel, E. Distinct conceptual and developmental domains: Social convention and morality. In H. F. Have (Ed.), *Nebraska Symposium on Motivation* (Vol. 25). Lincoln: Univ. of Nebraska Press, 1978.

Williams, J., Bennett, S., & Best, D. Awareness and expression of sex stereotypes in young children. *Developmental Psychology*, 1975, *11*, 635–642.

Youniss, J. The nature of social cognition: A conceptual discussion of cognition. In H. McGurk (Ed.), *Issues in childhood social development*. London: Methuen, 1979.

Youniss, J. Moral development through a theory of social construction: An analysis. *Merrill-Palmer Quarterly*, 1981, *27*, 385–404.

Author index

Subject index

A

Abstraction principle, and counting, 12–13

Adult(s)
and prosocial behavior, 181
qualities characterizing intellectual ability of, 127–128
responses of, to infants and gender, 44–46

Affect, communicating, and friendship, 171–174

Aggression
attitudes towards, 231
concept of, 231
developmental studies of, 241–243

Allocations
outcome, causes of individual differences in, 210–213
and sex, 212

Antiauthoritarianism, 302

Antisocial character disorder, concept of, 226, 227–228

Authority-dependency conceptions, and social inequality, 313

Authority rule, 209

B

Behavior, internal standards for, and intelligence concepts, 139–140, 150

Behavioral expectations, and gender, 45, 46

Biracial family
gender identity in, 55–56
racial identity in, 55–56

C

Cardinality principle, and counting, 12–13

Categorical self, 280

Causal reasoning, 2
and functional reasoning, 23–24, 34

Centration
and social class concepts, 104
in social cognition, 2

Change
conflict-driven model of, 307
social, development of concepts of, 92, 100–101

Children
black
prowhite bias of, 52, 53, 54, 61, 63, 68, 258, 259
same-race preference of, 61, 68, 260
blind, racial awareness of, 51
interracial
and gender identity, 55–56
and racial identity, 55–56
qualities characterizing intellectual ability in, 127

number perception of, 6–7, 16
qualities characterizing intellectual ability in, 125–127
Injustice, *see also* Justice
and cognitive distortion, 300
Intelligence
academic, 122, 123, 155, 157
constancy and malleability of, 112, 117–118, 132, 147
definitions of, 112, 113–114, 130
development of comparisons of, 149–150
general, 155
lack of, and roles, 152–153
across life span, 123–129
measurement of, impact of, 110
nature and nurture, influence of, 112, 116–117, 131–132
practical, 122
qualities associated with, 112, 116, 119–121, 131
and reading ability, 122–123
self-assessment of, 112, 115, 118, 131
social, 122
visible signs of, 112, 114–115, 130
Intelligence concepts, 109–133, 135–160
cognitive-developmental approach to, 135–160, 313
and cohesive bond with group members, 147–148
and comparisons, 138
and compensatory education, 144
and conceptual abstractness, 111, 119
and concrete operational thinking, 137, 149
and constancy and malleability of intelligence, 112, 117–118, 132, 147
and decentration, 138–139, 148, 149
and differentiation, 111, 116, 118, 119, 121, 123
and education, 135, 154–157
and intellectual ability across life span, 123–129
and internalization, 111, 119
and internal standards of behavior, 139–140, 150
levels of, 142–145
and metacognitive qualities, 148–149
and moral judgment, 136–137, 139, 140
and motivation, 143, 144, 146, 150, 153, 154

and obedience, 136–137, 139, 140, 142–143, 146, 148, 154, 313
and peer associations, 147
and person perception, 137, 138, 142–143, 146, 148
qualitative nature of, 113–114
quantitative nature of, 113, 114
and self-direction, 150, 151, 153, 155
and role theory, 150–152
and rule-following behavior, 151, 153
and self-assessment, 112, 115, 118, 131
and social comparison, 138–139, 149
and social competence, 137, 145, 146, 147, 148, 152, 154, 155
and social interaction, 142, 144–145, 146, 148, 154–157
and socialization, 145
and socialization of thought, 147
and studying, 143, 146, 150
and support, 144, 145, 148, 152
and test performance, 143, 147, 149, 154, 314
and visible signs of intelligence, 112, 114–115, 130
International Association for the Evaluation of Educational Achievement (IEA) study, 301–305, 307
Interpersonal equality concepts, 256, 257, 261, 262–267, 277, 278
Intimate relationships, 176
Introjection, 233

J
Justice
distributive, *see* Distributive justice
and laws, 292, 293, 294–296, 298
and moral development, 291–296
negative, 213
and rules, 292
social, perception of, *see* Social justice, perception of
and social conventions, 293–294
Just world, perceptions of, 300

K
Kindness, *see also* Prosocial behavior
and friendship, 168–169, 170

L
Labeling, and racial awareness, 66

and relative deprivation theory, 269–270
and status attribution theory, 271
Social–political order, construction of, 289–291
Social skills, individual differences in, and friendship, 167–168
Social systems role-taking, 91
Social transmission, 322–324
Society, conflict within, 98
Sociocentric conceptions, and social class concepts, 90, 91, 92, 94, 95–96, 97, 103, 105, 299
Socioeconomic status, *see also* Social class differences; Stratification
and antiauthoritarianism, 302
and distributive justice judgments, 212
and peer relations, 265
and perception of political conflict, 304
and prosocial behavior, 187–188
and scores on Distributive Justice Scale, 265–266, 279
and self-esteem, 276–277
Spatial strategies, in assessing quantity, 8–10, 18, 33
Speech, inner, and control of impulsive behavior, 140
Stable-order principle, and counting, 12, 13
Standards, setting of
in friendship, 165
in parent–child relationship, 164–165
Status attribution theory
and perception of social justice, 271
and stratification, 276
Stereotypes
and cognitive schema, 325
rigidity of, 313
Strange person phenomenon, 52–53, 54
Stratification, *see also* Social class differences; Socioeconomic status
awareness, development of, 272–273
awareness, effect of on self-esteem, 273–274
concept of, 271–277
and conflict theory, 275–276
and equity theory, 276
and functionalist theory, 275
legitimation of, 274–277
and status attribution theory, 276

Studying, and intelligence concepts, 143, 146, 150
Subitizing
versus counting, 15–17, 18
in quantitative equality and inequality, establishment of, 14–18, 33
Sullivan, H. S., theories of, 162–166, 174–176
Support
deviant behavior, changing of, 227
and intelligence concepts, 144, 145, 148, 152

T
Tactile cues, and gender awareness, 49
Tagging, in counting, 11–12, 13, 18
Talents, individual differences in, and friendship, 167
Tasks, performance on, 35
Television, and racial attitudes, 66, 67
Test performance, and intelligence concepts, 143, 147, 149, 154, 314
Thought, socialization of, and intelligence concepts, 147–148
Toys, gender-typing of, 45, 46, 50, 55
Transductive reasoning, and gender-role development, 60
Trust, in friendship, 173, 174

U
Unkindness, and friendship, 169–170

V
Values
and allocations, 210–211, 212
and social institutions, 303–307
Visual cues, and gender awareness, 49
Vitiligo, 70
Voice pitch, and gender awareness, 48–49

W
Withdrawal behavior, concept of, 227, 231
Women's rights, *see* Rights, women's

Y
Youth culture, 254

DEVELOPMENTAL PSYCHOLOGY SERIES

Continued from page ii

EUGENE S. GOLLIN. (Editor). *Developmental Plasticity: Behavioral and Biological Aspects of Variations in Development*

W. PATRICK DICKSON. (Editor). *Children's Oral Communication Skills*

LYNN S. LIBEN, ARTHUR H. PATTERSON, and NORA NEWCOMBE. (Editors). *Spatial Representation and Behavior across the Life Span: Theory and Application*

SARAH L. FRIEDMAN and MARIAN SIGMAN. (Editors). *Preterm Birth and Psychological Development*

HARBEN BOUTOURLINE YOUNG and LUCY RAU FERGUSON. *Puberty to Manhood in Italy and America*

RAINER H. KLUWE and HANS SPADA. (Editors). *Developmental Models of Thinking*

ROBERT L. SELMAN. *The Growth of Interpersonal Understanding: Developmental and Clinical Analyses*

BARRY GHOLSON. *The Cognitive-Developmental Basis of Human Learning: Studies in Hypothesis Testing*

TIFFANY MARTINI FIELD, SUSAN GOLDBERG, DANIEL STERN, and ANITA MILLER SOSTEK. (Editors). *High-Risk Infants and Children: Adult and Peer Interactions*

GILBERTE PIERAUT-LE BONNIEC. *The Development of Modal Reasoning: Genesis of Necessity and Possibility Notions*

JONAS LANGER. *The Origins of Logic: Six to Twelve Months*

LYNN S. LIBEN. *Deaf Children: Developmental Perspectives*